THE LIMITS OF FUNDAMENTAL RIGHTS PROTECTION BY THE EU

School of Human Rights Research Series, Volume 79.

The titles published in this series are listed at the end of this volume.

THE LIMITS OF FUNDAMENTAL RIGHTS PROTECTION BY THE EU

The Scope for the Development of Positive Obligations

Malu Beijer

intersentia
Cambridge – Antwerp – Portland

Intersentia Ltd
Sheraton House | Castle Park
Cambridge | CB3 0AX | United Kingdom
Tel.: +44 1223 370 170 | Fax: +44 1223 370 169
Email: mail@intersentia.co.uk
www.intersentia.com | www.intersentia.co.uk

Distribution for the UK and Ireland:
NBN International
Airport Business Centre, 10 Thornbury Road
Plymouth, PL6 7 PP
United Kingdom
Tel.: +44 1752 202 301 | Fax: +44 1752 202 331
Email: orders@nbninternational.com

Distribution for Europe and all other countries:
Intersentia Publishing nv
Groenstraat 31
2640 Mortsel
Belgium
Tel.: +32 3 680 15 50 | Fax: +32 3 658 71 21
Email: mail@intersentia.be

Distribution for the USA and Canada:
International Specialized Book Services
920 NE 58th Ave. Suite 300
Portland, OR 97213
USA
Tel.: +1 800 944 6190 (toll free) | Fax: +1 503 280 8832
Email: info@isbs.com

ISBN 978-1-78068-455-0
Depot no. D/2017/7849/8
NUR 828

British Library Cataloguing in Publication Data. A catalogue record for this book is available from the British Library.

ABOUT THE AUTHOR

Malu Beijer (1986) graduated from Utrecht University, the Netherlands, in 2012, where she obtained a bachelor's degree in law (with distinction) and a master's degree in Legal Research with a specialisation in European Public Law (cum laude). During her studies, Malu Beijer undertook several research projects on European migration law, internal market law and EU fundamental rights. She worked as a legal intern at the Dutch Council of State, the Dutch Ministry of Foreign Affairs, and the law firm, Pels Rijcken & Drooglever Fortuijn. She also worked as a student-assistant at Utrecht University, where she organised two legal conferences, and took part in an exchange with Tsukuba University, Japan.

In 2012 Malu Beijer received a Research Talent grant from the Netherlands Organisation for Scientific Research (NWO). She carried out her research under the supervision of prof. dr. J.H. (Janneke) Gerards at the law faculty of the Radboud University, Nijmegen. At this university, Malu Beijer has taught several classes on EU fundamental rights law and EU judicial protection, and continues to do so. She is a member of the European law working group of the Netherlands Committee of Jurists for Human Rights (NJCM) and is a board member of the Dutch young network for European Law (STER). She also writes a weekly newsletter on ECtHR and ECJ cases.

Malu Beijer has participated in, and co-organised several legal conferences and has published in international and Dutch legal journals. She continues her work as a researcher and lecturer in the field of EU law and fundamental rights at Radboud University alongside her work as a judicial assistant.

ACKNOWLEDGEMENTS

Writing my PhD over the course of the past four years was a challenging but ultimately very rewarding experience. For a long time much of my work was only stored on a small USB device that I have carried with me during the journeys from Utrecht to Nijmegen and back. It has been difficult to work on a project that never is quite complete. Even after days, weeks and months of work, there are always further thoughts that remain and projects that are left unfinished. Now I am very pleased to be able to show the final results of my work in this book.

I would not have succeeded without the excellent guidance provided by Janneke. At every stage of the project, Janneke made time to listen to my thoughts and struggles with the materials, and to give me most helpful feedback on my work. Janneke has given me the confidence to write my PhD and to speak out about topics of EU law and human rights which have become very dear to me. For many reasons Janneke is a very important person who has helped me to complete this project and has been there for me on a personal level as well. I could not have wished for a better supervisor.

Of course there are others to thank too. I have met some inspiring people along the way in Nijmegen as well as in other places. I am grateful to the department of International and European Law of the Radboud University which has offered me a great working environment, and which has allowed me to keep learning about topics of International and European law. I have been able to learn more about human rights in practice, by attending the Venice Academy of Human Rights and the regular meetings of the working group of European law of the *NJCM*. I am especially grateful to have been allowed to share my work at the Realaw Research Forum of 2015 and at the seminar in Utrecht on positive obligations. Ellen – thank you for the smooth and fun cooperation! Further thanks to John Morijn for the opportunity to discuss my research and to Herman van Harten for writing about *Dhahbi v. Italy*.

Thanks to Marc for providing distractions and a lot of 'gezelligheid' during the final stages of my PhD, as well as to Jasper for sharing thoughts on our common research interests, and of course to the *Jonghe Gaerde* for other fun experiences. I am grateful to my friends from Utrecht and from the LRM, in particular Eduardo, Wouter and Frank. Special thanks to Irene and Caroline for their lasting friendship and for being my 'paranimfen'. Further thanks to my family (in law).

This list would not be complete, far from it, if I did not mention Jie-Heda. You have been there for me for many years. I am very lucky to have you in my life.

CONTENTS

PART I: THE CONCEPT OF POSITIVE OBLIGATIONS WITHIN THE CONTEXT OF THE EUROPEAN CONVENTION ON HUMAN RIGHTS

ABBREVIATIONS

A-G	Advocate General
BVerfG	Bundesverfassungsgericht
EC	European Community
ECJ	European Court of Justice
ECHR	European Convention on Human Rights ('the Convention')
ECSR	European Committee on Social Rights
ECtHR	European Court of Human Rights
EU	European Union
GC	General Court of the European Union
IACHR	Inter-American Court of Human Rights
TEC	Treaty establishing the European Community
TEU	Treaty on European Union
TFEU	Treaty on the Functioning of the European Union
UDHR	Universal Declaration of Human Rights
UN	United Nations
US	United States of America

GENERAL COURT

EUROPEAN COMMITTEE ON SOCIAL RIGHTS

INTER-AMERICAN COURT OF HUMAN RIGHTS

AFRICAN COMMISSION ON HUMAN AND PEOPLE'S RIGHTS

PERMANENT COURT OF INTERNATIONAL JUSTICE

BUNDESVERFASSUNGSGERICHT (GERMAN CONSTITUTIONAL COURT)

U.S. SUPREME COURT

CHAPTER 1
INTRODUCTION

1.1. BACKGROUND TO THIS STUDY

1.1.1. TWO SUPRANATIONAL COURTS IN EUROPE DECIDING ON FUNDAMENTAL RIGHTS CASES

In today's pluralistic European legal order there are two supranational courts that both interpret the scope and the meaning of fundamental rights. Fundamental rights are a set of individuals rights and freedoms which, for example, include the right to life and freedom of expression, and can also be found in national constitutions.[1] At the supranational level, the European Court of Human Rights (ECtHR) firstly plays an important role in interpreting the fundamental rights set out in the European Convention on Human Rights (ECHR or 'the Convention'). The ECtHR (and its predecessor, the European Commission of Human Rights), entered the scene in the 1950s, allowing individuals, as well as states, to bring claims regarding violations of the mainly civil and political rights of the Convention. From that moment on, the ECtHR has delivered judgments in a wide range of cases where fundamental rights were allegedly interfered with, and in those judgments it has fleshed out the meaning and scope of the rights laid down in the Convention.[2] The ECtHR has also played an important part in the development of fundamental rights doctrines.[3] The case-law of this Court has generated important effects on the way in which fundamental rights are protected at the national level. The states parties *inter alia* have had to make legislative changes in response to specific judgments of the ECtHR on individual cases.[4] Today, the detailed case-law of the ECtHR and its fundamental rights doctrines are therefore of interest for various areas of law.

---

1 The term 'human rights' is also often used in this context and commonly refers to the right laid down in international human rights treaties such as the Universal Declaration of Human Rights ('UDHR'). The term 'fundamental rights', which is used in this study, encompasses a broader category of rights, and also include the rights found in the constitutions of the member states. Furthermore, the term fundamental rights in this study does not include the 'other' general principles of law that have been developed by the ECJ, nor the fundamental freedoms under EU law, which are sometimes also referred to as fundamental rights under EU law.

2 For a further historical overview of the ECtHR, see Bates (2010).

3 Harris, O'Boyle, Bates & Warbrick (2014), p. 34.

4 Harris, O'Boyle, Bates & Warbrick (2014), pp. 34–35.

On the same European continent, albeit in respect of fewer states, the Court of Justice of the European Union (ECJ), now also plays a role in the protection of fundamental rights.[5] The ECJ interprets and safeguards the correct application of the law of the European Union (EU). Its primary aim is not to ensure respect for fundamental rights, since it was established for different reasons. It was set up to focus on an economic type of integration between the European states. It has become clear, however, that actions taken by EU institutions and EU member states under EU law can affect the protection of fundamental rights. The right to property may, for example, be interfered with because of arrangements made at the EU level to establish an internal market. Moreover, the EU member states have agreed to cooperate in matters of immigration and civil and criminal matters in the area of freedom, security and justice, which can affect important fundamental rights such as the prohibition of inhuman and degrading treatment. While, initially, the ECJ ensured through its case-law that fundamental rights were guaranteed as general principles of Community law, and later of EU law, the EU Treaties now clearly mandate for fundamental rights to be protected. Since 2009, the EU has its own written and binding catalogue of fundamental rights, the Charter of Fundamental Rights ('the Charter').

So far, the foregoing will be a very familiar story for many readers, especially for those working in the field of fundamental rights protection in Europe. They will know that the ECJ has found a clear place alongside the ECtHR as a court that can offer protection of fundamental rights in Europe. The ECJ is competent to interpret fundamental rights in cases that fall within the scope of EU law, and it can decide that EU legislation or other decisions taken by the EU institutions are void if they fail to secure respect for these rights. In several areas, such as privacy law, asylum law and non-discrimination law, the ECJ has delivered important decisions and has recognised important principles.[6] Increasingly, the ECJ is being requested to determine how fundamental rights are to be protected within the context of EU law, especially since the Charter has become legally binding.[7]

The ECJ remains, however, quite a novel player in the field of fundamental rights protection. It still needs to clarify how fundamental rights are to be protected within the context of EU law, especially on the basis of the EU Charter. Seeing that the ECJ has less

---

5 The Court of Justice of the European Union is comprised of three courts: the Court of Justice, the General Court and the Civil Service Tribunal. In this study the term ECJ is used to refer primarily to the first of these courts, i.e., the Court of Justice, which is the highest court. Only the Court of Justice is competent to respond to the questions referred to by the national courts under the preliminary reference procedure. The Court of Justice is further competent to deal with applications for annulment actions and actions for failure to fulfil EU obligations, and with appeals against the judgments of the General Court.

6 See e.g. ECJ 13 May 2014, C-131/12, *Google Spain*; ECJ 6 October 2015, C-362/14, *Schrems*; ECJ 8 April 2014, Joined cases C-293/12 and 594/12, *Digital Rights Ireland*; and ECJ 21 December 2011, Joined cases C-411/10 and C-493/10, *N.S. and others*.

7 For a statistical overview of the numbers of questions that have been raised by national courts from 2009 onwards, see European Commission, Staff Working Document on the Application of the EU Charter of Fundamental Rights in 2015, SWD(2016), 158 final, p. 8.

experience in dealing with fundamental rights cases, comparisons are often made to the way in which other courts interpret and apply fundamental rights. The ECtHR is an obvious comparator in this respect, because it protects the same range of fundamental rights as the ECJ and it is, moreover, also situated at the supranational level.

Another reason for choosing the ECtHR as a comparator is substantive in nature. It is considered desirable that fundamental rights are interpreted and applied in the same way in the context of EU law as they are under the Convention, especially since many states will need to comply with the judgments of both of these courts.[8] The ECJ itself has also explicitly relied on the interpretations which have been provided by the ECtHR in its case-law, and it declared early on that the fundamental rights guaranteed by the Convention are of special significance in that respect.[9] It has even been agreed that the EU itself should accede to the Convention, and since 2010, negotiations have been taking place to make specific arrangements to realise such accession. As a consequence, the ECtHR would be able to hear claims brought by individuals against the EU for violation of the rights laid down in the Convention. In this way, the ECtHR would have an important role in ensuring that the EU complies with the minimum standards laid down in the Convention and to prevent divergence of the standards of fundamental rights between the Convention and the EU. However, in December 2014, the ECJ raised important objections to the arrangements laid down in a draft accession agreement.[10] Under the proposed arrangements, several of the specific characteristics and important principles of EU law would be interfered with. Since then, the accession process has been on hold, and it is expected to take quite some time before it is continued.[11]

The ECJ thus still has the final say on how fundamental rights are to be protected within the EU context. For reasons of consistency, however, it is generally expected that the ECJ would have resort to principles similar to those which the ECtHR has developed for the interpretation and application of fundamental rights. The ECtHR has, for example, developed its famous margin of appreciation doctrine, which leaves states a certain discretion in their legislative, administrative or judicial choices in areas where fundamental rights are at stake. It has also developed elaborate standards on the proportionality assessment that states must undertake to justify restrictions of fundamental rights. The ECJ has been somewhat slow in developing similar fundamental rights doctrines in its own case-law, and it has been criticised in that regard.[12] Fundamental rights doctrines can help to bring clarity, certainty and predictability for

8 Article 52(3) of the Charter also specifically requires such consistency.

9 See ECJ 18 June 1991, C-260/89, *ERT*.

10 ECJ 18 December 2014, *Opinion 2/13*.

11 The lack of progress in the accession process since *Opinion 2/13* is also confirmed in European Commission, 2015 Report on the application of the EU Charter of Fundamental Rights, SWD(2016), 158 final, p. 8.

12 See Gerards (2015), p. 47; Douglas-Scott (2011), p. 649; Sánchez (2012), p. 1592; Gerards (2011a), p. 90; and Kühling (2009), p. 490. The ECJ has, however, paid an important contribution in developing the concepts of direct and indirect discrimination in its case-law, see Gerards (2015), p. 47.

the actors who are subject to this particular fundamental rights regime.[13] Development of such doctrines is considered all the more necessary because of the concerns that continue to exist over the democratic legitimacy of decisions that are made at the EU level.[14] Moreover, by developing fundamental rights doctrines the ECJ could finally remove doubts over the reality of its intention to protect fundamental rights and it could change its current image, as a court that mainly protects interests of an economic kind.[15]

At the same time, it should be noted that the ECJ is, indeed, a rather different court compared to the ECtHR. It has different interests to protect under EU law, it employs a rather different judicial style, and also takes a different position towards individuals and the national and EU authorities. It can therefore be questioned whether and to what extent certain fundamental rights doctrines can really be expected to be developed within the context of EU law in a similar way by these two different courts.

Against this background, this study focuses on the potential for the development by the EU of one particular fundamental rights doctrine – that of positive obligations. Originally developed by the ECtHR, the question is raised whether and to what extent it can be incorporated by the EU Courts, especially in light of the considerations discussed above. The following section first briefly explains what the concept of positive obligations means (section 1.1.2.) and, secondly, what types of questions have been raised regarding this concept in the academic debates on the EU system of fundamental rights protection (section 1.1.3.). The main question of this research is then presented (section 1.1.4.), followed by the aims and objectives of this study (section 1.2.), and the methods and approaches used to answer the main question of this study (section 1.3.). Next, in order to set a solid baseline for the discussion that is undertaken in this study, a working definition is provided of the concept of positive obligations in relation to the notion of fundamental rights within the context of EU law (section 1.4.). Finally, the outline of this book is provided (section 1.5.).

1.1.2. THE CONCEPT OF POSITIVE OBLIGATIONS

Various courts and bodies in (international) human rights law have recognised a concept of positive obligations in their judgments.[16] The ECtHR, in particular, has clearly accepted positive obligations in its case-law.[17] The ECtHR has explained that

---

13 Kühling (2009), p. 490.

14 Kühling (2009), p. 490; and Gerards (2012b).

15 Douglas-Scott (2011), p. 681.

16 For examples of judgments of such international bodies, see IACHR 29 July 1988, Inter-Am.Ct.H.R. Series C No 4, *Vélasquez Rodríguez v. Honduras* (Merits), paras 160–166 and 174–177; and African Commission on Human and People's Rights No 211/89 (1 May 2001), *Legal Resources Foundation v. Zambia*, para. 62. For an overview of the recognition of positive obligations by different international and national legal systems, see Dröge (2003), pp. 268–284; and Stachel (2006), pp. 20–29.

17 See Mowbray (2004); and Xenos (2012). This development in particular is discussed in chapter 3.

the protection of fundamental rights traditionally requires states to abstain from interfering with the individual freedoms of citizens, which means that states incur a negative obligation. Fundamental rights protection can, in addition, give rise to positive obligations, meaning that states must take active measures to ensure the protection of individuals' fundamental rights in a practical and effective manner. This applies both in their relation to the state and in their private relations. The positive obligations which have been imposed by the ECtHR on states range from obligations in the legislative sphere that ensure respect for the right to privacy of same-sex couples, to obligations to take practical measures to ensure peaceful demonstrations, and to obligations to provide a more general framework in the legislative, policy or practical area to combat human trafficking. The case-law of the ECtHR has been criticised *inter alia* for showing unwarranted judicial activism and disrespect for the principle of subsidiarity.[18] Nonetheless, over time, the ECtHR has developed a highly influential case-law which reveals the standards and methods it uses in recognising these obligations. The recognition of positive obligations is generally considered to be justified by the principle of the effective protection of fundamental rights. The concept of positive obligations has now been more broadly accepted in modern democracies.[19]

1.1.3. THE DEBATE ABOUT POSITIVE OBLIGATIONS WITHIN THE CONTEXT OF EU LAW

So far, it is difficult to see a concept of positive obligations in the case-law of the ECJ.[20] In 1999, De Witte noted that:

> 'The ECJ's case-law on human rights is, in fact, still developing. It has dealt only quite recently with another well-known issue of the fundamental rights doctrine of both national constitutional courts and the European Court of Human Rights, namely the question whether fundamental rights also impose *positive duties* on governments (in our case, on the Community Institutions as well as on the Member States acting within the scope of EC law).'[21]

De Witte was referring to one particular judgment, the case of *T. Port*, in which the ECJ seemed to have defined a positive obligation for the Community institutions to protect the fundamental rights of undertakings in their transition to the common market, which is explained further at section 1.4.[22] Since then, only a few researchers have noted

---

18 See e.g. the critiques of former judge Fitzmaurice in his dissenting opinion to ECtHR 13 June 1979, no. 6833/74, *Marckx v. Belgium*; and Van Kempen (2008).

19 See generally Fredman (2008).

20 Stubberfield (2012); Besson (2011a), p. 115; Ahmed & Butler (2006), p. 794; De Schutter (2004); Van der Velde (2009), pp. 74–78; and Heringa & Verhey (2001), pp. 19–20.

21 De Witte (1999), p. 882.

22 Others have also pointed to this case as an example of the formulation of a positive obligaton by the ECJ, see Weiler & Fries (1999), p. 156. Section 1.4. provides a brief discussion of this case in order to explain the definition of positive obligations. The case of *T. Port* is also discussed in section 11.5.5.

other types of positive obligations, which seem to have been developed incidentally in the case-law of the ECJ. In particular, such obligations have been identified in the field of national procedural law, where states have been required to introduce new remedies and powers for national authorities.[23]

It has more often been held that EU fundamental rights have a predominantly negative character.[24] This is to say that fundamental rights essentially set limits on the exercise of powers by the EU. Ahmed and Butler, in particular, have held that:

> 'The nature of human rights protection within the EU is essentially 'negative'. That is, the EU is seen to be under a duty not to violate human rights when it takes steps to fulfil the obligations arising from the Treaty. It is considered to be under a duty not to violate human rights whenever it takes action, but without any general competence to take positive action on human rights.'[25]

An important explanation that is often given for the more limited development of positive obligations under EU law is that the EU does not have a general competence to protect fundamental rights.[26] Indeed, it can be doubted whether positive obligations can be recognised if there are limited competences for the EU to take measures to protect fundamental rights, as such obligations would entail requirements to introduce legislative provisions or to implement financially burdensome measures.[27]

There is, however, potential for the development of positive obligations, especially because of the way in which fundamental rights have been laid down in the Charter. The Charter contains a wide array of rights, some of which evidently require positive action to be taken.[28] There are, for example, various socio-economic rights included in the 'Solidarity' Title of the Charter which are generally expected to give rise to positive obligations for states if they are to be fully realised. Article 51(1) of the Charter also requires the EU institutions and member states, when implementing EU law, to respect the rights, observe the principles and *promote* the application thereof. Clearly, this implies that the Charter contains more than a mere limit to the actions of the EU and a set of purely negative obligations.[29] The Charter also explicitly holds that the same meaning and scope must be given to the rights of the Charter that correspond to

---

23 See in particular Prechal & Widdershoven (2011); Van Cleynenbreugel (2012a); and Van Cleynenbreugel (2012b).

24 Stubberfield (2012), p. 125; Besson (2011b), p. 43; Kühling (2009), p. 492; Ahmed & Butler (2006); De Schutter (2004), pp. 3–4; and Alston & Weiler (1999), pp. 10–11. The approach of the ECJ towards fundamental rights has, at least in the past, also been characterised as defensive and instrumental, see De Schutter (2004), pp. 3–16.

25 Ahmed & Butler (2006), p. 794. Cf. also Stubberfield (2012), p. 125.

26 See in particular ECJ 28 March 1996, *Opinion 2/94*, para. 27; Besson (2011b), pp. 50–53; Van der Velde (2009), pp. 74–78; De Schutter (2004), pp. 29–31; Heringa & Verhey (2001), pp. 19–20.

27 See Eeckhout (2002); Von Bogdandy (2008); Craig (2011a), p. 219; Craig & De Búrca (2015), p. 397; and the sources mentioned in *supra* n. 26.

28 See also Gersdorf (1994), pp. 400–426.

29 Eeckhout (2002), p. 980.

those laid down in the Convention.[30] Therefore, it could be expected that the positive obligations which have been developed under the Convention could be incorporated into EU law.

At the same time, the fact remains that the limited competences of the EU to protect fundamental rights are stressed in various places in the Charter. Article 51(2) of the Charter, in particular, stipulates that: '[t]he Charter does not extend the field of application of Union law beyond the powers of the Union or establish any new power or task for the Union, or modify powers and tasks as defined in the Treaties.'[31]

Consequently, there is a continuing concern as to whether positive obligations could indeed be recognised within the limits that are placed on the protection of fundamental rights by the EU. In relation to Article 51(2) of the Charter, Prechal, De Vries and Van Eijken have remarked that:

> The intentions of the drafter are clear. However, apart from being considered as judicially enforceable standards, in contemporary understanding fundamental rights are also tasks and mandates for the legislature, policymakers and the administration. Often they call for proactive measures that are necessary to realize fundamental rights, such as the right to a clean environment, the right to social protection, or adequate protection in criminal proceedings. In other terms, there is some intrinsic dynamism in these rights that puts limitations such as those in Article 51 of the Charter under pressure.[32]

There is thus a fear that the protection of fundamental rights by the EU may lead to an unwarranted expansion of its competences.[33] Some scholars find it hard to see how the concept of positive obligations could be protected within the scope of EU law without widening the competences of the EU.[34] There is a concomitant apprehension that the measures which could be required to fulfil positive obligations simply could not be met by the EU, if it has only limited competences to protect fundamental rights. At the same time, there are also fears that by firmly adhering to, and even stressing, the concept that the limited competences of the EU must be preserved, it will not be possible for fundamental rights to be protected effectively within the context of EU law.[35] Some

30 See Article 52(3) of the Charter.

31 Similar considerations are included in the fifth section of the preamble of the Charter; the second sentence of Article 51(1) of the Charter; the explanations to Article 51(2) of the Charter; the second sentence of Article 6(1) TEU; Declaration No. 1 to the Lisbon Treaty; as well as Articles 1(3) and 9(1) of the Draft Agreement for the Accession of the EU to the European Convention for Human Rights, 47+1(2013)008rev2, Final Report to the CDDH, 10 June 2013.

32 Prechal, De Vries & Van Eijken (2010), p. 239.

33 Cf. Craig & De Búrca (2011), p. 397; Besson (2011b), pp. 44–55; Van der Velde (2009), pp. 74–78; De Schutter (2004), pp. 29–31; De Búrca (2003), p. 2; Eeckhout (2002), p. 979; and Heringa & Verhey (2001), pp. 19–20.

34 See Prechal, De Vries & Van Eijken (2010), p. 239; Van der Velde (2009), pp. 74–78; and Heringa & Verhey (2001), pp. 19–20.

35 Besson (2011a), p. 115.

scholars have found that the ECJ has, so far, taken a far too cautious approach in its case-law towards the recognition of positive obligations.[36]

Overall, looking at the Charter and the discussions surrounding the accession of the EU to the Convention, as well as the debate about the expanding competences of the EU, the development of positive obligations within the EU context raises many questions. What scope does EU law really leave for the development of positive obligations within the context of EU law? To what extent does the ECJ already recognise a concept of positive obligations to protect fundamental rights in its case-law? Is there some potential for the ECJ to develop further such obligations in the future? It is uncertain whether positive action in relation to fundamental rights could actually be required within the context of EU law, what kinds of obligations this would encompass and how such obligations could be formulated without coming into conflict with the specific character of EU law, such as the limited competences of the EU. A doctrine of positive obligations that would help to answer such questions needs to be developed.[37]

1.1.4. THE MAIN RESEARCH QUESTION OF THIS STUDY

Against this background, this study centres around the following question. To what extent is there scope for recognition of a concept of positive obligations to protect fundamental rights under EU law, and in what manner can the ECJ develop a doctrine of positive obligations?

1.2. AIMS AND OBJECTIVES

The primary aim of this study is to attempt to bring more clarity as to how, if at all, positive obligations could be developed within the context of EU law.[38] The goal is to establish what scope EU law provides for a development of positive obligations, and what limits would apply to such a development under EU law. While questions have often been raised in academic debates about potential conflicts with the doctrine of limited competences of the EU, the question of if and how this doctrine would allow for positive obligations to be incorporated into EU law has not yet been analysed. It is

36 Ahmed & Butler (2006), p. 795.

37 Some suggestions have been advanced in the literature. So far, however, they all seem to point in different directions, and they draw different conclusions as to the extent to which the concept of positive obligations can be accepted and whether gaps in the protection of fundamental rights under EU law may be expected. See, e.g. De Schutter (2004). Cf. Ahmed & Butler (2006), p. 794. These approaches are discussed in section 8.4.1.

38 This section, as well as the sections on the specific research questions, the delimitation of the research and its methodology, are based to a large extent on the proposal that was written by the present author to apply for the Research Talent Grant of 2011 of the Social Sciences of the Netherlands Organisation for Scientific Research.

therefore valuable to attempt to develop a doctrine of positive obligations that can be taken into account by the ECJ in its judgments and that fits well in the EU system and its underlying principles.

As such, this study does not seek to establish which positive obligations could be incorporated into specific areas of EU law. However, as explained in the following section, specific case law examples are used as an illustration of the types of situations in which positive obligations could become relevant under EU law. These examples can also help to determine the limits and the scope for a development of positive obligations.

By exploring the particular topic of positive obligations, more general insights into the specific system of EU fundamental rights protection will also be generated. Given the growing importance of fundamental rights in the EU, the EU Courts, national judges and legal practitioners, such as lawyers, are faced with an increasing number of cases involving EU fundamental rights. It is still unclear how the EU system of fundamental rights relates to core EU principles such as conferral of limited powers, subsidiarity and proportionality. It is, therefore, also unclear what kinds of fundamental rights cases can be dealt with by the ECJ and how far this Court is able to go. The aim of this study is to bring further clarification of the specific system of protection of fundamental rights of the EU, which is also of particular interest for determining the scope for a development of positive obligations. This necessitates a discussion of the limited competences of the EU as well as a number of other relevant topics, including the institutional role and the judicial style of the ECJ and the limited scope of application of EU fundamental rights.

Thirdly, this study aims to contribute to the critical debate regarding the system of EU fundamental rights protection. As has been explained to some degree already, some scholars suggest that the limited competences of the EU to protect fundamental rights could cause gaps in the protection of fundamental rights to arise. This study aims to bring clarity regarding the types of situations in which it is *not* possible to recognise positive obligations on the basis of EU law. It will be discussed whether that is necessarily problematic, and the resulting findings may provide some 'food for thought' in relation to the accession of the EU to the Convention. Some scholars expect a further development of positive obligations under EU law after the accession has taken place.[39] The discussion of the potential scope for a development of positive obligations in EU law in this study will shed new light on this discussion.

1.3. METHODS AND APPROACH

In answering the main question underlying this study, and the various sub-questions of this study, the following methods and approaches are used.

39 See Stubberfield (2012). The accession of the EU to the Convention also cannot affect the limited competences of the EU, see Article 6(2) TEU.

1.3.1. DEFINING THE CONCEPT OF POSITIVE OBLIGATIONS AND ITS IMPLICATIONS

As an important starting point, further clarity is brought as to what the development of a concept of positive obligations to protect fundamental rights really means. This is necessary to be able to discuss whether, and to what extent, a concept of positive obligations could be accepted within the specific context of EU law. The primary source of inspiration for such insights in this research is the case-law of the ECtHR and the academic theory which is directly related thereto. Importantly, as explained in section 1.1, the concepts that have been developed by the ECtHR are considered to form the most relevant source of inspiration for the ECJ with regard to the interpretation of the fundamental rights that are recognised under EU law.[40] There is a rich source of commentary available for studying this concept which has been written in the language of the present author's own legal background (Dutch), and there also are numerous studies in the English language.[41] The case-law of the ECtHR has been extensively discussed and can therefore provide useful further insights as to what positive obligations actually entail, what important features they have, what criticism they raise and also how such criticism can be counteracted. Drawing on these findings, concrete recommendations can be directed at the EU Courts (regarding their application of the doctrine), as well as to national authorities (regarding the possibility of influencing the application of the doctrine on the EU level, for example, by formulating preliminary questions in court procedures) and to legal practitioners.

1.3.2. IDENTIFYING THE SCOPE AND LIMITS FOR THE DEVELOPMENT OF POSITIVE OBLIGATIONS UNDER EU LAW

As a second step, the scope and the limits of fundamental rights protection in the EU are examined, in particular with a view to the development of positive obligations. A legal theoretical study is therefore undertaken of the main principles and values that are relevant for the functioning of the doctrine of positive obligations in the context of the EU legal system. The various principles and their potential impact on the doctrine of positive obligations have been traced and analysed on the basis of a study of legal theoretical writings and on the basis of their application in the case-law of the ECJ. The main values and principles investigated are the principles of conferral of limited powers; the principle of subsidiarity; the principle of proportionality; and the protection of fundamental rights. Further research has also been undertaken on the specific role which the ECJ plays in the field of fundamental rights protection and

---

40 Article 6(3) TEU specifically mentions the Convention as such as a source of inspiration for the development of general principles of EU law.

41 Examples thereof include Lawson (1995a and 1995b); Mowbray (2004); Van Kempen (2008); Gerards (2011b); and Xenos (2011).

the specific position that it may adopt towards the EU institutions and the member states, which, as is often noted, is reflected in the reasoning of its judgments.[42] This allows a deeper understanding of the underlying principles, values and interests that determine the division of competences between the EU level and the national level, and the mechanisms determining the relationship between the EU and the Convention. Such understanding can help to structure and nuance the current political and media debates on 'competence creep', especially in the field of fundamental rights protection.

1.3.3. STUDYING SPECIFIC CASE-LAW EXAMPLES

To be able to draw further conclusions regarding the extent to which a development of positive obligations can take place within the context of EU law, and whether such a development would give rise to any conflicts with specific EU law principles, the ECJ case-law showing relevant examples of positive obligations for the context of EU law has been examined. These examples have been selected on the basis of a study of the literature, as well as by further studying the judgments of the ECJ and the opinions of the Advocates General on fundamental rights matters that were delivered between December 2009 and June 2016. The different sources of literature for the most part only revealed relevant examples of cases dating from the period before the Charter entered into force. Therefore, to supplement this with more recent examples, a further study was carried out regarding the case-law of the ECJ and the opinions of the Advocates General since December 2009. A further reason for taking December 2009 as a starting point for this in-depth study is that this is the date of the entry into force of the Charter as a binding document. Since that date, there has been a clear increase in the number of cases of the ECJ on fundamental rights, and these cases appear to have been overlooked in the literature discussing the development of a concept of positive obligations.

This case-law analysis provides some further insight into the specific kinds of positive obligations that could become relevant for the EU, and the specific situations in which such positive obligations would arise. Such examples include the case of *T.Port* (also discussed further below) in which Community institutions were put under an obligation to take meaures to protect the right to property of traders in their transition to the common market; the case of *Chatzi* (discussed in section 7.2.2.) in which the member states incurred a legislative obligation to protect the right to equal treatment with respect to parents of twins and their right to parental leave; and the case of *Abdida* (discussed in section 11.5.4.) in which the member states incurred an obligation to provide for the basic needs of a seriously ill third-country national, as well as interim measures while he or she awaits the appeal of a transfer decision. A selection of cases are further assessed in light of the conclusions reached in part II to find out whether, and at what point, any conflicts with the specific principles of EU law take place.

---

42 See Gerards (2016); and De Witte (1999).

Within the EU's legal order, the ECJ is just one of the institutions that could further define the scope and meaning of fundamental rights, since the EU legislature and the executive are also increasingly engaging with fundamental rights protection. A different approach might have been to study whether and how the EU institutions, in combination with the national legislature, would incorporate the concept of positive obligations into the EU legal order, in a similar way to the ECtHR. This present study, however, focuses on the ECJ and its case-law. The ECJ still plays an authoritative role in the interpretation of fundamental rights within the EU context.[43] Legal scholarship, moreover, expects that the ECJ in particular will deal with the concept of positive obligations in the EU context.[44] As will be explained in this study, positive obligations may often not be defined beforehand by legislatures or other public authorities.[45] They are, rather, revealed in concrete circumstances and in individual cases brought to the courts, showing that certain gaps exist in state policies. Indeed, the definition of positive obligations by Courts raises the most intricate questions, as the first part of this study, in particular chapter four, will reveal. Even though this research is therefore not focused on legislation at the EU and at the national level, it should be emphasised and recognised that the EU legislature can provide important guidance to the various actors involved as to how positive obligations to protect fundamental rights in relevant fields of interest for EU law can be accommodated and, for example, the limits which must be respected.

Considering the three steps discussed above, it can be seen that, overall, this study takes a predominantly legal positivist approach as to answering the central question. This is valuable, since so much is as yet unknown about the potential scope for a development of positive obligations doctrine under EU law. For that reason, a further normative study of the doctrine of positive obligations and the protection of fundamental rights within the EU context is not specifically called for, nor is it undertaken in this study.

1.4. WORKING DEFINITION OF POSITIVE OBLIGATIONS WITHIN THE CONTEXT OF EU LAW

In academic discussions, only a few writers have explained how they would define a concept of positive obligations for EU law. Most refer in general to the concept of positive obligations as it has been defined by the ECtHR or to the tripartite duty to respect, protect and fulfil human rights as it has been developed in international human

43 Besson has, for example, explained that the EU legislature and the member states may still not be sufficiently aware of how to apply and explain fundamental rights in relation to their policies and actions under EU law, see Besson (2011b), p. 68.

44 Besson (2011b), pp. 59 and 68; and Fontanelli (2011), E-26.

45 Besson (2011b), p. 59.

rights law.[46] This study, as discussed earlier, also takes inspiration from the case-law of the ECtHR on the development of positive obligations, including its definition. As explained further in chapter 3, the basic definition provided by the ECtHR is that of an obligation for states to take active measures to protect fundamental rights.[47]

There is more, however, to defining positive obligations within the context of EU law. This is because of the specific role played by provisions of EU primary or secondary EU law which must also be taken into account. These provisions play an important role because they bring situations within the scope of application of EU fundamental rights. Provisions of secondary EU law may already provide (quite clearly) the conditions and the actions that must be undertaken by the EU institutions or the member states. However, if such conditions and detail are missing, and the actions which need to be taken by the EU institutions or the member states are mostly defined by provisions of fundamental rights and the interpretation given thereof by courts, it can be concluded that an obligation to take active measures is indeed established on the basis of provisions of fundamental rights. This is when positive obligations are created under EU law according to the meaning given to this concept in this study.

Thus a positive obligation within the context of EU law is defined as 'An obligation to take active measures which is based on the protection of fundamental rights and which is not already specified by EU (secondary or primary) law.'

To explain the choice for this particular definition, a closer look can be taken at a specific example, that is, the case of *T. Port*.[48] This case has frequently been cited as a prime example of where the ECJ has recognised in a clear manner the existence of a positive obligation for the Community institutions.[49] In that judgment, the ECJ held that:

> The Community Institutions are required to act in particular when the transition to the common organization of the market infringes certain traders' fundamental rights protected by Community law, such as the right to property and the right to pursue a professional or trade activity.[50]

Here, the ECJ clearly stated that the EU institutions are under an obligation to take active measures to protect the fundamental rights of traders. This positive obligation was formulated by the ECJ in response to a case brought by Port, which was a German trading company which suffered adverse effects from a quota system which was established under a Community Regulation for the import of bananas. In accordance

---

46 Ahmed & Butler rather define the concept of positive obligation on the basis of the tripartite typology of 'respect, protect, and fulfil', which is more commonly used in international human rights law, see Ahmed & Butler (2006), p. 796; and section 3.3.2.

47 See section 3.2.2.

48 ECJ 26 November 1996, C-68/95, *T. Port*.

49 Cf. Weiler & Fries (1999), p. 147; De Witte (1999), p. 882; and Ahmed & Butler (2006), p. 795.

50 ECJ 26 November 1996, C-68/95, *T. Port*, para. 38.

with that Regulation, Port had obtained licences for the import of a certain quantity of bananas which was based on its sales numbers in a certain reference year. That particular year, Port's sales were particularly low due to a breach of contract by one of its suppliers. The licences subsequently allocated to Port were insufficient for the company to meet its previously contracted financial obligations. Port complained about irreparable infringements of its property rights before the national courts under these circumstances. The national court referred questions to the ECJ, which, among others, addressed the failure of the European Commission to take measures. The European Commission had been given the power under the Regulation to take measures 'to assist the transition from arrangements existing before the entry into force of this Regulation to those laid down by this Regulation, and in particular to overcome difficulties of a sensitive nature'. In some respect, therefore, the measures which the Community institutions were required to take on the basis of the judgment of the ECJ were related to a positive act that was already defined in secondary Community law.[51] At the same time, the provision of secondary EU law had granted a discretionary power for the Commission to take action in relation to transitional arrangements that needed to be made.[52] The European Commission was under no obligation under the Regulation to take such measures, nor was it required by the Regulation actively to ensure the protection of fundamental rights. It may therefore be argued that the Commission incurred the obligation to exercise its power to protect the fundamental rights of traders only on the basis of the interpretation of the specific provision that was given by the ECJ in the case of *T. Port*.

To show the difference, the example of a positive obligation that follows directly from the provisions of secondary EU law can be given. In its judgment in the case of *Parliament v. Council* the ECJ held that this situation arose.[53] There, it had to assess the compatibility of certain provisions of Directive 2003/86 on family reunification in light of fundamental rights. Under this Directive, member states were allowed to restrict the right to family reunification in respect of children over the age of 12 or, in certain circumstances, the age of 15.[54] The member states could also make use of waiting lists. In interpreting the relevant provisions, the ECJ took into account the positive

51 According to Ahmed & Butler, the case of *T. Port* does not illustrate a 'true example' of a positive obligation. It only concerns a 'corrective' measure which would be taken to repair the damages suffered by the violation of a certain fundamental right, see Ahmed & Butler (2006), pp. 794–795. This distinction between negative and positive obligations is further discussed in in relation to the case-law of the ECtHR in section 3.2.3. and in relation to the case-law of the ECJ in section 11.2.

52 Article 30 of Regulation No. 404/93 of 13 February 1993 on the common organisation of the market in bananas [1993] OJ L47/1.

53 ECJ 27 June 2006, C-540/03, *Parliament v. Council*.

54 See Articles 4(1), 4(6) and Article 8 of Directive 2003/86/EC of 22 September 2003 on the right to family reunification [2003] OJ L251/12.

obligations that havebeen defined by the ECtHR under Article 8 ECHR requiring states to let persons enter into and reside on their territory.[55] It held that:

> Article 4(1) of the Directive imposes precise positive obligations, with corresponding clearly defined individual rights, on the Member States, since it requires them, in the cases determined by the Directive, to authorise family reunification of certain members of the sponsor's family, without being left a margin of appreciation.[56]

Thus, by providing the conditions under which member states were required to grant family reunification, the Directive itself laid down a positive obligation on the member states.[57] The ECJ therefore did not need to define further the actions that would have to be undertaken by the member states.

Importantly, the definition provided above is only a working definition, which is in need of refinement. In particular, in defining positive obligations it is important to take account of the different types of positive obligations that exist, as well as the distinction that can be made between negative and positive obligations. These issues are discussed in chapters 3 and 11.[58]

1.5. OUTLINE OF THIS STUDY

This study has been structured as set out below.

1.5.1. PART I: THE CONCEPT OF POSITIVE OBLIGATIONS WITHIN THE CONTEXT OF THE EUROPEAN CONVENTION ON HUMAN RIGHTS

The first part of this study explains how the ECtHR has developed positive obligations and what criticism the development of this concept has raised. First, chapter 2 gives

---

55 ECJ 27 June 2006, C-540/03, *Parliament v. Council*, paras 52–54. The ECJ specifically refers to the positive obligations in the cases of ECtHR 21 December 2001, no. 31465/96, *Sen v. the Netherlands*, para. 31; ECtHR 19 February 1996, no. 23218/94, *Gül v. Switzerland*, para. 38; and ECtHR 28 November 1996, no. 21702/93, *Ahmut v. the Netherlands*, para. 67. In the case of *Parliament v. Council*, the ECJ may have been inspired by arguments brought forward by the European Parliament and the discussion thereof by Advocate General Kokott in her Opinion to the case, see Opinion of AG Kokott in C-540/03, paras 64–71.

56 ECJ 27 June 2006, C-540/03, *Parliament v. Council*, para. 60.

57 In this context, in particular, it is difficult to distinguish between positive obligations and negative obligations, see e.g. Lawson (1995a), p. 558. Cf. ECtHR 28 May 1985, nos. 9214/80 to 9474/81, *Abdulaziz, Cabales and Balkandali v. the United Kingdom*; and ECtHR 11 July 2000, no. 29192/95, *Ciliz v. the Netherlands* paras 61–62. For further examples, see Xenos (2012), p. 69.

58 See sections 3.2.2., 3.2.3., and 11.2. where it is explained how the distinction between positive and negative obligations can be made. See further sections 3.3. and 11.4. for the existence of different types of positive obligations.

a brief background sketch of some important elements of the legal system of the Convention. Chapter 3 explains how the ECtHR has developed positive obligations in its case-law, including a definition of the concept of positive obligations, as well as the different types of positive obligations that can be distinguished. Chapter 4 discusses in more detail the various problematic features which are related to a development of positive obligations by the ECtHR. Chapter 5 collects the main conclusions of part I.

1.5.2. PART II: THE SCOPE FOR A DEVELOPMENT OF POSITIVE OBLIGATIONS WITHIN THE CONTEXT OF EU LAW – AN ANALYSIS OF THE SPECIFIC PARAMETERS OF THE EU LEGAL ORDER AND THE EU SYSTEM OF FUNDAMENTAL RIGHTS PROTECTION

The second part of this study turns towards the system of fundamental rights protection of the EU. Chapter 6 discusses a number of general features of this system, including the rationale of fundamental rights protection within the context of the EU system, some general and important provisions of the Charter, and the particular interrelationship between EU law and the Convention. Chapters 7 to 9 address in more detail the parameters that are of particular relevance to determine the potential and the limits of a development of positive obligations by the ECJ. Chapter 7 discusses the institutional position and the judicial style of the ECJ. Chapter 8 looks into the complicated issue of the limited competences of the EU to protect fundamental rights. Chapter 9 addresses the limited scope of application of fundamental rights under EU and Chapter 10 presents the main conclusions of the second part of this study.

1.5.3. PART III: SYNTHESIS

The third and final part of this study brings together the findings and the conclusions of the two preceeding parts. Chapter 11 provides an overview of the various kinds of positive obligations that can be found in the case-law of the ECJ and evaluates how the Court has developed such obligations in its case-law on the basis of the conclusions reached in parts I and II. Finally, chapter 12 sets out the final conclusions of this study as well the recommendations for how the development of positive obligations by the ECJ could take place.

PART I

THE CONCEPT OF POSITIVE OBLIGATIONS WITHIN THE CONTEXT OF THE EUROPEAN CONVENTION ON HUMAN RIGHTS

CHAPTER 2

THE SYSTEM OF FUNDAMENTAL RIGHTS PROTECTION UNDER THE EUROPEAN CONVENTION ON HUMAN RIGHTS

2.1. INTRODUCTION

In order to understand the meaning of the recognition of positive obligations under the Convention, it is first important to take into account the particularities of the Convention system. This is because a positive obligation may bear different meanings for each court or body and legal system in which it is applied. The ECtHR, in particular, has derived positive obligations from a catalogue of mainly civil and political rights under the Convention. These rather negatively formulated rights are understood by the ECtHR, principally, as obligations for states to refrain from taking action.[1] How has this system thus allowed for the recognition of positive obligations, which demand an active interference by states?

This chapter provides a further background to the Convention system, which, as such, will be helpful for those looking for some general context of the Convention. It is also of interest for the analysis of the development of positive obligations within this system in the following chapters.[2] Specific topics that are dealt with in this chapter are the background and purpose of the Convention (section 2.2.); its enforcement mechanisms (section 2.3.); the subsidiarity principle (section 2.4.); the role of the ECtHR (section 2.5.); the tools of interpretation of the ECtHR (section 6.); the effects of the Convention in the national legal order (section 2.7.); and the horizontal effect of Convention provisions (section 2.8.). The discussion of these topics is followed by a brief conclusion (section 2.9.).

---

1 See e.g. ECtHR 13 June 1979, no. 6833/74, *Marck v. Belgium*, para. 31.

2 On the Convention system generally, see e.g. Harris, O'Boyle, Bates & Warbrick (2014); Van Dijk & Arai-Takahanshi (2006); and Gerards (2011a).

2.2. BACKGROUND AND PURPOSE OF THE EUROPEAN CONVENTION ON HUMAN RIGHTS

The Convention was adopted in 1950. It was drafted within the Council of Europe, an international organisation that was established to achieve peace and unity in Europe after the Second World War.[3] At around the same time the European Coal and Steel Community and the European Atomic Energy Community, and later the European Economic Community, were established. These predecessors of the current EU essentially had the same ideal as the Council of Europe; however, they have mainly sought an economic form of cooperation between states.[4] The Convention was, instead, oriented towards the protection of human rights. Its main aim was to prevent the atrocities committed during World War Two from reoccurring and to protect the democratic ideals of Western Europe especially at the time when communist regimes were in place in the Eastern part of Europe.[5] Initially, only 10, Western European, states ratified the Convention, but over time membership has grown. There was a particularly sharp increase in the number of ratifying states in the 1990s after the fall of the Berlin Wall and the dissolution of the Yugoslav Republic.[6] The geographical expansion of membership to the Convention to Eastern Europe, which since 1998 also includes Russia, has generally had an effect both on the workload of the ECtHR, as well as on the types of fundamental rights issues with which the ECtHR is now confronted.[7] The Convention itself has further evolved into, what is called by some, a 'European Bill of Human Rights' with a very important role played by the ECtHR.[8] The Convention provides an important (minimum) standard for the protection of fundamental rights for all of the European states.[9] Large numbers of complaints are still, and especially, brought by individuals regarding violations of fundamental rights by all of the states parties.

---

3 Convention for the Protection of Human Rights and Fundamental Freedoms signed in Rome, 4 November 1950, ETS 5; 213 UNTS 221 (as amended by Protocols No. 11 and No. 14). The aims of the Council are set out in the preamble and Article 1 of the Statute of the Council of Europe 1949, ETS 1; 87 UNTS 103.

4 For an historical overview of the establishment and development of the European Economic Community, see Urwin (1995).

5 Bates (2010), pp. 46–47.

6 Bates (2010), p. 22. At present, there are 47 states parties to the Convention. The ratification of the Convention by these Eastern European States constitutes an important step for those states to be able to join the European Economic Community, see Bates (2010), p. 451.

7 Most of the complaints are concerned with a lack of respect for the rule of law, the right to liberty and security, and the right to a fair trial, see Bates (2010), p. 483. For a statistical overview of the types of violations see Registry of the European Court of Human Rights, Annual Report 2015, p. 193, available online at <www.echr.coe.int>.

8 Bates (2010), p. 5; and Harris, O'Boyle, Bates & Warbrick (2014), p. 4.

9 On the effects of the Convention and the judgments of the ECtHR on the national legal order, see Gerards & Fleuren (2013).

Substantively, the Convention draws from the rights laid down in the Universal Declaration of Human Rights which was adopted by the United Nations in 1948.[10] The Convention contains a range of civil and political rights, and a few more socially flavoured rights, such as the right to private and family life and the right to freedom of association. Most social rights have, however, been left out of the Convention. It was found problematic at the time to include social and economic rights as they were not considered to form clear enforceable rights. It was also held that such rights were already recognised and accommodated in the Western European democracies.[11] Since then, specific fundamental rights instruments have been adopted, such as the European Social Charter which provides guarantees of social and economic rights. However, it has a different and less forceful enforcement mechanism.[12] More recently, social and economic rights can also be found in the Charter of Fundamental Rights of the EU.[13] Also, some concessions have been made to the substantive guarantees in the Convention by the addition of multiple Protocols to the Convention. Therefore, the right to protection of property, the right to education, the right to equality between spouses, and a self-standing right to non-discrimination have been included.[14] Further, the ECtHR has played an important role in developing certain social and economic components in its case-law on the protection of the civil and political rights laid down in the Convention.[15]

2.3. ENFORCEMENT MECHANISMS

In comparison to most other international human rights treaties, the Convention stands out for its enforcement mechanisms. Individuals can complain directly before the ECtHR. The judgments of the ECtHR are binding for the parties to the case and they can become final.[16] Both individuals and states can bring applications before the ECtHR regarding violations by one of the states parties to the Convention.[17]

---

10 The preamble of the Convention also states that the states parties are resolved to 'take the first steps for the collective enforcement of certain of the rights stated in the Universal Declaration'. For this reason, the Convention is considered more effective in comparison to the UDHR, see Bates (2010), p. 110.

11 Bates (2010), pp. 63–68.

12 There is now also a collective complaints procedure, which can be used to enforce the rights laid down in the European Social Charter. The European Committee on Social Rights has delivered a few influential (although not binding) judgments, for example, on the conditions for the reception of illegally staying migrants, see ECSR 14 November 2014, no. 90/2103, *Conference of European Churches v. the Netherlands.*

13 See further section 6.10., explaining that a particular distinction can apply between rights and principles and their justiciability, which could particularly affect the social and economic rights under the Charter.

14 Protocols nos. 1, 4 and 12. These protocols have been ratified by most, but not all, of the states parties.

15 See further Leijten (2015).

16 Articles 46(1) and 32 ECHR.

17 Articles 33 and 34 ECHR. Protocol No. 11 of 1998 has made the right to individual application and the jurisdiction of the Court compulsory for all states parties.

In practice, however, very few inter-state applications are actually made.[18] The Convention is usually enforced through the delivery of judgments by the ECtHR in individual cases. The ECtHR itself has also recognised the significance of such individual applications by stating that 'the Convention right to individual application … has over the years become of high importance and is now a key component of the machinery for protecting the rights and freedoms set forth in the Convention'.[19] However, the number of individual applications being made has led to an overwhelming case load for the ECtHR.[20] Any person, non-governmental organisation or group of individuals, irrespective of nationality may bring a claim before the ECtHR alleging the breach of one or more Convention rights against one of the states parties. Important admissibility conditions are the exhaustion of domestic remedies and certain time limits which must have been met (Articles 34 and 35 ECHR).

The execution of the judgments of the ECtHR is further supervised by the Committee of Ministers (Article 46(2) ECHR), which is composed of representatives of the states parties' governments. The Convention also provides for a system of reports on states' compliance (Article 52 ECHR), but this mechanism is seldom used.

2.4. SUBSIDIARY SYSTEM OF PROTECTION OF FUNDAMENTAL RIGHTS

The principle of subsidiarity is an important principle underlying the Convention system as such, and it is also key to understanding the role of the ECtHR and some of the interpretative principles which it uses (see sections 2.5. and 2.6. below).[21] The principle of subsidiarity is specifically mentioned in Article 1 of Protocol No. 15, but this Protocol has not yet entered into force.[22] The subsidiarity principle has been held to follow generally from Article 1 ECHR which encapsulates the basic idea that states are primarily responsible for securing the rights and freedoms of the Convention to

18 The annual report of 2015 of the European Court of Human Rights reveals that there was a small number of inter-state applications pending in 2015. The annual report is available on <http://www.echr.coe.int/Documents/Annual_report_2015_ENG.pdf>.

19 ECtHR 4 February 2005, nos. 46827/99 and 46951/99, *Mamatkulov and Askarov v. Turkey*, para. 122.

20 Current numbers can be found in the Facts and Figures which are available on <http://www.echr.coe.int>.

21 The ECtHR has described the principle of subsidiarity as 'primordial' to the system of protection of the Convention, see ECtHR 1 March 2010, nos. 46113/99 to 21819/04 (adm. dec.), *Demopoulos and others v. Turkey*, para. 69. See further Villiger (2007), pp. 623–637. Within the EU context, there is a somewhat different meaning that can be ascribed to the principle of subsidiarity, as it is also employed specifically to govern the division of powers between the EU and the member states, see section 8.4.3.

22 Protocol No. 15 was adopted in 2013 as a response to reforms concluded to in the Brighton Declaration of 2002. At the time of writing (February 2016), Protocol No. 15 is still open for signature and ratification by the states parties, see <http://www.coe.int/en/web/conventions/full-list/-/conventions/treaty/213/signatures>.

everyone within their jurisdiction.[23] Thus, in this respect, the Strasbourg system of supervision is subsidiary to the national system. The ECtHR may intervene only if national authorities have failed to fulfil their obligations under the Convention.[24] Moreover, the Convention intends to provide only a minimum standard of fundamental rights for Europe.[25]

The subsidiary character of the Convention system has several important implications.[26] First, states should be offered the opportunity to redress alleged infringements of Convention rights before the ECtHR becomes involved. Secondly, states are generally considered to be better placed to assess the factual and legal circumstances of a particular case than the ECtHR, and so the ECtHR allows states to decide which measures they consider appropriate for remedying fundamental rights violations. Thirdly, while it is the ECtHR's task carefully to review states' fulfilment of their obligations under the Convention, it must also pay attention to the national identities and the diversity of the states parties. It must, after all, deal with 47 states which have a cultural, historical and moral diversity.[27]

In effect, the principle of subsidiarity thus governs the division of tasks between the national authorities and the ECtHR.[28] The ECtHR only deals with individual complaints on the condition that all national remedies have been exhausted (Article 35(1) ECHR), and states must make sure that remedies are available for individuals at the national level if they experience a violation of fundamental rights (Article 13 ECHR).

In a substantive sense, subsidiarity also has a role to play. Subsidiarity is apparent from the restraint that is adopted by the ECtHR in the interpretation and application of the Convention. The margin of appreciation doctrine, which defines the intensity of the review by the ECtHR of national decisions and measures, is a particular expression of such a deferential approach.[29] Further, the Convention allows for a higher level of protection of fundamental rights at the national level (Article 53 ECHR), but this provision is rarely applied by the ECtHR.[30] The ECtHR has developed several techniques in its case-law that aim to ensure respect for its subsidiary position in its review of the protection of fundamental rights. It has, for example, developed the

---

23 See ECtHR 7 December 1976, no. 5493/72, *Handyside v. the United Kingdom*, para. 48. A basis for the principle of subsidiarity is generally found in Articles 1, 13 and 35(1) ECHR.

24 See ECtHR 23 July 1968, nos. 1474/62 to 2126/64, *Belgian Linguistic case*, para. 10 *in fine*.

25 The ECtHR interprets a range of terms in the Convention autonomously. This applies to the terms 'criminal charge' within the meaning of Article 6(1) ECHR, and 'home' within the meaning of Article 8(1) ECHR, see ECtHR 8 June 1976, nos. 5100/71 to 5370/72, *Engel and others v. the Netherlands*, paras 81–82; and ECtHR 18 November 2004, no. 58255/00, *Propokovich v. Russia*, para. 36. Although the meaning of a term in the Convention is not necessarily identical to the meaning of the term at national level, the Court does rely and draw inspiration from national meanings for its autonomous interpretations.

26 Villiger (2007), pp. 634 ff.

27 ECtHR 23 July 1968, nos. 1474/62 to 2126/64, *Belgian Linguistic case*, para. 10 *in fine*.

28 Villiger (2007), p. 634.

29 Villiger (2007), p. 629. See further section 2.6.3.

30 Cf. ECtHR 15 October 2009, no. 17056/06, *Micallef v. Malta*, para. 60.

so-called 'in for a penny, in for a pound' approach, in which it aims to exercise judicial review of nationally protected fundamental rights.[31] This implies a review by the ECtHR regarding whether certain fundamental rights which are recognised at the national level but not at the Convention level are, nonetheless, protected in conformity with the requirements of the Convention. For example, the ECtHR has examined whether the right to adoption, which is not protected by the Convention as such, was at least applied by public authorities to individuals in a non-discriminatory manner.[32] This approach ultimately seeks to secure that fundamental rights are protected at the national level more effectively.

Another specific way in which the ECtHR aims to bridge the concerns of a subsidiary and ineffective review is by conducting a procedural type of review.[33] In this approach, the ECtHR has regard to the quality of the decision-making process and to the existence of procedural safeguards in order to find out whether sufficient protection of fundamental rights has (already) been provided at the national level. There are different variations of such procedural review. One variation could be that if the ECtHR is indeed satisfied with the quality of the 'process' at the national level, the ECtHR will not look in more detail at whether the substantive standards of the Convention have also been complied with.[34] The benefit of the approach is that by shifting the focus of fundamental rights protection to the national level, and by strengthening the available national administrative frameworks, individuals gain better opportunities to complain of fundamental rights violations at national level. It further increases the objectivity of the Court's judgments, because it does not need to substitute the assessment that has already been made by the national court by its own assessment on the merits.[35]

2.5. THE ROLE OF THE ECtHR

As has been explained already, the delivery of judgments by the ECtHR is of considerable importance for the enforcement of the guarantees laid down in the Convention. The ECtHR essentially reviews whether states parties have observed their engagements under the Convention in individual applications (Article 19 ECHR) in light of its subsidiary and supervisory role.[36] The ECtHR thereby interprets and applies

---

31 Gerards (2013), pp. 79–82.

32 ECtHR 22 January 2008, no. 43546/02, *E.B. v. France*, para. 49.

33 Dubout (2007); and Brems & Lavrysen (2013). See further section 3.3.1. Interestingly, a procedural type of review has also been recognised within some judgments of the ECJ on fundamental rights, see Lenaerts (2012b) and section 7.5.2.

34 See e.g. ECtHR 27 September 1995, no. 18984/91, *McCann and others v. the United Kingdom*, para. 153. Cf. Tulkens & Van Drooghenbroeck (2012), Gerards (2012a), pp. 187–189; and Xenos (2012), pp. 65–69. The ECtHR does not consistently refer, however, to those procedural violations when examining a state's positive obligations, see Van de Westelaken (2010), pp. 147–148.

35 Dubout (2007), p. 402.

36 See also ECtHR 13 August 1981, nos. 7601/76 and 7806/77, *Young, James and Webster v. the United Kingdom*, para. 53.

the Convention (Article 32 ECHR).[37] The ECtHR is not a court of fourth instance in relation to the national courts, as it has explicitly stated.[38] The ECtHR also does not deal with errors of facts or law committed by national courts, unless it appears that the assessment made by the national courts is flagrantly and manifestly arbitrary.[39]

The interpretations which are provided by the ECtHR of the Convention *de facto* have an impact that goes beyond the individual cases to which the judgment formally relates.[40] The ECtHR delivers its judgments in a way that allows its interpretation of the Convention rights to be applied more generally. The interpretations given by the ECtHR on the rights laid down in the Convention have acquired a certain authoritative force. States have accepted the *res interpretata* of the judgments of the Convention even in cases which have been brought by individuals against one of the other states parties.[41] In particular, the Grand Chamber develops further authoritative interpretations of the Convention in the cases that are brought before it. The Grand Chamber is competent to deal with serious questions affecting the interpretation or application of the Convention (Articles 30 and 43 ECHR). In addition, the introduction of pilot judgment has allowed the ECtHR to develop the interpretation of the Convention in a more general way. Pilot judgments are delivered in so-called 'clone cases', where several cases in combination reveal a systemic problem with the compliance by one of the states parties with the guarantees of the Convention.[42]

The question is sometimes raised whether the ECtHR should transform into a constitutional court, which should also be considered against the background of its high workload.[43] This would mean that the ECtHR would focus on major fundamental rights problems in Europe rather than on individual complaints. The constitutional nature of the Convention has for many years been the subject of extensive academic debate, where it is as much criticised as it is welcomed.[44] Presently, the ECtHR is

---

37 Prior to 1998, the European Commission of Human Rights provided interpretations of the Convention by deciding on the admissibility of cases and by issuing reports on the merits of admitted cases. The Commission was abolished by Protocol 11; also as a result of that Protocol, the ECtHR became a full-time permanent body.

38 See e.g. ECtHR 24 November 1994, *Kemmache v. France (No. 3)*, no. 17621/91 para. 44.

39 See e.g. ECtHR 24 July 2008, no. 36376/04, *Kononov v. Latvia*, para. 108.

40 On the relation between the Convention, the judgments of the ECtHR and national law, see section 3.2.7.

41 The Court has held that 'The Court's judgments in fact serve not only to decide those cases brought before the Court but, more generally, to elucidate, safeguard and develop the rules instituted by the Convention' and 'Although the primary purpose of the Convention system is to provide individual relief, its mission is also to determine issues on public policy-grounds in the common interest, thereby raising the general standards of protection of human rights and extending human rights jurisprudence throughout the community of Convention States'. See respectively ECtHR, 18 January 1978, no. 5310/71, *Ireland v. the United Kingdom*, para. 154; and ECtHR, 24 July 2003, no. 40016/98, *Karner v. Austria*, para. 26.

42 Rule 61 of the Rules of Court, inserted on 21 February 2011. The Court delivered its first pilot judgment in ECtHR 28 September 2005, no. 31443/96, *Broniowski v. Poland*.

43 Other reforms introduced to reduce the workload of the ECtHR include the possibility of single judges making decisions on the admissibility of applications (Article 27 ECHR).

44 Cf. e.g. Alkema (2000), pp. 41–63; and Wildhaber (2002), pp. 161–165.

described as a quasi-constitutional court, because it is generally considered to provide the final interpretation of fundamental rights within Europe.[45]

While the ECtHR may thus play quite an active role in the protection of fundamental rights, it is also aware of its subsidiary function, as has been discussed above.[46] In general, the ECtHR therefore remains careful in pronouncing on decisions which are politically sensitive for the states parties.[47]

2.6. TOOLS OF INTERPRETATION OF THE EUROPEAN COURT OF HUMAN RIGHTS

As any international treaty, the Convention is interpreted according to the rules on interpretation of Treaties laid down in the Vienna Convention, which the ECtHR also considers itself bound by.[48] The ECtHR has, however, also described the Convention as a 'law-making treaty', which would make it distinct from other international treaties that merely create contractual obligations.[49] The ECtHR thus approaches the Convention as being of a special kind in the area of international law. By reason of the special nature of the Convention, the ECtHR has held that 'it is … necessary to seek the interpretation that is most appropriate in order to realise the aim and achieve the objective of the treaty, not that which would restrict to the greatest possible degree the obligations undertaken by the Parties.'[50]

Given the special 'law-making character' of the Convention, the 'object and purpose' of the Convention play a crucial role in the interpretation of the rights set forth in the Convention.[51] As explained earlier, the aims of the Convention are to ensure the 'protection of individual human beings' and to 'maintain and promote the ideals and values of a democratic society'.[52] The ECtHR has explained that these objects and

45 The Court has expressed on several occasions that the Convention is a 'constitutional instrument of European public order', see ECtHR 23 March 1995, no. 15318/89, *Loizidou v. Turkey* (preliminary objections), para. 75; and ECtHR 4 March 1991, nos. 15299/89 to 15318/89 (adm. dec.), *Chrysostomos, Papachrysostomou and Loizidou v. Turkey*, para. 22. See further Frowein (1990).

46 See section 2.4.

47 Gerards (2011b), pp. 201–202.

48 Articles 31 to 33 of the Vienna Convention on the Law of Treaties (1969). The ECtHR does not often refer to provisions of the Convention. See e.g. ECtHR 21 February 1975, no. 4451/70, *Golder v. the United Kingdom*, para. 29.

49 Brölmann (2005), pp. 383–387.

50 ECtHR 27 June 1968, no. 2122/64, *Wemhoff v. Germany*, para. 8.

51 Article 31(1) and (2) of the Vienna Convention on the Law of Treaties give weight to the object and purpose of a treaty for the interpretation of the treaty's provisions. The ECtHR applied these provisions in the *Golder* case to discover whether a right of access to court was indeed guaranteed by Article 6(1) ECHR, see ECtHR 21 February 1975, no. 4451/70, *Golder v. the United Kingdom*, paras 24–36.

52 ECtHR 7 July 1989, no. 14038/88, *Soering v. the United Kingdom*, para. 87; and ECtHR 7 December 1976, nos. 5095/71 to 5926/71, *Kjeldsen, Busk Madsen and Pedersen v. Denmark*, para. 53.

purposes justify certain specific methods for the interpretation of the Convention.[53] The ECtHR strongly focuses on a teleological interpretation of the Convention. Other methods of interpretation are less important for the case-law of the ECtHR, in particular the historical method of interpretation.[54] This can be explained by the fact that the text of the Convention and the *travaux préparatoires* date back more than 60 years.[55] States parties in Europe at that time faced rather different fundamental rights' challenges as compared to those seen now. Also, over the years many new states, including Eastern European states, which did not participate in the drafting process have become parties to the Convention.

The principle of effectiveness and the principle of evolutive or dynamic interpretation both play important roles in the interpretation of the Convention. These principles help the ECtHR to realise the object and purpose of the Convention, and they can be viewed as interpretative principles which follow from the special character of the Convention.[56] Another important tool of interpretation which is specifically used by the ECtHR is the 'margin of appreciation' doctrine. This doctrine plays an important role in the judgments of the ECtHR. It gives clear expression of the subsidiary nature of the Convention. In view of their importance, these three tools of interpretation are briefly explained below.

2.6.1. THE PRINCIPLE OF EFFECTIVENESS

The Convention provisions are, generally, to be interpreted and applied in line with the principle of effectiveness.[57] The ECtHR has often held that 'The Convention is intended to guarantee not rights that are theoretical and illusory but rights that are practical

53 ECtHR 21 February 1975, no. 4451/70, *Golder v. the United Kingdom*, para. 36. Judge Fitzmaurice argued for a far more cautious and conservative approach, exactly so because of the special character of the Convention that enforces individuals' rights against the states, see the separate opinion of Judge Fitzmaurice to the judgment of the ECtHR in this case, in particular at paras 38–39.

54 See Gerards (2011a); and ECtHR 23 March, no. 15318/89, *Loizidou v. Turkey* (preliminary objections), para. 71. The ECtHR has held that the *travaux préparatoires* may be used as a supportive, rather than a decisive, source and that they may be overruled, see ECtHR 1 July 1961, no. 332/57, *Lawless v. Ireland*, para. 14.

55 Cf. also Article 32 of the Vienna Convention on the law of treaties where the *travaux préparatoires* are mentioned as a supplementary interpetation method. Yet, some of the Protocols annexed to the Convention were introduced much more recently. The *travaux préparatoires* corresponding to those Protocols may then indeed be considered of importance for the interpretation of the rights they contain, see Gerards (2011b), p. 69.

56 See Senden (2011), pp. 46 and 69. A distinction can be made between interpretative principles and interpretation methods (e.g. textual interpretation), see Senden (2011), pp. 44–47. It has been questioned whether the Convention actually holds a special character and whether its interpretation methods can really be considered unique in comparison to other international legal systems, see e.g. Christoffersen (2009).

57 See e.g. ECtHR 4 February 2005, nos. 46827/99 to 46951/99, *Mamatkulov and Askarov v. Turkey*, para. 101; and Gerards (2011b), p. 31.

and effective'.[58] According to the ECtHR, the effective interpretation of fundamental rights forms an objective of the Convention.[59] To be able to guarantee 'practical and effective rights' means that the Convention cannot remain theoretical and illusory.[60] States must ensure that individuals can enjoy fundamental rights in the reality of everyday life. An example of this approach is the judgment of the ECtHR in the case of *Airey v. Ireland*.[61] In this case, Mrs Airey wanted to divorce from her violent husband, but the national procedure she needed to follow to obtain a divorce was complex and held before a specialised court. The assistance of a solicitor proved indispensable to follow such a procedure. Mrs Airey could not afford to hire a solicitor, and so access to court was not realistically available to her. Before the ECtHR, she complained that her right of access to court (Article 6(1) ECHR) was violated. The ECtHR decided that the right of access to court was not effectively protected in this case, and moreover, that in such circumstances the state may need to provide for legal aid. This led to a positive obligation that needed to be fulfilled by the states parties.[62]

To ensure the effectiveness of Convention rights may further imply that states are held responsible for prospective or potential breaches of the Convention. This is shown by the judgment of the ECtHR in the case of *Soering v. the United Kingdom*.[63] This case was about a young German national who was detained in a prison in England. He was waiting to be extradited to the United States where he would be faced with charges of murder, and where he might incur the death penalty. Although it was not certain that the death penalty would actually be imposed in his case, the ECtHR held that the prohibition of torture (Article 3 ECHR) would be not be protected in an effective manner if the applicant were to be extradited to the United States. There was a real risk of ill-treatment, to which the United Kingdom needed to pay attention.[64] The ECtHR thus established that a violation had taken place even though the actual ill-treatment had not taken place.

Applying the principle of effectiveness to fundamental rights protection might also mean that the territorial reach of the jurisdiction of the ECtHR is extended, as the judgment in *Soering v. the United Kingdom* shows.[65] More generally, the scope of Convention rights and obligations has been widened considerably as a result of the Court's interpretation of fundamental rights based on the principle of effectiveness. An effective interpretation implies that the permissible limitations of the Convention rights

58 ECtHR 9 October 1979, no. 6289/73, *Airey v. Ireland*, para. 24.
59 Senden (2011), p. 73.
60 Mowbray (2005), p. 75.
61 ECtHR 9 October 1979, no. 6289/73, *Airey v. Ireland*.
62 ECtHR 9 October 1979, no. 6289/73, *Airey v. Ireland*, para. 24.
63 ECtHR 7 July 1989, no. 14038/88, *Soering v. the United Kingdom*.
64 ECtHR 7 July 1989, no. 14038/88, *Soering v. the United Kingdom*, para. 87. Factors that *inter alia* were taken into account by the Court were the conditions of the detention (being on death row) and the personal circumstances of the applicant (the young age and the psychiatric conditions in which the crimes were committed), see para. 111 of the judgment.
65 Harris, O'Boyle, Bates & Warbrick (2014), p. 18.

are interpreted in a narrow sense by the ECtHR.[66] Lastly, the ECtHR has also decided to interpret the notion of a 'victim' within the meaning of the right to individual petition (Article 34 ECHR) on the basis of the principle of effectiveness, which means that a wider array of claims can be lodged before the ECtHR.[67]

2.6.2. THE PRINCIPLE OF DYNAMIC OR EVOLUTIVE INTERPRETATION

The ECtHR has rather famously held: 'The Convention is a living instrument which … must be interpreted in light of present-day conditions.'[68] With this statement, the ECtHR announced that it will apply a dynamic or evolutive interpretation to the rights of the Convention in its judgments.[69] The ECtHR thereby adopts a flexible approach to the interpretation of fundamental rights.[70] It takes into account that societies and their standards of living evolve and that therefore fundamental rights can, over time, acquire new meanings. Thus, the ECtHR does not strictly hold to the interpretation of the Convention that was prevalent at the time when it was adopted, but adapts the interpretation of Convention rights in accordance with the contemporary standards of living and thinking in the Council of Europe. The ECtHR has regard to the developments of certain areas of law, including changes in public opinion, in relation to the interpretation of the applicable Convention rights.[71] The penal policies and family laws of the states parties have, for example, developed significantly over time.[72] Seeing that such an evolution can take place, the ECtHR may therefore also, over time, deliver different judgments on the same issues.

The ECtHR will only accept a different interpretation of the fundamental rights of the Convention due to the changing standards of the states parties in a gradual manner. The ECtHR makes use of the consensus method to determine whether a certain interpretation can be accepted.[73] This method of comparative interpretation means that the ECtHR has regard to the prevalent standards that are recognised by national and international laws, taking account of interpretations as well as practices. The ECtHR looks at the extent to which a certain interpretation of a fundamental right is accepted

---

66 Senden (2011), p. 76.

67 ECtHR 6 September 1978, no. 5029/71, *Klass and others v. Germany*, para. 34.

68 ECtHR 25 April 1978, no. 5856/72, *Tyrer v. the United Kingdom*, para. 31.

69 Gerards (2011b), p. 75.

70 Senden (2011), p. 70.

71 See e.g. ECtHR 13 June 1979, no. 6833/74, *Marckx v. Belgium*, para. 41; and ECtHR 25 April 1978, no. 5856/72, *Tyrer v. the United Kingdom*, para. 31.

72 A clear example of a dynamic interpretation can also be found in the Court's case-law regarding the legal recognition of transsexuals, which has led it to adopt a different and evolved interpretation of the right to private and family life (Article 8 ECHR) over time, see ECtHR 27 September 1990, no. 10843/84, *Cossey v. the United Kingdom*; and ECtHR 11 July 2002, no. 28957/95, *Christina Goodwin v. the United Kingdom*.

73 Gerards (2009), p. 17.

in the states parties, and it requires a certain level of uniformity. It generally needs to be satisfied that, at least, the majority of states parties appreciate the same standard. Preferably, this should be a great majority of the states.[74]

2.6.3. THE MARGIN OF APPRECIATION DOCTRINE

The ECtHR may decide to grant a margin of discretion to the national authorities in the fulfilment of their obligations under the Convention, which is better known as a margin of appreciation.[75] The margin of appreciation doctrine is expressly inspired by the subsidiary nature of the Convention system.[76] National authorities are generally considered to be better placed than the ECtHR to implement Convention law, and to strike a fair balance between all the interests involved. The 'room for manoeuvre' that is allowed in the protection of the Convention rights is, however, subject to the supervision of the ECtHR.

The margin of appreciation doctrine is used by the ECtHR when it examines the proportionality and the reasonableness of interferences of states parties with Convention rights. The doctrine is therefore relevant especially to those rights which have limitation clauses, which most notably concerns Articles 8 to 11 ECHR. These provisions allow states parties to restrict Convention rights as long as a restriction strikes a fair balance of interests and meets a number of other requirements.[77] The application of the margin of appreciation doctrine by the ECtHR may mean that it adjusts the intensity of its assessment. Generally, the ECtHR will limit its examination to whether national authorities have made a careful assessment of all facts and interests at stake. The ECtHR could decide to assess only whether adequate procedural safeguards were available at national level, or whether the balance of interests that was struck by the national authorities was not manifestly without reasonableness or proportionality.[78] Thus, so-called non-derogable rights, such as Article 2 ECHR on the right to life and Article 3 ECHR on the prohibition of inhuman and degrading treatment, in principle do not leave room for a similar deferential assessment.

The ECtHR can accord a wide, a narrow, or a *certain* margin to states depending on the specific context of the case. Considerable deference is generally applied by the

---

74 See e.g. ECtHR 13 June 1979, no. 6833/74, *Marckx v. Belgium*, para. 41.

75 ECtHR 7 December 1976, no. 5493/72, *Handyside v. the United Kingdom*, paras 48–49.

76 ECtHR 23 July 1968, nos. 1474/62 to 2126/64, *Belgian Linguistic case*, para. 10 *in fine*; and ECtHR 13 June 1979, *Marckx v. Belgium*, no. 6833/74, para. 41. Indeed, the margin of appreciation is also expressly mentioned in Article 1 of Protocol no. 15, see section 2.4.

77 Exceptionally, the margin of appreciation has been applied by the ECtHR to determine the material scope of a Convention right, see: e.g. ECtHR 8 July 2004, no. 53924/00, *Vo v. France*, paras 81–82. In this case the Court was confronted with the question whether the right to life could be applied to the situation of an unborn child.

78 See further Arai-Takahashi (2002); and Gerards (2011b), chapter 3.

ECtHR if a case concerns the economic and social policies of a state.[79] At the same time, generalisations on the scope of the margin of appreciation are hard to make. There are many factors which the ECtHR takes into account, such as the nature of the right, the importance of the right for the individual, the nature of the interference, the object pursued by the interference, and the consensus in Europe on the issues at stake.[80] Arguably, with so many factors to take into account, and due to the lack of clarity as to the relations between these factors, the application of the doctrine by the ECtHR is rather unpredictable.[81]

The margin of appreciation doctrine is also of special interest in relation to the formulation and development of positive obligations by the ECtHR. It is particularly relevant when the ECtHR deals with infringements of fundamental rights that have been caused by private parties. It can be expected that the margin of appreciation in this field is generally wide, although there is also room for exceptions.[82]

2.7. THE EFFECTS OF THE EUROPEAN CONVENTION ON HUMAN RIGHTS IN THE NATIONAL LEGAL ORDER

Because of the subsidiary nature of the Convention system, the Convention needs to rely on the national authorities for effectuating the rights and freedoms it sets forth. In this regard, the responsibility of the states parties is paralleled with a high level of autonomy. States may, in principle, decide for themselves how they wish to give effect to the Convention.[83] They need to make sure that Convention rights are guaranteed to the individuals within their jurisdiction (Article 1 ECHR) and provide individuals with effective remedies before their national courts in the event of a violation of Convention rights (Article 13 ECHR). On the basis of these obligations, the effects of the Convention on the national legal orders would seem to be limited.[84]

Yet, all of the state parties have chosen to incorporate the Convention in some way or another in their domestic legal systems, meaning that individuals can rely on Convention provisions – or at least the rights protected by the Convention – before the

---

79 See e.g. ECtHR 21 February 1986, no. 8793/79, *James and others v. the United Kingdom*, para. 46.

80 Cf. ECtHR 4 December 2008, nos. 30562/04 and 30566/04, *S. and Marper v. the United Kingdom*, para. 102; ECtHR 27 May 2004, no. 66746/01, *Connors v. the United Kingdom*, para. 82; and ECtHR 10 April 2007, no. 6339/05, *Evans v. the United Kingdom*, para. 77.

81 Harris, O'Boyle, Bates & Warbrick (2014), p. 17. See also Spielmann (2012).

82 See e.g. ECtHR 8 July 2003, no. 36022/97, *Hatton and others v. the United Kingdom*, paras 100–103 and 122–123. Specifically in relation to the concept of positive obligations, see sections 3.2.6. and 4.7.1.

83 Harris, O'Boyle, Bates & Warbrick (2014), p. 26. It has also been confirmed by the ECtHR that 'neither Article 13 nor the Convention in general lays down for the Contracting States any given manner for ensuring within their internal law the effective implementation of any of the provisions in the Convention', see ECtHR 6 February 1976, *Swedish Engine Driver's Union v. Sweden*, no. 5614/72, para. 50.

84 Leach (2005), p. 150.

national courts.[85] States are not legally obliged to do so.[86] The ways in which Convention rights can be enforced and protected through and by the national courts, legislature and executive may differ between the states parties.[87] Nonetheless, academic research has shown that, over the past years, the Convention has increasingly been relied on in national courts throughout Europe.[88]

States parties are further legally bound to abide by the judgments of the ECtHR (Article 46(1) ECHR). The obligations of the states in individual judgments are generally confined to what is stated in the *dictum*, that is, the operative part of the judgment. In the *dictum*, the ECtHR formally concludes the judgment with its findings on the admissibility and the merits of the case, and, eventually, awarding just satisfaction.[89] The binding effect of the judgment applies to all organs of the state, including the legislature.[90] Decisions of the ECtHR made in specific judgments are restricted to the states that were party to it, which excludes a general *erga omnes* effect.[91] The ECtHR considers, however, that its judgments establish precedents, which it considers to be in the interest of legal certainty, foreseeability and equality before the law.[92] An *erga omnes* effect is therefore *de facto* present when it comes to interpretations given by the ECtHR on the terms of the Convention. This is often called the 'interpretative force' or *res interpretata* of its judgments.[93] It means that states are expected to follow the interpretation of fundamental rights that has been provided by the ECtHR in cases to which they were not a party.

The judgments of the ECtHR are declaratory, which implies that the ECtHR decides in its judgments whether a state has violated the Convention or not.[94] The ECtHR

85 The United Kingdom, with its dualist system, for example, has made provision for the incorporation of the Convention in the Human Rights Act 1998, which implies that individuals must have recourse to the Human Rights Act to receive the protection that is offered by the Convention. In the Netherlands, the Convention is implemented according to a monist tradition.

86 The ECtHR considers incorporation as a 'particularly faithful reflection' of the intention to secure the Convention rights in the national legal order, see ECtHR 18 January 1978, no. 5310/71, *Ireland v. the United Kingdom*, para. 239; and Bates (2010), p. 159.

87 It has to do with the choices that have been made at national level with regard to the reception of international law. The direct effect of the Convention is also dependent on the self-executing character of a specific right, meaning that it must be precise and clear. See Gerards & Fleuren (2013), p. 49.

88 Polakiewicz (2010), pp. 50–52. See more generally Barkhuysen & Van Emmerik (2005), Keller & Sweet (2008); and Martinico & Pollicino (2010).

89 Article 41 ECHR states that just satisfaction is awarded if the Court deems it necessary. Also, the dictum reveals the distribution of votes of the judges.

90 ECtHR 26 July 2011, no. 41416/08, *M. and others v. Bulgaria*, para. 136.

91 Resolution 1226/2000, Execution of judgments of the European Court of Human Rights, Parliamentary Assembly (30th Sitting), Council of Europe, point 3.

92 The Court may, nevertheless, deviate from earlier interpretations if there is a good reason to do so, for example, if fundamental rights standards have evolved, see e.g. ECtHR 18 January 2001, no. 24882/94, *Beard v. the United Kingdom*, para. 81.

93 Resolution 1226/2000, Execution of judgments of the European Court of Human Rights, Parliamentary Assembly (30th Sitting), Council of Europe, point 3. This implies that the ECtHR's interpretations must, generally, be followed and therefore generally produce an orientation effect for the Court as well as for the domestic authorities, see Ress (2005), p. 374.

94 ECtHR 13 June 1979, no. 6833/74, *Marckx v. Belgium*, para. 58.

cannot order a state to make use of particular means to remedy the violation, nor can it nullify the decision taken by the national authorities. States are generally free to choose the (individual or general) means by which they wish to execute the judgments of the ECtHR, as long as their action is in compliance with the Court's conclusion set out in the judgment.[95]

Sometimes, the ECtHR provides indications of which general or individual measures must be taken by states to execute particular judgments.[96] General measures may, in particular, be called for when there is a structural problem at the national level that underlies the violation.[97] Examples of individual measures recommended by the ECtHR include the immediate release of a prisoner who was held in detention unlawfully; the return of land to an applicant following unlawful expropriation; and the retrial of an applicant whose case had not been dealt with by an independent and impartial tribunal.[98] The ECtHR explained that it indicated such measures in the relevant judgments, because there was in reality no choice left to the states in the execution of the judgment; there was an urgent need for the measures to be taken; and that resort to national remedies would needlessly prolong procedures for the applicant.[99] The Court's pilot judgments also offer a suitable framework within which the ECtHR is able to prescribe such general measures.[100] The Committee of Ministers supervises whether states have taken general and/or individual measures to execute particular judgments of the ECtHR.

Although the ECtHR has always stressed that it is not its task to review the national legislation of states parties in light of the Convention *in abstracto*, in relation to the general obligation of Article 1 ECHR it expects states parties to undertake to ensure the compatibility of their national legislation with the Convention requirements, especially

---

95 See e.g. ECtHR 26 June 2012, no. 26828/06, *Kurić and others v. Slovenia*, para. 406; ECtHR 13 July 2000, nos. 39221/98 and 41963/98, *Scozzari and Giunta v. Italy*, para. 249; and ECtHR 10 January 2012, *Ananyev and others v. Russia*, nos. 42525/07 and 60800/08, para. 180. The discretion allowed to states in the execution of the Court's judgment follows from Article 1 ECHR, see ECtHR 23 January 2001, no. 28342/95, *Brumărescu v. Romania (Article 41)*, para. 20. The competences of the Court can be contrasted with those of the Inter-American Court of Human Rights which has the explicit power, under Article 63(1) of the American Convention of Human Rights to rule that the 'consequences of the measure or situation that constituted the breach of such right or freedom be remedied …'.

96 Sutton (2010), pp. 56–59. The Court incidentally held that 'States that are parties to a case are *in principle* [emphasis added] free to choose the means whereby they will comply with a judgment', see ECtHR 31 October 1995, no. 14556/89, *Papamichalopoulos and others v. Greece* (Article 50), para. 34.

97 See e.g. ECtHR 3 November 2011, no. 12793/03, *Balitskiy v. Ukraine*, para. 54.

98 See respectively ECtHR 8 April 2004, no. 71503/01, *Assanidze v. Georgia,* point 14 of the dictum; ECtHR 31 October 1995, no. 14556/89, *Papamichopoulos v. Greece* (Article 50), para. 38; and ECtHR 30 October 2003, no. 32984/96, *Alfatli and others v. Turkey* (as regards the applicant Mahmut Memduh Uyan), para. 52.

99 Cf. ECtHR 8 April 2004, no. 71503/01, *Assanidze v. Georgia,* par 202; ECtHR 17 September 2009, no. 10249/03, *Scoppola v. Italy* (No. 2) para. 154; ECtHR 31 October 1995, no. 14556/89, *Papamichalopoulos and others v. Greece* (Article 50), para. 40; and ECtHR 9 October 2007, no. 14484/04, *Hasan and Eylem Zengin v. Turkey*, para. 84.

100 The Committee of Ministers has explicitly invited the Court to do so, see Committee of Ministers, Resolution RES(2004)3, 12 May 2004, 114th session; and Resolution RES(2004)6, 12 May 2004, 114th session. See further Ress (2005), pp. 379–380; and Gerards (2012c), pp. 381–384.

if their legislative actions clearly interfere with Convention rights.[101] Bringing national legislation in conformity with the Convention is to be considered in the interest of preventing further violations for the individual's case, as well as preventing future violations for other individuals.[102]

Therefore, in this respect, it can already be expected that states will undertake certain active measures to ensure compliance with the Convention and with the judgments of the ECtHR.[103] Generally, states are, however, given some discretion to make their own choices as to how to comply with the Convention and the judgments of the ECtHR.

2.8. HORIZONTAL EFFECT OF CONVENTION PROVISIONS

The direct horizontal effect of fundamental rights, which would mean that these rights are directly applied in the relations between private parties, is excluded under the Convention. Individuals can only invoke the Convention provisions before the ECtHR in respect of the actions or omissions of states parties. This follows from the (restrictions to the) right to individual petition as laid down in the Convention (Article 34 ECHR). However, the ECtHR has, to a certain extent, allowed for the indirect horizontal effect of the Convention rights. It has held states parties responsible for private infringements and it has also accepted the indirect horizontal effect by accepting that states have a positive obligation to prevent the fundamental rights of individuals *vis-à-vis* other individuals.[104] As an example, in the case of *Moreno Gómez*, the ECtHR held that the Spanish state was responsible for a violation of the right to private life of an individual living in the vicinity of bars, restaurants and night clubs in the city centre of Valencia that created disturbances, such as noise nuisance.[105]

Indirect horizontal effect of the Convention rights is thus often established by the ECtHR by attributing responsibility for infringements to states parties (Article 1 ECHR)[106] or through the imposition of positive obligations.[107] States can be called upon to prevent, remedy or sanction individual's actions in order to protect the fundamental

---

101 See ECtHR 27 September 1995, no. 18984/91, *McCann and others v. the United Kingdom*, para. 153. The Court has examined the compatibility of certain national legal provisions in abstract as to their compliance with the Convention. See e.g. ECtHR 29 April 1988, no. 10328/83, *Belilos v. Switzerland* (concerning a reservation made by a state party to Article 6 ECHR); ECtHR 6 September 1978, no. 5029/71, *Klass and others v. Germany*, para. 33 (concerning a law that allows restrictions of the confidentiality of mail, post and telecommunications); and ECtHR 25 February 1982, nos. 7511/76 to 7743/76, *Campbell and Cosans v. the United Kingdom*, para. 26 (concerning a law allowing corporal punishment in schools).

102 See ECtHR 17 February 2004, no. 39748/98, *Maestri v. Italy*, para. 47.

103 This is also further examined in relation to the positive obligations which states incur under the Convention in section 4.4.1.

104 See generally Gerards (2011b), pp. 263 ff.

105 ECtHR 16 November 2004, no. 4143/02, *Gómez v. Spain*.

106 Cf. also ECtHR 13 July 2004, no. 69498/01, *Pla and Puncernau v. Andorra*.

107 See e.g. ECtHR 26 March 1985, no. 8978/80, *X and Y v. the Netherlands*.

rights of the Convention.[108] It is not clear, however, at what point states will be held liable more generally for omissions in the private sphere.[109] This is also discussed in chapters 3 and 4 in relation to the doctrine of positive obligations.

2.9. CONCLUSIONS

The civil and political rights under the Convention have been enforced successfully within the states parties, which has depended on the existence of the right of individuals to lodge complaints before the ECtHR. This chapter has explained that the ECtHR delivers judgments which provide individual justice, and which also develop the standards set by the Convention more generally. The Convention provides an important minimum standard of fundamental rights protection for its states parties, and as a result, has had effects on the laws of states parties and their fundamental rights obligations, even though the Convention has, formally, only limited legal effect. In its interpretation of the Convention, the ECtHR has regard to the object and purpose of the Convention, that is, to achieve individual justice, and it has developed several tools of interpretation which are specific for the Convention. By interpreting the Convention rights effectively and dynamically, states parties' obligations have been extended considerably and have come to cover obligations to regulate private relations. At the same time, the ECtHR also aims to respect certain important limits such as those constituted by the subsidiary character of the system of the Convention, which is expressed first and foremost in its doctrine of the margin of appreciation.

108 See generally Gerards (2011b), pp. 264–280.
109 Harris, O'Boyle, Bates & Warbrick (2014), p. 24.

CHAPTER 3

THE DEVELOPMENT OF POSITIVE OBLIGATIONS UNDER THE EUROPEAN CONVENTION ON HUMAN RIGHTS

3.1. INTRODUCTION

This chapter aims to define the meaning of the concept of positive obligations and its implications for the Convention system. A clear basis of the concept of positive obligations is needed so that it can be applied and further examined within the specific context of EU law (see part II). Scholars such as Mowbray, Xenos and, most recently, Lavrysen have undertaken important studies on the development of positive obligations by the ECtHR, which will be relied on in this chapter.[1] These studies also show that there continues to be discussion on some aspects of the development of positive obligations by the ECtHR. Therefore, a further study of the case-law of the ECtHR itself is also undertaken here in order to discover how the ECtHR specifically understands and defines the concept of positive obligations.[2]

This chapter begins by describing how the ECtHR introduced the concept of positive obligations in its case-law (section 3.2.1.). It then looks at how the ECtHR defines positive obligations (section 3.2.2.); how the distinction between positive and negative obligations is made (section 3.2.3.); the general rationale expressed for recognising positive obligations (section 3.2.4.); which explicit legal bases are used (section 3.2.5.); and the methodology applied by the ECtHR in order to determine the existence of positive obligations under the Convention (section 3.2.6.). The first part of this analysis is followed by an overview of several typologies of positive obligations that can be made (section 3.3.), and a discussion of the implications of the recognition of the different kinds of positive obligations, both for states and for individuals (section 3.4.). Thereafter, important limitations on the scope of positive obligations that can be found in the case-law of the ECtHR are highlighted (section 3.5.). A few main observations on the concept of positive obligations are brought together in the conclusions (section 3.6.).

---

1 Mowbray (2004); Xenos (2012); Lavrysen (2013); and Lavrysen (2016). Other important studies which will be referred to include Lawson (1994a); Lawson (1995b); Dröge (2003); Akandji-Kombé (2007); Van Kempen (2008); and Klatt (2011).

2 Dröge (2003), p. 3; Klatt (2011), p. 692; Xenos (2012), p. 6; and Lavrysen (2016), p. 14.

3.2. THE DEVELOPMENT OF POSITIVE OBLIGATIONS BY THE ECtHR

3.2.1. THE BELGIAN LINGUISTIC CASE: INTRODUCING POSITIVE OBLIGATIONS

The ECtHR introduced the concept of positive obligations for the first time in the *Belgian Linguistic* case in 1968, which was only its sixth judgment.[3] In this judgment, the ECtHR provided important reasoning on how the concept of positive obligations was to be understood within the context of the Convention, and it is therefore dealt with here in detail.

This case was about the effects of the Belgian linguistic laws on children attending schools in certain regions of Belgium. These linguistic laws divided the Belgian territory into linguistic regions and established that public schools would teach either in Flemish or in French. Some children who were raised to speak French by their parents lived in regions where all of the nearby schools were obliged to teach in Flemish. A group of these children's parents decided to lodge a complaint before the ECtHR against the Belgian government, alleging that the right to education (Article 2 of the First Protocol) and their right not to be discriminated in the enjoyment of their family life (Articles 8 and 14 ECHR) was breached. The Belgian government, however, argued that it could not be held responsible for either of these violations.[4] It had already complied with what was (literally) required of it under the Convention. It did not as such and deliberately hinder the applicants' children's access to educational institutions. The Belgium government also argued that such matters of national languages, education and subsidisation of public facilities were to be dealt with internally by the Belgian legislature, not by the ECtHR which was a supranational court. There was therefore no infringement, because the issue wholly fell outside of the scope of the Convention.

The ECtHR did not agree with the Belgian government. As to the alleged violation of the right to education in this case, the ECtHR held that:

> The negative formulation [no person shall be denied the right to education] indicates, as is confirmed by the 'preparatory work' …, that the Contracting Parties do not recognise such a right to education as would require them at their own expense, or to subsidise, education of any particular type or at any particular level. However, it cannot be concluded from this that the State has no positive obligation to ensure respect for such a right as is protected by Article 2 of the Protocol. As a 'right' does exist, it is secured, by virtue of Article 1 of the Convention, to everyone within the jurisdiction of a Contracting State.
>
> To determine the scope of the 'right to education', within the meaning of the first sentence of Article 2 of the Protocol, the Court must bear in mind the aim of this provision. It notes in this context that all member states of the Council of Europe possessed, at the time of

3 ECtHR 23 July 1968, nos. 1474/62 to 2126/64, *Belgian Linguistic case*, para. 3.
4 ECtHR 23 July 1968, nos. 1474/62 to 2126/64, *Belgian Linguistic case*, Part A of the judgment.

> the opening of the Protocol to their signature, and still do possess, a general and official educational system. There neither was, nor is now, therefore, any question of requiring each State to establish such a system, but merely of guaranteeing to persons subject to the jurisdiction of the Contracting Parties the right, in principle to avail themselves of the means of instructions existing at a given time.
>
> The Convention lays down no specific obligations concerning the extent of these means and the manner of their organisation or subsidisation. ... However the right to education would be meaningless if it did not imply in favour of its beneficiaries, the right to be educated in the national language or in one of the national languages, as the case may be.[5]

The ECtHR thus recognised, despite the fact that the Convention itself does not specify particular obligations that must be fulfilled by states parties, nor textually enunciates an active approach towards protecting fundamental rights, that positive obligations can be imposed on the states parties. This interpretation by the ECtHR of the Convention rights requires the states to move beyond a formal and textual reading of the rights of the Convention. Fundamental rights protection would, in the view of the ECtHR, become meaningless for certain groups of individuals if the obligations for the states parties were reduced to what is stated in the exact words of the Convention. The children of the applicants, for example, would not be able to enjoy the right to education meaningfully if education was not accessible in one of the national languages.

In the *Belgian Linguistic* case, the ECtHR ultimately did not specify the content of any particular positive obligation that would have to be fulfilled under the Convention. In fact, most of the complaints of the applicants were dismissed. Nonetheless, the *Belgian Linguistic* case paved the way for the further development of positive obligations by the ECtHR in the subsequent cases of *Marckx v. Belgium*, *Airey v. Ireland* and *X. & Y. v. the Netherlands*.[6] In these cases the ECtHR actually did impose 'novel' positive obligations on the states parties and these cases are much more well known. They show a range of the different kinds of situations that can give rise to positive actions for states. These cases help to clarify what positive obligations may entail under the Convention, and they are therefore briefly discussed here and in the following subsections to show how the ECtHR defines positive obligations, the rationale that guides the development of positive obligations in such cases, as well as the legal bases and methods used to determine the content and scope of positive obligations.

First, the case of *Marckx v. Belgium* was about an unmarried mother whose family ties with her daughter were not automatically legally recognised by Belgian laws because the birth of the child had taken place outside of marriage.[7] Both the mother and daughter complained before the ECtHR about a violation of their right to family

---

5 ECtHR 23 July 1968, nos. 1474/62 to 2126/64, *Belgian Linguistic case*, para. 3 *in fine*.

6 ECtHR 13 June 1979, no. 6833/74, *Marckx v. Belgium*; ECtHR 9 October 1979, no. 6289/73, *Airey v. Ireland;* ECtHR 26 March 1985, no. 8978/80, *X. and Y. v. the Netherlands*. For an interesting insight into the historical background of the *Belgian Linguistic case*, see Bates (2010), p. 237.

7 ECtHR 13 June 1979, no. 6833/74, *Marckx v. Belgium*.

life under Article 8 ECHR. The ECtHR came to the conclusion that Belgium had failed to fulfil its positive obligation under Article 8 ECHR, as it held that:

> when the State determines in its domestic legal system the regime applicable to certain family ties such as those between an unmarried mother and her child, it must act in a manner calculated to allow those concerned to lead a normal family life. As envisaged by Article 8, respect for family life implies in particular, in the Court's view, the existence in domestic law of legal safeguards that render possible as from the moment of birth, the child's integration in his family life. In this connection, the State has a choice of various means ...[8]

Secondly in the case of *Airey v. Ireland*, which was briefly addressed in chapter 2, the ECtHR established a positive obligation in connection to the right to a fair trial laid down in Article 6 ECHR. In this case, the applicant, Mrs Airey, sought a divorce from her violent husband, but was unable to start the requisite court proceedings, because she could not afford a solicitor.[9] She found that her right of access to a court under Article 6 ECHR had been effectively denied by the Irish government. The Irish government argued before the ECtHR that it did not, as such, prevent access to the applicant in this case and that, moreover, free legal aid was not provided for under Article 6(1) ECHR. This provision only specifically requires states to make legal aid available in criminal cases, and not expressly in civil cases. The ECtHR determined nonetheless that:

> Article 6 para. 1 may sometimes compel the State to provide for the assistance of a lawyer when such assistance proves indispensable for an effective right of access to court either because legal representation is compulsory, as is done by the domestic law of certain Contracting States for various types of litigation, or by reason of the complexity of the procedure or of the case.[10]

As a third example, the case of *X. and Y. v. the Netherlands* provides a helpful illustration of how the ECtHR has recognised a positive obligation under the Convention. This case was about a father who complained about the situation of his daughter who was mentally handicapped and lived in a privately run home for mentally handicapped children, where she had been sexually assaulted. The perpetrator of this crime could not be prosecuted because, under the Dutch laws of that time, victims needed to lodge complaints personally. His daughter could not, however, physically sign the complaint due to her condition. The father therefore complained of a violation of the right to private and family life under Article 8 ECHR, for which the Netherlands was responsible. In its judgment, the ECtHR agreed that:

> the protection afforded by the civil law in the case of wrongdoing of the kind inflicted on Miss Y is insufficient. This is a case where fundamental values and essential aspects of private life are at

---

8 ECtHR 13 June 1979, no. 6833/74, *Marckx v. Belgium*, para. 31.

9 ECtHR 9 October 1979, no. 6289/73, *Airey v. Ireland*.

10 ECtHR 9 October 1979, no. 6289/73, *Airey v. Ireland*, para. 26.

> stake. Effective deterrence is indispensable in this area and it can be achieved only by criminal law provisions.[11]

Thus, the Dutch government had failed to provide sufficient protection for the right of the applicant under Article 8 ECHR in this case and incurred a positive obligation in the area of criminal law provisions.

All these three cases are considered to form landmark judgments of the ECtHR in developing positive obligations in its case-law. They have received much attention (and criticism) and have led to an intense debate as to how far the ECtHR's conception of positive obligations actually reaches.[12]

3.2.2. DEFINING THE CONCEPT OF POSITIVE OBLIGATIONS

The ECtHR, in general, explains in the cases mentioned above that a positive obligation entails that states must 'do something', 'take action' or 'undertake affirmative action'.[13] It therefore does not provide a very particular definition of the concept of positive obligations in its case-law. The ECtHR holds, for example in relation to Article 8 ECHR, that:

> the object of the Article is 'essentially' that of protecting the individual against arbitrary interference by the public authorities ... Nevertheless it does not merely compel the State to abstain from such interference: in addition to this primarily negative undertaking, there may be positive obligations inherent in an effective 'respect' for family life.[14]

The ECtHR has further declined to develop a general theory on how the concept of positive obligations must be defined under the Convention.[15] It has held that 'as far as those positive obligations are concerned, the notion of "respect" is not clear-cut',[16] and that 'having regard to the diversity of practices followed and the situations obtaining in the Contracting States, the notion's requirement will vary considerably from case to case'.[17]

---

11 ECtHR 26 March 1985, no. 8978/80, *X. and Y. v. the Netherlands*, para. 27.

12 The various points of criticism are further discussed in chapter 4.

13 See respectively Akandji-Kombé (2007), p. 7; the dissenting opinion of Judge Martens to ECtHR 19 February 1996, no. 232184/96, *Gül v. Switzerland*; and Mowbray (2004), p. 2.

14 ECtHR 13 June 1979, no. 6833/74, *Marckx v. Belgium*, para. 31.

15 ECtHR 21 June 1988, no. 10126/82, *Plattform "Ärtze für das Leben" v. Austria*, para. 31.

16 ECtHR 28 May 1985, nos. 9214/80 to 9474/81, *Abdulaziz, Cabales and Balkandali v. the United Kingdom*, para. 67.

17 ECtHR 27 September 1990, no. 10843/84, *Cossey v. the United Kingdom*), para. 37.

3.2.3. THE DISTINCTION BETWEEN NEGATIVE AND POSITIVE OBLIGATIONS

Importantly, the ECtHR organises a dichotomy of Convention obligations. It explains that the Convention either gives rise to negative obligations, which are viewed as the traditional and essential obligations in the protection of fundamental rights, or to positive obligations which are viewed as an addition to negative obligations, but which are also 'inherent' to the rights of the Convention.[18] This dichotomy between positive and negative obligations helps to further define the concept of positive obligations under the Convention more clearly. There are three different features which are further explored here. These features can be derived from the case-law of the ECtHR and are also often discussed in the literature.

3.2.3.1. *Traditional versus Implied Obligations*

Negative obligations logically follow from the text of the Convention. The ECtHR has therefore explained in its case-law that negative obligations form the traditional obligations under the Convention.[19] The Convention enunciates a traditional liberal view on the protection of fundamental rights, which applies in particular to the type of rights that the Convention protects, that is, (mostly) civil and political rights.[20] The rights laid down in the Convention are interspersed with negative formulations, such as 'no one shall be deprived of …', 'no one shall be subjected to …' and 'no one shall be required to …'.[21] The existence and definition of negative obligations further logically follow from the structure of the Convention provisions.[22] Most of the Convention provisions contain a clause or separate paragraph that exceptionally allow for acts of interference by public authorities, such as Articles 8 to 11 ECHR. These sections stipulate certain requirements which must be met for interferences to be objectively justified. The interference must be 'in accordance with the law', pursue a 'legitimate interest' and be 'necessary in a democratic society'. This implies that state action in the field of fundamental rights protection provides the exception rather than the rule.[23]

---

18 ECtHR 13 June 1979, no. 6833/74, *Marckx v. Belgium*, para. 31.

19 ECtHR 23 July 1968, nos. 1474/62 to 2126/64, *Belgian Linguistic case*, para. 7 in fine.

20 See Connelly (1986), pp. 571–572; Harris, O'Boyle, Bates & Warbrick (2014), p. 21; and Bates (2010), pp. 64–68.

21 See Articles 2(1), 3, 4(2), 5(1), 7(1–2) ECHR. A negative approach to fundamental rights protection also follows from the second paragraph of Articles 8, 10 and 11 ECHR which allow interferences as exceptions if certain criteria are met.

22 See generally Gerards & Senden (2009). Cf. Connelly (1986), pp. 571–572; and Gerards (2011b), p. 233. In comparison, the provisions guaranteeing civil and political rights laid down in the EU Charter of Fundamental Rights are formulated in a much more neutral and less negative way.

23 Cf. Xenos (2012), p. 2.

States are thus required, foremost, to abstain from intruding in the lives of individuals under the Convention.[24]

The ECtHR has held on several occasions that positive obligations arise only in addition to the negative obligations.[25] Some Convention provisions do, however, lay down fairly specific positive obligations for states parties. Article 2(1) ECHR, for example, requires the right to life to be protected *by law*. Article 6 ECHR also comprises a list of several specific actions which must be undertaken by the state to guarantee the right to a fair trial. It specifies, for example, that legal aid and interpreters must be provided in relation to criminal cases. Article 6 ECHR as a whole, moreover, requires the existence of a fully-fledged judicial system which allows the public to attend.[26] Likewise, the right to education laid down in Article 2 of the First Protocol to the Convention presupposes the existence of educational facilities.[27] The right to free elections laid down in Article 3 of the same Protocol also very logically gives rise to particular legal and practical actions by the state in order to realise elections.[28] Lastly, the right to marry, laid down in Article 12 ECHR, would be made redundant if states parties did not provide the legal possibility to enter into marriage. Thus, there are various provisions of the Convention which demonstrate that states must, to a certain extent, undertake certain actions to protect fundamental rights.[29] The stated examples of explicit positive obligations, such as the provision of a judicial system, evidently flow directly from the provisions of the Convention, and these could readily be foreseen by states parties when they signed the Convention, as opposed to implied positive obligations.[30] The content of implied positive obligations, such as those that were defined in the cases of *Marckx v. Belgium*, *Airey v. Ireland*, and *X. and Y. v. the Netherlands* does not logically follow from the Convention itself, but has been defined by the ECtHR.[31] The specific actions which were required in those cases, such as that family ties need to be recognised (in the case

---

24 Cf. ECtHR 2 March 1987, no. 9267/81, *Mathieu-Mohin and Clerfayt v. Belgium*, where the Court held in para. 50: '… the fact that the primary obligation in the field concerned [Article 3 of Protocol No. 1] is not one of abstention or non-interference, as with the majority of the civil and political rights, but one of adoption by the State of positive measures to "hold" democratic elections'.

25 See e.g. ECtHR 13 June 1979, no. 6833/74, *Marckx v. Belgium*, para. 31.

26 Cf. the reasoning of the Court with regard to Article 6 ECHR in ECtHR 21 February 1975, no. 4451/70, *Golder v. the United Kingdom*, paras 25 and 36.

27 ECtHR 23 July, nos. 1474/62 to 2126/64, *Belgian Linguistic case*, para. 5 *in fine*.

28 Cf. ECtHR 6 October 2005, no. 74025/01, *Hirst v. the United Kingdom* (no. 2), where the Court held in para. 57: 'Indeed it was considered that the unique phrasing [of Article 3 of the First Protocol] was intended to give greater solemnity to the Contracting States' commitment and to emphasise that this was an area where they were required to take positive measures as opposed to merely refraining from interference …'

29 Cf. Dröge (2003), pp. 7–8.

30 Bates (2010), p. 104.

31 Van Dijk (1998), pp. 17–18; Harris, O'Boyle, Bates & Warbrick (2014), p. 22; and Mowbray (2004), p. 226. Cf. Fredman (2008), p. 70. Fredman explains that positive obligations are frequently, but incorrectly, characterised as indeterminate, programmatic and resource intensive, and negative obligations as determinate, immediately realisable and resource free.

of children born out of wedlock), are not expressly or directly indicated by the relevant provision under the Convention.[32] Such positive obligations only become evident in the specific circumstances of the cases brought before the ECtHR. The case-law of the ECtHR shows that positive obligations can, in principle, be formulated in relation to all of the Convention rights.[33]

3.2.3.2. *State Action versus State Omission*

Since positive obligations require states to take action, they, in some way, relate to the omissions of states. By contrast, negative obligations, which require states to abstain from interfering, relate to the (positive) acts of states.[34] Positive obligations have thus sometimes been characterised as 'sanctions to the inaction of states'.[35] In the case of *Marckx v. Belgium*, it can, for example, be said that the state omitted to provide for legal safeguards specifically to ensure the protection of the rights to privacy and family life to children born out of wedlock. In the case of *Airey v. Ireland*, the state omitted to provide for (practical and legal) arrangements to ensure that individuals who lacked financial resources were able to start court proceedings and actually obtain a divorce. In the third case, *X. and Y. v. the Netherlands*, the state failed to provide for criminal law provisions which would ensure the protection of the right to privacy of one vulnerable individual from another individual.[36]

It can, however, be difficult to determine whether a violation of the Convention results from the positive acts of a state or from states' omissions. It has often been noted that the ECtHR could have approached certain cases on positive obligations as matters involving a negative obligation for the state. In the case of *Marckx v. Belgium*, for example, the ECtHR could have held that the state had failed to fulfil its negative obligation under

---

32 It has been argued that positive obligations result in an extensive reading of the Convention, see Van Dijk (1998), p. 18; and Russell (2010), p. 283. Cf. also ECtHR 21 February 1975, no. 4451/70, *Golder v. the United Kingdom*, para. 36. The Court held that 'it follows that the right of access constitutes an element which is inherent in the right stated by Article 6 para. 1 (art. 6–1). This is not an extensive interpretation forcing new obligations on the Contracting States: it is based on the very terms of the first sentence of Article 6 para. 1 (art. 6–1) read in its context and having regard to the object and purpose of the Convention, a law-making treaty ...'. By contrast, implied positive obligations can be regarded as an extensive interpretation of Convention rights.

33 Thus far, positive obligations have been determined by the ECtHR in relation to Articles 2, 3, 4, 5, 6, 8–11, 13 and 14 ECHR specifically. Yet, it is imagined that positive obligations arise under any of the Convention's fundamental rights, see Van Dijk (1998), p. 26. For a provision-based overview of the Court's development of positive obligations, see Mowbray (2004); and Harris, O'Boyle, Bates & Warbrick (2014).

34 Cf. Lavrysen (2016), p. 10.

35 Vande Lanotte & Haeck (2005), p. 99.

36 The ECtHR more recently emphasised the vulnerability of children in such cases, see ECtHR 12 December 2013, no. 5786/08, *Söderman v. Sweden*, para. 81.

the Convention because the application of its marital laws had adversely affected the enjoyment of a particular individual's rights under the Convention.[37]

Lavrysen has also explained that, in establishing positive obligations under the Convention, the ECtHR takes into account the existing structures that could ensure the protection of fundamental rights in the states parties. If the required protection would imply that the states parties would have to modify their existing structures, such as in cases on the recognition of gender transformation and adoption, then the ECtHR can decide to impose a 'positive obligation' on the state.[38] Thus in cases on positive obligations, states may have taken certain positive acts already. According to the ECtHR a clear distinction between positive and negative obligations does not always need to be made.[39] It has held that:

> [The] … fulfilment of a duty under the Convention on occasion necessitates some positive action on the part of the State; in such circumstances, the State cannot simply remain passive and 'there is … no room to distinguish between acts and omissions.'[40]

Perhaps for that reason, the ECtHR has indeed not attempted to clarify how the distinction between positive and negative obligations can be made.[41] The distinction between positive and negative obligations is not always easy to make because there are state acts as well as state omissions involved in fundamental rights cases, as explained above. Fundamental rights violations can thus result from a complex set of causes. Positive obligations can relate to interferences with fundamental rights that are caused by private parties, as well as interferences that are caused by the state itself.[42]

For the purpose of this research, it is of importance to be able to distinguish, broadly, between the two concepts of 'positive' and 'negative' obligations. The point is that when positive obligations are imposed, they essentially require some action to be taken to secure the rights of certain individuals which have not yet received sufficient attention in the policies of the state. A state may have failed to ensure the protection of especially vulnerable persons, for example, in relation to the positive acts which it has already undertaken. The establishment of such positive obligations on the basis of fundamental rights provisions can still have important consequences, as explained further below.[43]

---

37 Cf. Xenos (2012), p. 22. Xenos reads the respective judgments differently, as he explains that the Court imposed positive obligations on the states parties in those judgments, because they all concerned obligations to protect fundamental rights from acts of private parties, instead of acts of state agents.

38 Cf. Lavrysen (2016), pp. 237–277.

39 Cf. Xenos (2012), p. 60.

40 ECtHR 9 October 1979, no. 6289/73, *Airey v. Ireland*, para. 25. Cf. ECtHR 10 March 1972, nos. 2832/66 to 2899/66, *De Wilde, Ooms and Versyp ('Vagrancy') v. Belgium* (Article 50), para. 22.

41 Cf. ECtHR 8 July 2003, no. 36022/97, *Hatton and others v. the United Kingdom*, para. 119; and Klatt (2011), p. 695.

42 Lavrysen (2016), p. 72. The different types of positive obligations are discussed in section 3.3.

43 See in particular section 3.4.

3.2.3.3. *Conjunctive versus Alternative Structure*

The last defining feature of positive obligations versus negative obligations can be rather briefly explained. It has been held, for example by Klatt, that negative obligations have a 'conjunctive structure', whereas positive obligations have an 'alternative structure'.[44] This means that in the case of negative obligations, the fulfilment of the requirement is straightforward: negative obligations do not really leave any choice as to how they must be fulfilled. States must simply refrain from interfering. Any type of action is forbidden. Positive obligations, however, generally leave open a range of measures that can be taken by states, as has also been recognised by the ECtHR.[45] A positive obligation generally implies that national authorities are left a choice as to the precise fulfilment of that positive obligation in the national legal order. Not all of these actions need to be taken by the state.

Although, as has been explained, it can thus be quite difficult to make a distinction between positive and negative obligations in all cases, the three defining features of positive and negative obligations mentioned are used as a basis for making the distinction throughout this study. It is therefore generally held that positive obligations (i) do not follow (directly) from provisions on fundamental rights and their structure, but need to be implied in individual cases; (ii) require states to take active measures; and (iii) generally leave a choice as to which measures need to be taken by the state.

3.2.4. RATIONALES FOR RECOGNISING POSITIVE OBLIGATIONS

In most cases, the ECtHR does not indicate a very clear and explicit legal basis for the recognition of positive obligations (see section 3.2.5.). Instead, it generally refers to the need to guarantee an effective protection of fundamental rights as the underlying ground or justification.[46] The ECtHR often explains that the effective protection of fundamental rights – which is necessitated by the object and purpose of the Convention – requires states to take action instead of refraining from taking action. Convention rights must be enjoyed in a meaningful way and their interpretation must be 'practical and effective', not 'theoretical and illusory'.[47] In the case of *Airey v. Ireland*, for example,

44 Klatt (2011), pp. 695–696.

45 Cf. Nieuwenhuis (2011), p. 189; and Van Dijk (1998), p. 22. The Court has held that 'While it is the duty of Contracting States to take reasonable and appropriate measures to enable lawful demonstrations to proceed peacefully, they cannot guarantee this absolutely and they have a wide discretion in the choice of the means to be used … In this area the obligation they enter into under Article 11 of the Convention is an obligation as to measures to be taken and not as to results to be achieved', see ECtHR, 21 June 1988, no. 10126/82, *Plattform "Ärzte für das Leben" v. Austria*, para. 34.

46 According to Klatt, providing justification for positive obligations is considered to form one of the main problems of the recognition of positive obligations by the Court, see Klatt (2011), p. 693.

47 See also section 2.6.1.

the ECtHR took into account the high court fees that were charged as well as the particularly complex court procedures, concluding that:

> the Court considers it most improbable that a person in Mrs. Airey's position can effectively present his or her case. ... hindrance in fact can contravene the Convention just like a legal impediment ... fulfilment of a duty under the Convention on occasion necessitates some positive action on the part of the State ...[48]

While access to court was formally made available in Ireland, the judicial system in Ireland was arranged in a way which made it almost impossible for certain individuals to access the judicial system in practice. The ECtHR accepts that interferences can be caused – directly or indirectly – by legislative, administrative or judicial acts of state agents, by acts of private parties, and by the vulnerabilities of particular individuals.[49] It has been argued that the ECtHR has thereby accepted a multidimensional perspective to fundamental rights protection.[50] This means that it holds states responsible for interferences with fundamental rights which go far beyond violations that are caused by their own acts. The attribution to states parties of violations caused by private parties, thus the horizontal violations, has significantly increased the range of circumstances in which states have incurred responsibility.[51] Having to fulfil the positive obligations that have been defined by the ECtHR in its case-law means that states must bring their national legislation into conformity with Convention rights, and that they must also undertake other forms of regulatory activities to be able to comply with the Convention, even though in respect of individual judgments the ECtHR cannot, in principle, impose particular legislative obligations on states.[52]

The approach of the ECtHR with regard to the development of positive obligations evidently requires justification as to why (and to what extent) states parties can be held responsible for fulfilling such wide-ranging fundamental rights and obligations. On occasion, in relation to the specific circumstances of a case brought before it, the ECtHR has expressed some thoughts on how the attribution of the infringements of fundamental rights in a broad array of circumstances can be justified. This can be of interest more generally.[53] In its very first judgment on positive obligations, the *Belgian Linguistic* case, the ECtHR held:

> The Court considers that the general aim set for themselves by the Contracting Parties through the medium of the European Convention on Human Rights, was to provide effective protection

---

[48] ECtHR 9 October 1979, no. 6289/73, *Airey v. Ireland*, paras 24–25.

[49] Cf. Xenos (2012), pp. 142–143.

[50] Cf. Dröge (2003), p. 386; and Van de Westelaken (2010), p. 138.

[51] See e.g. ECtHR 26 March 1985, no. 8978/80, *X. and Y. v. the Netherlands*, para. 23; Cf. ECtHR 21 June 1988, no. 10126/82, *Plattform "Ärtze für das Leben" v. Austria*, para. 32; ECtHR 25 April 1996, no. 15573/89, *Gustafsson v. Sweden*, para. 45; and ECtHR 13 July 2004, no. 69498/01, *Pla and Puncernau v. Andorra*. Some scholars consider that this formed the initial reason why the Court developed a concept of positive obligations in its case-law, see Xenos (2012), p. 19.

[52] See further section 2.7.

[53] Cf. Xenos (2012), p. 4.

> of fundamental human rights, and this, without doubt not only because of the historical context in which the Convention was concluded, but also because of the social and technical developments in our age which offer to States considerable opportunities for regulating the exercise of these rights.[54]

The ECtHR thus takes into account the fact that states (nowadays) have the power to influence the enjoyment of fundamental rights protection, and that it is therefore reasonable to require states to use their influence since individuals do not have the ability to counteract fundamental right violations which they may experience, whether in relations with other individuals or as they arise from their own vulnerability.[55] This rationale has also been described as 'the obligation of effective power'.[56]

In relation to this, the ECtHR has on various occasions also explained that the responsibility for fundamental rights violations of states results from the fact that they have (already) decided to undertake regulatory activities to control certain affairs and thus also to ensure fundamental rights protection in that area. States must then make sure that their legislation respects *everyone*'s fundamental rights.[57] In the case of *Marckx v. Belgium*, the ECtHR specifically explained that:

> when the State determines in its domestic legal system the regime applicable to certain family ties such as those between an unmarried mother and her child, it must act in a manner calculated to allow those concerned to lead a normal family life. As envisaged by Article 8, respect for family life implies in particular, in the Court's view, the existence in domestic law of legal safeguards that render possible as from the moment of birth the child's integration in his family.[58]

The same rationale is noticeable in the *Belgian Linguistic* case (although the ECtHR refrained from imposing any particular positive obligation). The ECtHR explained in its judgment on this case that the (active) protection of the right to education imposes an obligation for states to organise their educational system in accordance with fundamental rights.[59] This may involve, as the circumstances of that case show, organisational and financial obligations. The ECtHR thus finds that such positive obligations do not upset the choices made in such national sovereign affairs, as the states had already set up particular official systems of education when they signed the Convention upon which fundamental rights protection is built. This is also how the ECtHR has explained that the states parties needed to adopt criminal law provisions

---

54 ECtHR 23 July 1968, nos. 1474/62 to 2126/64, *Belgian Linguistic case*, para. 5 *in fine*.

55 Cf. Xenos (2012), p. 143.

56 As explained by Sen, there is a certain asymmetry of power, e.g. between a mother and a child, or a state and its citizens, which implies that there is responsibility for the one in power to create more justice, see Sen (2010), p. 205. Cf. further Xenos (2012), pp. 2 and 142–143; and Bates (2010), p. 236.

57 Cf. ECtHR 9 October 1979, no. 6289/73, *Airey v. Ireland*, para. 23; ECtHR 13 June 1979, no. 6833/74, *Marckx v. Belgium*, para. 31; and ECtHR 22 June 2004, no. 31443/96, *Broniowski v. Poland*, at para. 184.

58 ECtHR 13 June 1979, no. 6833/74, *Marckx v. Belgium*, para. 31.

59 ECtHR 23 July 1968, nos. 1474/62 to 2126/64, *Belgian Linguistic case*, para. 9.

to ensure in the case of *X. and Y. v. the Netherlands* that the private life of the applicant could effectively be protected.[60] The ECtHR explicitly said that 'indeed it is by such provisions that the matter is normally regulated. Moreover, ..., this is in fact an area in which the Netherlands has generally opted for a system of protection based on the criminal law.'

Thus if states are engaged in a certain area they must ensure the 'all inclusiveness' of their national laws and they can be required to remedy certain 'gaps' in their legislation in order to protect the rights of certain individuals.[61] It may be said that the same rationale applies here as in the application of the 'in for a penny – in for a pound' approach that was discussed in chapter 2.[62] States parties need to make sure that they confer fundamental rights protection under their national laws in conformity with the requirements of the Convention, and thus in a non-discriminatory way.

Lastly, the ECtHR has also justified the recognition of positive obligations in its case-law by pointing out that states are to be considered responsible for the fundamental rights violations of certain private parties, if they have adopted acts that could explicitly condone, legalise or otherwise approve the behaviour of such private parties. For example, in the case of *Moreno Gómez v. Spain*, the ECtHR concluded that the state could be held responsible for the violation of the right to privacy of Ms Moreno, who experienced considerable noise nuisance and suffered from sleep disturbance from the activities of the many bars, restaurants and night clubs in the city centre of Valencia. The ECtHR reasoned that:

> Although the Valencian City Council has used its powers in this sphere to adopt measures (such as the bylaw concerning noise and vibrations) which should in principle have been adequate to secure respect for the guaranteed rights, it tolerated, and thus contributed to, the repeated flouting of the rules which it itself has established during the period concerned.[63]

The ECtHR potentially applies such considerations in other circumstances where states have granted licences to certain undertakings whose activities may affect the

---

60 ECtHR 26 March 1985, no. 8978/80, *X. and Y. v. the Netherlands*, para. 27.

61 In the case of *X. and Y. v. the Netherlands*, the ECtHR held that 'This is a case where fundamental values and essential aspects of private life are at stake. Effective deterrence is indispensable in this area and it can be achieved only by criminal-law provisions ... The only gap, so far as the Commission and the Court have been made aware, is as regards persons in the situation of Miss Y; in such cases, this system meets a procedural obstacle which the Netherlands legislature had apparently not foreseen', see ECtHR *X. and Y. v. the Netherlands*, para. 27.

62 See section 2.4.

63 ECtHR 16 November 2004, no. 4143/02, *Moreno Gómez v. Spain*, para. 61. For similar considerations, see ECtHR 13 August 1981, no. 7601/73 and 7806/77, *Young, James and Webster v. the United Kingdom*, where the Court held in para. 49: '... hence, if a violation of one of those rights and freedoms is the result of non-observance of that obligation in the enactment of domestic legislation, the responsibility of the State for that violation is engaged. Although the proximate cause of the events giving rise to this case was the 1975 agreement between British Rail and the railway unions, it was the domestic law in force at the relevant time that made lawful the treatment of which the applicants complained.' See also ECtHR 28 June 2001, no. 24699/94, *VgT Verein Gegen Tierfabriken v. Switzerland*, para. 47.

enjoyment of fundamental rights of individuals living nearby. If such undertakings infringe fundamental rights in a serious way, states may be said to have knowingly tolerated such behaviour and therefore can incur positive obligations based on their responsibilities under the Convention.[64]

In conclusion, while the ECtHR generally recognises positive obligations in a wide range of circumstances mainly by expressing the rationale of the effective protection of fundamental rights, it may also, in specific circumstances, take into account other considerations for attributing state responsibility, such as that states have the effective power to be able to make a difference in the lives of individuals. The ECtHR may have regard to the existing legal framework of the state which already provides a certain level of protection, in order to be able to impose positive obligations by reason of the 'all-inclusiveness' of the national regulatory system, and to require states to remedy certain gaps in their legal systems. Lastly, the ECtHR may take into account that states have already legalised certain behaviour or, instead, decided to take action to control other kinds of unwanted behaviour (such as noise nuisance).

3.2.5. EXPLICIT LEGAL BASES

As such, the principle of effective protection of fundamental rights is thus used by the ECtHR as a ground to justify the recognition of positive obligations under the Convention. The ECtHR has also pointed out that there is a further basis to be found for legitimising the existence of positive obligations in the specific text of the Convention.[65] The ECtHR has explained, for example, that the term 'respect for' in Article 8 ECHR was deliberately chosen by the drafters of the Convention instead of terms such as 'acknowledge' or 'take into account'. This would imply, according to the ECtHR, that positive obligations can be found in relation to this provision.[66] The ECtHR has also held in relation to Article 2 ECHR which requires the right to life to be protected by law, that it contains a basis for states to put in place an administrative and legislative framework.[67]

---

64 ECtHR 9 December 1994, no. 16798/90, *López Ostra v. Spain*. Cf. ECtHR 9 June 2005, no. 55723/00, *Fadeyeva v. Russia*, paras 89–93.

65 See Xenos (2012), p. 21, who explains that the use of the terms 'everyone has the right to …', or 'no person shall be …', also form general reference points for the active protection of fundamental rights.

66 See ECtHR 25 February 1985, nos. 7511/76 and 7743/76, *Campbell and Cosans v. the United Kingdom*, para. 37. The ECtHR has also applied this reasoning in relation to Article 9 ECHR, despite the fact that 'respect for' is not included in that provision as such, see ECtHR 20 September 1994, no. 13470/84, *Otto-Preminger-Institut v. Austria*, para. 47.

67 See ECtHR 9 June 1998, no. 23413/94, *L.C.B. v. the United Kingdom*, para. 36. Cf. Lavrysen (2016), p. 93. In relation to the other Convention rights which, under the second paragraph, require restrictions to be provided for by law, the ECtHR regards the legislative obligations flowing therefrom as 'negative obligations' as opposed to 'positive obligations'. See further Xenos (2012), p. 26; Akandji-Kombe (2007), p. 7; and Van Dijk (1998), p. 26.

More generally, the ECtHR has indicated Articles 1 and 13 ECHR as the basis for the recognition of positive obligations.[68] Article 1 ECHR requires the states parties to 'secure' the fundamental rights of the Convention. This general obligation must always be read in conjunction with a specific Convention right and cannot lead to a self standing violation of the Convention.[69] The ECtHR has clarified that Article 1 ECHR establishes a binding obligation for states to *always* secure fundamental rights.[70] Article 1 ECHR engages the responsibility of states for compliance with the Convention within their territory generally.[71] Violations that result from national legislation, administrative acts or other forms of state action are therefore attributed to the states parties.[72] In combination with Article 14 ECHR, the ECtHR has also held that Article 1 ECHR implies a general obligation for states parties to prevent or remedy breaches of the Convention rights at national levels.[73] The obligation under Article 1 ECHR is held to be one of result.[74]

Article 13 ECHR entails an obligation for the states parties to provide for effective remedies at national level. Article 13 ECHR is, in a way, closely connected to the realisation of the general obligation of Article 1 ECHR. By requiring the states parties to provide remedies at national level for individuals whose Convention rights are violated, the provision aims to secure, procedurally, that the Convention rights are effectively protected at national level.[75] Article 13 ECHR also has an accessory character: according to the Court's case-law, Article 13 ECHR can only be invoked by individuals if there is an 'arguable claim' of a violation of the (rights under the) Convention.[76] Article 13 ECHR allows the states parties discretion in choosing the manner of fulfilling this procedural obligation of the Convention.[77] The ECtHR, however, rarely applies the term positive

68 In relation to Article 1 ECHR, see ECtHR 23 July 1968, nos. 1474/62 to 2126/64, *Belgian Linguistic case*, para. 3 *in fine*; ECtHR 27 September 1995, no. 18984/91, *McCann and others v. the United Kingdom*, para. 161; and ECtHR 31 May 2007, no. 7510/04, *Kontrová v. Slovakia*, para. 51. In relation to Article 13 ECHR, see ECtHR 30 November 2004, no. 48939/99, *Öneryildiz v. Turkey*, para. 92. Cf. Xenos (2012), p. 21; and Mowbray (2004), p. 5.

69 See ECtHR 18 January 1978, no. 5310/71, *Ireland v. the United Kingdom*, para. 238.

70 See ECtHR 18 January 1978, no. 5310/71, *Ireland v. the United Kingdom*, para. 239.

71 Also of relevance is Article 26 of the Vienna Convention on the Law of Treaties, which holds that treaties are binding upon parties and they must be performed in good faith.

72 See ECtHR 13 August 1981, nos. 7601/76 to 7806/77, *Young, James and Webster v. the United Kingdom*, para. 49.

73 See ECtHR 18 January 1978, no. 5310/71, *Ireland v. the United Kingdom*, para. 239.

74 Cf. Barkhuysen (2004), p. 32.

75 ECtHR 26 October 2000, no. 30210/96, *Kudla v. Poland*, para. 152. However, as the ECtHR held, 'Article 13 ECHR does not go so far as guarantee a remedy allowing a Contracting State's laws as such to be challenged before a national authority on the ground of being contrary to the Convention or to equivalent domestic legal norms', see ECtHR 21 February 1986, no. 8793/79, *James and others v. the United Kingdom*, para. 85.

76 See e.g. ECtHR 6 September 1978, no. 5029/71, *Klass and others v. Germany*, para. 64; and more recently, ECtHR 4 July 2013, no. 21788/06, *Balakin v. Russia*, para. 33, where the ECtHR concluded that Article 13 ECHR was not applicable in relation to domestic procedures to obtain social housing, as it did not constitute an arguable claim of a violation of a substantive Convention right.

77 ECtHR 26 October 2000, no. 30210/96, *Kudla v. Poland*, para. 154.

obligations when imposing procedural obligations on the states parties on the basis of Article 13 ECHR, even though the actual requirements developed under Article 13 ECHR are very similar to the requirements which are developed by the ECtHR when it develops positive obligations on the basis of other provisions of the Convention.[78] This could be explained by the fact that Article 13 ECHR recognises in a more explicit way that active requirements need to be taken – that is, by providing remedies – and positive obligations follow more implicitly from other provisions of the Convention.[79]

3.2.6. METHODOLOGY FOR DETERMINING THE EXISTENCE OF POSITIVE OBLIGATIONS

The Convention provisions itself have been drafted with a view to states' negative obligations which does not give much structure for defining states' positive obligations. The criteria which have been laid down in the Convention provisions, in particular where it concerns 'interferences' are, in the Court's perspective, not fully applicable to positive obligations.[80] Therefore, in determining the existence of positive obligations, the ECtHR has clarified that it applies a fair balance test.[81] The application of the fair balance test in cases of positive obligations has been explained by the ECtHR in its judgment in *Rees v. the United Kingdom* as follows:

> In determining whether or not a positive obligation exists, regard must be had to the fair balance that has to be struck between the general interests of the community and the interests of the individual, the search for which balance is inherent in the whole of the Convention … In striking this balance the aims mentioned in the second paragraph of Article 8 may be of a certain relevance, although this provision refers in terms only to 'interferences' with the right protected by the first paragraph – in other words is concerned with the negative obligations flowing therefrom …[82]

To some extent, the fair balance test is thus similar to the test that must be carried out according to the terms of the provisions of Convention rights that specifically allow for restrictions to be made (such as Article 8(2) ECHR). In the Court's view, the terms 'pursues a legitimate interest' and 'the interests of a democratic society' might be of relevance. It is not so logical to apply the term 'prescribed by law' in cases on positive obligations, considering that a legislative framework is usually absent in circumstances that give rise to a positive obligation on the part of the state.[83] Thus, (only) some

78 Lavrysen (2016), p. 52.
79 Lavrysen (2016), p. 53.
80 Cf. Van Dijk (1998), p. 25; and Gerards (2011b), p. 233.
81 See Gerards (2011b), p. 236. Cf. e.g. ECtHR 27 September 1995, no. 18984/91, *McCann and others v. the United Kingdom*, para. 161.
82 ECtHR 17 October 1986, no. 9532/81, *Rees v. the United Kingdom*, para. 37.
83 Cf. Lawson (1995b), pp. 728 and 730; and Gerards (2011b), p. 238.

elements related to the test of balancing can be used in regard to negative as well as positive obligations.

The fair balance test in cases on positive obligations implies a merging of the two stages of review. The fair balance test determines both whether a right exists – thus whether an individual's claim falls within the scope of a Convention right – and whether it has been legitimately compromised by the state – thus whether an infringement can be objectively justified.[84] Those two stages are generally kept separate in respect to negative obligations. This implies that the Court's assessment for determining whether a state has fulfilled its positive obligations is less structured as compared to negative obligations.[85]

In most cases, the ECtHR carries out the fair balance test by determining first which interests are involved, that is, the interests of the individual and the general interests of the community, and subsequently whether the state has carried out a reasonable assessment in balancing those interests.[86] The ECtHR will look at the national administrative and legislative frameworks as a benchmark for finding which interests need to be taken into account and whether the public authorities have struck a fair balance of those interests.[87]

On occasion, the Court applies the fair balance test in a different way, by first defining which particular positive action arises on the basis of a specific Convention right and then by examining whether the state has fulfilled that particular positive obligation, or whether the failure to fulfil that obligation can be objectively justified according to the criteria for justifying interferences of fundamental rights.[88] This assessment is evidently more structured as compared to the assessment discussed above and it also provides much more clarity over the content of the positive obligations which can follow from the Convention provisions. However, the ECtHR only rarely applies this approach.

In several cases it has appeared that the ECtHR may also apply a 'knowledge' test to determine whether the state incurs positive obligations. In the case of *Osman* in particular, the ECtHR has explained that it will examine whether 'the authorities knew or ought to have known at the time of the existence of a real and immediate risk to the life of an identified individual or individuals from the criminal acts of a third party'.[89] The criterion of knowledge is particularly relevant in relation to positive obligations which are concerned with violations of fundamental rights between private parties.

---

84 See Gerards & Senden (2009), p. 634; and Xenos (2012), p. 59. See e.g. ECtHR 8 July 2003, no. 36022/97, *Hatton and others v. the United Kingdom*.

85 See generally Gerards & Senden (2009).

86 Gerards (2011b), p 234.

87 See further Xenos (2012), pp. 65–69.

88 See e.g. ECtHR 27 September 1995, no. 18984/91, *McCann and others v. the United Kingdom*; and ECtHR 10 February 2011, no. 30499/03, *Dubetska and others v. Ukraine*, paras 105 ff. See further for the merits of this approach, Lavrysen (2013).

89 ECtHR 28 October 1998, no. 23452/94, *Osman v. the United Kingdom*, para. 116.

This criterion has been applied by the ECtHR in relation to matters such as child abuse and in cases concerning industrial dangerous activities.[90]

States parties may be allowed a margin of appreciation in complying with the positive obligations under the Convention.[91] The margin of appreciation is generally wide when the active protection of Convention rights gives room for alternative measures to be taken and when there is little consensus in the states parties as regards the positive action that follows from Convention provisions, especially if the case at hand involves social or economic rights.[92] The width of the margin of appreciation is, however, determined under similar conditions as would be the case for negative obligations.[93] There appears to be no significant difference in its application, although this has been subject of debate.[94]

While the ECtHR has thus devised a separate test for determining the existence of positive obligations, the ECtHR has also clarified that:

> Whether [a] case is analysed in terms of a positive duty on the State to take reasonable and appropriate measures to secure the applicant's rights under paragraph 1 of Article 8 or in terms of an 'interference by a public authority' to be justified in accordance with paragraph 2, the applicable principles are broadly similar.[95]

By trivialising the distinction between negative and positive obligations, the Court seems to have wanted to make clear that states do not need to identify whether fundamental rights violations result from acts or omissions; instead, states must focus on providing effective protection of individuals' rights.[96]

3.3. TYPOLOGIES OF POSITIVE OBLIGATIONS

The discussion above has concluded that the ECtHR applies quite a broad definition of positive obligations. The concept of positive obligations therefore in fact comprises a

---

90 ECtHR 26 March, no. 8978/80, *O'Keeffe v. Ireland*, para. 144; and ECtHR 30 November 2004, no. 48939/99, *Öneryildiz v.Turkey*, para. 73.

91 See e.g. ECtHR 26 May 1994, no. 16969/90, *Keegan v. Ireland*, para. 49.

92 Cf. Van Dijk (1998), p. 22. See e.g. ECtHR 30 June 2009, no. 32772/02, *Verein gegen Tierfabriken Schweiz (VgT) v. Switzerland (no. 2)*, para. 81.

93 See section 2.6.3.

94 See further Gerards (2011b), pp. 254–256. Cf. Lavrysen (2016), pp. 217–218 who argues that in the examination of the fulfilment of positive obligations under Articles 8 to 11 ECHR, the ECtHR applies a lower level of intensity.

95 See ECtHR 21 February 1990, no. 9310/81, *Powell and Rayner v. the United Kingdom*, para. 41. Cf. ECtHR 7 July 1989, no. 10454/83, *Gaskin v. the United Kingdom*, para. 41; ECtHR 9 December 1994, no. 16798/90, *López Ostra v. Spain*, para. 51; and ECtHR 4 December 2007, no. 44362/04, *Dickson v. the United Kingdom*, para. 70.

96 In relation to the determination of states' positive obligations, the ECtHR has, however, clearly expressed several limitations that must be taken into account, as discussed further below, see section 3.5.

multitude of different types of actions that can be taken by the state and such obligations may arise in very different circumstances. This section aims to provide insight into the existence of the different types of positive obligations which can arise from the Convention.[97] It discusses the (basic) typology of positive obligations that can be found in the case-law of the ECtHR, as well as various other typologies that have been put forward in the literature.

3.3.1. TYPOLOGY DEVELOPED BY THE ECtHR

The judgments of the ECtHR do not provide much systematisation for the positive obligations which it has developed. The ECtHR has generally developed positive obligations on a case-by-case basis and always in relation to specific Convention rights.[98] The ECtHR makes a distinction only between substantive, or material, and procedural positive obligations in its judgments.[99] The same distinction can be found concerning negative obligations in the case-law of the ECtHR.[100] In making the distinction, what matters is the content of the required action.[101] The substantive positive obligations, especially, show a great variety of measures that must be taken by states under the Convention, and are heavily case-based.[102] States have, for example, incurred positive obligations to ensure that lawful demonstrations proceed peacefully; to provide for conditions of detention that respect human dignity; to enable the legal recognition of the sexual identity of transsexuals; and to protect the Gypsy way of life.[103] Such obligations typically impose social and economic demands on states parties and have effects on the relations between individuals.[104] States parties could discharge the substantive positive obligations by taking action at the legislative, the judicial or the administrative level.[105]

Procedural positive obligations are concerned with the organisational dimension of fundamental rights protection. The Convention itself provides for explicit procedural positive obligations in Articles 6 and 13 ECHR, as these provisions require states to have various kinds of procedural safeguards in place.[106] The ECtHR has developed

97 The many different typologies that can be identified are also explained by Lavrysen (2016).
98 For a provision-based overview, see Mowbray (2004); and Harris, O'Boyle, Bates & Warbrick (2014).
99 See e.g. ECtHR 9 April 2009, no. 71463/01, *Silih v. Slovenia*, para. 158; and ECtHR 30 November 2011, no. 48939/99, *Öneryildiz v. Turkey*, paras 89 ff.
100 Dröge (2003), p. 7.
101 Cf Akandji-Kombe (2007), p. 16.
102 Gerards (2011b), p. 239.
103 See, respectively ECtHR 21 June 1988, *Platform 'Ärzte für das Leben' v. Austria*, paras 31–34; ECtHR 2 December 2004, no. 4672/02, *Farbtuhs v. Latvia*, para. 51; ECtHR 11 July 2002, no. 28957/95, *Christine Goodwin v. the United Kingdom*, para. 71 and 93; and ECtHR 18 January 2001, no. 27238/95, *Chapman v. the United Kingdom*, para. 96.
104 Gerards (2011b), p. 240.
105 Gerards (2011b), p. 239.
106 Cf. Akandji-Kombe (2007), p. 16.

further 'implied' procedural positive obligations, particularly in relation to Articles 2 and 3 ECHR. The ECtHR has held that effective investigation must be undertaken into suspicious deaths and into complaints about inhuman or degrading treatment.[107] The ECtHR has also established that there is an obligation on states to undertake effective investigations on the basis of Article 2 ECHR, which it has even qualified as a separate and autonomous duty under the Convention.[108] Procedural obligations can further be found in respect to almost all other substantive rights of the Convention, although the ECtHR may not always define the procedural obligations as such in terms of positive obligations.[109] Clear examples of procedural obligations can be found, however, in the case-law of the ECtHR on adoption and custody cases. In such cases, the ECtHR has required there to be procedures in place to allow the persons involved to participate in the decision-making process and to have access to remedies, to ensure the effective protection of the right to private and family life under Article 8 ECHR.[110]

There are judgments to be found in which the ECtHR imposes both substantive and procedural positive obligations on the states parties, and where the interaction between the two types of obligations is noticeable. On some occasions, the ECtHR examined first whether a state party had complied with a substantive obligation, and then whether the national legal and administrative framework had provided for the requisite procedural safeguards to protect Convention rights.[111] In more recent years, the ECtHR has increasingly focused on whether states parties have fulfilled certain positive procedural obligations under the Convention, which can be regarded as the way in which it aims to respect the subsidiary nature of the Convention system, as discussed in chapter 2.[112] This tendency has also been depicted as the 'proceduralisation movement' of the ECtHR, in which the ECtHR has shown to pay special attention to the quality of the administrative, judicial or even legislative procedures which are relevant to the specific circumstances in which the alleged interference with a fundamental right has taken place.[113]

---

107 Cf. ECtHR 27 September 1995, no. 18984/91, *McCann and others v. the United Kingdom*, para. 161; and ECtHR 30 November 2004, no. 48939/99, *Öneryildiz v. Turkey*, para. 65.

108 ECtHR 9 April 2009, no. 71463/01, *Šilih v. Slovenia*, paras 154 and 159.

109 Brems (2013).

110 See ECtHR 16 December 2010, no. 25579/05, *A.B. and C. v. Ireland*, para. 267; ECtHR 20 March 2007, no. 5410/03, *Tysiaç v. Poland*, paras 117–118; and ECtHR 8 July 1987, no. 9840/82, *B. v. the United Kingdom*, para. 63. The obligation to involve 'stakeholders' in the decision-making process can also be found in the case of *Hatton and others* on the protection of the right to private life with regard to the expansion of an airport, see ECtHR 8 July 2003, no. 36022/97, no. 36022/97, *Hatton and others v. the United Kingdom*, para. 128.

111 See e.g. ECtHR 16 December 2010, no. 25579/05, *A. B. and C. v. Ireland*..

112 Akandji-Kombe (2007), pp. 16–17. See further Brems & Lavrysen (2013); and Brems & Gerards 2017 (forthcoming).

113 Xenos (2012), pp. 67–69. See e.g. ECtHR 24 June 2014, no. 33011/08, *A.K. v. Latvia*, para. 86.

3.3.2. TYPOLOGIES DEVELOPED IN ACADEMIC LITERATURE

There are many different typologies of positive obligations which provide useful insight into the types of implementing measures which states could take to fulfil the positive obligations under the Convention, as well as what different relations these positive obligation can apply to.

First, the types of measures which states could take to implement the positive obligations under the Convention could be considered. Xenos, in particular, has concentrated on this, and distinguishes between positive obligations to legislate, positive obligations to provide for an administrative framework, and positive obligations to take practical measures to protect fundamental rights.[114] The ECtHR itself has also clarified on different occasions that fundamental rights require, by their very nature, that there must be a legislative and administrative framework to protect fundamental rights or that amendments must be made thereto.[115]

Secondly, to be able to classify further the positive obligations which can be found in the case-law of the ECtHR, it may be useful to look at the classic typology of the duties to respect, protect and fulfil.[116] This tripartite typology was originally developed in relation to the protection of social, economic and cultural rights, although it can also be applied to the protection of civil and political rights.[117] The duty to respect entails a duty to refrain from interfering in the exercise of fundamental rights by individuals. The duty to protect constitutes a duty to prevent human rights violations caused by private parties. The duty to fulfil is a duty for states to take complementary legal, administrative and other kinds of measures in order to guarantee the enjoyment of fundamental rights.[118] All three duties are considered to be inherent to all fundamental rights, and are necessary to fully realise fundamental rights.[119] It is often suggested that – compared to the negative/positive dichotomy which is applied by the ECtHR – this typology manifests more clearly the indivisible nature of fundamental rights and the multiple types of obligations that can be imposed on states.[120]

---

114 Xenos (2012), pp. 107–118. Cf. Russell (2010).

115 See e.g. ECtHR 23 July, nos. 1474/62 to 2126/64, *Belgian Linguistic case*, para. 5 *in fine*; ECtHR 26 March 1985, no. 8978/80, *X. and Y. v. the Netherlands*, para.107; and ECtHR 30 November 2004, no. 48939/99, *Öneryildiz v. Turkey*, para. 89. See Xenos (2012), pp. 107, and 110. Xenos develops the argument that a legislative and administrative framework and practical measures form the 'core content of positive obligations' for states parties.

116 Shue (1980), p. 51. Shue develops the tripartite duties, consisting of the 'duty to avoid depriving', the 'duty to protect from deprivation' and the 'duty to aid the deprived'.

117 Cf. Koch (2005), p. 82.

118 Koch (2005), p. 82.

119 Most commentators recognise, at the least, a duty to protect in many of the Court's judgments on positive obligations, see Dröge (2003), pp. 6–7; and Xenos (2012), pp. 19 and 142–143.

120 See Koch (2005), pp. 82 and 84; Harris, O'Boyle, Bates & Warbrick (2014), p. 22; and Mowbray (2004), pp. 222–225.

Related to this typology is one which distinguishes between positive obligations of a horizontal nature and positive obligations of a vertical nature.[121] Horizontal positive obligations relate to the protection of fundamental rights in the relations between individuals, whereas vertical positive obligations relate to the relations between the state and an individual.[122] Dröge has also further distinguished between the horizontal positive obligations which have a social dimension.[123] Such positive obligations are concerned with the realisation of the effective enjoyment of fundamental rights in social reality. Where positive obligations with a social dimension are encountered, the fundamental rights violations are not caused directly by any act of a state agent, nor by acts of other private parties, but rather arise from the situation 'on the ground'. Also, Xenos seems to consider that there is such a positive obligation with a social dimension to be found in the case-law of the ECtHR. According to Xenos there are positive obligations which arise in the absence of state interference, and relate to the vulnerability of specific groups of individuals, such as immigrants or the elderly.[124]

It can be very difficult to distinguish clearly between these vertical, horizontal and social types of positive obligations in practice. Scholars themselves may even come to different conclusions over what type of positive obligations were defined by the ECtHR in specific cases.[125] Also, the tripartite typology of positive obligations discussed earlier is very difficult to trace on the basis of the case-law of the ECtHR on positive obligations.[126] The differences between these typologies may in fact relate to the objective of the analysis that was undertaken when they were developed.[127] These typologies may, however, more generally show the types of relations to which positive obligations may apply (to state-individual, to two individuals, or to the societal relations of individuals). It is therefore also useful to examine the types of positive obligations which may be found in the case-law of the ECJ, which will be discussed further in parts II and III.[128]

Lastly, an interesting typology has been developed by Van Kempen.[129] This typology focuses on the degree to which the positive obligations of the ECtHR follow from the negative obligation that can legitimately be derived from the provisions of the

121 See Lavrysen (2016), pp. 72 ff. Xenos, however, considers that positive obligations are always concerned with the relations between individuals, see Xenos (2012).

122 See e.g. Xenos (2012), pp. 19 and 142–143.

123 Dröge (2003), p. 382.

124 Xenos (2012), p. 143.

125 Xenos, for example, is convinced that the ECtHR defined a horizontal type of positive obligation in the case of *Marckx v. Belgium*, whereas Dröge regards this case as an example of a positive obligation of a social dimension, see Xenos (2012), p. 19; and Dröge (2003), p. 382.

126 Lavrysen (2016), p. 11.

127 Dröge's typology intends to clarify the normative content of positive obligations, and concentrates on what causes underlie a fundamental rights violation. Xenos' analysis concentrates on identifying the criteria for determining the scope of states' positive obligations under the Convention, with the objective of defining the scope of positive obligations better and in a more 'realistic, consistent and predictable manner', see Xenos (2012), p. 57.

128 See sections 11.3. and 11.4.

129 Van Kempen (2008), pp. 16–20.

Convention. Van Kempen analysed the Court's development of positive obligations, particularly in the field of criminal law. He put forward six types of positive obligations that can be arranged on a scale that is based on a negative concept of freedom. The negative concept of freedom, according to Van Kempen, is essential to the guarantees which are provided by fundamental rights. On one end of the scale, one can find the so-called *dependent* type of positive obligations. This positive obligation is imposed on states when they breach the negative obligation not to interfere in the lives of individuals. For example, when states restrict the liberty of a detainee, they must take action to guarantee the basic facilities to protect the health and safety of detainees. Such obligations logically follow from the negative obligations that can be found in fundamental rights provisions. Next on the scale, there are positive obligations which are *supportive* to negative obligations, that is, obligations which must, in particular, be fulfilled by the addressees of fundamental rights provisions. Van Kempen indicates the positive obligation for suitable training to be provided for police officers in order to prevent torture, inhuman or degrading treatment as an example. Further along the scale one can find positive obligations that are *intrinsic* to particular fundamental rights, such as the right to free elections and the right to education, which logically require the state to set up certain institutions and take organisational measures. At the opposite side of dependent positive obligations, Van Kempen positions the so-called *autonomous* or *repressive* positive obligations. He considers this type of positive obligation to be the most detached and distant from the fundamental right to which the obligation is related (and therefore the most problematic). Examples of such positive obligations are obligations to prevent human trafficking and terrorist activities. Autonomous or repressive positive obligations require the most extensive interpretation of the Convention provisions.[130] This typology can, in particular, be useful when looking at the legitimacy of deriving certain positive obligation from fundamental rights.

Clearly, there are many different typologies of positive obligations to be made, and this section has not discussed all of them. The typologies that have been discussed here are those which will firstly be used in chapter 4 to examinine various problematic features of the development of (some) positive obligations. Secondly, these typologies will be especially relevant when discussing the concept of positive obligations in the following parts of this study on the EU context. The different typologies are applied in order to be able to characterise the types of positive obligations which may be found in the case-law of the ECJ, and also to discuss their problematic aspects.[131]

130 Van Kempen also identifies positive obligations which can cause 'secondary violations of fundamental rights'. An example is where the ECtHR requires states to fulfil positive obligations to protect the rights of children to have knowledge about their biological father, even though the biological father's right to privacy will be affected.

131 See section 11.4.

3.4. IMPLICATIONS OF POSITIVE OBLIGATIONS FOR THE PROTECTION OF CONVENTION RIGHTS

The recognition of positive obligations has significantly influenced the system of fundamental rights protection of the states parties to the Convention and it has greatly increased the opportunities of those seeking protection of fundamental rights.[132] This section pays some further attention in explaining how the acceptance of positive obligation has affected the scope of Convention rights and obligations. It draws on some of the general issues discussed in the previous sections. First, the implications are examined from the viewpoint of the states parties and then from the viewpoint of individuals. This mainly analytical section may disclose some of the various problematic features of the development of the concept of positive obligations, however, a more in-depth critical appraisal is undertaken in chapter 4.

3.4.1. THE POSITION OF STATES PARTIES

First, one important implication of the development of positive obligations is that, although the ECtHR establishes positive obligations in individual judgments, they have clear implications for all states parties of the Convention. The states parties can already incur obligations to amend legislation or administrative structures as part of the requirement to take individual and general measures under Article 46(1) ECHR.[133] The main difference, however, is that the individual and general measures prescribed under Article 46 ECHR are only imposed on one particular state, that is, the respondent state to a certain case, and they directly follow from the dictum of a judgment which that particular state must abide by. In contrast, positive obligations are developed by the ECtHR as obligations which are inherent to Convention rights – they are 'clarifications' of the terms and notions of the Convention given by means of interpretation.[134] Since these interpretations can be considered to form part and parcel of the text of the Convention, and thereby of the obligations undertaken by the signatory states, positive obligations *de facto* have *erga omnes* effect. The reach of positive obligations is therefore generally much broader than general and individual measures imposed under Article 46 ECHR.

Secondly, the Court's recognition of positive obligations as part of the states' obligations under the Convention has had a significant effect on the role that is played by states parties under the Convention. The state obtains a rather different role than is

---

[132] For a comprehensive analysis of the implications of the Court's recognition of positive obligations under the Convention, see Xenos (2012), particularly pp. 1–5.

[133] See further section 2.7.

[134] ECtHR 13 June 1979, no. 6833/74, *Marckx v. Belgium*, para. 31; ECtHR 9 October 1979, no. 6289/73, *Airey v. Ireland*, para. 23; and ECtHR 28 May 1985, nos. 9214/80 to 9474/81, *Abdulaziz, Cabales and Balkandali v. the United Kingdom*, para. 67. Cf. Gerards (2011b), p. 231.

given by its negative obligations to respect fundamental rights. The state is no longer, possibly, the 'violator' of fundamental rights (negative obligations), but becomes the 'protector' of fundamental rights due to the acceptance of positive obligations under the Convention.[135] In other words, states have become 'duty-bearers' under the Convention.[136] States bear duties to protect individuals from violations inflicted by state agents, but also from violations caused by private parties or which result from the vulnerabilities of particular groups of individuals. To perform their role as protectors of fundamental right, states must have regard to the requirements of fundamental rights protection prior to all the acts of state agents.[137] States must therefore take responsibility in all situations in which human rights issues can be reasonably be considered to play a role and they must design proactive, preventive, compensatory or remedial measures accordingly.[138] The recognition of positive obligations under the Convention thus implies a departure from a more formal understanding of the protection of the fundamental rights under the Convention.

Thirdly, the incorporation of positive obligations into the Convention has extended the fundamental rights obligations of the states parties beyond the 'sphere of rights' that they knowingly and willingly contracted to respect under the Convention. Positive obligations under the Convention may also imply obligations that lie in the field of social and economic rights. The ECtHR has clearly recognised this by stating that:

> the mere fact that an interpretation of the Convention may extend into the sphere of social and economic rights should not be a decisive factor against such an interpretation; there is no water-tight division separating that sphere from the sphere covered by the field covered by the Convention.[139]

The ECtHR thus does not limit itself to the exact codification of fundamental rights in the Convention, as this does not seem to leave room for implied positive obligations in general and social and economic obligations in particular. The ECtHR also continues to develop substantially new positive obligations in its case-law. Some recent examples of positive obligations that have been recognised include obligations to take measures to protect the environment and to take action against human trafficking.[140] States may have little certainty as regards the positive obligations they incur under the Convention, and they clearly need to keep track of the case-law of the ECtHR to understand what obligations they must abide by in relation to the Convention.

---

135 Dröge (2003), pp. 1 and 380. Dröge speaks of the states as the 'guarantor' and the 'violator' of fundamental rights.

136 Russell (2010), pp. 281–282.

137 See Xenos (2012), p. 3 where Xenos holds that 'the uniqueness of positive obligations is that the active protection of human rights is demanded *right now* or should have *already* been provided by the state's mechanism in circumstances in which there are known human rights issues'.

138 See further Xenos (2012), pp. 97–100.

139 ECtHR 9 October 1979, no. 6289/73, *Airey v. Ireland*, para. 26.

140 Dröge (2003), p. 3. See e.g. ECtHR 9 June 2005, no. 55723/00, *Fadayeva v. Russia*; and ECtHR 7 January 2010, no. 25965/04, *Rantsev v. Cyprus and Russia*.

Incorporating positive obligations into the Convention thus has significant implications for the states' role in protection of fundamental rights. Their role has been expanded and transformed in relation to the protection of fundamental rights. In terms of the obligations they incur, those cannot easily be circumscribed, and they may also evolve due to developments in the case-law of the ECtHR.

3.4.2. THE POSITION OF INDIVIDUALS

Individuals play an important role in the development of positive obligations by the ECtHR, since the existence of particular fundamental rights violations requiring positive action becomes apparent in judgments in cases brought by individual applicants, on a case-by-case basis.

The development of positive obligations by the ECtHR can be seen as an improvement of the legal position of individuals. Where the state incurs a positive obligation to protect fundamental rights, the individual obtains a right to positive action by the state.[141] Positive obligations for states thus often imply positive, enforceable rights for individuals. Traditionally, where negative obligations are concerned, individuals are entitled to be protected from interferences by state agents. The recognition of positive obligations may imply much stronger guarantees, as the individual is entitled to an active response by the states parties in terms of legislative, administrative or practical measures.[142] The recognition of positive obligations therefore empowers the individual *vis-à-vis* states parties. The empowerment of individuals is sometimes considered to be the most powerful argument to justify the development of positive obligations by the judiciary in general.[143]

At the same time, it has been argued that the recognition of positive obligations can also have a detrimental impact on the legal status of individuals. The right to positive action by the state for one individual may imply that another individual's rights are restricted. This concern is especially relevant in relation to the development of horizontal types of positive obligations. For example, in the case of *X. and Y. v. the Netherlands*, the ECtHR imposed a requirement on the state to protect the right to family life of a young individual who had been sexually assaulted.[144] The state needed to adopt criminal measures against the perpetrator, according to the ECtHR, which evidently had a detrimental effect on the rights of that second individual. Also, in the case of *Von Hannover*, the ECtHR imposed a positive obligation on the national court to protect the right to privacy of a well-known individual whose pictures had been

141 See Alexy (2002), chapter 9.
142 Xenos (2012), p. 2.
143 Xenos (2012), pp. 4 and 86.
144 Cf. Xenos (2012), p. 131.

published in newspapers without consent.[145] The fulfilment of this positive obligation, on the other side, restricted the right of the media to freedom of expression.

By recognising positive obligations in individual judgments, the ECtHR has further allowed the individual to set the state apparatus of all of the contracting parties in motion to implement the interpretation given to the Convention rights. The individual is not empowered, as such, to lay claim to any particular kind of action by the public authorities – due to the alternative structure of positive obligations.[146] Still, the judicial actions taken by the individual give rise to public debate and fundamental rights protection is put on the (political) agenda, although the ECtHR can leave room for public debate as to how particular positive obligations must be fulfilled. Positive obligations create an opportunity for individuals to participate in the democratic process and contribute to a deliberative democracy, where the state accounts for its actions and omissions through the adjudicative forum, and eventually, realises active protection of fundamental rights.[147] Through democratic procedures, individuals have the ability to influence state politics and thus decisions on how to fulfil positive obligations. The supervisory mechanism created by the Convention and the recognition of positive obligations therefore enables the individual to bring fundamental rights violations to the attention of states, even if they may otherwise be ignored by majoritarian politics.[148] As a result, positive obligations do not only result in stronger protection of rights and direct empowerment of the individual, but also in enhanced participation in national democratic decision-making.

3.5. LIMITATIONS ON THE SCOPE OF POSITIVE OBLIGATIONS

As has become clear from the discussion so far, there is a broad range of circumstances in which states can incur positive obligations, and a broad range of types of measures which states can be expected to take. In theory it seems that an endless range of positive obligations is conceivable. As has been explained, the principle of effectiveness generally guides the ECtHR's examination of the content of positive obligations under the ECtHR.[149] What the effective protection of fundamental rights requires can be examined only in very concrete situations. It will also depend on the particular type of Convention right that is involved, on the specific circumstances of the case and the different interests which are at stake, and sometimes even on the identity of the

---

145 ECtHR 24 June 2004, no. 59320/00, *Von Hannover v. Germany*. Cf. ECtHR 13 July 2004, no. 69498/01, *Pla and Puncernau v. Andorra*.

146 See section 3.2.3.

147 Cf. Sathanapally (2012), pp. 58–60.

148 Xenos (2012), p. 1.

149 Xenos (2012), p. 91. On the principle of effectiveness, see further section 2.6.1.

respondent state.[150] The principle of effectiveness is thus very open-ended. The scope of states' positive obligations may even change over time, because the ECtHR considers that the Convention must be interpreted as a 'living instrument'.[151] Xenos, for example, has therefore concluded that 'the problem with positive obligations is that their scope appears to be open-ended'.[152]

It can thus be very difficult to define the states' positive obligations in relation to the protection of fundamental rights. The ECtHR has, however, also made clear on occasions that there are some limitations which apply in this context. The ECtHR has generally held that, in comparison to negative obligations, the scope of positive obligations is *inherently* limited.[153] It also considers that positive obligations arise (only) in addition to negative obligations.[154] With respect to the protection of fundamental rights in horizontal relations, in which positive obligations are of concern, the ECtHR has moreover clarified that 'the Court is not in theory required to settle disputes of a purely private nature'.[155]

Other, more specific, limitations on the scope of positive obligations can also be found in the case-law of the ECtHR. The ECtHR requires the existence of knowledge, a direct and immediate link, and no impossible or disproportionate burdens to be able to accept (some) positive obligations.[156] These limitations have been developed especially in relation to provisions that are very indeterminate in nature, such as Article 8 ECHR, and Articles 2 and 3 ECHR, which have given rise to very detailed positive obligations under the Convention.[157] These limitations will be discussed in more detail

---

150 Van Dijk (1998), p. 22; and see ECtHR 16 December 2010, no. 25579/05, *A.B. and C. v. Ireland*, para. 248. In that judgment, the ECtHR summarised that 'certain factors have been considered relevant for the assessment of the content of those positive obligations on States. Some factors concern the applicant: the importance of the interest at stake and whether "fundamental values" or "essential aspects" of private life are in issue …; and the impact on an applicant of a discordance between the social reality and the law, the coherence of the administrative and legal practices within the domestic system being regarded as an important factor in the assessment carried out under Article 8 … Some factors concern the position of the State: whether the alleged obligation is narrow and defined or broad and indeterminate …; and the extent of any burden the obligation would impose on the State …'

151 Cf. Dröge (2003), p. 386.

152 Xenos (2012), p. 4.

153 See e.g. ECtHR 14 May 2002, no. 38621/97 (adm. dec.), *Zehnalova and Zehnal v. the Czech Republic*, where the Court held that 'the sphere of State intervention and the evolutive concept of private life do not always coincide with the more limited scope of the State's positive obligations. The Court considers that Article 8 of the Convention cannot be taken to be generally applicable each time the first applicant's everyday life is disrupted; it applies only in exceptional cases where her lack of access to public buildings and buildings open to the public affects her life in such a way as to interfere with her right to personal development and her right to establish and develop relationships with other human beings and the outside world.'

154 See e.g. ECtHR 13 June 1979, no. 6833/74, *Marckx v. Belgium*, para. 31.

155 ECtHR 13 July 2004, no. 69498/01, *Pla and Puncernau v. Andorra*, para. 59; and ECtHR 16 December 2008, no. 23883/06, *Khurshid Mustafa and Tarzibachi v. Sweden*, para. 33.

156 See Xenos (2012), pp. 100–107 and 146–171; Nieuwenhuis (2011), pp. 187–195; Xenos (2009), pp. 593–608; and Lavrysen (2016), pp. 121–193.

157 Cf. the speech by Jean-Paul Costa delivered at Zagreb University, 30 March 2009, available online at <http://www.echr.coe.int>.

in the following section in order to clarify how they are applied. In addition to this, it can be said that there also are some further limitations which apply generally to the scope of Convention rights, which are therefore also relevant for the scope of positive obligations. The wording of the Convention provisions and the comparative approach are considered most important in this regard.[158] Those limitations are derived mostly from interpretative principles, thus, they determine what kind of fundamental rights issues can reasonably be brought within the scope of the Convention rights.

3.5.1. KNOWLEDGE OF FUNDAMENTAL RIGHTS VIOLATIONS

The existence of knowledge by a state is an important condition limiting the scope of states' positive obligations.[159] It determines whether a particular action can be reasonably expected of a state in relation to situations where violations are committed by private parties. If it cannot be established that the state knew or ought to have known of fundamental rights violations committed by such actors, the state does not incur any positive obligations.[160] The ECtHR held so, very clearly, in the case of *Osman v. the United Kingdom*, which was about the protection of the right to life:

> it must be established to its satisfaction that the authorities knew or ought to have known at the time of the existence of a real and immediate risk to the life of an identified individual or individuals from the criminal acts of a third party and that they failed to take measures within the scope of their powers which, judges reasonably, might have been expected to take that risk.[161]

There are various ways in which the ECtHR has established that the state has or could have knowledge of fundamental rights violations. Xenos has explained that knowledge can be established, inter alia, by the presence of reports on particular fundamental rights violations, by complaints which are lodged by individuals at the offices of public authorities, and by repetition of certain incidents in the past.[162] In some cases it can be seen that the state has knowledge from specific circumstances where certain (vulnerable) individuals were involved. For example, if state authorities are aware of domestic violence that has taken place against a certain individual (in the past), it can be required to perform positive obligations to protect that individual in the future as well. In other cases, the ECtHR imposes positive obligations on the state on the basis of the knowledge which they could more generally be considered to have because of the

---

158 Dröge (2003), p. 387.

159 Xenos (2012), p. 75.

160 Xenos (2012), p. 75. Cf. Leach (2006), p. 124.

161 ECtHR 28 October 1998, no. 235452/94, *Osman v. the United Kingdom*, para. 116. Cf. ECtHR 10 May 2001, no. 29392/95, *Z. and others v. the United Kingdom*, para. 73.

162 See further Xenos (2012), pp. 73–91. See e.g. ECtHR 28 January 2014, no.35810/09, *O'Keeffe v. Ireland*, para. 161.

violations that take place in a particular area.[163] In its judgment in the case of *O'Keeffe v. Ireland*, for example, the ECtHR decided that the state ought to have known about the risk of sexual abuse for children in public educational systems.[164]

The element of knowledge is also especially relevant to determine whether the state can be held responsible for violations of Articles 2 and 8 ECHR in relation to certain dangerous industries or circumstances. In *Öneryildiz v. Turkey*, the ECtHR has explained that the positive obligation to take appropriate safeguards to protect the right to life applies 'a fortiori … in the case of industrial activities, which by their very nature are dangerous, such as the operation of waste-collection sites'.[165] The ECtHR concluded in this case that at different levels the authorities knew or ought to have known that there was a real and immediate risk for the people living near the site of such industry, which implied that the state had a positive obligations to take preventive measures.[166] The ECtHR derived this from the fact that there were administrative and municipal departments responsible for supervising and managing the specific industry, as well as specific regulations on the matter, and from the existence of reports which revealed the risks related to the specific industry. The Court's more recent judgment in the case of *Cavit Tinarlioglu v. Turkey* provides a helpful overview of the positive obligations that have been established by the ECtHR in similar circumstances. This judgment reveals that states can be held responsible for violations in relation to child abuse in school systems; for large numbers of stray dogs causing nuisance in city centres; and for the health risks posed by professional diving and by the release of asbestos into the environment.[167]

The element of knowledge is thus important to establish when states can be held responsible for fundamental rights violations between private individuals. In some cases knowledge is generally accepted by the ECtHR, while in other cases there is much more specific material available for it. The existence of the element of knowledge is not explicitly discussed by the ECtHR in all cases; however, it is still often, as Xenos has explained, implicit in the judgments of the ECtHR on positive obligations.[168]

---

163 Lavrysen (2016), p. 126.

164 ECtHR 28 January 2014, no. 35810/09, *O'Keeffe v. Ireland*, para. 152.

165 ECtHR 30 November 2001, no. 48939/99, *Öneryildiz v. Turkey*, para. 71. The ECtHR even held that 'the more predictable a hazard, the greater the obligation to protect against it' in ECtHR 20 December 2011, nos. 18299/03 and 27311/03, *Fingenov and others v. Russia*, para. 243.

166 ECtHR 30 November 2001, no. 48939/99, *Öneryildiz v. Turkey*, para. 101.

167 ECtHR 2 February 2016, no. 3648/04, *Cavit Tinarlioglu v. Turkey*, paras 60–67. Further, see ECtHR 28 January 2014, no.35810/09, *O'Keeffe v. Ireland*, paras 147–1478 and 152; ECtHR 26 July 2011, no. 9718/03, *Georgel and Georgeta Stoiescu v. Romania*, para. 56; ECtHR 5 December 2013, nos. 52806/09 and 22703/10, *Vilnes and others v. Norway*, para. 239; and ECtHR 24 July 2014, nos. 60908/11 to 62338/11, *Brincat and others v. Malta*, paras 105–107.

168 Xenos (2012), p. 82.

3.5.2. DIRECT AND IMMEDIATE LINK/MINIMUM LEVEL OF SEVERITY

On several occasions, the ECtHR has decided that particular claims were inadmissible and did not fall within the scope of Convention rights, because there was no *direct and immediate link* between the measure that was sought by the individual and the Convention right which was claimed. The ECtHR established this particular limit in its judgment in the case of *Botta v. Italy*, which was about a physically disabled man who complained that he could not access the beach at a holiday resort in Italy due to his condition.[169] He asked for special facilities, such as access ramps, lavatories and washing rooms to be installed by the Italian authorities. The Court responded to those claims as follows:

> the right to gain access to the beach and the sea at a place distant from his normal place or residence during his holidays, concerns interpersonal relations of such broad and indeterminate scope that there can be no conceivable direct link between the measures the State was urged to take in order to make good the omissions of the private bathing establishments and the applicant's private life.[170]

Although this was the first time the ECtHR explained this general limit in a judgment, it held that the requirement of a direct and immediate link had already existed in its earlier case-law. It thereby referred to the cases of *Airey v. Ireland*, and *X. & Y. v. the Netherlands*, which appeared to demonstrate the existence of a direct and immediate link.[171] In the case of *Airey v. Ireland*, for example, it was clear that the required action by the state – the granting of legal aid – was immediately and directly relevant to secure the protection of the fundamental rights of Ms. Airey, who sought to apply for a divorce, but was not able to start the very costly court proceedings.

In the case of *Botta v. Italy*, the Court also made mention of its earlier judgments in the cases of *López Ostra v. Spain*, and *Guerra and others v. Italy*.[172] In both rulings, the Court applied the principle of a minimum level of severity as a limitation to the scope of positive obligations. In these cases the Court was respectively asked to determine whether the right to private life (Article 8 ECHR) gave rise to active protection by states parties in order to protect the individuals from nuisance caused by environmental pollution and from a potentially dangerous situation as a result of the activities of a

169 ECtHR 24 February 1998, no. 21439/93, *Botta v. Italy*.

170 ECtHR 24 February 1998, no. 21439/93, *Botta v. Italy*, paras 34 and 35. Cf. ECtHR 8 July 2003, no. 27677/02 (adm. dec.), *Sentges v. the Netherlands*.

171 ECtHR 9 October 1979, no. 6289/73, *Airey v. Ireland*; and ECtHR 26 March 1985, no. 8978/80, *X. & Y. v. the Netherlands*.

172 ECtHR 9 December 1994, no. 16798/90, *López Ostra v. Spain*; and ECtHR 19 February 1998, no. 14967/89, *Guerra and Others v. Italy*.

chemical industry.[173] The Court held with regard to both cases that there must be a minimum level of severity for a claim to fall within the scope of Convention rights. The requirement of a minimum level of severity as such constitutes a requirement that was originally developed by the ECtHR to determine whether treatment constitutes ill-treatment within the meaning of Article 3 ECHR.[174] In the context of positive obligations, the requirement of a minimum level of severity has been developed by the ECtHR in order to narrow down the scope of protection for environmental claims on the basis of Article 8 ECHR, arguably so as to avoid a flood of claims in the area of environmental protection.[175] A minimum level of severity constitutes a high threshold for claims to fall within the scope of Article 8 ECHR. By using this requirement, the ECtHR in particular aims to make clear that not every instance of inconvenience in life gives rise to a well-founded claim of action under the Convention.

3.5.3. NO IMPOSSIBLE OR DISPROPORTIONATE BURDENS

The ECtHR has also recognised that there is a limit to what states parties may be required to do under the Convention to actively protect an individual's fundamental rights in terms of finances and organisation. In cases involving social and economic obligations, in particular, the Court has expressed that the particular measures which were claimed by the applicant could not impose an impossible or disproportionate burden on states parties.[176] The measures which are claimed by individuals under the Convention must be considered reasonable. Therefore, the Court has held, for example in cases where an applicant sought medical care or housing and special living facilities, that it must not cause an impossible or disproportionate burden for states to protect an individual's rights in those circumstances.[177] This limitation is also relevant in relation to positive obligations arising from the right to life and the prohibition of torture and other inhuman and degrading treatment under Articles 2 and 3 ECHR. The ECtHR has established that states have duties to investigate killings and other crimes, such as

---

173 See ECtHR 9 December 1994, no. 16798/90, *López Ostra v. Spain*, para. 51; and ECtHR 19 February 1998, no. 14967/89, *Guerra and others v. Italy*, para. 60. See also ECtHR 16 November 2004, no. 4143/02, *Moreno Gómez v. Spain*, para. 58; and ECtHR 9 June 2005, no. 55723/00, *Fadeyeva v. Russia*, para. 70.

174 See e.g. ECtHR 26 October 2000, no. 30210/96, *Kudla v. Poland*, para. 91.

175 See e.g. ECtHR 14 May 2002, no. 38621/97 (adm. dec.), *Zehnalova and Zehnal v. the Czech Republic*; and ECtHR 31 May 2007, no. 26828/06 (adm. dec.), *Makuc and others v. Slovenia*, para. 199. See further Lavrysen (2013).

176 Cf. ECtHR 9 June 2009, no. 33401/02, *Opuz v. Turkey*, no. 33401/02, para. 129; and ECtHR 30 June 2009, *Verein gegen Tierfabriken Schweiz (VgT) v. Switzerland*, para. 81; ECtHR 16 March 2000, no. 23144/93, *Özgür Gündem v. Turkey*, para. 43; and ECtHR 28 October 1998, no. 23452/94, *Osman v. the United Kingdom*, para. 116.

177 See e.g. ECtHR 4 January 2005, no. 14462/03 (adm. dec.), *Pentiacova and 48 others v. Moldova*; and ECtHR 18 January 2001, no. 27238/95, *Chapman v. the United Kingdom*, para. 91.

domestic violence. Those duties are limited, as the ECtHR explained in its judgment in the case of *Osman v. the United Kingdom*, where the applicant alleged a failure on the part of the authorities to protect the right to life of her son and husband, who were respectively wounded and killed in the same incident.[178] The ECtHR considered that:

> Bearing in mind the difficulties in policing societies, the unpredictability of human conduct and the operational choices which must be made in terms of priorities and resources, the scope of positive obligations must be interpreted in a way which does not impose an impossible or disproportionate burden on the authorities. Not every claimed risk to life, therefore, can entail for the authorities a Convention requirement to take operational measures to prevent that risk from materialising.[179]

Positive obligations must therefore not impose an impossible or disproportionate burden on states in cases that (directly) involve state agents, and also in cases that concern violations which are committed by private parties.

The ECtHR often looks at whether states have discharged their positive obligations under the Convention on the basis of the existence of a legal and administrative framework, and it stresses the importance of the actual implementation of such measures.[180] It does so rather than specifying which specific or practical measures would have to be taken by the state. It has taken this approach both in respect of Articles 2 and 3 ECHR, and in respect of Article 8 ECHR.[181] The requirement to have a regulatory framework in place is considered by Xenos to be of fundamental importance. According to Xenos, this even concerns the 'core content of positive obligations arising under paragraph 1 of Convention rights'.[182]

3.6. CONCLUSIONS

The ECtHR has introduced positive obligations to ensure that Convention rights are effectively protected. The concept of positive obligations implies that an active approach must be undertaken by states parties to fulfil the obligations of the Convention. Within the context of the Convention, the recognition of the concept of positive obligations has been considered both important and novel, especially because the Convention originally provided guarantees for the non-interference of states in the lives of individuals, which

---

178 ECtHR 28 October 1998, no. 23452/94, *Osman v. the United Kingdom*.

179 ECtHR 28 October 1998, no. 23452/94, *Osman v. the United Kingdom*, para. 116.

180 See further Lavrysen (2016), pp. 103–109; and cf. ECtHR, 16 November 2011, no. 4143/02, *Moreno Gomez v. Spain*, para. 61.

181 See e.g. ECtHR 17 January 2001, no. 32967/96, *Calvelli and Ciglio v. Italy*, para. 49; ECtHR 18 January 2001, no. 27238/95, *Chapman v. the United Kingdom*, para. 92; and ECtHR 16 July 2014, no. 37359/09, *Hämäläinen v. Finland*, para. 63.

182 Xenos (2012), p. 107.

clearly appears from the text of the Convention. According to the ECtHR, positive obligations are nonetheless inherent to the rights laid down in the Convention.

The ECtHR has adopted a broad approach to defining violations in terms of positive obligations, including situations where states have already taken certain positive acts. It can be difficult therefore, to clearly distinguish between positive and negative obligations, taking into account that state interfere in an increasing number of areas. Positive obligations can (still) essentially be defined by contrasting them to negative obligations. Contrary to negative obligations, positive obligations (i) do not directly follow from the text of fundamental rights provisions; (ii) they relate to state omissions rather than state acts, and (iii) they have an alternative structure, leaving states different choices to fulfil these obligations.

The development of positive obligations in the case-law of the Court has resulted in the recognition of different types of positive obligations. The Court itself has made a general distinction between substantive and procedural positive obligations. A further distinction is often made between vertical positive obligations, which relate to states' obligations in their relation with individuals; horizontal positive obligations, which relate to states' obligations in horizontal relations; and social positive obligations, which relate more broadly to the societal conditions in which fundamental rights violations may take place. Also of importance from an implementation perspective is the typology of measures that must be taken to fulfil positive obligations, namely legislative, administrative and practical measures. Lastly, a critical typology has been developed which recognises the extent to which positive obligations are connected to the negative concept of freedom within fundamental rights. According to this typology positive obligations range from being closely related to the fundamental right to being completely self-standing.

By imposing positive obligations on states parties, the ECtHR has expanded the responsibility of states for violations of fundamental rights, as this goes beyond responsibility for interferences caused directly by its agents, and even includes responsibility for violations caused by private parties or breaches caused by the particular vulnerabilities of individuals. The Court has not set out clearly how and to exactly what extent obligations to prevent violations can be imposed on the states parties. The main rationale for the recognition of positive obligations seems to be that states have an obligation to ensure effective protection of the Convention rights.

Positive obligations are discovered by balancing individual and general interests. This approach aims to define effective protection of an individual's fundamental rights, rather than to determine at which point states' responsibility arises. On different occasions, the ECtHR has set out certain limitations which further help to define the scope of positive obligations more clearly, which include the existence of knowledge, the requirement of a direct and immediate link, and that no impossible or disproportionate burden may arise for the states parties.

CHAPTER 4

A CRITICAL APPRAISAL OF THE DEVELOPMENT OF POSITIVE OBLIGATIONS UNDER THE EUROPEAN CONVENTION ON HUMAN RIGHTS

4.1. INTRODUCTION

The concept of positive obligations has become a familiar concept in the case-law of the ECtHR. In its judgments the ECtHR reconfirms and refines particular positive obligations which it has established in the past and also continues to develop new obligations.[1] Nevertheless, the concept of positive obligations and the Court's case-law on positive obligations have remained controversial. Various points of criticism have been expressed by scholars, as well as by judges of the ECtHR.[2] This chapter discusses that there is a certain amount of controversy over the very idea of inferring positive obligations from fundamental rights (section 4.2.). The Convention in particular is considered to leave no room for the implication of such obligations. Further, there are some who are critical of the far-reaching effects that positive obligations impose on relations between individuals (section 4.3.). Others find that the ECtHR, by determining the content of positive obligations, has entered the forbidden field of political decision-making, or that it has unduly created socio-economic obligations which had been deliberately excluded from the scope of the Convention by its drafters (section 4.4.). Also, the supranational position of the ECtHR is considered to be problematic in that respect (section 4.5.). The positive obligations doctrine continues to be considered unpredictable and incoherent and it has been criticised for its lack of well-defined limits (section 4.6.). Lastly, the methodological choices which the ECtHR has made in the development and application of positive obligations have met with considerable

---

1 See Mowbray (2004), pp. 229–231.

2 See further Lawson (1995a); Lawson (1995b); Van Dijk (1998); Dröge (2003); and Van Kempen (2008). See the dissenting opinion of Judge Terje Wold to ECtHR 23 July 1968, nos. 1474/62 to 2126/64, *Belgian Linguistic case*; the partly dissenting opinion of Judge Matscher and the partly dissenting opinion of Judge Pinheiro Farinha, both to ECtHR 13 June 1979, no. 6833/74, *Marckx v. Belgium*; and the dissenting opinions of Judge O'Donoghue and Judge Thór Vilhjálmsson, both to ECtHR 9 October 1979, no. 6289/73, *Airey v. Ireland.*

disapproval (section 4.7.).[3] These critiques of the positive obligations doctrine need to be discussed, as they would need to be evaluated and taken into account if the ECJ were to incorporate and develop a doctrine of positive obligations on its own. This chapter also considers, throughout the different sections, how such criticism can be dealt with. The main points of attention for developing a doctrine of positive obligations are brought together in the conclusions (section 4.8.).

4.2. ARE POSITIVE OBLIGATIONS *INHERENT* IN FUNDAMENTAL RIGHTS PROTECTION?

There are three types of criticism which have been expressed with respect to the Court's view that positive obligations are inherent to fundamental rights. Criticism has come from an originalist perspective, from a contemporary debate about the nature of fundamental rights, and out of concern regarding human rights inflation. These three points are consecutively discussed.

4.2.1. CRITICISM BASED ON ORIGINALISM

The development of positive obligations by the ECtHR can be viewed critically from an 'originalist' perspective. Originalism requires the law to be interpreted as it was originally written.[4] The Convention provisions are textually negatively phrased, and the declaration of intentions of the drafters of the Convention are considered to disclose a limited scope for the Convention.[5] It could therefore be argued that, originally, the Convention did not provide room for positive obligations, and that the few existing explicit positive obligations must be regarded as exceptions. Of the (former) judges of the ECtHR, Sir Gerald Fitzmaurice is most renowned for taking an originalist view with regard to the interpretation of the Convention. He expressed his views when serving at the ECtHR in the 1970s, which is precisely the period in time when the Court started to develop its positive obligations doctrine that provision.[6] In his dissenting opinion to the judgment of the ECtHR in the case of *Marckx v. Belgium*, Judge Fitzmaurice held that the Court had over-extended the scope of Article 8 ECHR by recognising a positive obligation under that provision. The object of the Convention was to provide protection for the individual

3 Such critiques have also been summarised by Klatt, see Klatt (2011), p. 694; and Klatt (2015), pp. 355–357.

4 Originalism perspectives have also been expressed in relation to the EU Charter, see Brittain (2015).

5 For an elaborate discussion of the drafting of the Convention, see Bates (2010), pp. 51–75 and pp. 80–94.

6 Dissenting opinion of Judge Sir Gerald Fitzmaurice to ECtHR 13 June 1979, no. 6833/74, *Marckx v. Belgium*; and dissenting opinion of Judge Sir Gerald Fitzmaurice to ECtHR 25 March 1978, no. 5856/72, *Tyrer v. the United Kingdom*.

from 'the whole gamut of fascist and communist inquisitorial practices' that was feared for in Europe since the two world wars.[7] The national regulation of family relationships had nothing to do with what the Convention was all about, and thus, according to Judge Fitzmaurice, the Court had illegitimately interpreted the Convention. It had been overly eager to produce a specific result, and had thereby abused its power in defining positive obligations in the case of *Marckx v. Belgium*.

Within the ECtHR, Judge Fitzmaurice found little support for these restrictive views. The majority of the Court's judges have, more generally, chosen to interpret the Convention as a living instead of a static instrument.[8] As a consequence, the Convention has been given a wider scope and interpretations have been chosen that clearly can go beyond a strictly textual and historical interpretation of the Convention.[9] This has been viewed critically by scholars, although they also recognise that the text of the Convention was drafted quite some time ago and does not necessarily reflect the current fundamental rights standards of the states parties. Some of the positive obligations which have been recognised by the ECtHR have therefore been added to the Convention by the ECtHR, whereas other positive obligations have as such (always) been rather more implicit in the Convention itself.[10]

Overall, it is important that when the ECtHR develops positive obligations in its case-law, that it has regard to the current fundamental rights standards of the states parties and/or that it explains that certain positive obligations flow more implicitly from the Convention provisions, so that it can ensure respect for the position of the states parties.

4.2.2. CONTEMPORARY DEBATES ON THE NATURE OF FUNDAMENTAL RIGHTS

The idea that positive obligations are as such *inherent* to fundamental rights remains contested. Some scholars argue that positive obligations are simply not part of the nature of fundamental rights, at least not when it comes to classic fundamental rights, that is, civil and political rights.[11] They argue that such classic fundamental rights are intended to guarantee the protection of an individual's freedom against intrusion and coercion by the state.[12] States are thus primarily required to abstain from taking action to realise fundamental rights protection. Finding a justification for states' practices of taking active measures on the basis of fundamental rights would run counter to the core value of freedom which fundamental rights ultimately aim to protect. The development

7 Dissenting opinion of Judge Sir Gerald Fitzmaurice to ECtHR 13 June 1979, no. 6833/74, *Marckx v. Belgium*, para. 7.
8 See section 2.6.2.
9 Bates (2010), p. 364. See further section 2.6.
10 Harris, O'Boyle, Bates & Warbrick (2014), p. 9.
11 Klatt considers that this constitutes the 'justification problem', see Klatt (2015), p. 955.
12 See generally Van Kempen (2008).

of positive obligations in relation to social, cultural and economic rights is, in this regard, approached differently. The realisation of those rights depends more obviously on active assistance by the state. Social, cultural and economic rights have even been characterised by some as second-generation rights.[13] The protection of such rights is considered less pressing than the protection of civil and political rights.[14] The Court has decided, nonetheless, to develop various social and economic positive obligations in relation to civil and political rights, and it does not draw a strict line between the two categories of rights.[15]

Starting from a primarily negative concept of freedom, scholars such as Van Kempen are very critical of the Court's development of positive obligations.[16] By accepting positive obligations, fundamental rights are, in a sense, used as a ground for legitimising states' practices of interfering in the lives of individuals. Van Kempen finds that the ECtHR does not pay due respect to the core value of freedom, that fundamental rights essentially seek to protect, and that it undermines the main rationale for guaranteeing an individual's fundamental rights.[17] An autonomous type of positive obligation is therefore objectionable, because it is far removed from a negative concept of freedom.[18] Some types of positive obligations can, however, be legitimately imposed on states according to Van Kempen, which is the case if they are inextricably linked to the fulfilment of the negative obligations of a state. Van Kempen finds that positive obligations can only be legitimately derived from fundamental rights if they are intended to guarantee the negative freedom of individuals. For example, if states detain prisoners, they have interfered with the right to liberty, even though such interferences may be justified and legitimate. For the very reason of having breached the negative obligation not to interfere in the liberty of individuals, states must take certain positive action, that is, provide basic living conditions for prisoners on the basis of fundamental rights. Positive obligations are in this view closely connected to the states' negative obligations as well as to negative freedom.[19] Van Kempen accepts that many other types of positive action can be considered generally desirable and in the interest of the fundamental rights of an individual or a group of individuals, but such actions really stem from values and interests which are not codified in a particular fundamental rights norm, and they therefore cannot be derived from the provision itself.[20]

---

13 The term 'second-generation rights' was introduced by Vasak, see Vasak (1977).

14 See e.g. Van Kempen (2008), p. 13. Cf. Fredman (2008), p. 66.

15 ECtHR 9 October 1979, no. 6289/73, *Airey v. Ireland*, para. 26.

16 See Van Kempen (2008).

17 Van Kempen's ideas on the doctrine of positive obligations are developed particularly in relation to the sometimes far-reaching case-law of the ECtHR in the field of criminal law. Especially in this area of law, maintaining a negative conception of freedom is of importance.

18 See section 3.3.2.

19 Van Kempen (2008), p. 14.

20 Van Kempen has suggested that therefore a different assessment can be undertaken in this respect, see section 4.7.2.

Evidently, the ECtHR has taken a different perspective on the kind of obligations that states must inherently guarantee under the Convention. The Court agrees that Convention rights essentially give rise to obligations for states to refrain from interfering (negative obligations).[21] The Court has developed a broad range of positive obligations, and does not appear to be particularly concerned about whether such obligations are derived from a negative or a positive notion of freedom. It has accepted states' obligations to protect individuals from interferences by other individuals, and obligations to assist those individuals which have particular vulnerable characteristics.[22] The ECtHR thus demonstrates a much broader and less negative conception of freedom than is held by Van Kempen. The development of the Court's concept of fundamental rights and positive obligations may have been inspired by the work of scholars such as Sen and Nussbaum.[23] These scholars have developed important ideas regarding the concept of freedom which fundamental rights seek to protect, which basically start from the perceived need to realise a situation where an individual is free (from obstacles) to choose the life he or she wants to live. Poverty, poor health or social inequalities must be considered to constrain the exercise of fundamental rights, just as much as hindrances or obstacles that are knowingly laid down by states.[24] This approach to freedom recognises that the protection of social, cultural and economic rights is as important as the protection of civil and political rights. The boundaries between those categories of rights cannot and should not be sharply drawn. They accept that states undertake various social and welfare functions in contemporary societies and that states can play an important role in influencing the enjoyment of the fundamental rights of individuals.[25] States become more and more involved in regulating private life, and as a result the public/private divide has become blurred. The distinction between negative and positive obligations therefore simply cannot be easily drawn.

This more 'positive' approach to fundamental rights and the concept of freedom arguably justifies a wider interpretation given to the rights laid down in the Convention. It implies that fundamental rights can be treated as values that are to be taken into account by all acts of states, including the legislature, the executive and the administrative apparatus.[26] From this perspective it could be accepted that positive obligations inherently follow from the Convention. It could therefore be regarded as problematic that the ECtHR applies a separate fair balance test to determine the existence of positive obligations. By doing so, the ECtHR undermines its own viewpoint that positive obligations are – just like negative obligations – inherent to fundamental

---

21 See e.g. ECtHR 13 June 1979, no. 6833/74, *Marckx v. Belgium*, para. 31; ECtHR 11 January 2006, nos. 52562/99 and 52620/99, *Sørensen and Rasmussen v. Denmark*, para. 57; and ECtHR 16 March 2000, no. 23144/93, *Özgür Gündem v. Turkey*, para. 42.

22 See Xenos (2012), pp. 142–146; and Dröge (2003), p. 179.

23 Sen (1999); and Nussbaum (2006). See further Dröge (2003), pp. 187–223; Xenos (2012), pp. 19–20; and Fredman (2008), p. 1.

24 Cf. Fredman (2008), p. 11.

25 See Connelly (1986), pp. 574–575; Xenos (2012), p. 21; and Mowbray (2004), p. 5.

26 Cf. Xenos (2012), p. 72.

rights.[27] At the same time, the ECtHR thus recognises that positive obligations differ from negative obligations and that different principles need to be taken into account in their examination. The different characteristics attributed to positive obligations, versus those of negative obligations can explain why the ECtHR applies a separate test for establishing positive obligations.[28] The ECtHR has also stated that there are certain limits which apply to the scope of positive obligations under the Convention.[29]

There is thus a theoretical debate on the foundations for the development of positive obligations. Some who very much adhere to a negative concept of freedom criticise the Court for its acceptance of positive obligations, or at least some types thereof. In contrast, others embrace a positive concept of freedom and would generally agree with the development of positive obligations in relation to the Convention.[30] To the extent that positive obligations are indeed far removed from guaranteeing the negative concept of freedom, it seems necessary for the ECtHR to take into account the detrimental impacts on the interests of other individuals in specific cases. In this regard it can be useful to take into consideration the particular typology which has been developed by Van Kempen, and specifically the autonomous or repressive type of positive obligation.[31]

4.2.3. THE CONCERN OVER HUMAN RIGHTS INFLATION

Apart from more theoretical disputes, there is perhaps a more practical risk that arises from accepting a broad conception of freedom and a similarly broad definition of positive obligations. The problem is that it makes it difficult to determine the exact scope of fundamental rights.[32] To some extent, the ECtHR itself has intensified this problem by holding on to a very wide conception of positive obligations, and by not (always) explaining its theory for the development of positive obligations under the Convention.[33] The ECtHR does not define the scope of positive obligations very well in its judgments, nor does it always provide clear limitations to the scope of positive obligations.[34] States are made (potentially) responsible for fundamental rights violations in a wide array of circumstances, including violations caused by the (in)direct

27 Cf. Xenos (2012), p. 119; and Lavrysen (2016), p. 218.

28 See sections 3.2.3. and 3.2.6. Some scholars, however, do not consider that a different test needs to be applied to positive and negative obligations, see in particular Lavrysen (2016), pp. 277–280.

29 See section 3.6.

30 Within the ECtHR, however, there remain differences of opinion with regard to the reach of positive obligations, see the dissenting opinion of Judges Zupančić, Gyulumyan, Kalaydjieva, De Gaetano and Wojtyzek to ECtHR 28 January 2014, no. 35810/09, *O'Keeffe v. Ireland*, paras 7 ff.

31 See section 3.4. This typology is also of interest as it could influence the extent to which the ECtHR may be required to specify and motivate how the recognition of particular types of positive obligations can be justified under the Convention.

32 Lawson (1995a), pp. 563–564.

33 Cf. Xenos (2012), p. 205.

34 Xenos (2012), p. 4.

involvement of its state agents, and also for violations caused by other individuals, and for the particular vulnerabilities of individuals.[35]

The problem of the so-called 'human rights inflation' may therefore arise, which means that claims for state action are increasingly being framed in terms of human rights, even if the relation of such claims to core fundamental rights issues is not always clear.[36] Human rights inflation is considered problematic for a variety of reasons. Among other things, it can blur the scope of human rights and it may affect legal certainty for claimants seeking judicial protection. The ECtHR has therefore been urged to provide a clearer justification for the recognition of positive obligations, for example by explaining to what extent the positive obligations under the Convention relate to the concept of negative obligations.[37] The ECtHR has also been urged to define the scope of Convention rights more clearly. The ECtHR indeed seems to have paid greater attention to this point of criticism, which will be further addressed in several of the following sections.

4.3. HORIZONTAL POSITIVE OBLIGATIONS

The ECtHR has developed positive obligations in its case-law which aim to protect the fundamental rights of individuals in their relations with other individuals. Actually, many of the positive obligations that have been recognised by the Court appear to have a certain horizontal dimension.[38] This type of positive obligation renders states indirectly responsible for fundamental rights violations that are committed by private parties and creates, albeit indirectly, a horizontal effect of fundamental rights (*Drittwirkung*).[39] Such effects have been considered problematic for various reasons. In the following subsections the limited personal scope of fundamental rights and the related problem of determining state responsibility for private acts are discussed.

4.3.1. THE LIMITED PERSONAL SCOPE OF FUNDAMENTAL RIGHTS

Fundamental rights are, in general, addressed to states and not to individuals.[40] For that reason, the ECtHR can hear claims brought by individuals against states but not

35 See further sections 3.3. and 3.4.

36 Cf. Sen (2010), p. 387. Sen argued that a solution for the fear of human rights inflation can be found in providing a public discussion on human rights claims. This will attest which claims are genuinely about human rights and which are not.

37 See Gerards (2012a), pp. 173–202; Lavrysen (2013); and Van Kempen (2008), pp. 12 and 73.

38 See e.g. ECtHR 26 March 1985, no. 8978/80, *X. and Y. v. the Netherlands*, para. 27. See further Xenos (2012), pp. 3, 19 and 39; and section 3.3.

39 The horizontal scope of EU fundamental righs is specifically addressed in section 6.7.2.

40 Van Kempen (2008), pp. 12–73.

against other individuals.[41] The Convention does not allow, whether substantively or procedurally, for a direct horizontal effect of Convention rights. By having accepted obligations to protect individuals from interference by other individuals, the ECtHR has been criticised for circumventing the limited outlook of the Convention. Moreover, there is some fear that the primary vertical effect of the Convention rights may be diluted as a result of the recognition of these types of positive obligations, as discussed in the previous section.[42] By accepting obligations to protect other individuals, the very foundation for fundamental rights could be jeopardised, that is, the need to protect the freedom of individuals from the power of the state.[43] The most problematic sitation is where the fundamental rights of other individuals are 'suppressed' by accepting positive obligations. Fundamental rights considerations may, for example, play a role in justifying the adoption of criminal investigation measures, the prosecution of suspects and the detainment of convicted criminals in order to prevent terrorism.[44] According to Van Kempen, such repressive types of positive obligations should be left outside the scope of protection of fundamental rights guarantees.[45]

To a certain extent, it must be acknowledged that one of the normal functions of states is to provide protection to individuals from harm caused by private parties, and to regulate the relations between private parties.[46] It is clear that states must act to protect individuals, for example, from interferences in their right to life (murder) and their right to property (theft) which can be effected by private parties as well as states parties. It can be disputed whether such obligations arise from the protection of fundamental rights or whether they arise from the states' sovereign responsibility to protect individuals from interferences by other individuals. The first scenario would mean that individuals could indeed claim and enforce a right to positive action by the state. This point then also essentially relates to the political nature of positive obligations which will be discussed elsewhere (see section 4.4.). Yet, it must be recognised by the ECtHR that it needs to take into account that the fundamental rights or interests of third parties can be affected by horizontal types of positive obligations. Therefore, if it imposes such positive obligations on states, it needs to make sure that it does not

41 Article 34 ECHR.

42 See generally Fredman (2008), pp. 73–76. Cf. ECtHR 21 June 1988, no. 10126/82, *Plattform "Ärtze für das Leben" v. Austria.*

43 Van Kempen (2008), para. 80.

44 Here, the right to safety as part of the right to liberty under Article 5 ECHR plays a role. See further Van de Westelaken (2010), p. 149. See also the partly dissenting opinion of Judge Wildhaber joined by Judges Kovler and Mularoni, all to ECtHR 20 December 2004, no. 50385/99, *Maraktzis v. Greece.*

45 In this regard, Van Kempen refers to the practice of the Supreme Court of the United States of America, which has specifically chosen to exclude duties to protect from the ambit of the protection that is offered by its constitution, see e.g. U.S. Supreme Court 27 June 2005, *Castle Rock/Gonzales*, 545 *U.S.* 189 (1989). The Supreme Court only recognises horizontal positive obligations if the individual who seeks protection finds itself in a state of dependency *vis-à-vis* the state and it is obvious that the individual cannot protect itself in such a situation (such as prisoners). See U.S. Supreme Court 6 June 1994, *Farmer/Brennan*, 511 *U.S.* 825 (1994).

46 Cf. De Meyer (1973), p. 273; and Xenos (2012), pp. 29 and 47.

run into conflict over the obligation of states to protect the fundamental rights of all individuals under the Convention.[47]

4.3.2. THE DETERMINATION OF STATE RESPONSIBILITY FOR PRIVATE ACTS

A problematic aspect to accepting horizontal positive obligations concerns the difficulty of determining state responsibility for interferences caused by private parties. Many violations of fundamental rights may be unknown to states. Purely horizontal violations could take place in private households. In some cases, these type of violations also cannot be controlled by state agents for other reasons. In contemporary societies, states have lost some control in certain areas, for example, by mandating many public tasks to private parties. Companies formerly owned by the state have been privatised or have become players on the commercial markets.[48] Also certain private parties such as multinationals and other powerful companies, such as banks, wield immense power that, as has been argued, goes beyond the states' control.[49]

The ECtHR holds, logically, that states parties are not relieved of the responsibility for guaranteeing fundamental rights protection in the execution of public tasks.[50] The question remains, however, to what extent states can be held responsible for all actions, or rather omissions, in a society in which the public/private divide is increasingly blurred.[51]

The case-law of the ECtHR on state responsibility for private acts is still case-based. It is not clear for what kind of private interferences and for what reasons states must take positive measures to protect individuals from fundamental rights violations caused by other individuals.[52] The ECtHR, for example, attributed state responsibility for fundamental rights violations in the case of *Öneryildiz v. Turkey* where it established that the Turkish state had not taken adequate measures to prevent an explosion at a rubbish tip, as a consequence of which many lives were lost.[53] Also in the case of *Guerra and others v. Italy*, the ECtHR held that the state failed to fulfil its positive obligation to provide information to inhabitants who were living near a site where an industry that was potentially very dangerous was operating.[54] The particular circumstances of

---

47 See the partly dissenting opinion of Judge Wildhaber joined by Judges Kovler and Mularoni, all to ECtHR 20 December 2004, no. 50385/99, *Maraktzis v. Greece*.

48 Fredman (2008), pp. 58–61. Cf. e.g. ECtHR 25 March 1993, no. 13134/87, *Costello-Roberts v. the United Kingdom*.

49 Dröge (2003), pp. 1–2.

50 See ECtHR 25 March 1993, no. 13134/87, *Costello-Roberts v. the United Kingdom*, para. 27, where the Court held that 'the State cannot absolve itself from responsibility by delegating its responsibilities to private bodies or individuals'.

51 See further Fredman (2008), pp. 40–58.

52 Van Kempen (2008), pp. 29–30.

53 ECtHR 30 November 2004, no. 48939/99, *Öneryildiz v. Turkey*, paras 92–94.

54 ECtHR 19 February 1998, no. 14967/89, *Guerra and others v. Italy*, paras 58–60.

those cases may have arguably given rise to positive obligations for those states, but the judgments do not explain in a more general sense how the scope of state responsibility for horizontal fundamental rights violations must be determined in such cases.

The ECtHR has developed a few limitations to the scope of positive obligations, as discussed in chapter 3, such as that states must have knowledge of fundamental rights violations.[55] This helps to bring some clarity over the situations in which states can be held responsible for violations of fundamental rights in horizontal situations. The ECtHR is still developing its case-law on this issue, however.

The ECtHR has not made clear to what extent it is also relevant to establish a certain causal link between state acts and fundamental rights violations. It seems that active interference by states in a given area, by adopting regulations or by taking other types of measures, is a relevant factor that could be taken into account. For example, the case-law of the ECtHR shows that states incur positive obligations for the very fact of having issued licences to undertakings that carry out certain harmful activities.[56] In that respect the positive obligation follows more logically from the fact of the state itself having failed to fulfil its negative obligation. According to the typology of Van Kempen, as discussed, it would then be less problematic to impose such a positive obligation on states.[57] There are some examples to be found in the case-law of the ECtHR which reveal that the ECtHR indeed takes into account the fact that states have actively intervened in certain circumstances, for example by establishing legislation while failing to fully respect the situation of certain (vulnerable) individuals in the given circumstances.[58] More generally, however, the case-law of the ECtHR on this issue is inconsistent.[59] It is therefore unclear to what extent the ECtHR also takes into account that a state has actively intervened in a certain area.

4.4. THE POLITICAL CHARACTER OF POSITIVE OBLIGATIONS

While there is now general agreement that fundamental rights protection can give rise to (some types of) positive obligations there is still disagreement as to whether the judiciary in particular is competent to impose positive obligations on the state.[60] One of the strongest critiques against the development of positive obligations is that it is at odds with the principle of separation of powers. Of relevance in this context also is the supranational position of the ECtHR, which will be discussed later (see section 4.5.).

55 See sections 3.2.6. and 3.5.
56 Lavrysen (2016), p. 130.
57 See sections 3.3.2. and section 4.2.2.
58 See sections 3.2.4. See e.g. ECtHR 26 May 1994, no. 16969/90, *Keegan v. Ireland*, para. 51.
59 See further Lavrysen (2016), pp. 246–251.
60 Fredman (2008), p. 92.

The discussion in the following sections thus focuses more generally on the arguments against the competence of the judiciary in general to determine positive obligations.

4.4.1. LACK OF DEMOCRATIC LEGITIMACY

In principle, it is problematic for the judiciary to determine which actions must be undertaken by the state, considering that judges are, after all, not democratically elected nor politically accountable.[61] The judiciary does not have the same capacity as the legislature and administrative bodies to consider all of the interests involved for determining which actions must be undertaken by the state. Positive obligations can generally be fulfilled by a range of possible actions and thus require political deliberation. Moreover, the fulfilment of certain positive obligations can impose a high burden on states resources in terms of finances as well as organisation.[62] Such decisions imply political choices which are generally not entrusted to the judiciary.

From this perspective, it can be maintained that courts should take a restrained approach in defining positive obligations related to politically sensitive decisions, especially those decisions in the field of social and economic policy with financial implications. It should, at the least, leave states parties a wide margin of appreciation as far as the further realisation of those obligations is concerned.[63]

Various judgments of the ECtHR on positive obligations have been criticised for this reason, especially where the ECtHR failed to provide clear reasoning for the choices it made in those judgments.[64] Van Kempen, in particular, is concerned over the practice of the ECtHR in which it indicates that states must undertake positive obligations in the area of criminal law.[65] The ECtHR does not always explain why criminal law measures in particular would be necessary to protect fundamental rights. Are there no other possibilities available to provide effective protection? Could prevention not have been chosen over repression?[66] These choices, it can be argued, should instead be made only after deliberation in the political domain.

Van Kempen therefore suggests that the ECtHR should adopt a different approach and refrain from specifying which positive (legislative) obligations should be undertaken by

---

61 Fredman (2008), pp. 32 ff.; and see ECtHR 21 February 1986, no. 8793/79, *James and others v. the United Kingdom*, para. 46, where the Court held: 'The Court, finding it natural that the margin of appreciation available to the legislature in implementing social and economic policies should be a wide one, will respect the legislature's judgment as to what is "in the public interest" unless that judgment be manifestly without reasonable foundation.'

62 Fredman (2008), pp. 69 ff.

63 Cf. Fredman (2008), pp. 95–96; and Nieuwenhuis (2011), pp. 191–195.

64 See Van Kempen (2008), p. 74.

65 See Van Kempen (2008), pp. 25–56 and 76; and Van de Westelaken (2010), pp. 135–152.

66 Van Kempen (2008), p. 78. See also the dissenting opinion of Judge Kjølbro to ECtHR 20 October 2015, no. 15529/12, *Balázs v. Hungary*, where it was held that the ECtHR had interfered too much in examining the choice over whether to criminally prosecute an individual involved.

the state.[67] The Court's recourse to such broad legal bases as Articles 1 and 13 ECHR, and the object and purpose of the Convention to provide effective fundamental rights protection, does not provide sufficiently precise legitimation for the far-reaching effects of positive obligations under the Convention.[68] The ECtHR could instead adopt an approach in which it first considers whether and/or which positive obligations are already recognised at the national level or in administrative structures. If such positive obligations can be recognised, the ECtHR can then examine whether the state fulfils such positive obligations without discriminating (on the basis of Article 14 ECHR and Article 1 of the Twelfth Protocol to the Convention).[69] States parties would then preserve the prerogative to determine whether and when to have recourse to particular methods – such as criminal law measures – in order to protect fundamental rights.[70]

This approach thus respects the principle of state sovereignty and the responsibility to protect. The concerns over the democratic legitimacy of judicial review are generally (also in relation to negative obligations) an important aspect to be aware of.[71] In developing positive obligations in its case-law, the ECtHR has explained in some cases that it looks at the choices that have already been made at national level which could secure the protection of certain fundamental rights. For example, in the case of *X. and Y. v. the Netherlands,* which was about a young and handicapped girl who was not able to lodge a complaint about sexual abuse that had taken place, the ECtHR held that:

> this is in fact an area in which the Netherlands has generally opted for a system of protection based on the criminal law. The only gap so far, as the Commission and the Court have been made aware, is as regards persons in the situation of Miss Y; in such cases, this system meets a procedural obstacle which the Netherlands legislature had apparently not foreseen.[72]

While the ECtHR had established in this case that a positive obligation to take measures in the field of criminal law derived from the right to protect private life, the ECtHR also explained that there is a certain basis that can be found under national law for taking such measures.

Furthermore, in the case of *X. and Y. v. the Netherlands*, the ECtHR explained that 'Effective deterrence is indispensable in this area and it can be achieved only by criminal-law provisions'.[73] The ECtHR thus clarified its choice for specific types of measures that need to be taken by states, in this case criminal law, while its choice is

---

67 Van Kempen (2008), pp. 87 and 89–94.

68 Van Kempen (2008), pp. 68–69.

69 A similar approach seems to be taken as the 'in for a penny – in for a pound' approach that was discussed in section 2.4.

70 This approach is also visible, to some extent, in the case of *Çam v. Turkey*, where the ECtHR was required to examine whether the state had violated the prohibition of discrimination in relation to the right to education in a case of a blind girl who was refused entry to a music academy on the basis of her sight impairment. See ECtHR 23 February 2006, no. 51500/08, *Çam v. Turkey*, para. 56.

71 See in particular Waldron (2006). Cf. Klatt (2015).

72 ECtHR 26 March 1985, no. 8978/80, *X. and Y. v. the Netherlands*, para. 27.

73 ECtHR 26 March 1985, no. 8978/80, *X. and Y. v. the Netherlands*, para. 27.

also further justified by the principle of effective protection of fundamental rights.[74] Providing such more specific directions as to the types of measures which can be taken will ultimately help states as well as litigants to find an appropriate way of securing effective fundamental rights protection. This approach is also visible in the practice of the ECtHR in which it indicates the general and individual measures that states must take to abide by its judgments under Article 46(1) ECHR. This provision only contains a very general obligation for states to comply with the judgments of the ECtHR.[75] The ECtHR, on occasion, also clarifies which particular individual as well as general measures need to be taken by the state in order to ensure that similar violations do not take place in the future.[76]

In relation to its case-law of positive obligations, it would thus generally help if the ECtHR were to explain why it chooses specific types of measures, in view of the fact that courts are frequently not well-placed to take such decisions, and therefore need to provide clear justifications.

4.4.2. EMPOWERMENT OF INDIVIDUALS

The ECtHR has accepted in its case-law that individuals are entitled to positive action by the state on the basis of its doctrine of positive obligations. The development of positive obligations by the ECtHR can be defended on the basis of the empowerment of individuals, as explained in chapter 3.[77]

There is some disagreement amongst scholars, however, as to whether the establishment of positive obligations by the judiciary can indeed be legitimated on the basis of this argument. Some argue that the interest of safeguarding the negative value of freedom is more important than empowerment, and this value would be overshadowed if it is also accepted that fundamental rights give rise to the need for positive action by states. In particular, this could be the case if the recognition of positive obligations would lead to interferences with the rights of other individuals.[78] The empowerment of individuals could be secured differently, namely through the accountability of politically elected parliament. Other scholars have instead proposed an intermediate approach. They believe that in a democracy governed by majoritarian rule, there is a legitimate role to be played by the judiciary in developing positive obligations. The judiciary has

---

74 See in particular Leach (2006), p. 126.

75 Under general international law, this means that states are required to end the violation (obligation of cessation), restore the situation as far as possible as it existed before the violation took place (*restitutio in integrum*) or, if reparation is not possible, make available appropriate satisfaction, see in particular *Chorzów Factory (Germany v. Poland) (Indemnity) (Merits)*, Permanent Court of International Justice, case PCIJ Rep Series A No 17, para. 47. See also Vande Lanotte & Haeck (2005), p. 704; and Ress (2005), p. 371.

76 See section 2.7.

77 See section 3.4.2.

78 See section 3.4.2.

an important role to play in protecting the rights of vulnerable individuals who are not able to voice their own particular interests under majoritarian rule. The recognition of positive obligations in judgments relating to individuals could therefore be necessary, and the judiciary would need to pay respect to certain constitutionally relevant criteria when accepting claims for positive obligations.[79]

Fredman, for example, argues that the judiciary can perform a corrective role in democratic societies when individuals cannot validate their fundamental rights claims through the electorate.[80] Judges then are competent to provide input in their judgments for a political discussion on the fulfilment of positive obligations, as long as they do not claim the power to have the final say as to which particular positive action must be taken. Fredman also finds that there are certain standards which must be met for the exercise of such power in the judicial process leading up to the definition of fundamental rights.[81] First, accountability is required, which demands that decision-makers should justify openly before courts their choice of particular actions. Standards of participation must also be met, which means that courts have to provide a forum for deliberation on perspectives. Lastly, the principle of equality must be applied, which demands that courts must address inequalities in the democratic process. Fredman considers the judiciary as a competent institution that can provide an appropriate forum for addressing inequalities, especially because judgments on positive obligations frequently concern individuals or groups of individuals who are vulnerable and/or face social inequalities, such as detainees, disabled persons and asylum seekers, who do not have a (majority) voice in the democratic process.[82]

The political character of positive obligations remains a critical factor in the development of such obligations by courts. Although it may be legitimated to contribute to the development of the fulfilment of states positive obligations for reasons of empowerment of individuals, it must still abide by democratic standards. Criticism can be raised, and it is therefore important that the ECtHR pays due respect to these points of criticism and sees that the standards developed by Fredman are met.

4.5. THE SUPRANATIONAL POSITION OF THE ECtHR

Several critics have stressed that there is further reason for restraint for the development of positive obligations by the ECtHR considering its supranational position.[83] Within the system of fundamental rights protection of the Council of Europe, the ECtHR must be careful to pay due respect to its subsidiary position.[84] The ECtHR can be considered to be at too great a distance from states to warrant far-reaching interventions in national

79 See Xenos (2012), pp. 48–49; and Klatt (2015).

80 Fredman (2008), pp. 100 ff. See also Xenos (2012); and Van Kempen (2008), pp. 85–86.

81 Fredman (2008), pp. 103–113.

82 See further Xenos (2012), chapter 3.

83 See Van Kempen (2008), p. 67.

84 See section 2.4.

law, and it may be insufficiently informed of the facts of the case and of all the interests involved in order to be able to carry out a balanced assessment to determine positive obligations.[85] According to the critics, therefore, the ECtHR should instead choose to leave a margin of discretion to the national authorities to decide which particular positive obligations must be fulfilled.

On various occasions the ECtHR has expressed that it is aware of its position and that, for that reason, it does not intend to substitute its own assessment on the fulfilment of positive obligations over the balancing of interests which has already been made by the public authorities. The ECtHR has, for example, held that:

> The balancing of individual interests that may well be contradictory is a difficult matter, and Contracting States must have a broad margin of appreciation in this respect, since the national authorities are in principle better placed than the European Court to assess whether or not there is a 'pressing social need' capable of justifying interference with one of the rights guaranteed by the Convention.[86]

Some politically sensitive positive obligations may also lead to high burdens for states, both in terms of organisation and finance. The Court has expressed awareness of this consequence, for example, in the case of *Rees v. the United Kingdom*, concerning the question whether the alteration of sexual identity must legally be recognised by national authorities:

> The introduction of such a system [i.e. the alteration of gender in birth registers from a given date] has not hitherto been considered necessary in the United Kingdom. It would have important administrative consequences and would impose new duties on the rest of the population.[87]

Because of the political sensitivity of the area in which claimants seek for particular actions by the state, the ECtHR has chosen on several occasions not to establish a positive obligation on the basis of the Convention at all.[88] The ECtHR has, for example, held that the Convention does not give rise to a general right to housing, free health care, or a clean environment.[89] The ECtHR also exercises much restraint regarding immigration law in view of the politically sensitive nature of that area.[90]

---

85 See Van Kempen (2008), pp. 54–55.

86 ECtHR 29 April 1994, nos. 25088/94 to 28443/95, *Chassagnou and others v. France*, para. 113.

87 ECtHR 17 October 1986, no. 9532/81, *Rees v. the United Kingdom*, para. 42.

88 Cf. ECtHR 28 May 1985, nos. 9214/80 to 9474/81, *Abdulaziz, Cabales and Balkandali v. the United Kingdom*, para. 68, where the Court concluded: 'The duty imposed by Article 8 cannot be considered as extending to a general obligation on the part of a Contracting State to respect the choice by married couples of the country of their matrimonial residence and to accept the non-national spouses for settlement in that country.'

89 See, respectively, ECtHR 18 January 2011, no. 272385/95, *Chapman v. the United Kingdom*, para. 99; ECtHR 26 May 2011, no. 27617/04, *R. R. V. Poland*, para. 198; and ECtHR 8 July 2003, no. 36022/97, *Hatton and others v. the United Kingdom*, para. 96.

90 ECtHR 28 May 1985, nos. 9214/80 to 9474/81, *Abdulaziz, Cabales and Balkandali v. the United Kingdom*, para. 67.

The ECtHR thus expresses awareness of the potential implications which the definition of a positive obligation in an individual's case can have for the particular state party, as well as for all of the states parties, arguably, due to its subsidiary position. At the same time, this exercise of restraint is in itself criticised. It is sometimes argued that such a deferential approach is at odds with the objective of realising the effective protection of fundamental rights.[91] It has been argued that the ECtHR should adopt a less deferential approach as regards fundamental rights violations for which the legislatures and judiciaries at national level cannot provide solutions. This would mainly apply to those issues which all European states deal with in isolation, but to which they do not seem to provide appropriate responses, such as the migration, international trade, cross-border movement of workers and environmental issues. These clearly cross-border issues require a concerted response at the regional or international level, and it appears especially difficult to conclude agreements between states in the short term, as the competences to deal with those issues remain, to a certain degree, at national level.[92]

There are therefore some different expectations on the role which the ECtHR must fulfil in the development of positive obligations under the Convention.[93] The ECtHR struggles with this, which it also does in respect of its case-law on negative obligations. One particular way of dealing with this criticism seems to be that the ECtHR increasingly pays attention to the national procedural framework to ensure an effective way of reviewing the compliance of states parties with the Convention, while respecting its subsidiary position, as further discussed in chapter 2.[94]

4.6. LEGAL UNCERTAINTY REGARDING THE SCOPE OF POSITIVE OBLIGATIONS

The scope of positive obligations can be quite open-ended.[95] The ECtHR has declined to develop a general theory on how the concept of positive obligations must be defined within the Convention. This is problematic because it frustrates the ability of states

---

91 See Xenos (2012), p. 5. According to Xenos, 'European judges are renowned for their low profile and cautiousness with states' sensitivities about the ever-decreasing national sovereignty that unavoidably results from the interaction of national legal systems with European human rights law. It is to their credit that they have always manage to sense carefully the international climate and the changing social dynamics in various corners of Europe before moving to modify steadily an progressively the intensity of their review on the state's legal system. There are numerous statements of the Court on the state's margin of appreciation and on the optional choice of the national incorporation of the Convention, but, in reality, what is observed is a considerable expansion of positive obligations and numerous rulings against the states that we present and discuss in the following chapters.'

92 See Xenos (2012), p. 48.

93 See further Xenos (2012), pp. 51–53.

94 See section 2.4. Interestingly, the ECtHR formulates positive procedural obligations in this context, which can itself be criticised. See e.g. ECtHR 27 September 1995, no. 18984/91, *McCann and others v. the United Kingdom*, para. 153; and cf. Van de Westelaken (2010), pp. 147–148.

95 See sections 3.2.6. and 3.5.; and cf. Xenos (2012), p. 4.

to foresee the obligations they will incur under the Convention, and for individuals to foresee which claims will be covered by the Convention.[96] With the lack of clearly defined limits to the scope of positive obligations, the possibilities for positive obligations to arise under the Convention may seem endless.[97]

Although the lack of specificity and predictability is problematic, it is difficult to blame the ECtHR for this. Fundamental rights generally provide only a very general framework, and the course of states' actions to protect such rights cannot directly be derived from the provisions in which fundamental rights have been laid down. Often, positive obligations are defined by the ECtHR on the basis of the specific circumstances of a case, which can be very hard for states to foresee. For example, the ECtHR accepted in the case of *Georgel and Georgeta Stoicescu v. Romania* that the state was under a positive obligation to take measures in response to the large number of stray dogs, because it needs to protect public health and prevent threats to the physical integrity of the population.[98]

The ECtHR can only determine in a very general and broad manner which positive obligations arise from the Convention, since it must leave the details and the manner of protection to be resolved through political debate.[99] Due to the political nature of positive obligations and the supranational position of the ECtHR, it is unavoidable that positive obligations can only be developed on a rather broad and vague basis. The ECtHR has, for example, held that states have a positive obligation under Article 8 ECHR 'to facilitate the gypsy way of life' in the case of *Chapman v. the United Kingdom*.[100] This positive obligation cannot directly create clear enforceable rights for individuals. Rather, it creates an indeterminate and open-ended positive obligation for states which should be filled in by the national authorities which will choose particular policies.[101] This is problematic as states will not be sure of what such an obligation actually entails and individuals may not be sure what they are entitled to and whether they will be able to start judicial proceedings to enforce compliance with such vague positive obligations.

On some occasions, the Court has been clear about which measures states must take to fulfil their positive obligations, for example, by clarifying that states needed to amend their criminal law provisions.[102] Inevitably, this raises objections from the point of the view of the separation of powers, in particular if it means that the Court delivers 'political' judgments. On other occasions, the Court has introduced specific limits to the scope of positive obligations, as set out in chapter 3.[103] Such limitations contribute at least somewhat to the task of defining the scope of positive obligations under the Convention more clearly.

---

96 Cf. Xenos (2012), pp. 4–5, pp. 78 and 205.

97 Cf. Xenos (2012), p. 91.

98 ECtHR 26 July 2011, no. 9718/03, *Georgel and Georgeta Stoicescu v. Romania*.

99 See sections 4.4. and 4.5.

100 ECtHR 18 January 2001, no. 27238/95, *Chapman v. the United Kingdom*, para. 96.

101 Van Kempen (2008), pp. 28 and 38–40.

102 See e.g. ECtHR 26 March 1985, no. 8978/80, *X. and Y. v. the Netherlands*.

103 See section 3.5.

The lack of certainty over the scope of positive obligations has led to proposals, put forward by different scholars, for the Court to provide a better understanding of the concept of positive obligations, to establish better-defined limits in individual judgments, and to improve the structure of its argumentation (see section 4.7.2.).[104] Considering the continuous development of positive obligations by the Court and their impact on national legislation of states parties, such strategies can generally be welcomed, especially since the Court has expressed its intention not to develop a theoretical framework regarding its doctrine of positive obligations and the possible methods for their implementation. At the same time, they can never fully remedy the unpredictability of the case-law of the Court.

4.7. AMBIGUOUS METHODS OF THE ECTHR FOR DETERMINING THE EXISTENCE OF POSITIVE OBLIGATIONS

4.7.1. CRITICAL EVALUATION OF THE FAIR BALANCE TEST

The Court's approach to determining the existence and fulfilment of states' positive obligations has been criticised for its technical flaws. It has already been mentioned that the fair balance approach of the ECtHR lacks clarity and fairness and the use of the margin of appreciation doctrine may be incorrect. Also, the usefulness of distinguishing between negative and positive obligations and of applying a different approach to determine the respective obligations under the Convention has been questioned. These three different points of criticism will be discussed, before some suggestions for improving the Court's technical approach will be briefly addressed.

4.7.1.1. Lack of Clarity, Structure and Fairness

The application of the fair balance test to determine positive obligations has been held to lack clarity, because the criteria which are used by the ECtHR are not fixed and the ECtHR does not base its judgments on a uniform approach.[105] The ECtHR does not consistently examine, with respect to the fulfilment of positive obligations by states, whether a state has a legitimate reason for seeking to escape its positive obligation to protect fundamental rights and whether this can be necessary in a democratic society.[106] Various judgments of the ECtHR further demonstrate that it does not always

---

104 See Lavrysen (2013); Xenos (2012); and Russell (2010).

105 Xenos (2012), p. 61; and Lawson (1995b), p. 728.

106 Van Dijk (1998), pp. 25–26. See e.g. ECtHR 18 January 2001, no. 24882/94, *Beard v. the United Kingdom*, para. 107.

fully perform a balancing exercise, that it concentrates only on specific interests[107] and that it simply assumes that particular positive obligations exist.[108] It is simply not clear how exactly the test is carried out.

Secondly, the fair balance test also has been said to lack structure. The test implies a merging of two stages, which are generally to be examined separately.[109] The ECtHR usually merges the questions of what constitutes an interference with a particular Convention right, and whether or not this interference can be objectively justified by the state, when it determines states' positive obligations. The precise scope of the positive obligations under the Convention is not frequently addressed by the ECtHR as a separate issue. The Court's judgments generally also do not make clear why and when particular claims to positive action will fall within the scope of the Convention. The Court's approach can cause confusion as to the distribution of the burden of proof between the claimant and the state.[110] The lack of clarity and structure of the Court's approach clearly increases the unpredictability and uncertainty over what positive obligations exist under the Convention.[111]

The third problematic aspect of the fair balance test is that it is considered to offer a lower level of protection of fundamental rights as compared to the test used to determine the fulfilment of a state's negative obligations – the assessment of which is regarded by some scholars as being much more structured.[112] In the fair balance test, the criteria are applied loosely instead of strictly.[113] It has been argued that the ECtHR applies the various proportionality criteria less stringently in case of positive obligations.[114] The lower level of protection is also a result of the Court's merging approach, where the ECtHR (incorrectly) applies the criteria for justifying restrictions of fundamental rights to determine the scope of states' positive obligations, and thus individuals' entitlements to positive action. This is because the ECtHR pays less attention to defining what rights individuals actually have, and more attention to whether or not it is reasonable to impose requirements on states to take certain active measures.

Overall, there thus seems to be a less strict and a rather confused approach to determine the fulfilment of states' positive obligations, which could affect the level of protection of an individual's fundamental rights.[115]

---

107 See e.g. ECtHR 8 July 2003, no. 36022/97, *Hatton and others v. the United Kingdom*. It has been argued that the Court overtly focused on economic arguments in the balancing act in this judgment, see Xenos (2012), p. 65. Cf. Tulkens & Drooghenbroeck (2002).

108 Van Dijk (1998), p. 24.

109 See generally Gerards & Senden (2009).

110 Gerards (2011b), p. 253.

111 Xenos (2012), pp. 91–97.

112 See Lawson (1995b), pp. 731 and 821.

113 See Lawson (1995b), p. 728.

114 See in particular Lavrysen (2016), pp. 209–218.

115 Cf. Van de Westelaken (2010), p. 150.

4.7.1.2. *The Incorrect Use of the Margin of Appreciation Doctrine*

In examining whether a state has complied with its positive obligations, the ECtHR usually has recourse to the margin of appreciation doctrine.[116] In particular, the ECtHR does so in cases concerned with the protection of Articles 8 to 11 ECHR.[117] Some scholars believe that a wide margin of appreciation must be afforded to states generally when they impose positive obligations.[118] They reason that initially, when states ratified the Convention, they had not given their consent to such obligations, which may entail financial or organisational burdens on states.[119] For these reasons, states should be allowed discretion in determining how they fulfil positive obligations under the Convention. According to other scholars, however, the margin of appreciation should not be applied differently to positive obligations and to negative obligations, and, in fact, it is generally to be just as wide or narrow for both types of obligations.[120] Also, it is only in cases on positive obligations that the ECtHR uses the argument that no impossible or disproportionate burdens can be placed on states.[121] By not expressing a similar limitation in cases on negative obligation, it could seem that a wider margin is too easily granted to states in cases on positive obligations.

The ECtHR has explained that the 'applicable principles' to the determination of states' positive and negative obligations are largely similar. This would imply that the ECtHR does not afford a different margin of appreciation to states in cases concerning positive obligations. Recent research, conducted by Lavrysen, suggests that, in practice, the ECtHR does adopt a lower intensity in its review of states compliance with their positive obligation under the Convention, particularly so in relation to violations of Articles 8 to 11 ECHR.[122] It is, however, difficult to discover whether the ECtHR really affords a wider margin of appreciation in cases of positive obligations than in negative obligations. Often, such cases can be about matters of socio-economic interests for the state or about matters for which there may not yet be sufficient consensus between states. These factors can influence whether the ECtHR will decide to grant a wide margin of discretion to the states parties. If the ECtHR indeed affords a different margin to the states in cases concerning positive obligations, it is important to find out how

---

116 See sections 2.6.3. and 3.2.6. The Court seldom holds in general that a wide margin of appreciation applies to positive obligations, except for ECtHR 3 February 2009, no. 31276/05, *Women on Waves v. Portugal*, para. 40, where it held: 's'il est vrai que, dans les deux hypotheses – obligations positives et negatives – l'État jouit d'une certain marge d'appréciation …, la Cour estime que cette marge d'appreciation est plus étroite s'aggisant des obligations negatives découlant de la Convention.'

117 Lavrysen (2016), p. 206. Lavrysen argues that the ECtHR applies a proportionality test which is less intense in cases on positive obligations cases than it is in cases on negative obligations, see on this point Lavrysen (2016), pp. 209–218.

118 See e.g. Van Dijk (1998), p. 22.

119 Campbell (2006), p. 411; and Van Dijk (1998), p. 22.

120 See Gerards (2011b), p. 256; and Lawson (1995b), p. 749.

121 Lavrysen (2016), p. 211.

122 Lavrysen (2016), p. 214.

the ECtHR exactly makes the distinction between positive and negative obligations, as discussed in the next subsection.

Another point of controversy is whether the ECtHR makes correct use of the margin of appreciation doctrine with regard to positive obligations because it merges the two stages which normally, in relation to negative obligations, are separated. A margin of appreciation should be offered to states only when determining whether restrictions of fundamental rights can be objectively justified, thus in the second stage of the review. Since the two stages are merged by the Court when determining the existence of positive obligations, the margin of appreciation for states affects both the scope of Convention rights and the justification of a restriction of Convention rights.[123] This is considered problematic, since all states parties should give the same meaning to the scope of Convention rights.[124] According to some critics, the margin of appreciation doctrine was therefore wrongly applied by the Court in various judgments, as it led to incorrect determination of the scope of Convention rights.[125] One widely cited example of an incorrect use of the margin of appreciation doctrine is the case of *Abdulaziz, Cabales and Balkandali v. the United Kingdom*, where the ECtHR explained that states have a wide margin of appreciation in the area of migration law and with regard to their obligations under Article 8 ECHR.[126]

4.7.1.3. Confused Approaches to Positive and Negative Obligations[127]

The ECtHR's distinction between positive and negative obligations has not always been very logical. It has not appeared easy to distinguish between the two, since the obligations may seem very much alike.[128] The Court has, for example, considered that the refusal by public authorities to grant residence permits was a failure to fulfil the negative obligation to respect the right to private and family life, but also a failure to

---

123 Xenos (2012), p. 64. Xenos finds that: 'At times, there is confusion with the term "margin" when it is used to describe a "choice" of measures to guarantee the active protection of human rights under paragraph 1, as opposed to examining the necessity/proportionality of the interference under paragraph 2 to which the principle of margin of appreciation is connected.'

124 Gerards & Senden (2009), p. 635.

125 See e.g. ECtHR 26 May 1994, no. 16969/90, *Keegan v. Ireland*, para. 49; ECtHR 17 October 1986, no. 9532/81, *Rees v. the United Kingdom*, para. 37; and ECtHR 8 July 2003, no. 36022/97, *Hatton and others v. the United Kingdom*, paras 99–100. See further Xenos (2012), pp. 93–95.

126 ECtHR 28 May 1985, nos. 9214/80 to 9474/81, *Abdulaziz, Balkandali and Cabales v. the United Kingdom*, para. 67. See dissenting opinion of judge Bernhardt to ECtHR 28 May 1985, nos. 9214/80 to 9474/81, *Abdulaziz, Balkandali and Cabales v. the United Kingdom*; and Van Dijk (1998), p. 25. Cf. further the dissenting opinion of judge Martens to ECtHR 27 September 1990, *Cossey v. the United Kingdom*, no. 10843/84; and cf. Xenos (2012), pp. 93–95.

127 See Connelly (1986), pp. 570–575. Connelly distinguishes between a negative and positive obligations approach with regard to the Court's interpretation of Article 8 ECHR.

128 Cf. the dissenting opinion of judge Wildhaber to ECtHR 25 November 1994, no. 18131/91, *Stjerna v. Finland*; and the dissenting opinion of Judge Martens to ECtHR 19 February 1996, no. 23218/94, *Gül v. Switzerland*. See further section 3.2.3.

fulfil the positive obligation to protect this right. The Court has further blurred its approach with regard to the examination of requests for legal recognition of name and sex changes in official registers in light of Article 8 ECHR.[129] In such cases, it is hard to explain why one or the other approach is applied by the ECtHR to examine states' infringements of fundamental rights.[130] Lavrysen has demonstrated that the ECtHR often looks at the 'existing status quo' in a state's legal and administrative framework to examine a case in terms of positive obligations or in terms of negative obligations.[131] This means that, for example, in the case of *Marckx v. Belgium* the ECtHR looked at whether states needed to take any kind of action on the basis of the legal framework that was already in place.[132] Positive acts had already been taken by the state to protect the family rights of children, but a certain gap had been left with regard to children born out of wedlock. As has been discussed before, it would then also appear possible to examine the case in terms of negative obligations.[133] States may often already have taken certain positive acts in an area where the omission to protect fundamental rights has taken place. There may be a combination of factors, including state actions or omissions, which create fundamental rights violations. Then, it cannot always be clearly determined whether a state has directly interfered with a fundamental right – which would most logically impose a negative obligation on the state – or whether it has failed to provide protection of fundamental rights – which would most logically impose a positive obligation.

It has sometimes been argued that the ECtHR does not need to distinguish between positive and negative obligations, especially if it holds that both types of obligations are inherent to the Convention. The criteria to be used for examining negative interferences can be used to examine the existence of positive obligations too, as explained in the following section.[134] The Court itself has also recognised at several occasions that the approaches are very similar.[135] It is therefore often recommended – in the interest of predictability, legal certainty and fairness – that the approaches for negative and positive obligations should be aligned. Some obligations for states parties could also be presented by the ECtHR as negative obligations, which has some (minor) positive implications.[136]

---

129 Cf. the examples provided by Lawson (1995b), pp. 732–734.

130 Xenos (2012), pp. 69 ff.; and Lawson (1995b), pp. 734–737 and 742–747.

131 See Lavrysen (2016), pp. 251 ff.

132 ECtHR 13 June 1979, no. 6833/74, *Marckx v. Belgium*.

133 See section 3.2.3. Different scholars have argued that the ECtHR did not necessarily have to review the violation in terms of a positive obligation, see Lawson (1995b), p. 563; Van Dijk (1998), pp. 18–19; and Xenos (2012), p. 69.

134 See e.g. Van Dijk (1998), p. 23; Lavrysen (2013) and Lavrysen (2016).

135 ECtHR 26 May 1994, no. 16969/90, *Keegan v. Ireland*, para. 49.

136 See Van Kempen (2008). Van Kempen develops a typology of positive obligations on the basis of the relation between positive obligations and negative obligations. Cf. Van Dijk (1998), pp. 24–25. Van Dijk argues that the term 'positive obligation' must only be used if there is a gap in the law or practices of states. Xenos also finds that the ECtHR should apply a more narrow definition of the term positive obligations in its case-law, see Xenos (2012), p. 78.

The ECtHR, however, has decided to make a distinction in its case-law between the positive and negative obligations which follow from the Convention. The ECtHR has stressed in some recent cases that it was necessary to examine the specific case in terms of a positive obligation, and not in terms of a negative obligation. In other cases, the ECtHR has instead stressed that it would examine those from the viewpoint of negative obligations, such as in cases on immigration and the protection of family rights.[137] It is still difficult to find out why the ECtHR makes the distinction in such cases, because it does not provide clear explanations for its choices.[138]

It is not in all areas that the ECtHR clearly expresses when a positive obligation instead of a negative obligation arises for states. In its case-law on the protection of Article 8 ECHR, states can incur legislative obligations, because they need to justify the restrictions of the right to private and family life on the basis of legal provisions.[139] However, the ECtHR does not use the term positive obligations when it imposes such legislative obligations. When examining violations of Article 2 ECHR, the ECtHR expressly looks into the 'positive' obligation for states to have an adequate legal framework in place.[140] In both situations, however, the content of the obligation is very similar.

While it may not as such be necessary for the ECtHR to always clearly express whether it finds that certain circumstances give rise to a negative or a positive obligation for states, it is important that the conceptual differences between the two types of obligations are taken into account. As discussed in chapter 3, the difference is, first, that positive obligations do not follow (textually) from fundamental rights, but they have to be implied by the ECtHR in its judgments. Secondly, positive obligations essentially still require certain actions to be taken by the state on the basis of fundamental rights provisions, and this is not the case for negative obligations. Thirdly, positive obligations have an alternative structure rather than a conjunctive structure, which means that states must generally be left discretion on how to fulfil those obligations under the Convention.[141]

---

137 Cf., on the one hand, the positive obligation approach in ECtHR 3 October 2014, no. 12738/10, *Jeunesse v. the Netherlands*, para. 105; and ECtHR 16 July 2014, no. 37359/09, *Hämäläinen v. Finland*, para. 63; and, on the other hand, the negative obligation approach in ECtHR 18 January 2001, no. 27238/95, *Chapman v. the United Kingdom*, para. 99; and ECtHR 26 April 2016, no. 62649/10, *İzzetin Doğan and others v. Turkey*, paras 96–97. Especially in relation to immigration cases and the right to respect for family life, De Vries has explained that 'the ECtHR still appears to be searching for the right way to qualify and examine the claims of aliens seeking admission for the purpose of family reunification. This seems to result from unwillingness on the part of the Court to recognise a right to family reunification as part of the right to family life, while at the same time not wanting to entirely exclude the possibility that a claim for family reunification could come within the scope of the Convention.' See De Vries (2011), p. 82.

138 See Xenos (2012), p. 69. For an explanation of this difference, see De Vries (2011), pp. 79–81.

139 Lavrysen (2016), p. 93.

140 ECtHR 24 March 2011, no. 23458/02, *Giuliani and Gaggio v. Italy*, para. 209.

141 Lavrysen, however, argues that there is no good reason to differentiate between negative and positive obligations on the basis of the argument that positive obligations would impose higher burdens on states' resources than in negative obligations cases, and this does not justify the broader margin which is granted to states for that reason, see Lavrysen (2016), pp. 208–209.

The ECtHR may want to demonstrate that it is aware of the implications which such positive obligations in its case-law have for states as well as for individuals, rather than take for granted that states can be held accountable for all types of fundamental rights violations, and individuals can claim their fundamental rights in all types of (private) situations.

It also seems especially relevant for the ECtHR to hold onto the distinction between positive and negative obligations in cases concerning the protection of the right to life and the prohibition of inhuman and degrading treatment. These are absolute rights which do not allow for any restrictions to be made in case of negative obligations. This does not hold for the positive obligations that can be developed on the basis of these provisions, such as the positive obligations requiring states to undertake investigations into suspicious deaths and into complaints about inhuman or degrading treatment.[142]

4.7.2. PROPOSALS TO IMPROVE THE STRUCTURE OF THE COURT'S APPROACH

Taking into account that the principles for examining negative obligations under the Convention can also be applied to positive obligations, several scholars have urged the Court to pay better attention to the structure of fundamental rights and no longer merge the first and the second stage.[143] By doing so, the Court would meet with the points of criticism which have been discussed above, such as the lack of clarity, certainty and fairness, and it would also conform to the view that positive obligations are inherent to fundamental rights. This would require the ECtHR to undertake two separate examinations. First, it needs to define the *scope* of the right ('definitional stage') and, second, it needs to determine the legitimacy of the *justification* for restrictions of the right ('justification stage') and take into consideration a state's margin of appreciation.[144] This two-stage examination is made obvious by the text of Articles 8 to 11 ECHR, which expressly allows for restrictions under several conditions. However, non-derogable rights, such as those of Articles 2 and 3 ECHR, do not expressly allow for restrictions to be made. When it concerns positive obligations in relation to these provisions, the ECtHR does accept restrictions.[145] The division of the examination into two stages would make it clear in which cases the ECtHR will accept jurisdiction and what obligations result for states. Also, by reviewing the justification of the restriction,

---

142 ECtHR 30 November 2004, no. 48939/99, *Öneryildiz v. Turkey*, para. 96.

143 See generally Lavrysen (2013); and see Klatt (2011), pp. 691–718; and Gerards & Senden (2009), pp. 619–653. Cf. the dissenting opinion of judge Wildhaber to ECtHR 25 November 1994, no. 18131/91, *Stjerna v. Finland*; the dissenting opinion of Judge Martens to ECtHR 19 February 1996, no. 23218/94, *Gül v. Switzerland*.

144 See Gerards & Senden (2009), pp. 620, and 634–636.

145 ECtHR 30 November 2004, no. 48939/99, *Öneryildiz v. Turkey*, para. 96.

the ECtHR could further clarify that arguments to justify restrictions that need to be put forward in cases on positive obligations.[146]

Currently, the Court pays very little attention to the definitional stage and most of its attention goes to the justification stage.[147] Exceptionally, the Court has paid attention to defining the scope of a positive obligation under a particular Convention right before examining whether a state's omission could be justified. It has done so mainly in relation to states' obligations under Articles 2 and 3 ECHR.[148] In its judgment in *Osman v. the United Kingdom*, for example, it explained elaborately:

> The Court notes that the first sentence of Article 2 § 1 enjoins the State not only to refrain from the intentional and unlawful taking of life, but also to take appropriate steps to safeguard the lives of those within its jurisdiction ... It is common ground that the State's obligation in this respect extends beyond its primary duty to secure the right to life by putting in place effective criminal-law provisions to deter the commission of offences against the person backed up by law-enforcement machinery for the prevention, suppression and sanctioning of breaches of such provisions. It is thus accepted by those appearing before the Court that Article 2 of the Convention may imply in certain well-defined circumstances a positive obligation on the authorities to take preventive operational measures to protect an individual whose life is at risk from the criminal acts of another individual.[149]

Here, the scope of a positive obligation is thus examined before it is made subject to a balancing of the interests to protect and to restrict a Convention right.

Both Lavrysen and Xenos have worked out in a fair amount of detail how the Court should go about the more structured assessment for determining the existence of positive obligations, and how to determine the core content of positive obligations.[150] The ECtHR could describe the initial scope of a positive obligation as the 'core' content of positive obligations – to distinguish it from the 'definitive' scope of positive obligations.[151] To define the core content of positive obligations, the ECtHR would have to determine whether an individual's claim falls within the scope of protection that is offered by the Convention.[152] After defining this core content of a positive obligation under a particular Convention right, the ECtHR would then proceed to determine whether the non-fulfilment of that obligation by states can be objectively justified, with

146 Moreover, the distinction is necessary as the stages require a different method of interpretation, see Gerards & Senden (2009), pp. 620 and 625. Also the distribution of the burden of proof becomes obvious, and the reason for protecting the human right is also more apparent, see Lavrysen (2013).

147 Xenos (2012), p. 92.

148 Gerards (2011b), p. 236. This approach is also visible in ECtHR 13 June 1979, no. 6833/74, *Marckx v. Belgium*, para. 31. See further Xenos (2012), pp. 24–26.

149 ECtHR 28 October 1998, no. 23452/94, *Osman v. the United Kingdom*, para. 115. Cf. also ECtHR 16 December 2010, no. 25579/05, *A, B and C v. Ireland*, para. 245.

150 See Xenos (2012), pp. 91 ff.; and Lavrysen (2013).

151 Xenos (2012), p. 91; and Lavrysen (2013).

152 Some scholars consider that the ECtHR should apply certain thresholds in determing whether a claim falls within the scope of protection that is offered by the Convention, see Gerards (2011b).

due respect for a states' margin of appreciation. The resulting positive obligation, which was defined in the justification stage, could then be described as a definitive positive obligation.

Undertaking this more structured assessment would help the ECtHR to overcome some of the criticism that has been raised to its approach on positive obligations.

4.8. CONCLUSIONS

The judges of the ECtHR and most scholars by now agree that positive obligations are part of the protection of fundamental rights by states. This chapter has discussed the fact that there still is some disagreement with regard to the development by the judiciary of states' positive obligations to protect fundamental rights on the basis of several features related to this development. Criticism still applies to whether or not certain types of positive obligations can indeed be derived from fundamental rights provisions, and also to the competences of the judiciary from a constitutional theory perspective. Opinions differ on the nature of fundamental rights more generally, and on the legitimate interpretation of the Convention by the ECtHR in particular. Although the ECtHR must tread with care in this area, it is also in the interests of predictability and certainty that the ECtHR provides greater clarity as regards the scope of positive obligations under the Convention.

A specific point which requires attention in the case-law of the ECtHR is the effect that the fulfilment of positive obligations may have on horizontal relations. It is not generally accepted that fundamental rights protection gives rise to a 'duty to protect' individuals from interferences by other individuals. Some scholars also argue that the acceptance of such duties goes against the very reason for guaranteeing the fundamental rights of an individual, that is, the protection of freedom. The ECtHR must, therefore, be sure to balance the interest of effectively protecting fundamental rights in horizontal relations, and the adverse effects of such 'duties to protect' on the protection of another individual's fundamental rights.

Another, often heard, point of criticism relates to the political character of positive obligations. The ECtHR should pay attention to the choices than can be made, and perhaps already have been made, by legislatures as to how positive obligations to protect fundamental rights can be fulfilled. A legitimate role can, however, be played by the ECtHR in determining the existence and the content of states' positive obligations if it appears that the protection of particular individuals is not respected under the majoritarian rule of the legislature.

The ECtHR is also required to take extra care in the development of positive obligations because of its subsidiary position in its relation with the states parties. This has led to a less precise determination of the positive obligations to be fulfilled by states under the Convention. In some particular areas, the ECtHR could consider being less deferential in the development of positive obligations, especially in cross-border situations where the states parties individually provide no appropriate solutions for violations of fundamental rights. Further, the Court could increase the effectiveness of the protection of fundamental rights by states by carrying out an examination of the procedural framework of states which must guarantee the protection of Convention rights at national level.

Lastly, there also remains ample room for the improvement of the technical approach of the ECtHR in the determination of states' positive obligation. It is generally agreed that the ECtHR could improve the structure of its approach and align its method for determining the fulfilment of states positive obligations to the criteria for the assessment of the fulfilment of states' negative obligations. Moreover, the ECtHR should often pay better attention to determining whether an individual's claim to positive action amounts falls within the scope of protection of a Convention right, before it proceeds to determine whether national authorities have struck a fair balance of the interests involved in such circumstances.

All of these points of criticism still appear relevant for the ECtHR to take into account in its development of positive obligations. They may therefore also be relevant for other courts to take into account, if they are confronted with cases where they need to determine the existence and content of positive obligations.

CHAPTER 5
PART I – CONCLUSIONS

5.1. THE MAIN FEATURES RELATING TO THE DEVELOPMENT OF POSITIVE OBLIGATIONS BY THE ECtHR

This chapter aims to bring together the conclusions of part I of this study, regarding the concept of positive obligations within the context of the Convention. This chapter focuses on some of the topics that will be especially relevant for part II of this study, which examines whether a similar development of positive obligations can take place within the EU's system of fundamental rights protection. Keeping that objective in mind, it is especially important here to formulate some conclusions regarding the definition of the concept of positive obligations in combination with the distinction that applies between positive and negative obligations (section 5.2.), as well as regarding the different types of positive obligations that can be identified in the case-law of the ECtHR (section 5.3.). The rationales used by the ECtHR for accepting the different types of positive obligations together with the possible effects of positive obligations are explained (section 5.4.). The main points of criticism related to this development are discussed (section 5.5.) and, lastly, some final remarks are provided with respect to the analysis presented in part II (section 5.6.).

5.2. THE DEFINITION OF POSITIVE OBLIGATIONS AND THE DISTINCTION BETWEEN POSITIVE AND NEGATIVE OBLIGATIONS

The ECtHR broadly defines a positive obligation as a requirement for states to take active measures to protect fundamental rights. It also has been seen in the preceding chapters that the ECtHR often applies the term 'positive obligations' in its judgments to indicate the obligations that states must fulfil to ensure the protection of a fundamental right within the relations between individual parties, and in its own relations with individuals. To some extent, it appears to be difficult to arrive at a more clear and helpful definition of the concept of positive obligations. The definition necessarily needs to be broad to cover the different types of positive obligations which are recognised by the ECtHR (see section 5.3.).

Perhaps a fuller understanding of the ECtHR's concept of positive obligations can be reached by looking at the distinction that applies between positive and negative obligations. The ECtHR has held that positive obligations arise in addition to the negative obligations that are traditionally to be found in the fundamental rights provisions of the Convention. Indeed, the fundamental rights guaranteed by the Convention are negatively phrased, and generally do not specify that certain actions need to be taken by the states. Even the structure of the Convention provisions is mainly oriented towards negative obligations – that is, most provisions specifically address the restrictions which can be made on those rights by public authorities. In that respect, positive obligations can be regarded as the mirror side of negative obligations – they simply are obligations for the states that are *not* negative. The ECtHR further has held that positive obligations generally leave states a choice as to the measures they have to take to fulfil those obligations, while negative obligations are usually regarded as obligations of result – states should simply refrain from interfering with fundamental rights (except when a justification can be given). Thus, by contrasting positive obligations and negative obligations, it becomes clear that there are certain differences, which may help to determine what positive obligations really are.

Admittedly, a clear-cut distinction between positive and negative obligations is hard to make in practice. The ECtHR itself has not always applied a very consistent or logical approach in every respect. In the case of *Marckx v. Belgium*, for example, the ECtHR imposed a positive obligation on the states parties to ensure legal recognition of the family rights of children born out of wedlock. In that case, the state had already taken certain positive action by establishing a legislative and administrative framework for the recognition of family rights. It could, therefore, also have been argued that the state violated its negative obligation in respect of children born out of wedlock. It is difficult to say in such a case whether it was the state's *failure to act* or rather its *actions* that caused an interference with a fundamental right. In addition, interference with fundamental rights can result from a complex set of causes that may involve state acts as well as omissions.

Such difficulties notwithstanding, in part I of this study it has been argued that it is still valuable to take the conceptual differences between negative and positive obligations into account when trying to understand when the ECtHR turns to applying positive obligations and how it defines the concept. In summary, the conceptual differences that can be taken into account here are that positive obligations, contrary to negative obligations, (i) do not follow (directly) from provisions on fundamental rights and their structure, but need to be implied in individual cases; (ii) require states to take active measures which can only relate to certain gaps in their policies; (iii) and have an 'alternative' structure, which means that they leave a choice as to the measures which need to be taken by states.

In combination, these features already reveal some inherent difficulties and specialties in recognising positive obligations. In particular, positive obligations cannot always be defined beforehand on the basis of provisions of fundamental rights. Rather they will reveal themselves in concrete circumstances, based on the question of what effective protection of a Convention right requires in the particular case on hand. This principle of effectiveness actually is very open-ended and its application can create some legal uncertainty. This broad approach to recognising positive obligations has given rise to various forms of criticism which are discussed further below (see section 5.5.).

5.3. TYPOLOGIES OF POSITIVE OBLIGATIONS

The broad definition of positive obligations provided for by the ECtHR allows it to cover various types of positive obligations. The ECtHR itself has only clearly distinguished between procedural and substantive positive obligations, but other typologies have been developed by scholars. These typologies can provide further insight into the different kinds of positive obligations that can arise from the Convention. These typologies also may help to reveal some of the effects that positive obligations may have, as well as the problematic consequences that some positive obligations may have. It is therefore useful briefly to summarise them before discussing the effects and criticism of the Court's case-law on positive obligations (see sections 5.4. and 5.5.).

Looking at the content of the measures needed to fulfil positive obligations, a distinction can be made between positive obligations to legislate, to provide for an administrative framework and/or to take practical measures to protect fundamental rights. In practice, however, it is difficult to trace this typology in the case-law of the ECtHR, as this court generally does not indicate what types of implementing measures would required to be taken. Nevertheless, it may be useful in a critical analysis of the Court's case-law, as it may help to determine if the Court has overstepped its judicial functions in imposing obligations on, for example, a national parliamentary body.

Secondly, a typology of vertical and horizontal positive obligations has been established. Vertical positive obligations concern the relation between the state and the individual, and horizontal positive obligations concern the relations between private parties. Horizontal positive obligations may be imposed to ensure that certain private parties do not violate the fundamental rights of a third party, which may, for example, occur in situations between an employer and an employee. Horizontal positive obligations may also be imposed on states to ensure that the fundamental rights of individuals are enjoyed in their broader societal relations. This then concerns horizontal positive obligations with a social dimension. Here, some groups of individuals can be especially vulnerable, such as immigrants or the elderly, and the violations are not caused deliberately by the state or by other individuals but, rather, they follow from a situation 'on the ground'. Both the vertical and horizontal types of positive obligations can be recognised in the case-law of the ECtHR. However, when looking at an ECtHR case, scholars may disagree over which of these two types of positive obligations have been established. Arguably, this is because it requires something to be said about the causes of the infringement (state, individual or social reality).

The third typology mainly focuses on the degree to which a positive obligation can be derived from the negative obligation to protect fundamental rights. On this basis, a distinction can be made between dependent, supportive, intrinsic, autonomous and repressive types of positive obligations. The first type (dependent obligations) is closest to the negative obligation to protect fundamental rights, while the last one (repressive obligations) is most detached from it. This typology has been developed to determine whether a certain positive obligation can legitimately be derived from provisions of fundamental rights. The autonomous and repressive types of positive obligations, in particular, are then held to be problematic. To some degree, this typology may overlap with the typology of vertical and horizontal positive obligations. The dependent type of positive obligation, for example, is imposed on states to ensure that they comply with their (negative) obligation not to interfere with an individual's fundamental rights. Therefore, it is mostly concerned with the (vertical) relation between the individual and the state, and can usually be classified as a vertical positive obligation. The autonomous type of positive obligation, by contrast, may not have any relation to the state, but may apply in a relation between private parties. Many autonomous positive obligations therefore could also be classified as horizontal types of positive obligations, potentially with a social dimension.

5.4. RATIONALE AND EFFECTS OF RECOGNISING POSITIVE OBLIGATIONS

In developing positive obligations in its case-law, the ECtHR has not been able to rely on the text and the structure of the fundamental rights under the Convention, nor on the other provisions laid down in the Convention.[1] As a guiding principle to discover, as well as justify, the recognition of positive obligations, the ECtHR has mainly had resort to the principle of effectiveness. On that basis, the judgments of the ECtHR have disclosed a wide variety of types of positive obligations, as the previous section has shown. However, the ECtHR also has expressed some other rationales in its case-law.

An example of such a rationale is that states are considered to have the power – especially nowadays – to effectively influence the protection of fundamental rights of individuals, also in their private relations, especially when they are vulnerable. It is reasonable, therefore, to impose positive obligations on states. Positive obligations thus may be imposed because they generally strengthen the rights which individuals may enjoy *vis-à-vis* the states parties. However, individuals cannot demand a particular action which must be taken by the state.

Another rationale may be defined as the 'responsibility rationale'. In several cases, the ECtHR has expressed interest in whether or not states have already undertaken

[1] The ECtHR does, however, use Articles 1 and 13 ECHR as a general basis, see section 3.2.5. In this regard, it is also necessary to take into account that the Convention was written 60 years ago. The ECtHR has chosen not to interpret the Convention as a static instrument, but as a living instrument. Therefore, it is the case-law of the ECtHR rather than the text of the Convention provisions which contains the main principles for the development of positive obligations.

regulatory activities to control certain affairs, and thereby left certain gaps. In the case of *Marckx v. Belgium*,[2] for example, the ECtHR pointed out that the state had already undertaken to legally recognise the family ties of children, but that it had not sufficiently taken into account the situation of children born out of wedlock, whose family rights also needed to be protected. The ECtHR considers it to be the state's responsibility to fill such a gap.

One of the main implications of the acceptance of positive obligations, regardless of their rationale, has been shown to be an increase in the obligations of states under the Convention, as well as the broadening of individuals' Convention rights. The ECtHR has made states responsible for a wide range of infringements of fundamental rights, which includes situations where the infringements are caused by private parties rather than state agents or bodies.

For both states and individuals, the recognition of positive obligations by the ECtHR may cause a certain amount of uncertainty. Positive obligations are developed by the ECtHR on a case-by-case basis, and they can be formulated either in a rather broad and vague manner, or with great precision and very closely geared to the individual circumstances of the case. As a result it is often not easy to predict what obligations will be incurred under the Convention, or what rights individuals could seek protection for under the Convention. The Court should not necessarily be blamed for this as fundamental rights provisions and the concomitant obligations by their nature may be very broad.

Another important implication of recognising positive obligations is that it may change, to some extent, the nature of fundamental rights protection by states. Fundamental rights may now provide a ground for state action, whereas, traditionally, fundamental rights were considered to provide guarantees *against* state interference. The recognition of positive obligations could therefore also have detrimental effects for certain individuals. Actively protecting the rights of certain individuals, for example by obliging the state to grant children access to information about their biological parents, means that the right to private life of another individual, in this example the biological parents, may be interfered with. Although this may be considered to be reasonable, it clearly opens up new and fundamental questions about where to strike a fair balance between right and interests, and about the scope of the positive obligations that can be imposed.

Overall, these different implications, that is, the expansion of states obligations and individual's rights; the legal uncertainty that is caused; and the effects on the fundamental rights of other individuals, must be taken into account in developing (a doctrine of) positive obligations. Although the ECtHR has clearly accepted such implications, they may give rise to some criticism of the doctrine. Indeed, when the objective is to assess whether positive obligations could be recognised in other contexts and by different courts, it is useful to take such criticism into account. These criticisms

---

2 ECtHR 13 June 1979, no. 6833/74, *Marckx v. Belgium*.

are explained in the next section together with some ways in which the ECtHR has aimed to counter some of these criticisms.

5.5. CRITICAL EVALUATION OF THE DEVELOPMENT OF POSITIVE OBLIGATIONS

The ECtHR has incurred much criticism over its development of positive obligations, which has been discussed extensively in chapter 4. The discussion in this section focuses on those lines of criticism which are of special importance to other courts that might consider developing (a doctrine of) positive obligations.

One of the main points of criticism relates to the political character of the imposition of positive obligations.[3] The definition of positive obligations could impose burdens on states in terms of financial resources as well as organisation. Such burdens are closely related to the kind of policy choices which are normally made by democratically elected and politically accountable bodies, rather than by courts. At the same time, scholars have rebutted such criticism by arguing that it can be necessary for courts to develop positive obligations, in particular to protect the rights of individuals whose voices may not have been heard under the majoritarian rule, such as those of minority ethnic groups. Arguably, courts could accept positive obligations in those circumstances if they meet certain standards, which have to do with the accountability of such decisions, the participation of the different parties in the proceedings, and the clarity of the inequalities that have appeared in such cases. Nevertheless, in by far the majority of cases, courts are expected to exercise a certain restraint in developing positive obligations for the reasons already mentioned. They must leave states a certain degree of choice as to the measures which they could take to fulfil positive obligations. The ECtHR has particularly been advised to ensure respect for the principle of state sovereignty in developing positive obligations by examining whether certain positive obligations are already recognised by the states parties in their legal and administrative structures (the responsibility rationale is discussed in section 5.4.). If the ECtHR finds that states have already adopted certain legislative provisions and/or administrative frameworks which are relevant to protect fundamental rights, but these leave some gaps or are applied in a discriminatory manner, the state may reasonably be asked to provide solutions.

The political nature of positive obligations is of continuing concern and thus requires the ECtHR to tread carefully and avoid making overly political choices. As a supranational court, the ECtHR is in an even more difficult position, because it may not be aware of national sensitivities and the specific circumstances of a case. While this would therefore call for even greater restraint by the ECtHR, there are also scholars who would encourage it to go further in developing certain kinds of positive obligations.

[3] See further section 4.4.

This may be required in particular where the problems concerned cannot be solved by states in isolation, such as migration or environmental issues. The ECtHR thus is confronted with different expectations on the role that it must play.

A second point of criticism has to do with the broad extent of the positive obligations that the ECtHR has recognised. The ECtHR has accepted, as explained earlier, vertical as well as horizontal positive obligations, and also those positive obligations with a social dimension. While all these positive obligations may be essential to come to a full realisation of the protection of fundamental rights, it has been argued that it may be difficult to impose so many different obligations on states. Some types of positive obligations are considered more difficult to accept on the basis of fundamental rights than others. It may be concluded, for example, that compared to horizontal obligations, vertical positive obligations may generally be imposed more easily. This is because of their relation to negative obligations which, under the Convention, very closely and logically follow from the fundamental right itself.

Horizontal types of positive obligations are more difficult to accept. As explained earlier, it is generally accepted that the state nowadays has an important role to play in ensuring the protection of the rights and interests of individuals, and this also applies to their private relations. Yet there are some potential problems to be taken into account. It has been argued, in particular, that the ECtHR must prevent the imposition of such positive obligations having negative effects on others. After all, as has been mentioned, by recognising positive obligations the rights of others can be affected, which could even result in a suppressive effect. Essentially, then, the negative concept of freedom that is inherent to fundamental rights is impeded. Another difficulty related to the development of horizontal types of positive obligations is that it can be quite hard to establish at exactly what point states can be held responsible for violations of fundamental rights in the private sphere. The case-law of the ECtHR includes some indications; however, it is also still developing and the case-law on this issue is regarded as somewhat unpredictable.

In its case-law, the ECtHR has sought to address some of these criticisms and concerns. It has done so by both developing a doctrine of positive obligations and recognising some important limitations to the development of positive obligations. The ECtHR has clarified, for example, that in some cases in order to incur a positive obligation under the Convention the state needs to have had knowledge of fundamental rights violations, there must be a direct and immediate link between a fundamental right and the positive obligation for the state, and the obligation should not give rise to an impossible or disproportionate burden. This also shows that, while the ECtHR may accept that states act to protect individuals from fundamental rights violations by other individuals, it may recognise a certain limit to imposing state responsibility for every type of violation which may take place, in particular those in the private sphere.

Although the ECtHR has thus developed a doctrine and some limits in its case-law, it has been criticised for its application, too. In particular, the doctrine is not always consistently applied and it still does not fully ensure the legal certainty and predictability that is so dearly needed. Scholars, applicants and practitioners very much want the

ECtHR to provide guidance on how fundamental rights are to be protected by the states parties. Thus, it is very important for the ECtHR to bring further clarity in its case-law on important topics such as the development of positive obligations.

Finally, an important point relating to the ECtHR's doctrine that has been critically evaluated is its use of the margin of appreciation doctrine. As explained in chapter 2, the ECtHR can decide to afford a wide margin of appreciation when it considers that the national authorities are better placed to judge over the proportionality or the reasonableness of fundamental rights interferences. In particular, the ECtHR may decide to grant a wide margin of appreciation to states when the issue concerns social or economic interests. Scholars have noted that the ECtHR does not always apply its margin of appreciation doctrine correctly, and that it too often affords a wide margin of appreciation to states when concerning their fulfilment of positive obligations under the Convention. Such consistent application of a wide margin of appreciation to states in cases on positive obligations would correspond to a consistent lowering of the level of intensity of review, and this has been argued to affect the protection of the rights of individuals. While the ECtHR thus may have good reason to allow a wide margin of appreciation to states, it may also need to be careful in not granting it too easily, because this may invite criticism.

5.6. CONCLUDING REMARKS LOOKING FORWARD TO THE ANALYSIS IN PART II

The development of positive obligations has many dimensions. Those that have been discussed in this chapter in the context of the ECtHR may be of interest for other courts which may be considering the development of (a doctrine of) positive obligations, such as potentially the ECJ. The ECtHR has used a concept of positive obligations for quite some time, which can provide a helpful source of inspiration as to what can be acceptable in the development of such a concept. As will be further explained in part II, the Convention is a very important instrument within the EU legal order, which may make it even more relevant for the ECJ to take the ECtHR's approach as an example. Yet, there are some clear differences between the EU law and the Convention which might make the ECtHR's doctrine less suitable to be applied by the ECJ. Such differences clearly need to be addressed to see to what extent a similar development of positive obligations could take place. One important aspect to take into account, for example, is that the ECtHR clearly is a human rights court, whereas the ECJ only deals with the protection of fundamental rights in some of the cases it delivers, even though the number of such cases are increasing in recent years. Moreover, there is the issue of competences which needs to be taken into account in the EU context, and such issues therefore will be central to part II of this study.

PART II

THE SCOPE FOR THE DEVELOPMENT OF POSITIVE OBLIGATIONS WITHIN THE CONTEXT OF EU LAW – AN ANALYSIS OF THE SPECIFIC PARAMETERS OF THE EU LEGAL ORDER AND THE EU SYSTEM OF FUNDAMENTAL RIGHTS PROTECTION

CHAPTER 6

MAIN PRINCIPLES OF THE EU SYSTEM OF FUNDAMENTAL RIGHTS PROTECTION

6.1. INTRODUCTION

Fundamental rights are protected in a very different framework by the EU as compared to the Council of Europe. The EU is not of itself a human rights organisation and it has never been given a general competence to protect fundamental rights. At the same time, the EU has adopted one of the most modern collections of fundamental rights. The EU is legally bound to comply with the Charter, and it has agreed to accede to the Convention. As a result of these (and other) developments, fundamental rights have been given an important place within the EU legal order.

This chapter aims to set out the main principles of the EU's system of fundamental rights protection. This mainly serves as an introduction to this system so that a selection of topics, which are of particular importance to further examine the concept and the doctrine of positive obligations, can be studied further in the next chapters.

First, a brief explanation of how fundamental rights have come to be recognised within the EU legal order and the EU Treaties is provided (section 6.2.). The next section points out that there are in fact several rationales for the protection of fundamental rights under EU law which are of importance in order to understand the further development of fundamental rights protection within this system (section 6.3.). Subsequently, the recent important institutional developments in the field of EU fundamental rights protection that have taken place are addressed (section 6.4.). After that, the content and the specific status of the Charter are explained (section 6.5.), while the general principles of EU law are also examined, since they continue to provide a basis for the protection of fundamental rights by the EU (section 6.6.). Then, the specific topics of the scope of application of the Charter (section 6.7.), the relationship between the protection of fundamental rights at EU level and at national level (section 6.8.), and the relationship between the EU and the Convention are discussed (section 6.9.). Some brief attention is also paid to the specific distinction that applies between rights and principles under the Charter (section 6.10.). Lastly, the the main findings of this chapter are set out (section 6.11.).

6.2. ORIGINS AND HISTORICAL DEVELOPMENT OF EU FUNDAMENTAL RIGHTS PROTECTION

From the time when the European Economic Communities were established up until today, a series of initiatives have been taken so as to ensure that fundamental rights were recognised within this specific legal order. Originally, no mechanism was provided to ensure fundamental rights protection.[1] Quite early on concerns were raised over the lack of this protection at Community level. This occurred particularly after the ECJ had developed the principles of direct effect and supremacy of Community law in the landmark cases of *Van Gend en Loos* and *Costa/ENEL*.[2] The ECJ explained that on the basis of these principles, national law, including national constitutional principles, could be set aside in case of a conflict with Community law. Consequently, national constitutional courts were concerned with the protection that they still needed to offer on the basis of the national constitutions and they referred preliminary questions to the ECJ on how to solve this conflict.[3] In a line of cases delivered in the early 1970s, the ECJ ultimately accepted that fundamental rights were to be protected by the Community.[4] Fundamental rights were to be protected under Community law as general principles of law;[5] and they were to be developed autonomously by the ECJ.[6] From that point on, the ECJ started to further develop these general principles of law in its case-law. It has taken the constitutions of the member states and international human rights treaties into account as an important source of interpretation, and it has pointed out that the Convention takes an especially important place.[7] Further, the ECJ has established in its case-law that these fundamental rights were to be protected by the EU institutions, as well as by the member states when they were implementing Community law.[8]

Eventually, recognition of this judge-made law was given, most clearly, by the Maastricht Treaty of 1994.[9] Subsequently, it was decided that the rights which were protected in the EU needed to be codified in the form of a written catalogue of

---

1 See e.g. Dauses (1985); and De Búrca (2011).

2 ECJ 5 February 1963, C-26/62, *Van Gend en Loos*; and ECJ 15 July 1964, C-6/64, *Costa v. ENEL*. Cf. BVerfG 29 May 1974, 2 BvL 52/7, *Solange I*.

3 ECJ 12 November 1969, C-29/69, *Stauder*; and ECJ 7 February 1970, C-11/70, *Internationale Handelsgesellschaft*.

4 Cf. De Witte (1999).

5 See ECJ 12 November 1969, C-29/69, *Stauder v Stadt Ulm*; ECJ 17 December 1970, C-11/70, *Internationale Handelsgesellschaft*; and ECJ 14 May 1974, C-4/73, *Nold*. Initially, the ECJ rejected fundamental rights claims, see e.g. ECJ 4 February 1959, C-1/58, *Stork & Cie. v High Authority*; and ECJ 15 July 1960, Joined cases C-36/59 and C-40/59, *Geitling v. High Authority*.

6 ECJ 13 December 1979, C-44/79, *Hauer*, para. 14.

7 Cf. ECJ 14 May 1974, C-4/73, *Nold*; and ECJ 13 December 1979, C-44/79, *Hauer*.

8 See ECJ 13 July 1989, C-5/88 *Wachauf*; and ECJ 18 June 1991, C-260/89, *ERT*. The determination of the scope of application of EU fundamental rights as regards member state action is further discussed in section 6.7.

9 See the Joint Declaration by the European Parliament, the Council and the Commission on fundamental rights of 5 April 1977 [1977] OJ L103/1.

fundamental rights.[10] The main aim was to increase the visibility of these rights.[11] This resulted in the Charter of Fundamental Rights, which was first proclaimed in 2000. After a failed attempt to adopt the Charter as part of the EU Constitution in 2005, the Charter was added, as a separate document, to the Lisbon Treaty, which came into force in December 2009. It has been given legally binding status as well as the status of primary law. In addition to this, the Lisbon Treaty has provided a legal basis for the accession of the EU to the Convention.[12] Earlier, the compatibility of the accession with the former Treaty on the European Community had been rejected by the ECJ in *Opinion 2/94*.[13] For that reason, the Lisbon Treaty thus provides a specific legal basis that allows, or rather obliges, the EU to accede. The accession is intended to allow external review by the ECtHR of the EU's compliance with fundamental rights, and it will further help to ensure consistency between the Strasbourg and Luxembourg approach to the protection of fundamental rights.[14]

All of these foregoing developments are now reflected in Article 6 TEU which sets out the current system of fundamental rights protection of the EU as follows:

> 1) The Union recognises the rights, freedoms and principles set out in the Charter of Fundamental Rights of the European Union of 7 December 2000, as adapted at Strasbourg, on 12 December 2007, which shall have the same legal value as the Treaties. The provisions of the Charter shall not extend in any way the competences of the Union as defined in the Treaties. The rights, freedoms and principles in the Charter shall be interpreted in accordance with the general provisions in Title VII of the Charter governing its interpretation and application with due regard to the explanations referred to in the Charter, that set out the sources of those provisions.
>
> 2) The Union shall accede to the European Convention for the Protection of Human Rights and Fundamental Freedoms. Such accession shall not affect the Union's competences as defined in the Treaties.
>
> 3) Fundamental rights, as guaranteed by the European Convention for the Protection of Human Rights and Fundamental Freedoms and as they result from the constitutional traditions common to the Member States, shall constitute general principles of the Union's law.

---

10 See the Presidency Conclusions of Cologne European Council of 3–4 June 1999, online available at http://www.europarl.europa.eu/summits/kol1_en.htm.

11 This is also expressed in the fourth section of the preamble of the Charter. Some scholars have questioned, however, whether the Charter only aimed to codify the status quo, or whether the intention was to go beyond a mere codification of rights which were already protected. Heringa & Verhey have held that 'the preamble to the Charter reflects a duality of approaches and shows that the various desires and perspectives as to what should be achieved in a Charter, have not been fully reconciled', see Heringa & Verhey (2001), p. 12.

12 Article 6(3) TEU.

13 ECJ 28 March 1996, *Opinion 2/94*.

14 See the Preamble to the Draft Agreement for the Accession of the EU to the European Convention for Human Rights, 47+1(2013)008rev2, Final Report to the CDDH, 10 June 2013.

Article 6 TEU thus shows that there are various sources of fundamental rights within the EU, which include the Charter, the general principles of EU law, national constitutional provisions, and the Convention. This raises a host of questions over the interrelationship between these various sources which will be discussed throughout this chapter (see sections 6.5. to 6.7.). Article 6 TEU also draws attention to one other important aspect that has not visibly changed over the years: the limited competences of the EU to protect fundamental rights. Article 6(1) TEU clearly stresses that the protection of fundamental rights may not lead to the extension or modification of the existing powers of the EU and that the limited competences must be respected.[15] Likewise, Article 6(2) TEU requires that the accession of the EU to the Convention cannot affect the competences of the EU. The relationship between the protection of fundamental rights and the limited competences of the EU is therefore of great importance. What exact competences the EU has to protect fundamental rights and how extensions of competences on the basis of the protection of fundamental rights nevertheless could take place is discussed in chapters 8 and 9.

Next to the changes that have been made to Article 6 TEU, it should also be noted that the protection of fundamental rights has been included as one of the values upon which the EU has been based. Article 2 TEU recognised the following democratic ideals as the foundations for the EU:

> The Union is founded on the values of respect for human dignity, freedom, democracy, equality, the rule of law and respect for human rights, including the rights of persons belonging to minorities. These values are common to the Member States in a society in which pluralism, non-discrimination, tolerance, justice, solidarity and equality between men and women prevail.[16]

Further, according to Article 3 TEU, the aim of the EU is to promote these values and the well-being of its peoples. The EU is required to 'combat social exclusion and discrimination, and it shall promote social justice and protection, equality between women and men, solidarity between generations and protection of the rights of the child'. In its external relations 'the Union shall [again] uphold and promote its values' and contribute to the protection of human rights. Thus, the EU nowadays has as a clear and express objective to protect fundamental rights.

---

15 See Article 51(2) of the Charter and Article 1(3) of the Draft Accession Agreement, see Final Report to the CDDH, 'Draft revised agreement on the accession of the European Union to the Convention for the Protection of Human Rights and Fundamental Freedoms', 10 June 2013, 47+1(2013)008rev2.

16 The connection between fundamental rights protection and the rule of law is also made in the preamble to the Charter, where it says that 'the Union is founded on ... the principles of democracy and the rule of law'.

6.3. RATIONALES OF FUNDAMENTAL RIGHTS PROTECTION WITHIN THE EU LEGAL ORDER

Before further discussing some of the institutional developments that have taken place since the entry into force of the Lisbon Treaty (see section 6.4.), it is useful first to clarify the underlying rationale of fundamental rights protection within the EU legal order.

It is important to understand that the EU has evolved into a very powerful entity which can take actions in different policy areas that include the 'traditional' internal market and the area of freedom, security and justice, as well as its external relations. In those areas, the actions of the EU can interfere with individuals' fundamental rights, either directly on the basis of actions taken by the EU institutions, or indirectly through the implementation of EU law by the member states. For this reason, the actions of the EU institutions as well as the member states, where they are acting on the basis of powers granted under EU law, must be constrained by fundamental rights guarantees.[17] Closely related to this rationale, the ECJ has also accepted the rule of law as an important rationale for the protection of fundamental rights. This was clearly so in the case of *Kadi*, where it held:

> ... it is to be borne in mind that the Community is based on the rule of law, inasmuch as neither its Member States nor its Institutions can avoid review of their acts with the basic constitutional charter, the EC Treaty, which established a complete system of legal remedies and procedures designed to enable the Court of Justice to review the legality of the acts of the institutions. ...
>
> It is also clear from settled case-law that respect for human rights is a condition of the lawfulness of Community acts ... and that measures incompatible with respect for human rights are not acceptable in the Community ...[18]

The protection of fundamental rights by the EU and the ECJ is further interwoven with some important principles of EU law which include the principle of supremacy, as well as the principles of the unity and effectiveness of EU law in combination with the principle of autonomy of EU law.[19] The need to safeguard the supremacy of EU law was indeed, as discussed above, initially an important factor leading the ECJ to accept the protection of fundamental rights within the community's legal order.[20] If the national constitutional courts were not to accept the supremacy of EU law based over the rights contained in the national constitutions and continued to build in reservations to accepting the supremacy of EU law, this would put the unity and effectiveness of EU

---

17 De Witte (1999), p. 866.

18 ECJ 3 September 2008, C-402/05 P, *Kadi and Al Barakaat International Foundation v Council and Commission*, paras 281 and 283. Cf. also the more recent case ECJ 18 July 2013, C-584/10 P, *Commission and others v Kadi*, para. 66.

19 Augenstein (2013).

20 Coppel & O'Neill (1992), p. 669; De Witte (1999), p. 866; and Besson (2011a), p. 114.

law at risk. As the ultimate guardian of the Treaties, it would only be for the ECJ, and not the national courts, to assess the validity of Community law, and the ECJ therefore sought to protect fundamental rights within Community law itself. The ECJ has clearly expressed such concerns in the case of *Hauer*:

> The question of a possible infringement of fundamental rights by a measure of Community institutions can only be judged in the light of Community law itself. The introduction of special criteria for assessment stemming from the legislation or constitutional law of a particular Member State would, by damaging the substantive unity and efficacy of EU law, lead inevitably to the destruction of the unity of the Common Market and jeopardizing of the Cohesion of the Community.[21]

The concern over the autonomous interpretation of EU fundamental rights remains of relevance today.[22] For example, this concern was expressed by the ECJ in *Opinion 2/13*, in which the ECJ deemed the draft agreement on the accession of the EU to the Convention to be incompatible with EU law.[23] Some more recent case-law of the ECJ also shows that the principle of supremacy, as well as the uniformity and effectiveness of EU law remain important rationales for the protection of fundamental rights by the EU.[24] In a revealing consideration, the ECJ held in the case of *Siragusa*, which concerned the scope of application of EU law, that:

> the objective of protecting fundamental rights in EU law ... is to ensure that those rights are not infringed in areas of EU activity, whether through action at EU level or through the implementation of EU law by the Member States. The reason for pursuing that objective is the need to avoid a situation in which the level of protection of fundamental rights varies according to national law involved in such a way as to undermine the unity, primacy and effectiveness of EU law.[25]

By themselves, EU fundamental rights are therefore necessary to protect the unity, primacy and effectiveness of EU law, even though their relation with the rule of law has also been recognised by the ECJ.[26]

---

21 ECJ 13 December 1979, C-44/79, *Hauer*, para. 14.

22 Augenstein (2013).

23 ECJ 18 December 2014, *Opinion 2*/13, paras 188–189; and ECJ 15 February 2016, C-605/115 *J.N.*, para. 47.

24 Recently, and most clearly, the ECJ has also clarified that the member states can only apply higher standards of fundamental rights in areas falling within the scope of EU law on the basis of their own constitutions to the extent that this would not affect the 'primacy, unity and effectiveness' of EU law, see ECJ 26 February 2013, C-399/11, *Melloni*, para. 60. See further section 6.8.

25 ECJ 6 March 2014, C-206/13, *Siragusa*, paras 31–32. This was reiterated in ECJ 10 July 2014, C-198/13, *Julian Hernández and others*, para. 47.

26 This rationale has raised clear criticism in the past, see further the discussion in section 7.6.2.1. on the approach of the ECJ in fundamental rights cases.

6.4. INSTITUTIONAL DEVELOPMENTS WITHIN THE FIELD OF FUNDAMENTAL RIGHTS PROTECTION

The ECJ has played an important role in the protection of fundamental rights, as already appeared from the historical developments briefly sketched in this chapter (see section 6.2.).[27] The ECJ continues to be a key actor in the protection of fundamental rights. Since the Charter became legally binding in 2009, national courts have increasingly raised questions to the ECJ on the interpretation and application of fundamental rights, and the ECJ itself is making more references to rights laid down in the Charter in its case-law.[28] In developing its case-law on fundamental rights in the years since the Charter has become legally binding, it has been noted that the ECJ has developed its own, to some extent, autonomous approach to protecting fundamental rights.[29] The ECJ now even primarily relies on the Charter as the main instrument for fundamental rights protection within the context of EU law.[30] The approach of the ECJ to protecting fundamental rights is discussed in greater depth in chapter 7.[31]

Aside from the interpretation and application of fundamental rights given by the ECJ, it is important to mention that the other EU institutions are also increasingly engaging in fundamental rights matters. After the Charter became legally binding in 2009, efforts have been made by the EU institutions to ensure compliance with fundamental rights in the exercise of their competences, and also to making their initiatives in this field more visible. The European Commission has, for example, adopted a strategy for the effective implementation of the Charter.[32] It *inter alia* publishes annual reports on the application of the Charter and has drawn up checklists for determining whether legislation is in compliance with the (limits) placed on their actions by the rights guaranteed in the Charter.[33] The other institutions of the EU have also adopted such

27 Cf. de Witte (1999); and Muir (2014a), p. 238.

28 For the statistics, see European Commission, Staff Working Document on the Application of the EU Charter of Fundamental Rights in 2015, SWD(2016), 158 final, pp. 7 and 8. See also Sánchez (2012), p. 1577. In respect of the application of the Charter by Dutch courts, see Van Harten & Grootelaar (2014). It has been explained that the increase in questions (also) coincides with the extension of the jurisdiction of the ECJ in the area of freedom, security and justice, see De Búrca (2013), p. 173.

29 Before 2009, the ECJ referred to the Charter only on some occasions, see e.g. ECJ 27 June 2006, C-540/03, *Parliament v Council*, para. 38. Advocates General have also referred to the Charter before it became legally binding.

30 See Augenstein (2013); and Sanchez (2012). This particular approach, as well as the further role played by the Court of Justice in the field of fundamental rights is also discussed in chapter 10.

31 See in particular section 7.6.2.

32 See Communication from the Commission: Strategy for the effective implementation of the Charter of Fundamental Rights by the European Union, COM(2010) 573, 19 October 2010; and cf. Butler (2012).

33 See European Commission, 2015 Report on the application of the EU Charter of Fundamental Rights, SWD(2016), 158 final; European Commission, Staff Working Document on the application of the EU Charter of fundamental rights in 2015, SWD(2016), 158 final; and European Commission Staff Working Paper, Operational Guidance on Taking Account of Fundamental Rights in Commission Impact Assessments, SEC(2011) 567, 6 May 2011.

checklists.[34] In addition, it has been observed that reference is increasingly being made to the provisions of the Charter, for example, in the recitals of legislative instruments of the EU institutions and in the provisions of such legislative instruments.[35] As discussed in more detail in chapter 8, the EU institutions have indeed adopted instruments in various areas that should ensure the promotion of fundamental rights. It is also noteworthy that a Fundamental Rights Agency has been established by the EU. This Agency mainly focuses on the provision of information and data on fundamental rights matters in the EU and does not have any enforcement powers as such.[36]

Hence, the aim of the Charter to strengthen the protection of fundamental rights within the EU by making fundamental rights more visible, has to some extent been realised. By contrast, the road to the accession of the EU to the Convention has been 'rocky'.[37] Protocol No. 8 relating to Article 6(2) TEU as well as Declaration No. 2 require that the specific characteristics of the EU and of EU law are protected in respect of the accession. Since the European Commission was designated as the negotiator of the accession process in June 2010, the technical matters of the accession have been extensively discussed in informal working groups of representatives of the member states of the EU and the states parties of the Council of Europe. Scholars have been closely following and reporting on the accession process.[38] In 2013, all of this led to the adoption of a package which includes a draft accession agreement and a draft explanatory report.[39] The draft accession agreement *inter alia* provides for a co-respondent mechanism which would allow the EU and its member states to become party to proceedings before the ECtHR involving violations of EU law, as well as a procedure of prior involvement so that the ECJ could determine the compatibility of provisions of EU law with fundamental rights prior to the review made by the ECtHR. The agreement was sent to the ECJ in a request for advice on its compatibility with the EU Treaties. Despite the creation of the different mechanisms and the establishment of other safeguards in the agreement, the ECJ found several aspects of the draft accession agreement to be incompatible with the EU Treaties.[40] As a result the accession process

---

34 See COREPER, Guidelines on Methodological Steps to be Taken to Check Fundamental Rights Compatibility at the Councils Preparatory Bodies, Council Document 10140/11, 18 May 2011, available online at <http://register.consilium.europa.eu/doc/srv?l=EN&f=ST%2010140%202011%20 INIT>. For a critical analysis of such checklists, see Morijn (2014).

35 See Muir (2014a); Muir (2014b); and Morijn & Van Sasse van Ysselt (2012).

36 Council Regulation No 168/2007/EC of 15 February 2007 establishing a European Union Agency for Fundamental Rights [1997] OJ L53/1.

37 As mentioned in C. Murphy, 'On the Rocky Road to Accession: Final Draft of the EU's Accession Agreement to ECHR approved', European Law Blog, 12/04/2013, http://europeanlawblog.eu/?p=1680.

38 See e.g. Gragl (2014b); and Lock (2011).

39 Final Report to the CDDH, Draft revised agreement on the accession of the European Union to the Convention for the Protection of Human Rights and Fundamental Freedoms, 10 June 2013, 47+1(2013)008rev2.

40 At the time of writing (June 2016), the European Commission is still in the consultation phase with respect to the issues that were raised by the ECJ in Opinion *2/13*, see European Commission, 2015 Report on the application of the EU Charter of Fundamental Rights, SWD(2016), 158 final, pp. 8–9.

has been put on hold; further steps have not yet been taken.[41] The finalisation of the accession itself is not expected for quite some time. Not only will the Commission have to modify the accession agreement in accordance with *Opinion 2/13*, the states parties of the EU and the Council of Europe would also still need to sign the agreement itself and thereafter ratify it.[42]

Lastly, it may be noted that over the past years, there has been much debate on the use of Article 7 TEU as a basis for action by the EU institutions to ensure fundamental rights protection.[43] If it appears that there is 'a clear risk for a serious breach by a member state of the values referred to in Article 2 TEU' – which includes the respect for human rights and for the rule of law – Article 7 TEU allows the Council to take certain actions. The Council must hear the member state involved and make recommendations, before it can resort to a more heavy sanction. The provision sets out a 'nuclear option', which entails that the voting rights of member states can be suspended if it is determined that there is a clear risk of a serious breach of human rights or the respect for the rule of law. So far, this provision has not been put to use, despite serious concerns which have risen over the protection of fundamental rights in some member states.[44] Politically, it has proven difficult to actually take concrete steps on the basis of this provision.[45] Therefore, actions are usually taken more indirectly and on an informal basis to address some of the more general rule of law issues in the member states which the EU seeks to address.[46]

6.5. THE CHARTER

With the Lisbon Treaty of 2009, as explained earlier, the Charter gained legally binding status and was given the same legal status as the EU Treaties.[47] The Charter contains a collection of civil, political, economic, social and cultural rights which are set out over

41 ECJ 18 December 2014, *Opinion 2/13*. See also the view of Advocate General Kokott in *Opinion 2/13*, which was delivered on 13 June 2014.

42 Some of the problematic effects of the incorporation of the Convention into EU law are discussed in section 6.9.

43 This provision has been included in the academic and the political debates on the problems occurring in Hungary as well as more recently in Poland concerning the alleged lack of respect for the rule of law and concerning fundamental rights issues related to the independence of the media and the position of the judiciary in those countries.

44 Cf. Editorial Comments (2012). Further mention must be made of Article 49 TEU, which establishes that respect for the foundational values of the EU (which includes respect for the rule of law and human rights) forms a condition for accession of new member states to the EU.

45 For the complications relating to Article 7 TEU see Editorial Comments (2016) and Editorial Comments (2015).

46 Recently the European Commission has started more informal dialogues and it has issued an opinion with respect to the concerns that have risen in Poland over the introduction of new rules affecting the independence of the judiciary as well as the media authority, see European Commission press release, 'Commission adopts rule of law opinion on the situation in Poland', Brussels 1 June 2016, IP/16/2015.

47 Article 6 TEU.

six different chapters headed by the titles 'Dignity', 'Freedoms', 'Equality', 'Solidarity', 'Citizens' rights' and 'Justice'. This primarily concerns a codification of rights which were either already recognised by the ECJ in its case-law, by the member states, or which could be found in other international or regional human rights treaties. There has thus been quite some debate about the added value of the Charter in relation to the rights that were already protected under EU law or by the member states' constitutions. After all, it mainly contains rights which can be found elsewhere and the EU was already bound to protect such rights on the basis of the general principles which have been developed by the ECJ in its case-law.[48] The intentions for drafting the Charter were, indeed, primarily to consolidate the rights which were protected within Europe and to give more visibility to these rights within the context of EU law.[49] Nevertheless, some rights contained in the Charter are considered to provide additional value to the rights which are guaranteed by the Convention. Examples thereof include the right to good administration, the right to conduct a business, the rights of the child, and several social and economic rights.[50]

Another important and 'novel' feature of the Charter is that it includes several provisions which further spell out how the Charter is to be applied in relation to national law and the ECHR, and how it is to be interpreted. These 'horizontal' provisions are contained in Article 51 to 54 of the Charter. They have appeared to be of great importance, and some of which will be discussed in some more detail in this chapter, as well as in chapters 8 and 9.[51] In addition, the 'explanations' which have been drafted to further clarify the provisions of the Charter must be taken into account. Article 52(7) of the Charter specifically requires the ECJ and the national courts to give due regard to these explanations in the interpretation of the Charter.[52] The explanations can be of great relevance, and the ECJ has already referred to these in its judgments.[53]

The ECJ is thus given various directions by the specific text of the provisions of the Charter, and the explanations of the specific provisions of the Charter, regarding how to determine the scope of the rights which individuals must be given under EU law as well as the obligations on the EU institutions and the member states. Seeing that these

48 Craig & De Búrca (2015), p. 396.

49 Cf. the fifth paragraph of the preamble of the Charter.

50 Gerards (2016), (section 1.). Cf. Heringa & Verhey (2001), pp. 13–14. Also, Article 47 of the Charter is not restricted, as Article 6 ECHR is, to civil and criminal cases.

51 Article 51(1) is discussed in section 6.7.; Article 53 is discussed in section 6.8.; Article 52(3) is discussed in section 6.9.2.; and Article 52(5) is discussed in section 6.10.

52 It has been questioned whether the explanations provide the most authoritative source of interpretation of the Charter, as Article 52(7) merely requires the EU and member states courts to have 'due regard' to these explanations which have been drawn up as a way of providing guidance in the interpretation of the Charter's provisions, see e.g. Lock (2009), pp. 383–385; and Gragl (2014), pp. 1742–1743.

53 See e.g. ECJ 15 February 2016, C-601/15, *J.N.*, para. 47.

provisions and explanations have been drafted relatively recently, it is expected that the ECJ will pay specific attention to these directions.[54]

6.6. THE GENERAL PRINCIPLES OF EU LAW

After gaining binding force, the Charter has quickly become the main source of fundamental rights within the EU for the ECJ as well as for the other EU institutions (see section 6.4.). General principles of EU law, which initially were the only basis which the ECJ used to protect fundamental rights, continue, however, to be a relevant source for the protection of fundamental rights under EU law. In principle, when a specific fundamental right can be found in the Charter itself, the ECJ seems to prefer to rely on that written provision instead of the corresponding general principle of EU law. However, the ECJ still often refers to the right to effective judicial protection as a general principle of EU law alongside the written version of that right laid down in Article 47 of the Charter, or sometimes even instead thereof.[55] General principles of EU law thus continue to be considered to provide some added value to the rights laid down in the Charter.[56] They also may function as a source of interpretation for the rights of the Charter. The right to effective judicial protection, for example, has been formulated very broadly in Article 47, while the more specific aspects recognised in the Court's case-law on fundamental rights as principles may help to provide for some detail in explaining this provision. The general principles of EU law can also function as a complement to rights which have been formulated (too) narrowly in the Charter. This applies in particular to Article 41 of the Charter on the right to good administration. This provision has been formulated in such a way that it is addressed only to the institutions of the EU, and the ECJ has indeed declared that Article 41 of the Charter is limited to those institutions. However, it has also clarified that when the authorities of the member states are implementing EU law, they nevertheless must respect the principles of good administration developed by the ECJ in its case-law, such as the principle of the rights of defence.[57] For this reason, and for the reasons mentioned earlier, general principles of EU law continue to play an important role for the protection of fundamental rights in the EU.

---

54 For a discussion of the importance of an originalist interpretation of the Charter, see Brittain (2015). In comparison, an historical interpretation of the Convention has been considered less important, because the Convention is much older. The ECtHR has interpreted the Convention as a living instrument, which means that its interpretation of fundamental rights has evolved over the years, see section 2.6.2.

55 The Court of Justice has also used its case-law on general principles of law, in particular, to further interpret Article 16 of the Charter on the freedom to conduct a business, cf. ECJ 22 January 2013, C-283/11, *Sky Österreich*, paras 41 ff.

56 See further Hofman & Mihaescu (2013).

57 ECJ 17 July 2014, Joined cases C-141/12 and C-372/12, *YS and others*, para. 67; ECJ 22 November 2012, C-277/11, *M.*, paras 81 ff.; and ECJ 5 November 2014, C-166/13, *Mukarubega*, paras 43 ff.

6.7. THE SCOPE OF APPLICATION OF EU FUNDAMENTAL RIGHTS

6.7.1. THE VERTICAL SCOPE OF APPLICATION OF EU FUNDAMENTAL RIGHTS

EU fundamental rights can only be applied to matters that fall within the scope of application of EU law. Article 51(1) of the Charter contains the main rule which governs the scope of application of the Charter's provisions. This provision is immensely important as it provides the starting point for determining if the provisions of the Charter need to be applied.[58] Article 51(1) stipulates that:

> The provisions of this Charter are addressed to the institutions, bodies, offices and agencies of the Union with due regard for the principle of subsidiarity and to the Member States, only when they are implementing Union law. They shall therefore respect the rights, observe the principles and promote the application thereof in accordance with their respective powers and respecting the limits of the powers of the Union as conferred on it in the Treaties.

The provisions of the Charter are accordingly addressed, first, to the institutions of the EU and, secondly, to the member states of the EU. Evidently, the EU institutions are bound to protect the rights of the Charter.[59] The application of EU fundamental rights to the actions of the member states is a more complicated matter. In fact, this topic has so far given rise to the greatest number of preliminary questions concering the Charter since it became legally binding.[60] The precise delimitation of the scope of application of EU fundamental rights to the actions of member states has not appeared to be easy.

For example, according to Article 51(1), the rights of the Charter are addressed to the member states in so far as they are 'implementing Union law'. In the case of *Åkerberg Fransson*, the ECJ delivered a seminal judgment on what this phrase means. It has first clarified that the provision laid down in Article 51(1) followed from its earlier case-law.[61] Also, the explanations relating to Article 51 of the Charter referred to the earlier judgments of the ECJ in *Wachauf*, *ERT* and *Annibaldi*. The former two cases in particular had provided important guidance on when EU fundamental rights needed to be complied with.[62] The case of *Wachauf* forms a classic situation of where

58 See also Sarmiento (2013), pp. 1270 and 1274.

59 Of interest in this regard is the decision of the ECJ in the case of *Ledra Advertising* which clarified that the Commission must ensure that actions taken in the context of the European Stablity Mechanism respect fudamental rights, in particular, the right to property, see ECJ 20 September 2016, Joined cases C-8/15 and C-10/15, *Ledra Advertising*, paras 58 and 66.

60 See most recently Dougan (2015); and Sarmiento (2013).

61 ECJ 26 February 2013, C-617/10, *Åkerberg Fransson*, para. 19.

62 The case of *Annibaldi* represents a situation in which EU fundamental rights do not apply. The Court of Justice did not find sufficient connection to specific rules of EU law that could have brought the situation within the scope of EU law, see ECJ 19 December 1997, C-309/96, *Annibaldi*.

EU fundamental rights need to be complied with by the member states. It concerns the situation where member states are implementing the provisions of a Directive.[63] In this situation, member states are considered to be acting on behalf of the Union, and this therefore is often referred to as the 'agency situation'.[64] The case of *ERT* concerns the second 'classic' situation where member states need to comply with EU fundamental rights. It concerns the situation where member states take measures that limit the fundamental free movement rights of the Treaty. When member states aim to justify such derogations from EU law, they need to comply with EU fundamental rights.[65] In the case of *Åkerberg Fransson*, the ECJ has more generally explained that:

> the fundamental rights guaranteed by the Charter must ... be complied with where national legislation falls within the scope of European Union law, situations cannot exist which are covered in that way by European Union law without those fundamental rights being applicable. The applicability of European Union law entails applicability of the fundamental rights guaranteed by the Charter.[66]

By developing this specific criterion of 'where national legislation falls within the scope of European Union law', the ECJ has established a wide scope of application of EU fundamental rights. This criterion allows for various situations to be caught by the application of the Charter, including those where national laws have not been adopted to give effect to provisions of EU law.[67] The ECJ has also accepted that member states must respect EU fundamental rights when they have been given discretion to take certain measures in the implementation of EU law.[68] The ECJ has even accepted that some situations fell within the scope of EU law, even though it is still not entirely clear why it deemed this to be so.[69] The ECJ has not provided for a clear categorisation of the different types of situations which fall within the scope of application of EU fundamental rights. Instead, it has approached the clarification of the scope of application of EU fundamental rights in a casuistic manner.

In several judgments following the case of *Åkerberg Fransson*, the ECJ has given further clarification as to the scope of application of EU fundamental rights, which seem to stress that there needs to be a sufficiently close connection to EU law to allow

---

63 ECJ 13 July 1989, C-5/88, *Wachauf*.

64 See e.g. Sarmiento (2013).

65 ECJ 18 June 1991, C-260/89, *ERT*, para. 43. This type of situation was affirmed more recently in ECJ 30 April 2014, C-30/12, *Pfleger and others*, para. 35.

66 ECJ 26 February 2013, C-617/10, *Åkerberg Fransson*, para. 21. In the explanations to the Charter a somewhat similar interpretation of Article 51(1) is given. In the second section thereof it is stated that 'the requirement to respect fundamental rights defined in the context of the Union is only binding on the Member States when they act in the scope of Union law'.

67 This is explained further in section 9.2.1. It had been questioned by the Advocate General in the opinion on this case whether there was indeed a sufficient connection to EU law, see Opinion A-G Cruz Villalón in C-617/10, *Åkerberg Fransson*, para. 40.

68 Cf. ECJ 21 December 2011, Joined cases C-411/10 and C-493/10, *N.S. and others*.

69 See e.g. ECJ 22 November 2005, C-144/04, *Mangold*; and ECJ 16 September 2010, C-149/10, *Chatzi*.

EU fundamental rights to be applied. In its judgment in the case of *Siragusa*, the ECJ has explained that:

> ... the concept of 'implementing Union law', as referred to in Article 51 of the Charter, requires a certain degree of connection above and beyond the matters being closely related or one of those matters having an indirect impact on the other ....
>
> In order to determine whether national legislation involves the implementation for the purposes of Article 51 of the Charter, some of the points to be determined are whether that legislation intended to implement a provision of EU law; the nature of that legislation and whether it pursues objectives other than those covered by EU law, even if it is capable of indirectly affecting EU law; and also whether there are specific rules of EU law on the matter or capable of affecting it ...[70]

This line of reasoning has also been reiterated in other cases.[71] In another series of judgments, the ECJ has clarified that various measures fall outside the scope of application of EU fundamental rights.[72]

Gradually, the ECJ is thus bringing clarity as to the exact scope of application of EU fundamental rights in respect of the actions of the member states.[73] There needs to be a sufficiently strong connection to obligations that are laid down in EU law, which is of particular importance to ensure that the competences of the EU do not expand.[74] The topic of the scope of application of EU law is discussed in detail in chapter 9 to find whether it allows for a development of positive obligations by the ECJ to take place.

6.7.2. THE HORIZONTAL SCOPE OF APPLICATION OF THE CHARTER

Another important dimension related to the scope of application of the Charter is its horizontal scope of application. The scope for the application of fundamental rights between two private parties is also of particular interest in relation to the development of positive obligations to protect fundamental rights under EU law. They are two different forms to secure that fundamental rights are respected in situations between two private parties.[75]

---

[70] ECJ 6 March 2014, C-206/13, *Siragusa*, paras 24–25.

[71] See ECJ 8 November 2012, C-40/11, *Iida*, para. 79; ECJ 10 July 2014, C-198/13, *Julian Hernández and others*, paras 32 ff.; and ECJ 27 March 2014, C-265/13, *Torralbo Marcos*, paras 32–36.

[72] Cf. ECJ 5 October 2010, C-400/10, *McB.*; ECJ 27 November 2012, C-370/12, *Pringle*, paras 179–182; and ECJ 7 March 2013, C-128/12, *Sindicato dos Bancários do Norte and others*; and ECJ 27 November 2012, C-370/12, *Pringle*, paras 179–182; and ECJ 11 November 2014, C-333/13, *Dano*.

[73] It has been suggested that the lack of clarity about the scope of application of EU fundamental rights has had a 'strong paralysing effect', see Morijn (2014), p. 132.

[74] This particular issue is further discussed in section 9.2.

[75] The ECtHR has ensured that fundamental rights can be applied indirectly in disputes between private parties by accepting developing positive obligations for states. Cf. the discussions over the horizontal application of the Convention in section 2.8., and in relation to the doctrine of positive obligations, section 4.3.

Article 51(1) of the Charter does not clarify of itself whether fundamental rights are to be given horizontal effect (see section 6.7.1.), because it is as such addressed to the EU institutions and the member states.[76]

So far, the ECJ has accepted the horizontal direct effect of EU law in certain situations in its case law, and it has also accepted a certain indirect horizontal effect of fundamental rights in its case-law.

In disputes with other individuals, the ECJ has established that individuals can directly rely on the EU's Treaty provisions on the free movement of workers and services as well as establishment.[77] In this type of case, a certain indirect effect of fundamental rights can also be applied, that is, when one of the parties invokes a fundamental right as a justification for the restriction of the free movement rights.[78] Furthermore, there can be an indirect effect of fundamental rights where individuals rely on certain provisions of EU secondary legislation in combination with provisions of fundamental rights in disputes with other private parties.[79] This may, in particular, occur in the area of employment law or in the area of privacy law, where there is specific EU secondary legislation that aims to secure the protection of fundamental rights in horizontal situations, such as the right to privacy and the protection of personal data which are protected by Articles 7 and 8 of the Charter.[80] In those cases, the indirect horizontal effect of EU fundamental rights in particular, and of EU law in general, is secured by the national courts that apply such rights. National courts have been required by the ECJ to interpret national law as far as possible in conformity with EU law (including fundamental rights), and to set aside national law which is not in conformity with EU law.[81] They may further accept state liability for the incorrect implementation of EU law on the basis of the principle of loyal cooperation, as protected by Article 4(3) TEU.[82]

It has further been debated, especially in recent years, whether the ECJ has also allowed for direct horizontal effect of fundamental rights on the basis of its judgments in the cases of *Mangold, Kücükdeveci* and *AMS*.[83] In the cases of *Mangold* and *Kücükdeveci*, the ECJ has required the national courts to apply the principle of non-

---

76 For different readings of this provision, cf. the Opinion of A-G Cruz Villalón in C-167/12, *AMS*, paras 28–33; and the Opinion of A-G Trstenjak in C-282/10, *Dominguez*, paras 80–83.

77 ECJ 12 December 1974, C-36/74, *Walrave and Koch*; ECJ 15 December 1995, C-415/93, *Bosman*; and ECJ 19 February 2002, C-309/99, *Wouters and others*.

78 See ECJ 11 December 2007, C-438/05, *Viking Line*.

79 De Vries & Van Mastrigt (2013), p. 274; and Hartkamp (2013), pp. 195–196.

80 See e.g. ECJ 24 January 2012, C-282/10, *Dominguez*; ECJ 27 March 2014, C-314/12, *UPC Telekabel Wien*; and ECJ 13 May 2014, C-131/12, *Google Spain*.

81 ECJ 26 June 2007, C-305/05, *Ordre des barreaux francophone and germanophone and others*, para. 28; and ECJ 29 January 2008, C-275/06, *Promusicae*, paras 68 and 70.

82 See ECJ 19 November 1991, Joined cases C-6/90 and C-9/90, *Francovich and Bonifaci v. Italy*; ECJ 24 January 2012, C-282/10, *Dominguez*, para. 43.

83 ECJ 22 November 2005, C-144/04, *Mangold*; ECJ 19 January 2010, C-555/07, *Kücukdeveci*; and ECJ 15 January 2014, C-176/12, *AMS*.

discrimination on grounds of age, as a general principle of EU law, in a dispute between an employer and an employee. These cases were brought within the scope of application of EU law on the basis of certain provisions laid down in EU Directives. However, in the case of *Mangold*, the provision had not been implemented correctly into national law, and in the case of *Kücükdeveci*, the provision had not yet been implemented because the period for implementing the Directive had not expired. In the cases of *Mangold* and *Kücücdeveci*, the ECJ decided that the national courts still needed to protect the principle of non-discrimination on grounds of age, and set aside national legislation if necessary to comply with that principle.[84] The ECJ has, however, always precluded the horizontal direct effect of provisions laid down in Directives itself, because Directives cannot by themselves confer obligations on individuals.[85]

So far the ECJ has not extended the approach which it developed in *Mangold* and *Kücükdeveci* to other cases on fundamental rights, and there seem to be as many proponents as opponents to its doing so.[86] In the *AMS* case, the ECJ clearly rejected a horizontal direct application of the right to information and consultation within the undertaking as guaranteed by Article 27 of the Charter.[87] The ECJ held that this provision did not in itself confer rights on individuals which they could invoke as such.[88] The minimal reasoning of the ECJ in these cases, however, provides much room for debate on the potential for the horizontal application of EU fundamental rights in other types of cases and in respect of other types of fundamental rights.[89]

6.8. THE SCOPE FOR THE PROTECTION OF NATIONAL FUNDAMENTAL RIGHTS UNDER EU LAW AND THE PRINCIPLE OF MUTUAL RECOGNITION

When national measures fall within the scope of application of EU law and EU fundamental rights, there are consequences for the scope of application of national standards of fundamental rights. Where member states are 'implementing Union law' within the meaning of Article 51(1) of the Charter, they need to comply with the EU standard of fundamental rights, as explained in the previous section. Article 53 of the

84 ECJ 22 November 2005, C-144/04, *Mangold*, para. 77; and ECJ 19 January 2010, C-555/07, *Kücukdeveci*, para. 53. It should also be mentioned that the ECJ did not as much confirm the substitution effect of fundamental rights (which implies the direct creation of rights and obligations for individuals), as it did the exclusionary effect (which implies the setting aside of national law), see De Mol (2011), p. 121.

85 ECJ 26 February 1986, C-152/84, *Marshall*.

86 Cf. e.g. the opinion of AG Trstenjak in C-282/10, *Dominguez*; and the opinion of AG Cruz Villalón in C-176/12, *AMS*.

87 ECJ 15 January 2014, C-176/12, *AMS*.

88 ECJ 15 January 2014, C-176/12, *AMS*, para. 47.

89 See in particular De Mol (2013).

Charter then allows the member states to provide for a higher level of protection of fundamental rights. This provision holds that:

> Nothing in this Charter shall be interpreted as restricting or adversely affecting human rights and fundamental freedoms as recognised, in their respective fields of application, by Union law and international law and by international agreements to which the Union or all the Member States are party, including the European Convention for the Protection of Fundamental Freedoms, and by Member States' constitutions.

Questions have been raised as to what this provision would exactly entail. Would it (always) allow for the highest standards of fundamental rights, on the basis of national or other sources of international law, to be applied? And how exactly does it aim to reconcile the application of parallel sources of fundamental rights? The ECJ has given an answer to some of these questions in the case of *Melloni*.[90] This case was about the execution of a European Arrest Warrant which was issued by the Italian authorities to execute a prison sentence determined in a judgment *in absentia* against Mr Melloni. The Spanish constitutional court had referred questions to the ECJ in this case because the surrender would interfere with an essential component of the right to a fair trial as guaranteed under the Spanish constitution, and this was not indicated by the four exceptions under the Framework Decision on the European Arrest Warrant that would allow national courts to refuse to agree to the surrender. The Spanish constitutional court asked the ECJ whether it could provide a higher level of protection on the basis of its national constitution in light of Article 53 of the Charter. In its judgment, the ECJ clarified that:

> ... Article 53 of the Charter confirms that, where an EU legal act calls for national implementing measures, national authorities and courts remain free to apply national standards of protection of fundamental rights, provided that the level of protection provided for by the Charter, as interpreted by the Court, and the primacy, unity and effectiveness of EU law are not thereby compromised.[91]

The protection of the primacy, unity and effectiveness of EU law thus needed to be given priority over the highest level of fundamental rights protection.[92] In this case, the principle of mutual recognition, which was an important principle underlying the Framework Decision, would have been put at risk if Spain had refused the surrender based on its national constitution. The ECJ also explained in *Melloni* that the Framework Decision reflected a consensus that had already been reached by the member states regarding the procedural rights that were to be given to persons who are the subject of a

---

[90] ECJ 26 February 2013, C-399/11, *Melloni*.

[91] ECJ 26 February 2013, C-399/11, *Melloni*, para. 60.

[92] ECJ 26 February 2013, C-399/11, *Melloni*, para. 60. Some scholars have reacted very critically to this judgment, see De Boer (2013).

European Arrest Warrant.[93] Based on such considerations, the ECJ determined that the Framework Decision was to be considered compatible with the right to effective judicial review as guaranteed under EU law.

Some scholars have provided a nuanced account of this judgment as still allowing the member states the discretion to apply their national fundamental rights standards, even in situations that do fall within the scope of EU law.[94] They consider that there is room for member states to apply their own fundamental rights standards in situations which are not completely determined by EU law, which the ECJ also clarified in its judgment in *Åkerberg Fransson*. In that case, there was clear discretion for the member states in the implementation of EU law. The ECJ also held, however, that national courts would first need to send a preliminary question to the ECJ if they were to have doubts about the scope for applying higher standards of protection under EU law.[95]

Especially in areas of EU law which are governed by the principle of mutual recognition, there can be a more limited scope for the application of higher standards of fundamental rights on the basis of national law, however. Under EU law, member states have decided to cooperate on civil, administrative and criminal matters on the basis of the principle of mutual recognition. This essentially means that they need to respect each other's (different) standards, and that there is mutual trust between the member states with regard to their compliance with (international) legal obligations, including the protection of fundamental rights. In several cases, concerns have been raised over whether other member states actually secured a sufficient level of fundamental rights protection based on their own national law. For example, in the case of *N.S. and others*, member states were required to send asylum seekers back to the the member state in which they had first arrived in the EU on the basis of the Dublin Regulation and on the basis of the principle of mutual recognition.[96] In that case, this would have meant that asylum seekers needed to be sent back to Greece, although there was a serious risk of violation of the prohibition of inhuman and degrading treatment as a result of the poor conditions for the reception of asylum seekers in that member state. In response to the questions referred to it by national courts, the ECJ made it clear that national courts cannot transfer asylum seekers back to the member state of first arrival 'where they cannot be unaware of the systemic deficiencies in the asylum procedure and in the reception conditions of asylum seekers in that Member State' that amount to a real risk of treatment contrary to the prohibition of inhuman and degrading treatment guaranteed by Article 4 of the Charter.[97]

This conflict with the principle of mutual recognition also arose in the case of *Aranyosi and Căldăru*, where national courts had asked questions to the ECJ about the

---

93 ECJ 26 February 2013, C-399/11, *Melloni*, para. 62.

94 Cf. Sarmiento (2013). See also section 9.3.4.

95 ECJ 26 February 2013, C-617/10, *Åkerberg Fransson*, para. 30.

96 ECJ 21 December 2011, Joined cases C-411/10 and C-493/10, *N.S. and others*. This case was based on ECtHR 21 January 2011, no. 30696/09, *M.S.S. v. Belgium and Greece*.

97 ECJ 21 December 2011, Joined cases C-411/10 and C-493/10, *N.S. and others*, para. 94.

execution of two European Arrest Warrants issued by Hungary and by Romania, because it had serious concerns about whether the detention conditions in those member states complied with fundamental rights standards.[98] Again, the ECJ accepted that to be able to execute a European Arrest Warrant member states need to assess whether another member state is complying with fundamental rights, if they are in the possession of evidence of a real risk of inhuman and degrading treatment of individuals detained in member state which issued the European Arrest Warrant. In its judgment, the ECJ set out in detail under which conditions this postponement could take place and, indeed, what the national authorities would have to do when faced with this type of situation.[99]

The cases of *N.S. and others* and *Aranyosi and Căldăru* show that the ECJ is willing to provide exceptions to the application of the principle of mutual recognition, especially where there are risks of serious interference with a fundamental right. However, the ECJ more generally stressed in *Opinion 2/13* that, save for exceptional circumstances, the member states need not check whether other member states are complying with EU law and with fundamental rights.[100]

6.9. THE RELATIONSHIP BETWEEN THE EU AND THE EUROPEAN CONVENTION ON HUMAN RIGHTS

6.9.1. THE STATUS OF THE EUROPEAN CONVENTION ON HUMAN RIGHTS AND JUDGMENTS OF THE ECtHR UNDER EU LAW

Although the Convention has not yet been given a legally binding status under EU law, it plays an important role in this legal order.[101] As has already been explained, the rights under the Convention originally provided an important reference for the ECJ in the development of general principles of EU law in its case-law. The same rights laid down in the Convention are now also to be found in the Charter, spread throughout its different chapters. The formulation of the rights in the Charter is often different, however, to the extent that modern adaptations have been made to the formulation of the provisions of the Convention.[102] For example, Article 5 of the Charter, which prohibits slavery and forced labour, specifically makes provision for the prohibition of human trafficking, and therefore adds to the rights protected by Article 4 ECHR.

98 ECJ 5 April 2016, Joined cases C-404/15 and C-659/15, *Aranyosi and Căldăru*, paras 92 and 104.

99 ECJ 5 April 2016, Joined cases C-404/15 and C-659/15, *Aranyosi and Căldăru*, paras 88 ff.

100 See ECJ 18 December 2013, *Opinion 2/13*, paras 191–192.

101 See ECJ 26 February 2013, C-617/10, *Åkerberg Fransson*, para. 44; and ECJ 24 April 2012, C-517/10, *Kamberaj*, para. 60; and ECJ 18 December 2014, *Opinion 2/13*, para. 179. As to the specific status which the Convention is expected to acquire under EU law, see also the View of Advocate General Kokott to *Opinion 2/13*, which was delivered on 13 June 2014, paras 197–207.

102 In comparison to the Convention, the rights of the Charter also are less negatively phrased.

Importantly, Article 52(3) of the Charter in general requires that the Convention must be taken into account in the interpretation of the rights laid down in the Charter. Article 52(3) of the Charter stipulates that:

> In so far as this Charter contains rights which correspond to rights guaranteed by the Convention for the Protection of Human Rights and Fundamental Freedoms, the meaning and scope of those rights shall be the same as those laid down by the said Convention. This provision shall not prevent Union law providing more extensive protection.

Article 52(3) thus aims to provide consistency between the interpretation of fundamental rights under the Charter and the Convention. In the explanations to the Charter, a precise list of the specific rights of the Charter which are held to correspond to the rights of the Convention is provided. Some of the rights in the Charter have a much wider scope as compared to the corresponding provisions in the Convention, however, as is also expressly allowed for under the last sentence of Article 52(3). Therefore, the explanations to the Charter include a list of rights which are to be given the same meaning as the corresponding Convention rights, but where the scope of the Charter provisions is wider. An important example is the right to a fair trial, which under Article 6 ECHR is limited to civil and criminal cases, while this restriction is not laid down in Article 47 of the Charter. This means that it applies to disputes in all areas of law, provided that they fall within the scope of EU law.

Article 52(3) of the Charter itself is not very clear about the degree to which the judgments of the ECtHR are to be taken into account in the interpretation of the corresponding Charter rights. The judgments of the ECtHR are specifically mentioned in the explanations to Article 52(3) as the authoritative source for the interpretation of the rights guaranteed by the Convention. There, it is held that:

> The meaning and the scope of the guaranteed rights are determined not only by the text of those instruments, but also by the case-law of the European Court of Human Rights and by the Court of Justice of the European Union. The last sentence of the paragraph is designed to allow the Union to guarantee more extensive protection. In any event, the level of protection afforded by the Charter may never be lower than that guaranteed by the ECHR.

Considering that the scope and the meaning of the rights of the Convention are to a great extent to be found in the case-law of the ECtHR, it seems quite evident that the judgments of the ECtHR are taken into account in the interpretation of the same rights laid down in the Charter. The ECJ has, especially in the past, made clear references in its case-law to specific judgments of the ECtHR which were relevant for it to interpret a fundamental right.[103] However, as has been mentioned earlier in this chapter, the current reasoning of the ECJ on fundamental rights matters is predominantly based on the EU's own provisions of fundamental rights which are contained in the Charter.

---

[103] Douglas-Scott (2006), pp. 644–650.

References to provisions of the Convention and the case-law of the ECtHR by the ECJ have decreased since 2009.[104] This has given rise to the fear that the ECJ will not be willing to take the judgments of the ECtHR into account, and that it may therefore interpret fundamental rights in a different way.[105]

Also, in the explanations to Article 52(3) of the Charter, a certain limitation is expressed with regard to the effect of the Convention under EU law. It holds that:

> This [Article 52(3)] means in particular that the legislator, in laying down limitations to those rights, must comply with the same standards as are fixed by the detailed limitation arrangements laid down in the ECHR, which are thus made applicable for the rights covered by this paragraph, without thereby adversely affecting the autonomy of Union law and of that of the Court of Justice of the European Union.[106]

The autonomous interpretation of EU law indeed has been of great concern to the ECJ, and this could be affected if the Court were to fully bind itself to Convention as well as the judgments of the ECtHR on the protection of fundamental rights. *Opinion 2/13* also seems to show that the ECJ is not willing to fully bind itself, in particular, to the judgments of the ECtHR. To briefly explain, in *Opinion 2/13*, in which the ECJ found several aspects of the draft accession agreement to be incompatible with EU law, the ECJ stressed that the accession agreement must take into account that the EU is not to be considered to be a state and that the EU has created a new kind of legal order which has specific characteristics that need to be preserved.[107] The ECJ held that the autonomy of EU law would be put at risk by the external judicial review of the ECtHR if the ECtHR were to judge over the division of competences between the EU and its member states.[108] Crucial concerns which the ECJ raised in its opinion included that the accession agreement had not sufficiently taken into account that in certain areas, such as the area of freedom, security and justice, the member states' obligations are governed by the principle of mutual trust which, according to the ECJ, precludes the member states from checking whether other member states have observed fundamental rights, save in exceptional circumstances.[109] Also, in respect of the arrangements which have been envisaged for the establishment of the co-respondent mechanism, the ECJ found that the assessment of the admissibility of a request by the EU or a member states to become co-respondent in a procedure before the ECtHR would put the autonomy of EU law at risk.[110] Any (future) assessment made by the ECtHR in this procedure over the question whether the EU or a member state is responsible for a breach of the Convention, or whether they are jointly responsible, would frustrate the EU's rules on

---

[104] See De Búrca (2013), p. 175.
[105] See in particular De Búrca (2013).
[106] See the last sentence of the third indent of the explanations to Article 52 of the Charter.
[107] ECJ 18 December 2014, *Opinion 2/13*, paras 154–158.
[108] ECJ 18 December 2014, *Opinion 2/13*, paras 179–186.
[109] ECJ 18 December 2014, *Opinion 2/13*, paras 191–195.
[110] ECJ 18 December 2014, *Opinion 2/13*, paras 215–235.

the division of competences between the EU and its member states. Also, the accession agreement does not provide for any specific arrangements as regards the jurisdiction of the ECtHR in the area of the common foreign and security policy.[111] In this particular area, the jurisdiction of the ECJ is restricted, and therefore, according to the ECJ, the jurisdiction of the ECtHR must be limited as well.

These concerns may partially explain why the ECJ has expressed its reservations to fully accepting the Convention and the judgments of the ECtHR. According to the ECJ, the autonomy of EU law would be affected if interpretations on fundamental rights provisions provided by external sources such as the ECtHR were to become binding on the EU.

Despite all this, the ECJ still refers to the judgments of the ECtHR, even after it delivered *Opinion 2/13*.[112] Indeed, since the scope and the meaning of the rights of the Charter cannot, in accordance with Article 52(3) of the Charter, be interpreted more restrictively under EU law, there does not in fact seem to be room for the ECJ to provide an interpretation that goes beyond the scope and meaning which has been given under the Convention.

The specific way in which the ECJ has dealt with the Convention and the judgments of the ECtHR is discussed from a more critical perspective in chapter 7.[113]

6.9.2. OVERLAPPING JURISDICTION BETWEEN THE ECtHR AND THE ECJ

Since all of the EU member states are also party to the Convention, it may happen that individuals bring complaints to the ECtHR on matters related to EU law. On several occasions, the ECtHR has been asked to decide on violations of the Convention by its states parties in situations where there was a clear connection to EU law. Therefore, there is, to some extent, an overlapping jurisdiction of the ECtHR and the ECJ and it is of importance for both courts to take each other's case-law into account. Particularly noteworthy is the judgment of the ECtHR in the case of *M.S.S. v. Belgium and Greece*.[114] This case concerned the transferral of asylum seekers under the EU Dublin Regulation (see section 6.8.). The case of *M.S.S.* showed that there were serious shortcomings in the conditions for the reception of asylum seekers in Greece, as well as in relation to the procedures for application for asylum there. The ECtHR decided that asylum seekers could not be sent back to a certain member state if there was ground to believe that

---

111 ECJ 18 December 2014, *Opinion 2/13*, paras 249–257.

112 See e.g. ECJ 18 December 2014, C-542/13, *M'Bodj*, paras 39–40; ECJ 18 December 2014, C-562/13, *Abdida*, para. 47.

113 See section 7.6.2.2.

114 ECtHR 21 January 2011, no. 30696/09, *M.S.S v. Belgium and Greece*. Of relevance also is ECtHR 4 November 2014, no. 29217/12, *Tarakhel v. Switzerland*.

they would be put at risk of facing treatment which was contrary to the prohibition of degrading treatment as protected by Article 3 ECHR.[115] Shortly after this judgment, the ECJ itself also affirmed this approach in *N.S. and others* – although seemingly under somewhat more narrow conditions.[116]

There are several other overlapping areas of law or topics in which both the ECtHR and the ECJ have delivered judgments. This includes *inter alia* the area of data protection as well as the detention conditions of asylum seekers.[117]

It can be said that the ECtHR secures a certain form of indirect review of the fundamental rights obligations of states under EU law when it decides on cases where member states are implementing EU law, such as in the case of *M.S.S. v. Belgium and Greece*. If states do not have any discretion, however, to deviate from their obligations under EU law, the ECtHR can be expected to apply a very deferential type of review. The ECtHR developed this particular approach in the case of *Bosphorus*.[118] In this case, the ECtHR clarified that states are not precluded from transferring competences to international organisations such as the EU, provided that the rights of the Convention are secured.[119] States parties remain responsible for all acts and omissions which are based on domestic and international law.[120] Where states parties implement obligations from an international organisation which protects fundamental rights in a manner which is at least equivalent to the Convention, the ECtHR will, however, apply a presumption that states parties act in conformity with fundamental rights. The ECtHR has explained that this presumption can be rebutted if it considers that the protection of fundamental rights in the specific case is manifestly deficient. In the case of *Bosphorus*, the ECtHR came to the conclusion that the EU indeed provided an equivalent level of fundamental rights protection, taking into account the various steps the EU has taken over the years to ensure protection of fundamental rights, and also that the protection that was provided to the applicant in that case was not manifestly deficient.[121]

To clarify, this *Bosphorus* approach does not apply to situations where member states have discretion in the implementation of EU law, nor in situations where the ECJ has

---

115 ECtHR 21 January 2011, no. 30696/09, *MSS v. Belgium and Greece*, para. 358.

116 ECJ 21 December 2011, Joined cases C-411/10 and C-493/10, *N.S. and others*, paras 88–89. Cf. in relation to this ECJ 18 December 2014, *Opinion 2/14*, paras 191–194; and the discussion in section 6.8.

117 Most recently on the right to protection of personal data, cf. ECJ 8 April 2014, Joined cases C-293/12 and 594/12, *Digital Rights Ireland*; ECJ 6 October 2015, C-362/14, *Schrems*; ECtHR 4 December 2015, no. 47143/06, *Zakharov v. Russia*. On the liability of internet search providers for individual comments, see ECJ 13 May 2014, C-131/12, *Google Spain*; and ECtHR 16 June 2015, no. 64569/09, *Delfi and others v. Estonia*. Also, in relation to the grounds for detention of aylum seekers, cf. ECJ 15 February 2016, C-601/15 PPU, *J.N.*; and ECtHR 22 September 2015, no. 62116/12, *Nabil and others v. Hungary*.

118 ECtHR 30 June 2006, no. 45036/98, *Bosphorus v. Ireland*.

119 See also ECtHR 18 February 1999, no. 24833/94, *Matthews v. the United Kingdom*, para. 33.

120 ECtHR 30 June 2006, no. 45036/98, *Bosphorus v. Ireland*, paras 152–157. See further Costello (2006).

121 ECtHR 30 June 2006, no. 45036/98, *Bosphorus v. Ireland*, paras 159–166.

not already exercised control of fundamental rights compliance through a preliminary reference procedure.[122]

This current limited approach of the ECtHR to the fundamental rights review of its states parties comprises one of the reasons why the accession of the EU to the accession is considered necessary. It is expected that, after accession, the ECtHR would no longer apply its *Bosphorus* doctrine,[123] and the EU would then be considered equal to other states parties to the Convention.[124]

6.10. THE DISTINCTION BETWEEN RIGHTS AND PRINCIPLES UNDER THE CHARTER

The Charter establishes a particular distinction between *rights* and *principles*. According to Article 52(5) of the Charter:

> The provisions of this Charter which contain principles may be implemented by legislative and executive acts taken by institutions, bodies, offices and agencies of the Union, and by acts of Member States when they are implementing Union law, in the exercise of their respective powers. They shall be judicially cognisable only in the interpretation of such acts and in the ruling on their legality.

Article 51(1) also mentions rights and principles; this provision stipulates that rights must be *respected* and principles must be *observed*. The distinction between rights and principles is mainly relevant for the enforceability of individual claims through the courts, which is clearly more limited for principles than it is for rights. Such a special, more limited status for principles appeared necessary to be included in the Charter, especially because the Charter contains many social rights, which the member states did not like to be directly justiciable for individuals.[125] Problematically, however, it is not exactly clear which of the Charter's provisions contain rights and which contain principles, nor are the implications of the divide immediately obvious. As has appeared from the discussions in part I, the distinction between clear rights and vague principles does not necessarily correspond to the distinction between civil and political rights as opposed to social, cultural and economic rights. Both types of

---

122 Cf. ECtHR 21 January 2011, no. 30696/09, *MSS v. Belgium and Greece*, para. 338; ECtHR 6 December 2012, no. 12323/11, *Michaud v. France*, paras 108–111.

123 To some extent, the ECtHR provides room for intensifying its review even pre-accession by holding that 'any such finding of equivalence could not be final and would be susceptible to review in the light of any relevant change in fundamental rights protection'. See ECtHR 30 June 2005, no. 45036/98, *Bosphorus v. Ireland*, para. 155. More recently, the ECtHR again applied the *Bosphorus* approach, see ECtHR 23 May 2016, no. 17502/07, *Avotiņš v. Latvia*.

124 See De Schutter (2014).

125 See further Craig (2011a), pp. 216–217.

rights may confer relatively clear and subjective individual rights.[126] Little guidance is provided by the Charter as to which fundamental rights laid down in the Charter may be characterised as rights and which as principles, and its provisions do not as such clarify whether they contain rights or principles. The explanations to the Charter mention that principles appear in the field of social law, in particular, and name as a few examples: Article 25 on the rights of the elderly, Article 26 on the integration of persons with disabilities and Article 37 on environmental protection. In addition, the explanations clarify that provisions of the Charter may contain both rights and principles at the same time, mentioning Article 23 on the equality between men and women, Article 33 on family and professional life and Article 34 on social security and social assistance as examples. Further clarifications as regards the distinction between rights and principles have deliberately been left to be explored further in case-law.

The difference between rights and principles may be held to relate mainly to the nature of principles, which, contrary to rights, are not formulated very clearly and do not confer subjective rights on individuals. For that reason, sufficient leeway must be given to the legislative and executive authorities in the implementation of principles and thus the assessments by courts of such legislative and administrative acts must be restrained. Indeed, in the explanations to the Charter it is provided that:

> Principles may be implemented through legislative or executive acts (adopted by the Union in accordance with its powers, and by the Member States only when they implement Union law); accordingly they become significant for the Courts only when such acts are interpreted or reviewed. They do not however give rise to direct claims for positive action by the Union's institutions or Member States authorities.[127]

Judicial review of principles must, according to the explanations, be limited to the interpretation and the assessment of the legality of EU law. Consequently, in the absence of any action taken by the EU, individuals cannot invoke principles as such as a ground for review. It remains somewhat unclear as to whether courts would only be able to interpret or review the legality of EU acts in light of a principle if those acts directly aimed at implementing a particular principle, or whether such review could go beyond such acts and be addressed in respect of a much broader range of legislative or executive acts in view where that principle would be of relevance. Interestingly, the divide between rights and principles in the Charter also has implications for the extent to which courts are allowed to define positive obligations.

So far, it appears that the ECJ has tried to stay clear of touching upon this Charter distinction. Several cases have been brought before the ECJ in which the interpretation of Article 52(5) of the Charter appeared relevant, but in all of them the distinction was

---

126 See Craig (2011a), p. 218.

127 Penultimate paragraph of the explanations relating to Article 52(5) of the Charter.

only discussed in the opinions of the Advocates General.[128] In the case of *AMS*, which was concerned with the application of Article 27 of the Charter guaranteeing the right of workers to information and consultation within an undertaking by national courts, the ECJ held that 'for the article to be fully effective, it must be given more specific expression in European Union or national law', but did not refer to Article 52(5) as such.[129] So far, it is only in the case of *Glatzel* that the ECJ addressed the matter.[130] This case was about the compatibility of the minimum standards of the physical fitness of drivers of motor vehicles, laid down in an EU Directive, *inter alia* in light of Article 26 of the Charter on the integration of persons with a disability. This provision has been indicated by the explanations to the Charter as an example of a principle and was addressed by the ECJ as follows:

> the principle enshrined by that article does not require the EU legislature to adopt any specific measure. In order for that article to be fully effective, it must be given more specific expression in European or national law. Accordingly, that article cannot by itself confer on individuals a subjective right which they may invoke as such ...[131]

The Court's interpretation confirms that the main difference between rights and principles relates to the lack of precision which is inherent to the nature of principles. A principle, therefore, does not confer individual subjective rights. Article 26 (which stipulates that 'The Union recognises and respects the rights of persons with disabilities to benefit from measures designed to ensure their independence, social and occupational integration and participation in the life of the community') does not confer subjective rights, nor does it contain much precision. Also, in the case of *Glatzel*, the ECJ concluded that it could apply the principle as a ground for interpreting and reviewing the legality of the Directive as it intended to implement that principle in its provisions.[132] The ECJ thus adopted quite a narrow view as to the material scope of application of the principle in the interpretation and the review of legality of EU law.[133] Moreover, this narrow view may be contested if it is taken into account that it would be very difficult to hold EU institutions responsible for not observing principles in their activities, as they could very easily plead that those act did not intend to implement particular principles. This would clearly undermine the effective protection guaranteed

---

[128] Cf. the opinion of AG Trstenjak in C-282/10, *Dominguez*, paras 49–50; and the opinion of AG Cruz Villalón in C-176/12, *AMS*, paras 43–80.

[129] ECJ 15 January 2014, C-176/12, *AMS*, para. 45.

[130] ECJ 22 May 2014, C-356/12, *Glatzel*, paras 74–76.

[131] ECJ 22 May 2014, C-356/12, *Glatzel*, para. 78.

[132] ECJ 22 May 2014, C-356/12, *Glatzel*, paras 74–76.

[133] Some scholars suggest that this narrow interpretation does not correspond with the interpretation which has been given by the Court of Justice *inter alia* to the precautionary principle. The precautionary principle, which is also mentioned in the explanations to the Charter as a principle that falls within the meaning of Article 52(5) of the Charter, has been used by the Court of Justice to assess the legality of EU acts which did not, as such, intend to implement that principle, see Craig (2011a), p. 220.

by these principles. Either way, however, scrutiny of EU law by the courts in light of principles will be restrained due to the generally broad formulation of principles, which do not provide clear-cut guidance to the courts.

6.11. CONCLUSIONS

The importance of protecting fundamental rights has clearly been recognised under EU law. At first, the ECJ played a strong role in the development of fundamental rights at the EU level, albeit under strong pressure by the national constitutional courts. By now, a clear political response has been given in order to ensure that fundamental rights are adequately protected within the scope of EU law. The entire range of actions which can be taken by the EU institutions and the member states in the different policy fields of the EU are constrained by fundamental rights norms. The main rationale for this, as has been explained in this chapter, is not only to protect the rights of individuals and companies, but also to ensure the protection of the primacy, unity and effectiveness of EU law.

At present, the Charter, which became legally binding in 2009, plays a central place in the protection of fundamental rights in the case-law of the ECJ, and it has become important to the political institutions. The rights laid down in the national constitutions and the rights guaranteed by the Convention also continue to be respected within the scope of EU law, in accordance with Article 6 TEU, and may still play a (limited) role.

Although since the Lisbon Treaty the EU is subject to an obligation to accede to the Convention, which could prevent divergences in the interpretation of fundamental rights, it has not yet complied with this obligation and the ECJ has expressed important reservations. Indeed, the ECJ currently appears to favour the development of the Charter over the incorporation of the Convention. In recent judgments the ECJ has made fewer references to the judgments of the ECtHR, and has paid more attention to interpreting the rights laid down in the Charter, including its 'horizontal clauses' (Article 51 to 54 of the Charter). Thereby, it has also responded to the increasing number of questions that have been raised on the interpretation of these horizontal clasuses. This has helped the Court to specify some rules on the scope of application of the Charter and the standards of fundamental rights applied at the national level and under the Convention. In the two landmark cases of *Åkerberg Fransson* and *Melloni*, the ECJ has made clear that the Charter has a wide scope of application, and that the member states can apply a higher level of fundamental rights protection to the extent that this does not affect the unity, primacy and effectiveness of EU law.

Much clarity has therefore already been provided regarding the protection of fundamental rights in the EU. Nevertheless, many questions on the Charter and the EU's system of fundamental rights protection are still waiting to be answered. These include the extent to which the notion of positive obligations can be recognised within the EU's system. The remainder of this study is devoted to an examination of this question.

CHAPTER 7

THE INSTITUTIONAL CHARACTERISTICS AND JUDICIAL CULTURE OF THE ECJ

7.1. INTRODUCTION

This chapter will explore further to what extent a development of positive obligations by the ECJ can be expected on the basis of its institutional position and its particular judicial culture. The ECJ has quite a different institutional position compared to the ECtHR, at least in some respects, and it also has a rather different judicial culture. There is a great complexity of factors which the ECJ must take into account and different 'audiences' to which the ECJ must listen that can pull it in different directions. These factors can have an impact on the potential for a development of positive obligations by this particular court.

This chapter starts off by discussing two specific judgments of the ECJ (section 7.2.). In one of these judgments, the ECJ decided not to recognise a positive obligation to protect a fundamental right (the case of *Bostock*); while in the other case, it did impose a positive obligation on the member states (the case of *Chatzi*). Both of these cases have been heavily criticised. It has been held that the ECJ did too little in the first case and too much in the second case. These are two types of criticism the ECJ may easily incur. The aim of this chapter is to place such judgments in the perspective of the different roles and judicial styles that the ECJ may adopt, and to examine whether and how the ECJ could respond to the arguments of its critics. After discussing the judgments of the ECJ in the cases of *Bostock* and *Chatzi*, and the criticism which these judgments have incurred, various specific factors relating to the judicial style as well as the institutional position of the ECJ are discussed that could explain its approach in these, as well as other judgments. These factors include the role and judicial style of the ECJ in general (section 7.3.); the procedures that are used to bring fundamental rights cases before the ECJ (section 7.4.); the institutional position of the ECJ *vis-à-vis* the EU institutions and the member states (section 7.5.); as well as the specific role played by the EU and the ECJ in the field of fundamental rights (section 7.6.). Lastly, some final conclusions are given on the extent to which the judicial style and the institutional position of the ECJ allow room for a development of positive obligations (section 7.7.).

7.2. DOING TOO LITTLE OR RATHER TOO MUCH?

7.2.1. THE *BOSTOCK* CASE

The *Bostock* case, which was brought to the Court in the early 1990s, was about the implementation of a Community Regulation on the common organisation of the market in milk and milk products.[1] Mr Bostock was a farmer in the United Kingdom who had leased a plot of land for the production of milk. He had made considerable improvements to the land to allow for milk production, and had been allocated certain quota under the said Community Regulation. After the lease of the land had been discontinued, he was left without any compensation by his landlord, nor was he compensated in any other way, and he suffered financial loss as a result. No obligation to compensate was provided for in the respective Community Regulation.[2] This led to the question whether the member states could be put under an obligation to take certain measures to protect the right to property of farmers under Community law, a question which was referred to the ECJ. The national court that considered this case in particular requested the ECJ to clarify whether a compensation regime needed to be introduced on the basis of Community law to protect the right to property for such tenants. The ECJ replied that:

> The right to property safeguarded by the Community legal order does not include the right to dispose, for profit, of an advantage, such as the reference quantities allocated in the context of the common organization of a market, which does not derive from the assets or occupational activity of the person concerned ...
>
> It follows that the protection of the right to property guaranteed by the Community legal order does not require a Member State to introduce a scheme for payment of compensation by a landlord to an outgoing tenant and does not confer a right to such compensation directly on the tenant.[3]

According to the ECJ, Community law thus did not (specifically) require member states to introduce a compensation regime to protect the right to property of a tenant.[4] This outcome, as well as the reasoning leading up to the Court's decision, has been fiercely criticised by Weiler and Lockhart.[5] According to Weiler and Lockhart, this judgment provides an example of how the ECJ has expressly allowed member states to breach the fundamental rights of an individual without offering them any means of compensation,

---

1 ECJ 24 March 1994, C-2/92, *Bostock*.

2 Article 4(1) of Council Regulation 857/84/EEC of 31 March 1984 adopting general rules for the application of the levy referred to in Article 5c of Regulation (EEC) No 804/68 in the milk products sector [1984] OJ L90/13.

3 ECJ 24 March 1994, C-2/92, *Bostock*, paras 19–20.

4 ECJ 24 March 1994, C-2/92, *Bostock*, paras 18–24.

5 Weiler & Lockhart (1995b), pp. 605–617.

even though the member states were clearly acting as 'agents of Community law' and they were bound to protect the right to property.[6] In the view of Weiler and Lockhart, the ECJ seemed to have established as much in the previous case of *Wachauf* on a very similar position. There, it had held that:

> ... Community rules which, upon the expiry of the lease, had the effect of depriving the lessee, without compensation, of the fruits of his labour and of his investments in the tenanted holding would be incompatible with the requirement of the protection of fundamental rights in the Community legal order. Since those requirements are also binding on the Member States when they implement Community rules, the Member States must, as far as possible, apply those rules in accordance with those requirements.[7]

On the basis of this judgment Weiler and Lockhart had expected that the ECJ would ensure the protection of the right to property by the member states in the case of *Bostock* as well. Community law itself had caused for the interference to take place, that is, by introducing a specific regime on milk production, and should therefore have also ensured that fundamental rights protection would be secured by the member states if they acted in that situation on the basis of Community law.[8] The Court, reasoning as it did, failed to ensure this protection.[9]

The judgment of the ECJ in the case of *Bostock* was rather brief, which is, as will be explained, characteristic of the Court's judgments, especially under the preliminary reference procedure. It is therefore difficult to discover why the ECJ took this particular approach. There are several possible explanations which could be given, which are further examined throughout this chapter. One of them is that the ECJ may have followed the position taken by the Advocate General in this case. In the opinion of Advocate General Gulman, it had been argued that Community law had actually intentionally granted wide discretion to the member states to implement the regime and to make arrangements to protect fundamental rights on the basis of their national laws.[10] Another possibility is that the ECJ had left the issue to be decided by the EU legislature. The ECJ may have wanted to avoid interfering in matters where the member states were competent to take action, thus respecting its subsidiary position in that regard.

7.2.2. THE *CHATZI* CASE

The Court's more recent judgment in the case of *Chatzi* seems largely opposed to its approach in the case of *Bostock*.[11] *Prima facie*, the question at issue in this case seemed

---

6 Weiler & Lockhart (1995b), pp. 609–610.
7 ECJ 13 July 1989, C-5/88, *Wachauf*, para. 19.
8 See section 8.4.4.
9 Weiler & Lockhart (1995b), p. 617.
10 Opinion A-G Gulman in C-2/92, *Bostock*, para. 33. See also section 8.4.1.
11 ECJ 16 September 2010, C-149/10, *Chatzi*. For a further discussion of this case, see section 11.5.2.

a simple one to answer: does the right to parental leave under EU law entitle the parents of twins to a double period of leave?[12] Under an EU Directive, member states were required to ensure that the right to parental leave was guaranteed for a period of at least three months.[13] Further room was left to the member states to provide more extensive protection. The question referred to in the case of *Chatzi* came from a court in Greece where the period of parental leave for one child was fixed at nine months.

The ECJ ruled that the right to equal treatment needed to be taken into account in order to ensure the protection of the rights of parents of twins, and also provided further reasoning as to what that would entail. The Court clarified that:

> The Member States can ... define, subject to compliance with the minimum three-month threshold imposed by the Framework Agreement in respect of the duration of parental leave, the detailed temporal rules under which parental leave may be taken. This discretion means in particular that, when Member States decide to set a period of parental leave that is longer than the minimum period prescribed by the Framework Agreement, they can lay down adjustments to the rules for the case of successive births of children.
>
> It follows that the national legislature has wide freedom of action when establishing the parental leave regime that is applicable to parents of twins and enables them to receive treatment that takes due account of their particular needs.
>
> In this regard, it should be stated that, generally, a duration appreciably longer than the minimum duration prescribed by the Framework Agreement and a certain degree of flexibility granted to the parents to take the leave on the basis of the age of the child are such as to make it easier to deal with the increased burdens connected with bringing up twins. Likewise, detailed implementing rules which, in accordance with paragraph 6 of the general considerations in the Framework Agreement, make substantial provision for flexible ways of organising work are such as to facilitate reconciliation of the requirements of work and the particular constraints that bringing up twins involves.
>
> However, it is also possible to conceive of and adopt other measures that are appropriate for the purpose of meeting the particular needs of the parents of twins, such as material assistance, in the form, for example, of a right of access to childcare centres, or financial aid, in the form, inter alia, of specific benefits allowing the method of care to be freely chosen.
>
> It is for the national court, which has sole jurisdiction to assess the facts of the dispute before it, to determine whether the body of national rules offers sufficient possibilities to meet, in a specific case, the particular needs of the parents of twins in their work and family life.
>
> In view of the foregoing considerations, the answer to the second question is that clause 2.1 of the Framework Agreement is not to be interpreted as requiring the birth of twins to confer entitlement to a number of periods of parental leave equal to the number of children born. However, read in the light of the principle of equal treatment, this clause obliges the national

[12] ECJ 16 September 2010, C-149/10, *Chatzi*, para. 75.

[13] Clause 2.1 of the framework Agreement on 14 December 1995 parental leave, set out in the annex to Directive 96/34/EC of 3 June 1996 on the framework agreement on parental leave concluded by UNICE, CEEP and the ETUC [1996] OJ L145/4.

> legislature to establish a parental leave regime which, according to the situation obtaining in the Member State concerned, ensures that the parents of twins receive treatment that takes due account of their particular needs. It is incumbent upon national courts to determine whether the national rules meet that requirement and, if necessary, to interpret those national rules, so far as possible, in conformity with European Union law.[14]

Hence, in contrast to *Bostock*, the ECJ in *Chatzi* made clear that there does exist a positive obligation for the national legislature to protect the right of equal treatment of parents of twins. The ECJ even rather elaborately explained what type of measures could be taken by the member states. Once again, however, this has invited some criticism, but of a different nature. The measures required by the judgment, it has been argued, would actually seem to fall within the scope of a more extensive protection that may voluntarily be provided by the member states at national level, and this would have justified a more deferential approach by the ECJ.[15] Chapter 11 will discuss the tension between this judgment and the limited powers of the EU in the field of fundamental rights protection.[16]

The question to be addressed in the present chapter, however, is what other factors might explain and justify this rather generous approach of the ECJ? In *Chatzi* it could have been that the ECJ was intent on providing an effective protection of fundamental rights, and wanted to play a stronger role in that field. Secondly, the uniform and effective application of EU law could have provided an interest which the ECJ was especially eager to protect. The direct imposition of a positive obligation on the national legislature instead of on the court is *prima facie* difficult to reconcile with the role that the ECJ is expected to play in the preliminary reference procedure; however, there have also been other examples of this more 'intrusive' approach, mainly where the uniform application and effectiveness of EU law was at stake.

7.3. THE ROLE AND JUDICIAL STYLE OF THE ECJ IN GENERAL

As can be gleaned from the two cases discussed above, the ECJ is not given the task only of providing an interpretation of fundamental rights. It inevitably also must do so in conjunction with provisions of EU primary or secondary law.[17] The ECJ must, in accordance with Article 19(1) TEU, ensure that 'in the interpretation and application of the Treaties the law is observed'. The EU Treaties and the various instruments of secondary

14 ECJ 16 September 2010, C-149/10, *Chatzi*, paras 70–75.
15 See De Mol (2012), pp. 28–29; and Muir (2013), p. 90.
16 See section 11.5.2.
17 Therefore, Article 51 of the Charter also requires there to be a connection to EU law in the application of EU fundamental rights, which is discussed in section 6.7. and chapter 9. Scholars also stress that it is important for the ECJ to take into account the choices which the EU legislature has already made in the field of fundamental rights protection, see Muir (2013), pp. 78–79 and 85.

law, such as Directives and Regulations, primarily, or in most cases, contribute to the functioning of the EU internal market or the area of freedom of security and justice without internal frontiers. The ECJ is competent to determine whether and how the EU institutions and the member states must comply with EU law, and it assesses the validity of EU law. The primary subjects of the judgments of the ECJ are the EU institutions and the EU member states and their courts. Although individuals are also regarded as important subjects of EU law, following from the establishment of the principle of direct effect that allows individuals to invoke EU law directly before their national courts, the ECJ does not often address individuals or their complaints directly.[18] Thus, the ECJ deals with quite different audiences and different subject matters compared to any other supranational court.

The role of the ECJ in shaping EU law is generally accepted to be an important one. The ECJ has *inter alia* developed the principles of direct effect and supremacy, which are considered foundational for the character and the effects of EU law.[19] Also, the ECJ has always played a crucial part in securing the Community's (main) objective, of achieving economic integration. In the field of the free movement rights, in particular, the ECJ has been willing to interpret concepts such as those of workers and services very broadly, and has quite easily accepted that the requirement of a trans-border movement would be fulfilled.[20] Such case-law has helped to expand the scope of EU law and its influence at national law considerably.[21] The economic free movement rules have been regarded by the ECJ as 'fundamental' rights or freedoms in themselves.[22] While this would seem to lead to the conclusion that the ECJ is mainly interested in economic integration, this would be a misconception.[23] The ECJ has also played an important role in achieving other goals, including the protection of fundamental rights, even if this would put the economic interests of the EU at risk (see section 7.6.).[24]

The important judgments of the ECJ in these different fields are not always very elaborately reasoned. The judgments of the ECJ have been characterised as 'short, tense and magisterial' or, put in a more negative way, as 'Cartesian' or 'cryptic and apodictic'.[25] This may make it difficult to find out what rationales and theories the ECJ actually uses to base its judgments on. The allegedly minimalistic style of reasoning of the ECJ also stands in stark contrast to the approach of the ECtHR, which elaborates in a much more detailed fashion what may be required to ensure the effective protection of the Convention provisions.[26] In its judgments, the ECJ generally relies on a 'linguistic,

18 Individuals may, moreover, become the subject of EU law by the adoption of decisions that could be of direct concern to them, see section 7.4.2.
19 Lenaerts (2013), pp. 1307–1308.
20 Prechal, De Vries & Van Eijken (2011), pp. 219–226.
21 Lenaerts (2013), pp. 1308–1309.
22 ECJ 12 June 2003, C-112/00, *Schmidberger*, para. 51.
23 Cf. Coppel & O'Neill (1992).
24 ECJ 14 October 2004, C-36/02, *Omega*.
25 Weiler (2001), p. 225; and Weiler (2013), p. 250.
26 See further De Búrca (2013).

systemic/constitutional and purposive' method of interpreting EU law. It rarely has regard to, for example, historical interpretation.[27]

The ECJ's brief and formal way of reasoning can partly be explained by the fact that the ECJ delivers its judgments in a collegiate fashion. To the dissatisfaction of some, there is no system of concurring or dissenting opinions, so that the judgments are written as if the ECJ only has one voice.[28] The ECJ must find consensus among all of the judges that have been assigned to a case. This implies that the rulings of the ECJ only consist of the very essential part to which all the judges were able to agree to.[29] Sometimes, the judgments of the ECJ do reflect that there are different views on a particular matter, for example when the judgment includes some of the viewpoints that have been submitted by the parties and the intervening parties to a case. The parties to the case (such as those before the national courts), the member states, and the EU institutions may submit written and oral observations.[30] Generally one would not, however, find non-governmental organisations represented in the procedures before the ECJ, as there is no general procedure which allows such third party intervention.[31] This may restrict the types of arguments that are presented to and dealt with by the ECJ in fundamental rights cases. It may therefore be the case that possibilities to define positive obligations to protect fundamental rights could escape the attention of the ECJ, seeing that it deals with different types of parties and different types of arguments.

The ECJ is advised by the opinions of Advocates General on its cases, which means that the EU system of adjudication can be characterised as a bifurcated system.[32] Advocates General deliver their opinions on a case prior to the judgment of the ECJ, and they are meant to assist the ECJ in its task of adjudication.[33] The ECJ often follows the judgments of the Advocates General, although there are also some noticeable exceptions to that rule.[34] In comparison to the judgments of the ECJ, the opinions of Advocates General are written in a much more elaborate fashion. They tend to provide the bigger picture as regards the underlying legal issues of a case, and they can be of a much more academic nature. The opinions of the Advocates Generals can be informative to the ECJ with regard to, for example, relevant legal doctrines, its own prior case-law or rather judgments from other courts, the arguments that were provided by the (intervening) parties during the oral or written hearings, and even sometimes the factual aspects of a

27 See Beck (2012), p. 6.

28 There have been some calls upon the Court to introduce a system of concurring or dissenting opinions within the ECJ, see J. Weiler (2013), p. 252; and De Búrca (2013).

29 Lenaerts (2013), pp. 1350–1351.

30 Article 23 of the Statute of the Court of Justice of the European Union.

31 Carrera & Petkova (2013), pp. 262–236. Carrera & Petkova explain that such intervention allows for further expertise to be brought to the Court as well as provide evidence and monitoring of fundamental rights violations for the ECJ.

32 Lasser (2004), p. 17. Cf. Bobek (2012).

33 Article 252 TFEU.

34 A notable example is the opinion of A-G Sharpston in C-34/09, *Zambrano*, where a broader scope of application of EU fundamental rights was advocated.

case. It is interesting to find that in these opinions, the doctrine of positive obligations has already been dealt with on several occasions.[35]

For the purposes of analyses such as that undertaken in the current study, it is generally of interest to have a look at the opinions of the Advocates Generals. They may provide for the theoretical underpinnings not expressed in the judgments of the ECJ itself, and they may also show additional arguments that have been brought by the different parties to a case. They may thus explain, for example, why the ECJ decided not to deal with the doctrine of positive obligations itself. In the case of *Bostock*, for example, the Advocate General had provided quite an elaborate argumentation as to why the ECJ would not need to recognise a positive obligation under Community law. The Advocate General had argued that there were sufficient mechanisms provided for at national level to secure that the right to property was protected.[36] Such opinions can often compensate for the deficits that can be experienced in the terse and formal reasoning of the ECJ.[37] It is important to mention, however, that in recent years, the role of Advocates General has been restricted. Changes have been made to enable the ECJ to cope with its workload and to deliver its judgments much more swiftly than it has done in the past (preliminary rulings on average taking 15 months).[38] These new regulations also allow for the ECJ to dispense with the opinions of the Advocates General in certain types of cases,[39] and in recent years it has frequently made use of this possibility.[40]

From this general characterisation of the judicial style of the ECJ and its specific judicial system, it can be seen why a theory of positive obligations would not necessarily be found in the case-law of the ECJ. The main focus of the ECJ is on interpreting specific provisions of secondary EU law, and it does not reason only on the basis of fundamental rights provisions. Its judicial style of reasoning is terse, which may also explain why the judgments do not clearly reveal whether the ECJ recognises a positive obligation or not.

---

35 See Opinion AG Gulmann. in C-2/92, *Bostock*; Opinion AG Tesauro in C-13/94, *P. v. S. and Cornwall County Council* (legal recognition and dismissal of transsexual employees); Opinion AG Kokott in C-540/03, *Parliament v. Council* (protection of the right to family life), paras 65–70; Opinion Trstenjak in C-282/10, *Dominguez*, paras 65 ff.; Opinion AG Jääskinen, in C-4/11, *Puid*, paras 60–63; Opinion AG Trstenjak in C-245/11, *K* (prevention of inhuman or degrading treatment), para. 70; Opinion AG Bot in C-300/11, ZZ; Opinion AG Sharpston in C-58/12, *Group Gascogne*, para. 118; Opinion AG Jääskinen in C-131/12, *Google Spain*, paras 119 and 134; Opinion AG Cruz Villalón. in C-176/12, *AMS*, paras 36 ff.

36 See also section 8.4.1.

37 Lasser (2004), p. 112.

38 Court of Justice of the European Union, Annual Report 2014, completed on 1 January 2015, pp. 9 and 88.

39 Article 20 of the Statute of the Court of Justice.

40 Cf. Court of Justice of the European Union, Annual Report 2014, completed on 1 January 2015, p. 8–9; See also Court of Justice of the European Union, Annual report 2015 judicial activity, completed on 1 January 2016, p. 10. In 2015, 43 per cent of the judgments of the ECJ were delivered without the opinion of an Advocate-General.

7.4. THE SPECIFIC CHARACTERISTICS OF THE PROCEDURES BEFORE THE ECJ

To be able to understand the style of reasoning of the ECJ further, it is of great importance also to look at the specific procedures which are used to bring fundamental rights challenges to the ECJ. It is especially of interest to take a closer look at the preliminary reference procedure, which is the main procedure through which the ECJ deals with issues related to fundamental rights.[41] This procedure can provide room for the national courts to decide about how the protection of EU law will best be secured within the national legal system, which means that the ECJ does not necessarily need to provide specific details on how fundamental rights would need to be protected, and what measures need to be taken. It is also of interest to look at the annulment procedure which can be started by individuals in quite limited circumstances to challenge fundamental rights protection, which, for that reason, will only briefly be discussed.

There are other procedures available under law EU law to challenge infringements of EU law which will not be discussed in much detail in this research. This includes the infringement procedure which the European Commission can initiate against member states if they fail to protect fundamental rights in the implementation of EU law. On some occasions the European Commission has initiated this procedure for that reason.[42] Also, the European Parliament can raise questions concerning the lack of fundamental rights protection, ultimately before the ECJ, if it finds that fundamental rights have not sufficiently been taken into account in certain legislative processes.[43] Lastly, it is interesting to note that the EU Treaties provide for a procedure which can be used by the EU institutions as well as the member states regarding the omissions of (other) EU institutions.[44] This could become of concern in relation to a lack of compliance with any positive obligations to protect fundamental rights. At the same time, it may prove difficult to fulfil the conditions to start this procedure, and it is rarely used.[45] For that reason, this procedure is not further considered in this chapter.

Another important aspect is that the ECJ has only limited jurisdiction to review the actions of the EU in the area of common, foreign and security policy on the basis of

---

41 European Commission, 2014 report on the application of the EU Charter of Fundamental Rights, pp. 160–176.

42 See European Commission, 2015 Report on the application of the EU Charter of Fundamental Rights, SWD(2016), 158 final, pp. 9–10. This report shows that the Commission has *inter alia* launched infringement procedures over the independence of the Hungarian data protection authority and the forced retirement of judges in Hungary; however, it also shows that the Commission did not clearly do so on fundamental rights grounds, see ECJ 6 November 2012, C-286/12, *Commission v. Hungary*; and ECJ 8 April 2014, C-288/12, *Commission v. Hungary*.

43 Cf. ECJ 27 June 2006, C-540/03, *Parliament v. Council*.

44 Article 265 TFEU.

45 This procedure first requires a request to be sent to one of the EU institutions to act before the ECJ can be requested to decide on the legality of the omission, and it requires that a specific obligation laid down by EU law can be identified. See also Craig & De Búrca (2015), pp. 537–539.

Article 275 TFEU. The Court has jurisdiction, however, to review restrictive measures taken against individuals in this area, such as the sanctioning measures which the EU has taken in attempts to combat terrorist activities and nuclear proliferation. This is addressed in section 7.4.2.

7.4.1. THE PRELIMINARY REFERENCE PROCEDURE

7.4.1.1. The Specific Function of the Preliminary Reference Procedure

Under the preliminary reference procedure, national courts can, and in some situations must, on the basis of Article 267 TFEU, refer questions to the ECJ on the interpretation of EU law and/or on the validity of acts of secondary EU law.[46] The effective functioning of the preliminary reference procedure is based on a system of cooperation between the national courts and the ECJ in which both have their own tasks.[47] Whereas national courts must ensure that EU law is applied correctly at national level, the ECJ has the prerogative of determining how EU law must be interpreted and of assessing the validity of the acts of the EU institutions. Article 267 TFEU stipulates that if questions are raised on the interpretation or validity of EU law before the national courts, and the answer to such questions is considered necessary to enable them to give a judgment, they may request the ECJ to give an answer to such questions. While there is discretion for the lower courts to make a reference to the ECJ, courts of last instance of the member states (against which there is no judicial remedy under national law) are obliged to do so. A further interpretation of the scope of the discretion of the lower courts, as well as of the scope of the obligation of the courts of last instance, is provided by the case-law of the ECJ.[48] National courts do not need to make a reference for a preliminary ruling when the ECJ has already provided an interpretation of a specific matter (*acte éclairé*), nor do they need to make a reference if the correct application of EU law 'may be so obvious as to leave no scope for any reasonable doubt as to the manner in which the question raised is to be resolved' (*acte clair*).[49]

The preliminary reference procedure is of great importance for the ECJ to be able to ensure the uniform and effective application of EU law at national level.[50] This procedure is also important for the ECJ to ensure that fundamental rights are interpreted in a uniform way and to ensure the effective protection of fundamental rights within the scope of EU law. From the very brief explanation of how the preliminary reference

---

46 See in general Broberg & Fenger (2014).

47 ECJ 6 October 1982, C-283/81, *Cilfit*, para. 7.

48 ECJ 6 October 1982, C-283/81, *Cilfit*, paras 10–20; and ECJ 27 March 1963, Joined cases C-28/62 to 30/62, *Da Costa*.

49 ECJ 6 October 1982, C-283/81, *Cilfit*, para. 16. More recently, the ECJ has refined the concept of *acte clair* in the case of *Ferreira da Silva*, see ECJ 9 September 2015, C-160/14, *Ferreira da Silva*.

50 Cf. Lenaerts (2013), pp. 1342–1350.

procedure works, it may already be clear, however, that the effective functioning of the preliminary reference procedure is dependent on a good relationship between the ECJ and the national courts.[51] National courts must be willing to bring relevant cases to the ECJ which would allow it to, for example, develop a concept of positive obligations under EU law.

7.4.1.2. The Dialogue with the National Courts

The preliminary reference procedure is based on a dialogue between the ECJ and the national courts.[52] If national courts refrain from referring questions to the ECJ, it may not be able to guarantee that EU law is interpreted uniformly at national level. The ECJ must thus ensure that it gives useful answers to the questions which are raised by the national courts, but not interfere too much in matters which the national courts are competent to resolve on the basis of national law. The subsidiary position of the ECJ *vis-à-vis* the member states (including their national courts) is more generally explained in section 7.5.2. National courts therefore also have an important role to play in bringing questions to the ECJ over the application of the doctrine of positive obligations in relevant areas of EU law.[53] Individuals may suggest in the national procedure that a preliminary question would be useful, but it is ultimately up to the national courts to decide about this.[54]

The ECJ is generally intent to answer only the questions raised by the national courts. In fact, as will also be discussed below, the ECJ is not inclined to take into account provisions of fundamental rights if it is not expressly invited to do so by the national courts; it rather aims to base its answer on provisions of primary and secondary EU law.[55] Generally, it seems that the degree of precision of the questions that are posed by the national courts, and the factual and legal guidance they may offer, are determinative for the level of detail of the answers given by the ECJ to those questions.[56] In the *Bostock* case, for example, the ECJ provided little more than a straightforward answer to the question that had been referred, and it was up to the national court to figure out how fundamental rights protection would have to be provided. In recent years, it has been

---

51 ECJ 6 October 1982, C-283/81, *Cilfit*, para. 7.

52 Cf. Bobek (2013).

53 It must be noted, however, that member states can incur liability if the national courts have interpreted EU law incorrectly, see ECJ 30 September 2003, C-224/01, *Köbler*. A further critical characterisation of the relations between the national courts and the ECJ under the preliminary reference procedure is given by Bobek, see Bobek (2013).

54 According to the case-law of the ECtHR, national (highest) courts must motivate their refusals to refer preliminary questions to ensure the protection of the right to a fair trial, see ECtHR 8 April 2014, no.17120/09, *Dhahbi v. Italy*. The ECJ has recognised that individuals do have an important role to play to protect fundamental rights before their national courts, see ECJ 5 February 1963, C-26/62, *Van Gend en Loos*, para. 24. See also section 7.6.2.2.

55 Lenaerts (2013), p. 1309.

56 Lenaerts (2013), p. 1344.

seen that national courts are increasingly raising questions on the application and interpretation of fundamental rights.[57] Although this could be seen as an invitation to further detail the interpretation of such fundamental rights, the answers of the ECJ to these questions may still be rather formal and brief.

Given that the preliminary reference procedure is characterised by cooperation between the ECJ and the national courts, the ECJ may decide to leave specific questions as to the application of its judgment to be resolved at the level of the national courts. In addition, the ECJ also often seems intent on answering only the particular legal problem that has been laid out in the specific case before it, rather than providing general principles that can be applied in other cases as well.[58] Lenaerts has explained that a certain 'judicial prudence' underlies this approach. The ECJ will wait until further questions reach the Court instead of addressing potentially difficult legal questions which may not be solved beforehand.[59]

Taking all this into account, it seems hard to explain the ECJ's judgment in the case of *Chatzi*.[60] Without being asked to do so directly by the national court, the ECJ there provided instructions to the national legislature on how the framework agreement would have to implemented in order to be faithful to the principle of equal treatment.[61] Indeed, this was an exceptional case: the ECJ very rarely gives such a direct task to the national legislature. It may only be speculated why the ECJ rendered the judgment it did. Perhaps the ECJ considered that it would be best for the national legislatures to ensure that discrimination in an important field of EU law would be prohibited, rather than having the national courts seeking for other solutions (judicially or administratively) to accommodate the judgment of the ECJ. However, it does not seem to fit well with the character of the preliminary reference procedure as the Court has developed it in its case-law.

Chatzi is also a-typical since the ECJ generally has been much more willing to impose quite far-reaching obligations on the national courts instead of the national legislatures. Several of the positive (procedural) obligations which it has imposed are discussed in chapter 11.[62] National courts have *inter alia* been required to set national provisions aside if they conflict with such fundamental rights and read national law in conformity with EU fundamental rights.[63]

---

57 European Union Agency for Fundamental Rights, Fundamental Rights Report 2016, FRA rapport, p. 39; and European Commission, 2015 Report on the application of the EU Charter, p. 10.

58 Lenaerts (2013), pp. 1355–1356.

59 Lenaerts (2013), p. 1356.

60 See section 7.2.2.

61 ECJ 16 September 2010, C-149/10, *Chatzi*, para. 75.

62 See section 11.3.2.

63 See ECJ 26 June 2007, C-305/05, *Ordre des barreaux francophone and germanophone and others*, para. 28; C-275/06, *Promusicae*, paras 68 and 70; ECJ 19 November 1991, C-6/90, *Francovich*, paras 31–37; and ECJ 16 February 2012, C-182/10, *Solvay*, para. 49. In horizontal disputes, see ECJ 22 November 2005, C-144/04, *Mangold*, para. 77; ECJ 19 January 2010, C-555/07, *Kücükdeveci*, para. 51; and ECJ 25 July 1991, C-208/90, *Emmott*, paras 21–23.

It can thus be concluded that the scope for a development of positive obligations will generally depend on the degree to which national courts specifically inquire about such issues at the Court. If asked by the national courts, the ECJ does seem willing to determine the solutions which must be provided at national level to ensure the effective application of fundamental rights. In the area of national procedural rules and remedies, it can be seen that the case-law of the ECJ is more elaborate and more detailed because the national courts have referred many questions.[64] In response to these, the ECJ has been willing to provide guidance on the requirements that follow from EU law. In other cases, the ECJ may not be asked specifically what the requirements may be, and perhaps some form of positive obligations would need to be fulfilled at national level. In such cases, it may rather be for the national courts to determine whether certain measures need to be taken by the legislative or administrative authorities to ensure the effective application of EU law.

7.4.2. DIRECT ACTIONS

There are fewer occasions in which individuals directly challenge EU acts or omissions directly before the ECJ. The relative rareness of this has to do with the criteria that have to be met by individuals in order to have *locus standi* before the ECJ based on Article 263 TFEU and which have been interpreted restrictively by the ECJ.[65] Individuals can challenge acts that are addressed to them, but they must be directly and individually concerned to be able to challenge legislative acts such as directives and regulations.[66] The latter do not constitute 'regulatory acts' for which the standing rights have been strengthened by the Lisbon Treaty, and which require individuals only to be directly concerned.[67]

Cases have been brought to the ECJ on alleged fundamental rights infringements by individuals in one area in particular. These are complaints that have been brought by individuals in relation to the sanction decisions which have been imposed on individuals who are considered to be affiliated to terroristic organisations, who have been associated with nuclear proliferation, or who have connections with certain governments that have been overthrown. The various judgments in the *Kadi* cases, in particular, have brought to light some of the serious shortcomings in the procedures that generally lead up to the adoption of such sanction decisions.[68] In this connection, the ECJ has quite actively developed a number of principles and procedures that would

[64] See also section 11.3.2. for examples of procedural positive obligations imposed by the ECJ on the member states.

[65] Fourth indent of Article 263 TFEU.

[66] See ECJ 15 July 1963, C-25/62, *Plaumann v. Commission of the EEC.*

[67] See ECJ 3 October 2013, C-583/11, *P Inuit Tapiriit Kanatami and others*, paras 58–59.

[68] ECJ 3 September 2008, Joined cases C-402/05 P and C-41/05 P, *Kadi and Al Barakaat*; and ECJ 18 July 2013, C-584/10 P, *Commission and others v. Kadi.*

need to be complied with by relevant institutions competent to take such decisions. Indeed, in this area the ECJ may be said to have developed quite a number of positive procedural obligations.[69]

The direct actions that are brought before the ECJ are by their very nature far more restrictive in comparison to the individual complaint procedure as is provided for under the Convention system. Greer and Williams find that this provides limited opportunities for social justice institutions or suffering individuals to actually bring their complaints before the ECJ.[70] Serious fundamental rights infringements are therefore not likely to reach the ECJ through direct actions.

It is much more common for fundamental rights issues to be raised before the ECJ via the preliminary reference procedure, and it is usually through this procedure that fundamental rights issues of individuals may be addressed by the ECJ, although in a more indirect way.[71] In that respect, there is a greater potential for a development of positive obligations under the preliminary reference procedure.

7.5. THE INSTITUTIONAL POSITION OF THE ECJ

7.5.1. SEPARATION OF POWERS AND THE SUPRANATIONAL POSITION OF THE ECJ

An examination of the development of positive obligations by the ECJ must take account of the specific function that courts generally exercise in modern democracies governed by the rule of law. If it would appear that the effective protection of fundamental rights requires far-reaching legislative or burdensome obligations to be fulfilled, this may be best decided by political institutions rather than by courts, let alone supranational courts.[72] Political institutions directly enjoy the legitimacy to take decisions on those matters, at EU level as well as at national level. Where judicial decisions would amount to the 'exercise of decision-making power', the ECJ could easily be accused of judicial activism.[73] In its relation with the national authorities, the supranational position of the ECJ could provide even greater reason for the ECJ to exercise caution in examining what the effective protection of EU law would require, as it could be at too great a distance to be able to adequately judge such situations.[74] The principle of subsidiarity thereby clearly is also involved, as was briefly addressed in section 7.4.1.2., but for the present context it relates to the constitutional division of powers in a democracy. In relation to the development of positive obligations, the ECJ may want to refrain from

69 See section 11.3.1.
70 Greer & Williams (2009), pp. 476–477.
71 See also 25 July 2002, C-50/00, *Unión de Pequeños Agricultores v. Council*, para. 42.
72 Cf. the discussions in sections 4.4. and 4.5. of part I.
73 De Búrca (1998), p. 230.
74 Muir (2014a), p. 243; De Búrca (1998), p. 219.

specifying too clearly what measures need to be established by the EU institutions or by the member states to effectively protect fundamental rights from the viewpoint of the principle of separation of powers (see section 7.5.2.) and also, for the national authorities, the principle of subsidiarity (see section 7.5.3.). The specific meaning of the principle of subsidiarity in relation to the proper distribution of competences between the EU and the member states is later discussed in chapter 8.[75]

The intensity of the ECJ's review more generally, thus with respect to the actions of the EU institutions and the member state, can also depend on the area of EU law that is at stake. Various scholars, such as Gerards and Craig, have noted that when it comes, for example, to the protection of the Treaty's free movement rules, the ECJ has been willing to examine quite carefully the reasonableness or the appropriateness of the decisions that were taken by the member states.[76] The ECJ has even be willing to exercise strict review of the member states' interferences with fundamental rights.[77] The ECJ could also take a step further and clarify what government action would be necessary to protect fundamental rights effectively in such areas. It must be acknowledged here, however, that the ECJ has yet to develop a very clear theory as to the intensity levels of its review.[78] It can be quite difficult to assess beforehand whether the ECJ will exercise strong or weaker forms of judicial review in specific cases. The approach of the ECJ in the field of fundamental rights, specifically, has, in the past, been characterised as one of great restraint.[79] However, more recently, the ECJ has shown that it is indeed willing to provide interpretation of fundamental rights in areas where it is much needed, and it has been willing to strike down EU legislation for violations of fundamental rights.[80] The more general roles played by the EU and the ECJ in the specific area of fundamental rights are discussed in section 7.6.

7.5.2. THE ROLE OF THE ECJ TOWARDS THE EU INSTITUTIONS

The ECJ has been said generally to exercise deferential review with respect to the legislative decisions that are taken by the EU institutions.[81] The ECJ has declared on various occasions that it would respect the discretionary powers which were given to the EU legislature on issues involving political, economic, social and technical questions, and therefore restricted its own review.[82] The ECJ is not easily willing to

75 See section 8.4.3.
76 Gerards (2011a), p. 91.
77 Gerards (2011a), p. 100.
78 Gerards (2011a), p. 90.
79 Besson (2011a), p. 116.
80 See e.g. ECJ 6 October 2015, C-362/14, *Schrems*.
81 De Búrca (1993), p. 146; and Gerards (2011a), p. 97.
82 ECJ 10 December 2002, C-491/01, *Britisch American Tobacco (Investments) and Imperial Tobacco*, para. 741; ECJ 8 June 2010, C-58/08, *Vodafone and others*, para. 52; and ECJ 22 May 2014, C-356/12, *Glatzel*, paras 52 and 64.

annul EU legislation that might be contrary to certain principles and rights laid down in the EU Treaties. In the past, the ECJ has not shown itself ready to strongly engage in the protection of fundamental rights and to declare EU legislation void on grounds of fundamental rights.[83] Muir had explained that also, more recently, the ECJ has not decided to annul EU legislation on the basis of incompatibility with fundamental rights, especially because EU legislation had specifically been adopted to ensure an effective protection of fundamental rights in a certain area.[84]

The ECJ has, however, also shown that on some occasions, including in fundamental rights cases, it may exercise a more stringent review of EU legislation.[85] The ECJ has done so where an important EU interest was at stake,[86] where violations of important fundamental rights were to be prevented,[87] as well as where there was a particularly serious interference with a fundamental right.[88] The intensity of the review of the ECJ in cases of EU legislation may thus depend on different factors.

A deferential type of review by the ECJ can, first of all, mean that the ECJ does not undertake an elaborate or full substantive assessment of EU legislation.[89] The ECJ will have regard to the specific choices that have already been made by the EU legislature, and it will only intervene if the measure that has been chosen is manifestly inappropriate in view of the objective which is pursued by that measure.[90] In fundamental rights cases, it can also been seen that the ECJ has regard to the specific recitals in the preamble of Directives and Regulations which reflect the wishes of the political institutions, and it does not further develop fundamental rights standards of its own.[91]

Interestingly, the ECJ has some other ways of showing a deferential review towards the EU institutions, which allow room for a development of positive obligations to protect fundamental rights. This includes a 'reconciliatory interpretation' and a procedural

---

83 See Coppel & O'Neill (1992). *Opinion 2/94* is sometimes regarded an example of where the Court deliberately provided discretion towards the political institutions of the EU and the member states on deciding over the desirability of the accession of the EU to the Convention. In this opinion the ECJ decided that the accession of the EU to the Convention was not compatible with EU law due to a lack of competence of the EU to protect field of fundamental rights, see ECJ 28 March 1996, *Opinion 2/94*.

84 Muir (2013), p. 95.

85 See Craig (2012), p. 424; and Gerards (2011a), p. 100.

86 ECJ 18 July 2013, C-584/10, *Commission and others v. Kadi*, para. 66 (concerning the protection of the rule of law).

87 Cf. ECJ 5 April 2016, Joined cases C-404/15 and C-659/15, *Aranyosi and Căldăraru*, paras 84–88; and ECJ 21 December 2011, Joined cases C-411/10 and C-493/10, *N.S. and others*, para. 84. See also Gerards (2011a), p. 100.

88 ECJ 8 April 2014, C-293/12, *Digital Rights Ireland*, para. 48.

89 The judgment of the ECJ in the case of *Sky Österreich* is a notable example, however, of a full substantive review in light of the proportionality principle laid down in Article 52(1) of the Charter, see ECJ 22 January 2013, C-283/11, *Sky Österreich*.

90 ECJ 10 December 2002, C-491/01, *Britisch American Tobacco (Investments) and Imperial Tobacco*, para. 741; ECJ 8 June 2010, C-58/08, *Vodafone and others*, para. 52; and ECJ 22 May 2014, C-356/12, *Glatzel*, paras 52 and 64.

91 Muir (2013), p. 86.

type of review. The 'reconciliatory interpretation' has been explained by Lenaerts as follows:

> in order to safeguard the legitimate objectives pursued by the EU legislator, the ECJ will first do everything within its jurisdiction to interpret secondary EU law in accordance with primary EU law. It follows that, in so far as the ECJ does not interpret secondary EU law in a *contra legem* fashion, the annulment or declaration of invalidity of an act adopted by the EU legislator operates as the *ultima ratio* in order to uphold the rule of law.[92]

Thus, according to Lenaerts, the annulment of EU legislation is generally not a helpful outcome of judicial review. Instead, and preferably, the ECJ could provide fundamental rights protection by further interpreting EU legislation in such a way that it also or still accommodates for the protection of fundamental rights. This technique may, as Muir has explained, either constrain or complement the actions that need to be taken on the basis of EU legislation.[93] Muir points to the case of *Chatzi* as an example of where the ECJ applied 'an interpretative technique tying the legislature's hands'.[94] In this case, as has been explained, the ECJ decided to interpret the provision of EU secondary legislation in such a way that it imposed a positive duty on the national legislature to ensure the effective protection of the principle of equal treatment. The ECJ held in this case that:

> under a general principle of interpretation, a Community measure must be interpreted as far as possible, in such a way as not to affect its validity and in conformity with primary law as a whole ..., including with the principle of equal treatment.[95]

Thus, this reconciliatory interpretation technique would seem to allow for the ECJ to develop certain positive obligations.

Several scholars have noted that the judgment of the ECJ in the case of *N.S. and others* forms another case where the ECJ re-interpreted EU legislation to 'save' its validity. This case was about the transfer of asylum seekers to other member states.[96] Under the Dublin Regulation, member states are required to send asylum seekers to the member state in which they first arrived and which is responsible for dealing with the asylum application. In the case of *N.S. and others*, the ECJ held that the obligations of the member states under the EU Dublin Regulation must be read in light of the prohibition of inhuman and degrading treatment as guaranteed in Article 4 of the Charter.[97] This means that the member states and their national courts cannot transfer an asylum seeker under the Dublin Regulation where they cannot be unaware of the fact that in the member state

---

92 Lenaerts (2013), pp. 1310–1311; and cf. Weiler (2013).

93 Muir (2013), pp. 88–89.

94 Muir (2013), p. 88.

95 ECJ 16 September 2010, C-149/10, *Chatzi*, para. 43.

96 ECJ 21 December 2011, Joined cases C-411/10 and C-193/10, *N.S. and others*. For a discussion of this case, see also sections 6.8., 6.9.2., 9.3.2.3. and 11.5.2.

97 ECJ 21 December 2011, Joined cases C-411/10 and C-193/10, *N.S. and others*, para. 88.

of first arrival there is a serious risk of treatment which is contrary to Article 4 of the Charter.[98] Again, this amounts to a certain positive obligation for the member state to ensure fundamental rights protection, as discussed further in chapter 11.[99] The other choice which the ECJ could have made was to conclude that the EU legislature failed to secure an effective protection of fundamental rights by laying down the specific obligations for the member states in EU secondary legislation, and it could perhaps have declared the Regulation null and void. Instead, however, the ECJ decided to read the obligations of the member states under the Dublin Regulation in light of Article 4 ECHR, and thus compatible with this provision.

By developing positive obligations for the member states in cases such as *Chatzi* and *N.S. and others*, the ECJ actually aims to respect its position towards the EU institutions, and it still allows for an effective protection of fundamental rights. It may, indeed, be considered more intrusive if the ECJ were to establish that a certain (well-considered) decision was contrary to EU law on substantive points than if the ECJ restricted itself to merely defining what additional requirements may need to be fulfilled to effectively protect fundamental rights. Such additional requirements can be expected to be of an administrative, judicial and procedural nature. The development of legislative obligations in particular, however, could be considered to be too intrusive a method of interfering in the powers of the EU institutions.[100]

Secondly, the ECJ has applied a procedural type of review in its case-law on the legality of EU legislation. This technique focuses on the procedural shortcomings in the adoption of EU legislation rather than on substantive shortcomings as such, and thereby also aims to respect the deferential position of the ECJ *vis-à-vis* the EU legislature.[101] A clear example of procedural review by the ECJ is shown in the case of *Volker und Markus Schecke*.[102] This case was about the validity of a provision laid down in an EU Regulation which required member states to publish information on the beneficiaries of European agricultural funds, which included the publication of the amounts received by those beneficiaries, the names of the natural or the legal persons and their municipality and, if available, the postal code of residence. In reviewing the proportionality of this measure, the ECJ noted that:

> [t]here is nothing to show that, when adopting [the contested provision], the Council and the Commission sought to strike such a balance between the European Union's interest in guaranteeing the transparency of its acts and ensuring the best use of public funds, on the one hand, and the fundamental rights enshrined in Articles 7 and 8 of the Charter, on the other hand.[103]

---

98 ECJ 21 December 2011, Joined cases C-411/10 and C-193/10, *N.S. and others*, para. 94.

99 See section 11.5.3.

100 See also the criticism which has been raised regarding the development of positive obligations by the ECtHR in section 3.4.1.

101 Lenaerts (2013).

102 Joined cases C-92/09 and C-93/09, *Volker und Markus Schecke*, 9 November 2010.

103 Joined Cases C-92/09 and C-93/09, *Volker und Markus Schecke*, 9 November 2010, paras 80–81.

The ECJ thus specifically had regard to whether the EU legislature itself had aimed to ensure the protection of fundamental rights, and seeing that it had not, the ECJ decided to annul the respective EU Regulation.

In other cases, a procedural type of review can also be noticed.[104] An example is the case of *Schrems*, which concerned the decision of the European Commission which established that the United States provided an adequate level of protection of personal data on the basis of the use of the safe harbour principles.[105] This decision had the effect that the EU member states and their undertakings could transfer the personal data of EU citizens to the United States. The CJEU indicated in its judgment on this case that the Commission decision itself did not provide any clarity over whether there existed rules in the United States intended to limit interferences with the rights to privacy and of personal data, and to provide effective legal protection against such interferences.[106] The ECJ decided to annul the Commission decision and it stated that in order for the Commission to adopt its (next) decision 'it must find, duly stating reasons, that a third country in fact ensures, by reason of its domestic law or its international commitments a level of protection of fundamental rights essentially equivalent to that guaranteed under the EU legal order …' .[107] The ECJ thus sent a clear signal to the European Commission that it had failed to do its own work of making the assessment, and the ECJ specifically required the Commission to explain in its own decisions how it aimed to ensure compliance with fundamental rights.

As stated in the beginning of this section, the ECJ has also shown that it sometimes is willing to exercise a fuller review of EU legislation, including on grounds of fundamental rights. Especially where important fundamental rights are at stake, or where there are serious interferences with fundamental right, the ECJ may decide to exercise stronger review. The ECJ attributed quite some importance to the seriousness of the interference with a fundamental right in the case of *Digital Rights*, for example.[108] A similar approach is visible in the *Kadi* judgment, in which the ECJ established that there had been serious shortcomings in the protection of certain procedural fundamental rights; these seemed to provide a reason for the ECJ to exercise strong review of the measures taken by the competent EU authorities.[109] In those cases, the ECJ is also willing to move away from its generally brief and formal reasoning, and to explain what the effective protection of fundamental rights would specifically require. The last judgment in *Kadi* is, in fact, very elaborate and detailed as to the types of procedural protection which the EU institutions need to provide when they decide to impose a sanction on an individual. The ECJ thereby also established certain positive procedural obligations for the EU institutions.[110]

---

104 See further Beijer (2017).
105 ECJ 6 October 2015, C-362/14, *Schrems*.
106 ECJ 6 October 2015, C-362/14, *Schrems*, paras 88–89.
107 ECJ 6 October 2015, C-362/14, *Schrems*, para. 96.
108 ECJ 8 April 2014, C-293/12, *Digital Rights Ireland*, para. 37.
109 Craig (2012), p. 424; and Gerards (2011a), p. 100.
110 See section 11.3.1.

In sum, there are various approaches which the ECJ can take in its review of EU legislation. While it mainly applies a deferential review of EU legislation, as explained earlier, this may actually give rise to positive (procedural) obligations for the member states or for the EU institutions themselves.

7.5.3. THE ROLE OF THE ECJ TOWARDS THE MEMBER STATES

It is rather difficult to discern to what extent the ECJ deliberately aims to express its subsidiary position towards the national authorities. In this context the ECJ rarely specifies the intensity of its review and, perhaps, it is not really necessary to do so. After all, the preliminary reference procedure, which is primarily used to ensure the correct application and interpretation of EU law at national level, is organised in such a way that it aims to be respectful of the subsidiary position of the ECJ. In the field of fundamental rights protection, the ECJ will rarely provide an interpretation of specific provisions of fundamental rights that may be relevant to a case if it is not specifically asked to do so by the national court, which can be seen as an expression of its subsidiary position in this field.[111] As explained in section 7.4.1., national courts are only required to ask for a preliminary ruling by the ECJ if they consider that it would be necessary to solve the particular dispute that lays before it. National courts rather than the ECJ are thus primarily competent to apply EU law at national level and therefore establish whether or not national authorities may have violated EU (fundamental rights) law in the particular circumstances of a given case. The ECJ engages in a dialogue primarily with the national courts over the interpretation of EU law at national level, and may not tell the national legislatures or administrative authorities directly whether they have violated EU law. The example of *Chatzi* has (therefore) been described as an incidental example of where the ECJ did choose to develop a positive obligation expressly for the national legislature.

Over time, the ECJ has introduced some hierarchical elements in relation to national law and its application by the national authorities. By developing the principle of supremacy, for example, the ECJ has made very clear that EU law takes priority over any national law that might stand in conflict with it.[112] Furthermore, in some cases, the ECJ is willing to undertake a stricter assessment of the application of EU law at national level by determining whether certain measures fulfil the requirements of a proportionality test. This is particularly visible in the context of the free movement rights.[113] While the ECJ has thus developed a more active approach in ensuring the protection of EU law at national level, it may be necessary for the ECJ to seek additional

111 Besson (2011a), pp. 116–117.
112 Besson (2011a), p. 115.
113 See e.g. ECJ 12 June 2003, C-112/00, *Schmidberger*, para. 51; and see De Vries (2013), pp. 173 and 178–179.

ways to respect its subsidiary position and to refrain from delivering all too intrusive rulings. There is good reason for doing so, because the ECJ is ultimately dependent on the national courts to continue to send questions that will allow it to ensure the uniform and effective application of EU law.[114]

Perhaps for that reason, in the specific context of the protection of the free movement rights, the ECJ has shown that it is willing to apply a more deferential type of review. The Court appears to do so in particular if the national authorities are pursuing certain objectives concerning which there is no consensus within the EU.[115] The cases of *Omega* and *Sayn-Wittgenstein* have been indicated as clear examples of this approach. In the case of *Omega*, the German government was seeking to protect the right to human dignity as it is protected under the German constitution to justify a restriction of the freedom to provide services.[116] The ECJ held that 'it is not indispensable in that respect for the restrictive measure issued by the authorities of a Member State to correspond to a conception shared by all Member States as regards the precise way in which the fundamental right or legitimate interest is to be protected'.[117] Thereby, the ECJ allowed room to the member states to decide how they would ensure protection of this fundamental right under EU law, and it also exercised quite deferential review of the proportionality of the restriction of the free movement provision in this case. The ECJ applied a similar approach in the case of *Sayn-Wittgenstein*, which concerned the restrictive use of titles of nobility. In this case, the ECJ even more explicitly recognised that member states were granted a margin of appreciation.[118] The ECJ also paid attention to the protection of Article 4(2) TEU on the respect for national identity, which provides a clear basis for allowing member states discretion in the application of EU law at national level.[119] The ECJ did not exercise strict review over the restriction of the right to free movement, and concluded that the measure taken did not seem to constitute an unjustifiable interference with EU law.

Most of the questions on the Charter that are referred to the ECJ by the national courts are concerned with the protection of the (procedural) right to effective judicial protection and the right to good administration.[120] The ECJ has been willing to develop certain far-reaching procedural standards in response to those questions, such as the requirement that national courts need to provide for interim measures.[121] This active development of procedural standards may be regarded as problematic from the viewpoint of the limited powers of the EU in this area. It may also be said, however, that

---

114 National courts could still decide to restrict the supremacy of EU law at national level, see Gerards (2011a), pp. 82–85.

115 Gerards (2011a), pp. 94–96; Lenaerts (2013), p. 1327; and De Vries (2013), pp. 179–181.

116 ECJ 14 October 2004, C-36/02, *Omega*.

117 ECJ 14 October 2004, C-36/02, *Omega*, paras 30 and 37.

118 ECJ 22 December 2010, C-208/09, *Sayn-Wittgenstein*, paras 86–87.

119 ECJ 22 December 2010, C-208/09, *Sayn-Wittgenstein*, para. 92.

120 European Commission, Staff Working Document on the application of the EU Charter of Fundamental Rights in 2015, SWD(2016), 158 final, p. 9.

121 See section 11.3.2.

the ECJ has in fact developed an approach in its case-law which is very much respectful of the arrangements made at national level. The ECJ has developed case-law in which it has always stressed that it respects the principle of national procedural law, and only on a very few occasions has it required for the national courts or authorities to provide for new remedies or new procedural rules.[122] The ECJ could impose further requirements on the basis of the procedural rights which are protected under the Charter or it could develop clearer procedural positive obligations on the member states.[123] However, the ECJ so far continues to stress the principle of national procedural autonomy in its case-law and, therefore, it clearly aims to allow member states discretion within the context of the procedural protection of EU law.[124]

The case of *DEB* shows an interesting example of where the ECJ has had specific regard to whether there was consensus at the level of the member states concerning the protection of a specific procedural fundamental right.[125] In this case, the ECJ was required to determine whether the right to legal aid, as protected by Article 47(3) of the Charter had to be granted to legal persons as well as natural persons. The ECJ held that this provision 'must be interpreted in its context, in the light of other provisions of EU law, the law of the Member states and the case-law of the European Court of Human Rights'.[126] The ECJ recognised that the grant of legal aid to legal persons was not yet a common principle that was shared by all member states. Further, it pointed out that those member states which did recognise legal aid for legal persons made a distinction between profit-making and non-profit-making legal persons.[127] The ECJ further had regard to the case-law of the ECtHR on this issue, from which it could derive various factors that needed to be taken into account to determine whether legal aid would need to be granted, and it concluded that the grant of legal aid to legal persons is not in principle impossible.[128] The ECJ showed a very careful approach in this case, which was geared to discovering whether there was a consensus between the member states. It was ultimately left to the national court to apply the principles which the ECJ had set forth in its judgment.[129]

On the basis of this approach, the ECJ could decide in future cases to first look at whether there is a certain degree of consensus as to the existence of a certain types of positive obligation, before it will impose this obligation on its own. The ECJ can, of course, undertake its own comparative assessment in this respect, but it may also have regard to the case-law of the ECtHR, which can reveal whether a certain type of positive obligation can already be recognised. If there does not appear to be sufficient consensus, the ECJ could be expected to allow further discretion to the member states

122 See ECJ 13 March 2007, C-432/05, *Unibet*, para. 37.
123 Prechal & Widdershoven (2011), p. 41.
124 See recently, for example, ECJ 6 October 2015, C-61/14, *Orizzonte Salute*, paras 46–48.
125 ECJ 22 December 2010, C-279/09, *DEB*.
126 ECJ 22 December 2010, C-279/09, *DEB*, para. 37.
127 ECJ 22 December 2010, C-279/09, *DEB*, para. 44.
128 ECJ 22 December 2010, C-279/09, *DEB*, para. 52.
129 ECJ 22 December 2010, C-279/09, *DEB*, paras 60–61.

to provide for fundamental rights protection based on their own (higher) standards. The member states may do so, on the basis of the ruling of the ECJ in the case of *Melloni*, as long as this does not affect the primacy, unity and effectiveness of EU law.[130]

In some exceptional cases, the ECJ has also specifically allowed the member states discretion to provide fundamental rights protection on the basis of their national law and on the basis of the Convention. In the case of *Dereci*, for example, an important question that needed to be answered was whether the national rules on residence requirements fell within the scope of EU law and whether the EU's standards of fundamental rights thus needed to be applied.[131] The ECJ clarified that:

> if the referring court considers, in the light of the circumstances of the disputes in the main proceedings, that the situation of the applicants in the main proceedings is covered by European Union law, it must examine whether the refusal of their rights of residence undermines the right to respect for private and family life provided for in Article 7 of the Charter. On the other hand if it takes the view that the situation is not covered by European Union law, it must undertake the examination in light of Article 8(1) ECHR.[132]

The ECJ thus clearly left room to the national court to decide whether its questions fell within the scope of EU law, but it was also willing to add that there might be other grounds that could be used for fundamental rights protection, such as protection on the basis of the Convention.

The ECJ adopted a similar approach in the case of *Willems and others*.[133] This case was about the compatibility of the EU's Regulation on Biometric Passports with the right to privacy or the right to the protection of personal data as are guaranteed by Articles 7 and 8 of the Charter. This Regulation imposes a requirement on the member state to obtain and to store certain biometric data of individuals (such as their fingerprints) in order to issue passports.[134] The Regulation does not establish further specific rules on the use and storage of this biometric data by persons and authorities at the national level for purposes other than verifying the identity of indivuals, such as for the detection and prosecution of criminal offences. In the case of *Willems and others*, individuals had complained before their national courts about the lack of safeguards that were provided for the use of their biometric data by the national authorities. Several national courts referred questions to the ECJ on this issue, including the question whether, in order to ensure the protection of the right to privacy and the right to the protection of personal data, the member states would need to guarantee by law that the biometric data collected on the basis of that Regulation would indeed not be used and stored

130 ECJ 26 February 2013, C-399/11, *Melloni*, para. 60. See also sections 6.8. and 9.3.4.

131 ECJ 15 November 2011, C-256/11, *Dereci*.

132 ECJ 15 November 2011, C-256/11, *Dereci*, para. 72.

133 ECJ 16 April 2015, Joined cases C-446/12 to C-449/12, *Willems and others*.

134 Regulation 2252/2004 of 13 December 2004 on standards for security features and biometrics in passports and travel documents issued by Member States [2004] OJ L385/1 as amended by Regulation 444/2009 of 6 May 2009 [2009] OJ L142/1.

for purposes other than those established by the Regulation.[135] In its response to the preliminary questions the ECJ decided that the rules regarding the use and the storage of the biometric data fell outside of the scope of the Regulation, and that it formed part of the exclusive competence of the member states. The ECJ pointed out that it had been made explicit in a specific provision and a recital that the Regulation 'does not provide a legal base for setting up or maintaining databases for storage of those data in Member States, which is strictly a matter of national law'.[136] As a consequence of this judgment, a legislative obligation to ensure the protection of the right to privacy and the right to the protection of personal data in relation to the storage and use of the biometric data could not be derived on the basis of EU fundamental right provisions.

It is of interest to note, however, that, after the ECJ explained in the case of *Willems and others* that the issue which was raised fell outside the scope of EU law, it held that:

> the foregoing considerations are without prejudice to any examination by the national courts of the compatibility of all the national measures relating to the use and storage of biometric data with their national law and, if appropriate, with the European Convention on the Protection of Human Rights and Fundamental Freedoms ...[137]

Clarification such as this can help the ECJ to overcome criticisms that it is not taking fundamental rights seriously, while it at the same time pays respect to the division of powers between the EU and the member states.[138]

7.6. THE EU AND THE ECJ'S ROLE IN THE FIELD OF FUNDAMENTAL RIGHTS

The foregoing sections have illustrated how the ECJ may take different approaches towards fundamental rights cases, depending on various factors. This section aims to explain and discuss more specifically what role the ECJ generally plays in its protection of fundamental rights, as well as the role that it is expected to play by the member states and their national courts and also by scholars. First, a brief background sketch is given on the discussions of the EU as a potential human rights organisation, since this also could influence the position which the ECJ is expected to take in fundamental rights cases (section 7.6.1.). Subsequently, the evolving role of the ECJ in the field of fundamental rights protection is explored in more detail (section 7.6.2.).

---

135 ECJ 16 April 2015, Joined cases C-446/12 to C-449/12, *Willems and others*, para. 24.

136 ECJ 16 April 2015, Joined cases C-446/12 to C-449/12, *Willems and others*, paras 47–50. See Article 4(3), and in particular recital no. 5 of the Regulation.

137 ECJ 16 April 2015, Joined cases C-446/12 to C-449/12, *Willems and others*, para. 51.

138 Such criticism is further explained in section 7.6.2.1.

7.6.1. THE EU AS A HUMAN RIGHTS ORGANISATION?

There has been quite some discussion as to whether or not the EU is to be regarded as a human rights organisation. Alston and Weiler are well known among the academic discipline for having advocated a strong EU human rights policy.[139] Ensuring respect for fundamental rights, in their view, would give rise to a wide range of measures that need to be undertaken by the EU. It would, for example, be necessary to appoint a specific Commissioner for Human Rights within the European Commission to help the member states in developing policies and initiatives to strengthen the protection of human rights. Moreover, the EU legislature would always have to attach a 'human rights clause' to its legislation dealing with issues such as transparency, the availability of information to interested parties, providing possibilities of appeal and the availability of legal aid. Also, the EU would need to address the problems relating to the standing rights for individuals before the ECJ.[140] Overall, Alston and Weiler suggest measures which would require important reforms to be undertaken by the political and the administrative bodies of the EU.

The EU is a very powerful organisation, having a great amount of financial resources and considerable political leverage, and it is therefore frequently called upon to use these means to protect fundamental rights.[141] The EU could, for example, fill in the gaps or complement the actions taken by other international organisations, such as the ECtHR.[142]

Others have seriously questioned whether such a comprehensive fundamental rights policy should be adopted by the EU.[143] As is often mentioned, the EU was never created to promote the protection of fundamental rights. Only later it was recognised that fundamental rights need to be secured at the Community level, primarily in relation to the actions taken by the institutions.[144] Notably, Von Bogdandy has provided an important counter-critique to the proposals of Alston and Weiler, arguing against bringing fundamental rights within the 'core' of the EU.[145] In his view, the main question that needed to be asked was whether there are serious shortcomings in the protection of fundamental right within the member states of the EU, and whether the existing mechanisms would not provide appropriate responses. Von Bogdandy pointed out that the Charter itself indicates that it is (mainly) meant to make fundamental rights more visible and enhance the protection of fundamental rights within the EU context.[146] Von Bogdandy further questioned whether a 'human rights policy' could be developed by the EU at all,[147] and he seriously doubted whether there would be

---

139 Alston & Weiler (1999).
140 Alston & Weiler (1999), pp. 21–22 and 25–26.
141 Alston & Weiler (1999), p. 13.
142 Besson (2006), p. 358; and Douglas-Scott (2011), pp. 657–658.
143 See section 8.3.5.
144 See De Búrca (2011), pp. 465–497.
145 Von Bogdandy (2000). For a more recent, similar, critique, see Rosas (2011).
146 Von Bogdandy (2000), p. 1312.
147 Von Bogdandy (2000), pp. 1310–1316.

sufficient political legitimacy to put the protection of fundamental rights at the core of the EU's activities.[148]

More recently, however, also Von Bogdandy and others have expressed their concern over the fundamental rights situation in several member states of the EU.[149] The protection of the rights of national and religious minorities and the treatment of asylum seekers by some of the member states of the EU has raised questions regarding the adequacy of the mechanisms at national level for protecting fundamental rights. Von Bogdandy and others have held that the very foundations of the EU could be threatened by such fundamental rights violations, especially in situations where the EU applies the principle of mutual recognition in its different policies. The EU must be able to rely on the democratic functioning of the member states, and their adherence to fundamental rights.[150]

Of increasing concern for the protection of fundamental rights within the scope of EU law are the legislative acts which have been adopted by the EU in the area of freedom, security and justice together with the acts taken by national authorities in the implementation thereof. In this area, national authorities and courts are required to cooperate with each other on the basis of the principle of mutual trust and mutual recognition. They must recognise each other's administrative and judicial decisions, while the protection of various fundamental rights can easily be at stake in such areas. Cases have been brought to the ECJ in which national courts have raised concern over the protection of the rights of the child and the right to family life, as well as the prohibition of inhuman and degrading treatment, in other member states.[151] On the basis of such cases, cooperation between the member states based on the principle of mutual recognition can be regarded as very problematic.[152]

Von Bogdandy and others have therefore explored whether the mechanisms provided for under EU law could be used to address such concerns. Taking into account the lack of political willingness to use the procedure prescribed for under Article 7 TEU, they suggest that individuals should be allowed to claim their rights before the national courts, by relying on fundamental rights guaranteed by EU law, if there appear to be systemic violations of those rights.[153] In their view, the presumption that the national authorities and national courts will respect the essence of fundamental rights must be applied. As a corollary, the EU would be required to take further action in the area of fundamental rights protection in certain exceptional situations, that is, when this presumption is rebutted.

---

148 Von Bogdandy (2000), pp. 1316–1317.

149 Von Bodandy, Kottmann, Antpöhler, Hentrei & Smrkolj (2012).

150 Von Bodandy, Kottmann, Antpöhler, Hentrei & Smrkolj (2012), pp. 489–492.

151 Cf. ECJ 21 December 2011, Joined cases C-411/110 and C-493/10, *N.S. and others*; and ECJ 5 April 2016, Joined cases C-404/15 and C-659/15, *Aranyosi and Căldăru*. These cases are briefly discussed in section 6.8.

152 Cf. De Schutter (2008), pp. 543–547.

153 Von Bodandy, Kottmann, Antpöhler, Hentrei & Smrkolj (2012), pp. 491–492. See section 6.4. on the use of the procedure of Article 7 TEU.

The various and developing viewpoints of scholars such as Alston and Weiler and Von Bogdandy reflect the different conclusions that could be reached as to what the endeavour of protecting fundamental rights in the EU would need to look like. On the one hand, it could be argued that the EU should indeed (and perhaps in a moral sense, must) make better use of its powers to make a difference with regard to the fundamental rights issues with which multiple member states struggle.[154] Also, the case has been made that the EU's modest approach with respect to the protection of fundamental rights within its internal legal order stands in stark contrast to what it aims to realise in its external relations.[155] It has been remarked that there is a discordance between the EU's internal and the EU's external powers seeing that the external fundamental rights powers of the EU are addressed much more clearly by the EU Treaties and that actions are indeed undertaken by the EU on the basis of these fundamental rights powers.[156] In its external relations, the EU is adopting specific action plans to protect human rights and democracy and it has developed the practice of including human rights clauses in agreements with third countries.[157] On the other hand, in its internal law, it is likely that the EU would be viewed with suspicion if it took a further, more 'activist' approach, seeing the more limited competences it has there.[158] Many would indeed agree that the EU is simply not intended to be a human rights organisation.[159]

As explained in chapter 6, the political institutions of the EU have taken a series of important steps which have, at least, given fundamental rights a more prominent place within the architectural design of the EU.[160] The EU has its own Charter, it has the obligation to accede to the Convention, and respect for human rights is clearly mentioned among the values upon which the EU is based.[161] Especially as a result of the changes brought about by the Lisbon Treaty, it has been argued that the EU has entered into a new phase in which the Charter must be taken into account in the legislative processes and the ECJ will also need to engage more clearly with the rights of the Charter.[162] The EU institutions themselves are more clearly paying attention to the protection of fundamental rights *inter alia* by drawing up checklists which they take into account when developing their policies.[163] In some areas, where the EU enjoys

154 Cf. Alston & Weiler (1999), p. 7. The existence of such powers is discussed in chapter 8.
155 Cf. Williams (2004).
156 See in particular Williams (2004). See Articles 3(5) and 21 TEU.
157 See Besson (2011a), para. 1.2.2.3. It is also of interest to note that the EU has acceded to the UN Convention on the Rights of Persons with Disabilities and, in that respect, it is bound to comply with its fundamental rights provisions in a similar way as the member states of the EU are bound themselves. See Council Decision 2010/48/EC of 26 November 2009 [2010] OJ L23/35.
158 Greer & Williams (2012), p. 479.
159 Lenaerts (2012a), p. 377.
160 See in particular sections 6.2. and 6.4.; and cf. Besson (2006), p. 344.
161 Some would argue however that human rights have been brought into the core of the activities of the EU, see Besson (2006), p. 345.
162 Lawson (2005), p. 28.
163 See European Commission, 2014 report on the application of the EU Charter of Fundamental Rights, pp. 160–176.

specific competences to take action, certain Directives have also been adopted by the EU, especially in the area of non-discrimination.[164] Some scholars have also held that the EU is increasingly making use of its indirect competence to protect fundamental rights, as explained in chapter 8.[165] Moreover, as discussed in the next section, the ECJ is more actively engaging in fundamental rights protection and it has delivered some important judgments in this field.

Despite the foregoing, it is still questionable whether the EU actually can be said to have developed a fundamental rights policy of its own. Douglas-Scott has adequately depicted this by stating that 'the protection of fundamental rights in the EU has evolved in an *ad hoc*, confusing, incremental way and that there exists no clear, conceptual underpinning to the rights protected in the EU'.[166]

Also, others have noted that, although fundamental rights have been given a more prominent place under EU law, it remains unclear which direction the EU should take in this field.[167] The competences of the EU to actively protect fundamental rights by adopting legislation are in particular still limited, as explained in chapter 8.

Seeing that the member states have thus not attributed a clear and broad competence to the EU to take action in this field, there continue to be calls for a more restricted development of the protection of fundamental rights at EU level.[168] On this basis, De Schutter has also held that 'the EU is called upon to better protect and promote human rights in its law and- and policy-making, [while] it is at the same time asked to act with restraint in this field'.[169]

There clearly is an ambivalence that is also reflected in the EU Treaties and in the Charter in various provisions governing the protection of fundamental rights by the EU. On the basis of Article 51(1) of the Charter, the EU is required to respect, protect and even observe fundamental rights, while Article 51(2) of the Charter stresses that the protection of fundamental rights cannot extend or modify the competences of the EU.[170] Various other provisions of the Charter also specifically call on further concretisation to be made either by means of national or EU law, such as Article 30 that holds 'Every worker has the right to protection against unjustified dismissal, in accordance with Union law and national law and practices'. This may concern a principle within the meaning of Article 52(5) of the Charter which would require the ECJ to provide for judicial restraint when interpreting such rights.[171] Overall, therefore, there do not yet seem to be very clear principles that could inform the EU at what point it is required to undertake action to protect fundamental rights.

---

164 Muir (2014a), p. 225. See also section 8.3.3. for such specific competences.
165 Muir (2014a), p. 226. See section 8.3.4.
166 Douglas-Scott (2011), p. 649.
167 Augenstein (2013), p. 1938.
168 See in particular Alston & Weiler (1999); and Von Bogdandy (2000).
169 De Schutter (2008), p. 511.
170 See sections 8.3.1. and 8.3.4.4.
171 See Article 52(5) of the Charter, and section 6.10.

7.6.2. THE ECJ AS A HUMAN RIGHTS COURT?

Of all the EU institutions, the ECJ is considered to have played (and still plays) an essential role in the protection of fundamental rights within the EU legal order. Below, the role the ECJ played before the Lisbon Treaty entered into force is explained (section 7.6.2.1.) and also the role it has played since this Treaty entered into force (section 7.6.2.2.). There is a certain continuity in the Court's approach, but there are also some notable differences between these two periods. The section thereafter reflects in more detail on the existence of and expectations for a development of fundamental rights doctrines by the ECJ, such as a doctrine of positive obligations (section 7.6.2.3.).

7.6.2.1. The Role of the ECJ Pre-Lisbon

At the very beginning, the ECJ was the primary actor among the EU institutions which dealt with fundamental rights challenges, mainly on request by the national courts through the preliminary reference procedure.[172] The ECJ was the first to recognise that fundamental rights were to be protected under Community law at the time when the Treaties of the European Community did not provide for a system of fundamental rights protection.[173] From that perspective, the ECJ has been regarded as an important guardian of the protection of fundamental rights within the EU.[174]

Initially, the ECJ was led to accept the protection of fundamental rights at Community level, because of the concerns that had risen over the supremacy of Community law.[175] The effects of EU law on national law, and in particular on the national constitutions, had become an important source of tension.[176] The ECJ responded to these concerns by accepting that fundamental rights were protected as general principles of Community law. Later on, the ECJ clarified on a few occasions that the protection of fundamental rights by the Community was also necessary to uphold respect for the rule of law.[177]

The original approach of the ECJ to protecting fundamental rights has been criticised. In particular, Coppel and O'Neill have questioned whether the ECJ was really willing to take fundamental rights seriously.[178] Coppel and O'Neill found that the ECJ had adopted a defensive approach in its protection of fundamental rights, because it chiefly aimed to protect the principle of supremacy of Community law, and only for that reason decided to accept fundamental rights at the Community level. Coppel and O'Neill further claimed that the ECJ employed an 'offensive approach' to fundamental

172 De Witte (1999), p. 863.
173 This was discussed in section 6.2.
174 Cf. De Witte (1999); and Muir (2013).
175 See sections 6.2. and 6.3.
176 See section 6.2.
177 Cf. ECJ 23 April 1986, C-294/83, *Les Verts v Parliament*, para. 23; and ECJ 28 March 1996, Opinion 2/94, para. 34.
178 Coppel & O'Neill (1992), pp. 670–671.

rights. According to them, the ECJ had deliberately extended its jurisdiction into a wide range of areas to be able to expand its influence, and not per se to genuinely ensure the protection of fundamental rights.[179] Coppel and O'Neill found it particularly problematic that the ECJ brought the *ERT* situation, that is the situation where member states derogate from the free movement provisions, within the realm of its fundamental rights jurisdiction.[180] They also alleged that the ECJ had, in most cases, let Community objectives prevail over interests of fundamental rights protection. According to Coppel and O'Neill:

> these common outcomes are not coincidental but follow directly from an instrumental manipulation of the nature and importance of the concept of fundamental rights protection. In each case the Court has manipulated the usage of fundamental rights principles, endowing these principles with just enough significance in Community terms to allow for the triumph of the Community will.[181]

This harsh criticism has, to some extent, been countered by Weiler and Lockhart.[182] They found that there was simply no clear evidence to substantiate the claim that the Court indeed only used fundamental rights in a defensive or even an offensive way. According to Weiler and Lockhart, Coppel and O'Neill put forward a one-sided and in some case even incorrect analysis.[183]

At the same time, Weiler and Lockhart also expressed concern over the approach of the ECJ. They particularly pointed to the case of *Bostock*, which was discussed in beginning of this chapter.[184] According to Weiler and Lockhart, the ECJ did too little in its judgment to ensure that the member states would indeed undertake action at national level to protect fundamental rights in this case, and it had left too much discretion in that regard.[185] The approach of the ECJ was rather restrained, and was not very fundamental rights friendly, which has also been noticed for other cases. The ECJ has accepted the competence to review national measures in light of fundamental rights, but in its judgments on fundamental rights cases it often left much discretion to the national courts to decide how they would ultimately secure the protection of those rights. Also commenting on such judgments, in contrast De Witte found that:

> The prudent attitude of the Court of Justice is commendable. There is no justification for going beyond and undertaking the full-scale 'incorporation' of Community fundamental rights into the national legal orders, as happened in the United States. Indeed, there is no glaring human rights deficit in the legal orders of the Member States, which the ECJ should set out to remedy.

179 Coppel & O'Neill (1992), p. 670.
180 This situation is explained in sections 6.7.1. and 9.3.2.2.
181 Coppel & O'Neill (1992), pp. 682–683 and 690.
182 See Weiler & Lockhart (1995b), p. 624.
183 Weiler & Lockhart (1995b), p. 623.
184 See section 7.2.1.
185 Weiler & Lockhart (1995b), pp. 605–617.

> In some of them, such as Germany, Italy, and Spain, there are sophisticated systems for the judicial protection of constitutional rights; in others, such as France, Belgium, and the Netherlands, the European Convention on Human Rights is enforced by the courts as a quasi-constitution. Also, all Member States are (unlike the EU) subject to the supervision of the European Convention organs in Strasbourg.[186]

The case of *Bostock* is illustrative of this generally restrained approach. As also proposed by the Advocate General in the opinion to the case, the ECJ may have wanted to refrain from substituting its own assessment over the choices that should be made by the Union or the domestic legislature. The ECJ's decision to expand the scope of the Community's standards of fundamental rights had only briefly been rendered previously in the case of *Wachauf*, which was considered controversial at the time. There is therefore something to be said for a deferential approach of the ECJ in the field of fundamental rights, especially in respect of member states' actions. Weiler and Lockhart have also explained that the ECJ is in a very delicate position, since it is not a fundamental rights court by nature. Nevertheless, Weiler and Lockhart advised the ECJ to prevent future 'attacks' on its position with regard to fundamental rights protection.[187] For this reason, they also held that the ECJ should have provided for better protection of fundamental rights in the case of *Bostock*. In particular, they explained that there was a sufficient basis under Community law, which would have allowed the Court to impose the said positive obligations on the member states.[188]

The difficult position in which the ECJ may find itself when deciding about fundamental rights, can also been seen in its case-law about the conflicts between free movement provisions and fundamental rights. In cases such as *Schmidberger* and *Omega*, the ECJ accepted that fundamental rights can be invoked as a justification for the restriction of fundamental rights.[189] The ECJ has approached the protection of fundamental rights in these cases as a form of interference with the free movement rights, and subjected the protection of these interests to a balancing test. The ECJ has established that the protection of fundamental rights must be necessary to allow interferences with the fundamental freedoms. This approach has raised questions as to whether, in the Court's view, the market values of the fundamental freedoms might rank higher than fundamental rights.[190] The ECJ is directly required to protect two different interests and must ensure the protection of both, since it has developed the free movement provisions as 'fundamental freedoms' of their own.[191] Seen from that perspective, the recognition of fundamental rights as interests which could override the 'economic' fundamental rights of the Community would be commendable. Still, in many cases the ECJ has ultimately chosen the protection of the free movement

---

186 De Witte (1999), p. 873.
187 Weiler & Lockhart (1992), pp. 624–625.
188 Weiler & Lockhart (1995b), pp. 605–617.
189 ECJ 12 June 2003, C-112/00, *Schmidberger*; and ECJ 14 October 2004, C-36/02, *Omega*.
190 See De Schutter (2004), p. 9; and Morijn (2006).
191 Biondi (2004), p. 54.

provisions over the protection of fundamental rights.[192] The ECJ thus will not always reach the most favourable outcome in terms of fundamental rights protection.

Overall, the ECJ has been closely followed and criticised even before the entry into force of the Lisbon Treaty. In this period, the ECJ has often been willing to make references to the Convention as well as the case-law of the ECtHR in the interpretation of fundamental rights as general principles of Community and of EU law.[193] The ECJ has also been willing to revise its previous interpretations of fundamental rights by following the interpretation that was later given by the ECtHR in similar cases.[194] Since the ECJ follows the ECtHR's approach it could be inferred that the ECJ is willing to take fundamental rights seriously, considering that the ECtHR is a human rights court and is better able to decide about fundamental rights cases. This has, moreover, also been in the interest of a consistent interpretation of fundamental rights seeing that the ECtHR and the ECJ have ended up deciding on very similar fundamental rights matters.[195] Nevertheless, it is equally true that the ECJ for this period has been accused of taking fundamental rights insufficiently seriously, in particular because in many cases, it seems that it has allowed economic and internal market interests to prevail over fundamental rights.

7.6.2.2. The Role of the ECJ Post-Lisbon

The Lisbon Treaty has brought about some notable effects and changes in comparison to the period before. For one thing, the ECJ is increasingly engaged in fundamental rights protection. National courts are increasingly referring questions to the ECJ on the application and the interpretation of the Charter.[196] The specific provisions of the Charter have given rise to many new questions, such as Article 51(1) which provides a limited scope of application of the fundametal rights laid down in the Charter.[197] Aside from providing further clarification of such novel provisions, the ECJ has also been more active in deciding that EU legislation is void because of an incompatibility with fundamental rights. In doing so, the ECJ has handed down some very important judgments on the protection of fundamental rights in Europe. The example of the *Digital Rights* case on the Data Retention Directive has shown that the ECJ is willing to annul EU legislation if it fails to secure adequate protection of fundamental rights.[198]

---

192 See ECJ 18 December 2007, C-341/05, *Laval*; and ECJ 11 December 20007, C-438/05, *Viking Line*.

193 De Búrca (2013).

194 Cf. ECJ 21 September 1989, C-46/87, *Hoechst*; ECtHR 16 December 1992, no. 13710/88, *Niemitz*; and ECJ 22 October 2002, C-94/00, *Roquettes Frères*.

195 There is a certain overlap between the jurisdictions of these courts, see section 6.9.2.

196 Cf. Muir (2014a).

197 See section 6.7. and chapter 9.

198 ECJ 8 April 2014, Joined cases C-293/12 and C-594/12, *Digital Rights Ireland*.

There are by now many more examples in which the ECJ has taken this decision.[199] For these reasons, further attention has been drawn in the recent years to what role the ECJ can play in the protection of fundamental rights in Europe.

It is interesting to find that the approach of the ECJ has to some extent changed as compared to its approach before the Lisbon Treaty entered into force. In its more recent case-law, the ECJ refers primarily to relevant provisions of fundamental rights as laid down in the Charter, and on fewer occasions, it refers to the provisions laid down in the Convention.[200] The ECJ thereby seems to maintain some distance from the Convention. In the case of *Åkerberg Fransson*, the ECJ explained that:

> it is to be remembered that whilst Article 6(3) TEU confirms, fundamental rights recognised by the ECHR constitute general principles of the European Union's law and whilst Article 52(3) of the Charter requires rights contained in the Charter which correspond to rights guaranteed by the ECHR to be given the same meaning and scope as those laid down by the ECHR, the latter does not constitute, as long as the European Union has not acceded to it, a legal instrument which has been formally incorporated into European Union law. Consequently, European Union law does not govern the relationship between the ECHR and the legal systems of the Member States, nor does it determine the conclusions to be drawn by a national court in the event of a conflict between the rights guarantee by that convention and a rule of national law (...).[201]

The ECJ thus expresses some reservations on the full effect of the Convention under EU law and, rather, seems intent on developing its own autonomous approach to fundamental rights. The concern of the ECJ for an autonomous interpretation of EU law has also been made apparent in *Opinion 2/13*, in which the ECJ pointed out various reasons why the draft accession agreement was incompatible with EU law.[202]

In other respects, the case-law of the ECJ shows a certain continuity. The ECJ has not, for example, radically altered its style of reasoning in response to its renewed role in fundamental rights cases, nor has it started to develop (many) fundamental rights doctrines in its case-law.[203] The ECJ often continues to rely on its traditional, rather formal and terse reasoning, as has been discussed in a previous section.[204] The

---

199 See in particular Joined cases C-92/09 and C-93/09, *Volker und Markus Schecke*, 9 November 2010; C-236/09, *Test-Achats*, 1 March 2011; Joined cases C-402/05 P and C-41/05 P, *Kadi and Al Barakaat*, 3 September 2008; C-584/10 P, *Commission and others v. Kadi*, 18 July 2013; and ECJ 6 October 2015, C-362/14, *Schrems*.

200 Cf. De Búrca (2013).

201 ECJ 26 February 2013, C-617/10, *Åkerberg Fransson*, para. 44; ECJ 24 April 2012, C-517/10, *Kamberaj*, para. 60; and ECJ 18 December 2014, *Opinion 2/13*, para. 179.

202 The preservation of the autonomy of EU law was also of great concern during the negotiations preceding the draft accession agreement and this can also be seen in the *Kadi* cases, see Muir (2013), pp. 80–81. For a critical reflection on the autonomous interpretation of the Charter by the ECJ, see De Búrca (2013), pp. 171–174; and cf. Augenstein (2013). The decision taken by the ECJ in *Opinion 2/13* is discussed further in section 6.9.1.

203 De Búrca (2013).

204 See section 7.3.

ECJ generally does not spell out in detail what specific requirements follow from the protection of fundamental rights.

The ECJ therefore still considers that its primary role is that of safeguarding EU law. It does not consider itself to be a human rights court.[205] The current President of the Court, Lenaerts, has also explained that the ECJ's formal approach must be maintained because it fits best with its task that it shares with the national courts.[206] The national courts must be given discretion to accommodate the rulings of the ECJ, and the ECJ may therefore not provide far-reaching solutions in respect of the national situation.

This particular approach of the ECJ post-Lisbon has been criticised. According to De Búrca, the minimalistic style of reasoning of the ECJ does not fully show the extent to which it actually takes into account the concerns that are related to fundamental rights protection, and the different viewpoints that can be taken.[207] It has also been submitted that the Court's traditional methods of interpretation (grammatical and teleological interpretation) are not suitable in fundamental rights cases.[208] Often it concerns very difficult cases, which confront the ECJ with the member states' most sensitive policies, and in which the ECJ needs to apply fundamental rights provisions that offer very little guidance as to how they must be interpreted. In such cases, more openness on the part of the ECJ with regard to its reasoning and the choices it makes could help to counter criticism of judicial activism, as has been argued by Gerards.[209] The particular line of case-law of the ECJ in the cases of *Mangold* and *Kücückdeveci*, in which the Court allowed for a certain horizontal effect of fundamental rights, for example, has especially been criticised because of the minimalistic and self-referential style of reasoning.[210] The Court has not clearly explained the rationale underlying its approach in these cases. Aside from claims of judicial activism,[211] this line of case-law has also caused much legal uncertainty.[212]

Moreover, the ECJ has been criticised because of its more recent position towards the Convention and the judgments of the ECtHR as explained above. The ECJ does not provide insight into whether, and to what extent, it has taken into account relevant judgments of the ECtHR.[213] This has given rise to fears, over whether the EU meets

205 This has appeared most clearly in a study that was undertaken on the practical use of the case-law of the ECtHR by the ECJ which was based on interviews that were held with various judges and Advocates general of the ECJ, see Krommendijk (2015).

206 Lenaerts (2013), p. 1304.

207 De Búrca (2013), pp. 176–177.

208 Gerards (2012b), pp. 27–28.

209 Gerards (2012b), pp. 40–41.

210 ECJ 22 November 2005, C-144/04, *Mangold*; and ECJ 19 January 2010, C-555/07, *Kücükdeveci*. These cases are explained in section 6.7.2.

211 See Muir (2013), pp. 92 and 96.

212 See De Mol (2011), p. 118; Pech (2012); and Bobek (2013).

213 See again De Búrca (2013).

the minimum level of fundamental rights protection that is guaranteed under the Convention.[214]

The ECJ does not consistently refer to the judgments of the ECtHR that could be relevant for the interpretation of fundamental rights. At the same time, this approach can be explained by its desire for an autonomous interpretation of fundamental rights. As explained in chapter 6, the explanations of the Charter also specifically requires attention to be paid to the autonomy of EU law and that of the ECJ in relation to the standards for limiting the rights of the Charter.[215] The explanations to Article 52(3) of the Charter state that the EU and national legislatures 'must comply with the same standards as are fixed by the detailed limitation arrangements laid down in the ECHR … without thereby adversely affecting the autonomy of Union law and that of the Court of Justice of the European Union'.[216] It might thus be expected that the ECJ would undertake a different assessment with regard to the limitation of fundamental rights as compared to the ECtHR. The Charter also has a specific clause for limiting fundamental rights, laid down in Article 52(1).[217] Some scholars have held that the case-law of the ECJ has indeed demonstrated a different approach towards the limitation of fundamental rights.[218]

It has already been mentioned that the ECJ takes into account the scope and meaning of fundamental right as developed by the ECtHR in its case-law.[219] There are plenty of cases in which the ECJ still refers to the judgments of the ECtHR as a further support in its fundamental rights cases.[220] Several authors have commended the ECJ for this. In particular when it is confronted with cases on sensitive and complex matters, it is considered valuable if the ECJ refers to judgments of the ECtHR as a further ground of support for its decision.[221]

There are several examples of cases in which the ECJ has specifically referred to the judgments of the ECtHR in order to impose a positive obligation on either the EU institutions or on the member states. The ECJ has, for example, specifically relied on the judgments of the ECtHR to establish that the right to an effective remedy as guaranteed

---

214 De Búrca (2013); and Krommendijk (2015).

215 See section 6.9.1.

216 See also ECJ 9 November 2010, Joined cases C-92/09 and C-93/09, *Volker und Markus Schecke and Eifert*, para. 35, where the ECJ holds that it must follow the limitation clause to Article 8 ECHR.

217 According to this provision 'Any limitation on the exercise of the rights and freedoms recognised by this Charter must be provided for by law and respect the essence of those rights and freedoms. Subject to the principle of proportionality, limitations may be made only if they are necessary and genuinely meet the objectives of general interest recognised by the Union or the need to protect the rights and freedoms of others.' This provision is also discussed with a view to the recognition of positive obligations, see section 8.3.4.4.

218 See Peers (2014), pp. 1461–1468.

219 Kühling (2009), p. 491.

220 See ECJ 18 December 2014, C-562/13, *Abdida*, paras 47 and 52.

221 Krommendijk (2015), p. 825.

by Article 47 of the Charter requires that a remedy must be provided before the General Court to allow undertakings to claim damages as a result of lengthy competition procedures.[222] The ECJ pointed out a certain judgment of the ECtHR which established that states must take measures to ensure that the right to a fair trial under Article 6 ECHR is guaranteed within a reasonable time, and if they fail to do so, they must provide for compensation.[223]

By contrast, there are also some examples of cases in which the ECJ has not yet recognised relevant case-law of the ECtHR.

First, there is the judgment of the ECtHR in the case of *Tarakhel v. Switzerland*.[224] In this case, the ECtHR decided that Switzerland would violate the prohibition of inhuman and degrading treatment under Article 3 ECHR by transferring a family with minor children back to Italy on the basis of the rules established under the Dublin Regulation. Under the Dublin Regulation, as explained earlier, the EU member states are required to send asylum seekers back to the specific member state where they first arrived in the EU, which, in this case, was Italy. The ECtHR took into account the extremely vulnerable position of a family with minor children and their specific needs and considered that they required particular protection.[225] The ECtHR established that Switzerland would need to request individual guarantees from Italy to ensure that upon arrival, the family would be accepted in conditions which were adapted to the age of children and that the family would be kept together.[226] The ECtHR thus imposed an obligation on the Swiss authorities to obtain insurances from the public authorities of another state party to which they send asylum seekers. Previously, the ECJ has expressly followed the interpretation of the ECtHR in the *M.S.S. v. Belgium and Greece* case on the Dublin Regulation. However, so far the ECJ has not embraced the position of the ECtHR in the case of *Tarakhel v. Switzerland*. Instead it held, very generally, in *Opinion 2/13*, that:

> when implementing EU law, the Member States may, under EU law, be required to presume that fundamental rights have been observed by the other Member States, so that not only may they not demand a higher level of national protection of fundamental rights from another Member State than that provided by EU law, but, save in exceptional cases, they may not check whether that other Member State has actually, in a specific case, observed the fundamental rights guaranteed by the EU.[227]

This interpretation of the ECJ could provide reason to believe that it would accept in very limited situations, perhaps more limited than the ECtHR, that member states need to seek individual guarantees from other member states to secure the protection

---

222 Cf. ECJ 26 November 2013, C-58/12, *Group Gascogne v. Commission*, para. 83.
223 ECtHR 26 October 2000, no. 30210/96, *Kudla v. Poland*.
224 ECtHR 4 November 2014, no. 29217/12, *Tarakhel v. Switzerland*.
225 ECtHR 4 November 2014, no. 29217/12, *Tarakhel v. Switzerland*, para. 119.
226 See further Beijer (2015), pp. 128 and 147–148.
227 ECJ 18 December 2013, *Opinion 2/13*, para. 192.

of fundamental rights when transferring an asylum seeker to another member state. It is of special importance, according to the ECJ that the member states should thus uphold the principle of mutual recognition in this context. The ECJ could be criticised for this particular position. However, in another more recent case, the ECJ took a different approach and allowed room for the member states and their national courts to apply exceptions to the principle of mutual recognition. In the case of *Aranyosi and Căldăru*, which was about the execution of a European Arrest Warrant, the ECJ allowed room for the member states and their national courts to set the principle of mutual recognition aside under certain circumstances, which the ECJ further clarified in its judgment.[228] This case, which was discussed in chapter 6, may show that the ECJ is thus willing to follow the approach of the ECtHR by specifically taking individual circumstances into account.

As a second illustration, the case-law of the ECtHR on the protection of the right to a fair trial of individuals in relation to the preliminary reference procedure has also not yet been recognised by the ECJ.[229] In its case-law, the ECtHR has established that national courts of last instance must provide reasoning for their refusal to refer a preliminary reference to the ECJ on questions of interpretation of EU law.[230] The ECtHR requires the national courts to explicitly mention the reasons which the case-law of the ECJ provides on the exceptions to the obligations of the national courts under Article 267 TFEU (the *Cilfit* case-law).

So far, the ECJ has not endorsed this interpretation of the ECtHR, although it is clearly relevant in respect of the obligations which the member states of the EU must fulfil within the scope of EU law. It is not clear whether the ECJ would also recognise an obligation for the member states to give reasons for their decision not to make a reference for a preliminary ruling. The ECJ has always held in its case-law that the preliminary reference procedure gives discretion to the national courts to decide whether a preliminary reference is necessary.[231] Under EU law, there are no remedies for individuals enabling them to obtain a reference for a preliminary ruling by the ECJ.[232] It is therefore questionable whether the ECJ would be willing to accept an obligation for the national court to provide reasons for their decisions not to refer a question to the ECJ, as it is difficult to square with the specific character of the preliminary reference procedure.[233] Moreover, the ECJ might consider this to be an issue that falls within the area of national procedural autonomy.[234]

---

228 ECJ 5 April 2016, Joined Cases C-404/15 and C-659/15, *Aranyosi and Căldăru*. See section 6.8.

229 ECtHR 20 September 2011, nos. 3989/07 and 38353.07, *Ullens de Schooten and Rezabek v. Belgium*; and ECtHR 8 April 2014, no. 17120/09, *Dhahbi v. Italy*.

230 ECtHR 8 April 2014, no. 17120/09, *Dhahbi v. Italy*, paras 31–33.

231 See recently ECJ 9 September 2015, Joined cases C-72/14 and C-197/14, *X. and T.A. van Dijk*, paras 54–61.

232 See also Lacchi (2016).

233 See also section 7.4.1.

234 See section 7.5.3.

There is thus some uncertainty over whether the ECJ would always arrive at the same decisions as the ECtHR has reached, especially in the cases mentioned here. As has been discussed, it is not unlikely that the ECJ will go its own way. This does not need to be problematic, but if the ECJ decides to provide for a different approach towards the protection of fundamental rights than the ECtHR, in matters falling within the scope of EU law, it would be desirable to pair this to a greater openness in its reasoning behind its judgments, as well to offer better insight into the choices the ECJ makes. This would be in the interest of providing legal certainty and could ensure a further legitimation of its decisions.

7.6.2.3. *The Development of Fundamental Rights Doctrines by the ECJ*

The ECJ has so far been slow in developing fundamental rights doctrines in its case-law.[235] However, the ECJ has developed certain doctrines in other areas, such as in the field of the free movement law, where it has accepted the horizontal effect of the free movement rights.[236] The ECJ has even established that member states are under a positive obligation to protect the free movement rules from interferences committed by private parties.[237] This might give rise to a certain expectation that such positive obligations would also be created by the ECJ to ensure the protection of EU fundamental rights. However, the ECJ has not clearly engaged in the development of such obligations, nor in the development of a clear doctrine of positive obligations.

There are some judgments of the ECJ on fundamental rights, in which the ECJ has provided a much more elaborate reasoning and insight into its approach. The *Sky Österreich* judgment is largely regarded as a good example of where the ECJ carefully examined whether the EU legislature had struck a right balance in the protection of the freedom to conduct a business and the right to freedom of expression under the Audiovisual Media Directive.[238] The ECJ thereby closely followed the proportionality assessment laid down in Article 52(1) of the Charter. Also, in several cases, the Court has specifically had regard to the seriousness of a fundamental rights interference.[239] If the interference with a fundamental right is serious, it seems that the Court will apply a more strict review. The ECJ has developed case-law in which it allows exceptions to the application of the principle of mutual recognition in the case of an interference with

---

235 See Gerards (2015), p. 47; Douglas-Scott (2011), p. 649; Sánchez (2012), p. 1592; Gerards (2011a), p. 90; and Kühling (2009), p. 490. The Court of Justice has, however, paid attention to concepts of indirect and direct discrimination in its case law, see Gerards (2015), p. 47.

236 Besson (2011a), p. 117. See also section 6.7.2.

237 See ECJ 9 December 1997, C-265/95, *Commission v. France*; and ECJ 12 June 2003, C-112/00, *Schmidberger*; and cf. De Vries & Mastrigt (2013), pp. 274–276; Trstenjak & Beysen (2013); and Alston & Weiler (1999), p. 10.

238 ECJ 22 January 2013, C-283/11, *Sky Österreich*.

239 See in particular ECJ 8 April 2014, C-293/12, *Digital Rights Ireland*; para. 48; and ECJ 6 October 2015, C-362/14, *Schrems*, para. 78.

an absolute fundamental right, such as Article 4 of the Charter on the prohibition of inhuman and degrading treatment.[240]

It has been argued that it is necessary for the ECJ to develop its fundamental rights doctrines further. Some scholars have also, in particular, encouraged the ECJ to start developing a doctrine of positive obligations.[241] The development of these and other doctrines has been considered necessary for various reasons. First, fundamental rights doctrines in general provide further clarity, certainty and predictability to the actors that are subject to a particular fundamental rights regime.[242] It has especially been held that it would be necessary for the ECJ to start developing fundamental rights doctrines, since it is now confronted with a greater number of cases that involve fundamental rights.[243] Several scholars also maintain that the development of fundamental rights doctrines would be necessary to enable the Court to play a strong role in the field of fundamental rights, and thereby enhance the legitimacy of EU law.[244] In that respect, the ECJ is expected to make up for the democratic deficits in the EU. Some authors cherish serious concerns over the legitimacy of the decisions that are taken by the EU institutions, and expect the ECJ to respond to those concerns by developing a clear fundamental rights discourse.[245] The ECJ would, in particular, need to ensure the legitimacy of EU decisions *vis-à-vis* the national constitutional courts seeing that these courts still express concerns over the existence of an adequate level of protection of fundamental rights at the EU level. EU law can have a clear impact on the rights of individuals as a result of the effect given to the principles of supremacy and of direct effect of EU law as well as other principles. Therefore, the ECJ needs to ensure that EU law is legitimated by democratic ideals, including the protection of fundamental rights.[246] In the view of these scholars, the ECJ needs to show that it takes fundamental rights seriously by undertaking a strong review of the measures of the EU institutions in light of fundamental rights. If it did so, the national courts would also be willing to entrust the ECJ with the power necessary to adjudicate in the field of fundamental rights.[247]

In developing fundamental rights doctrines, the ECJ has been urged to consider the doctrines and methods of interpreting fundamental rights which the ECtHR has developed, including the methods of interpretation of meta-teleological reasoning, autonomous or consensus interpretation, and a margin of appreciation doctrine.[248]

---

240 See ECJ 21 December 2011, Joined cases C-411/10 and C-493/10, *N.S. and others*, para. 86; and ECJ 5 April 2016, Joined cases C-404/15 and C-659/15, *Aranyosi and Căldăru*, paras 85–87.

241 Kühling (2009), p. 492.

242 Kühling (2009), p. 490.

243 Gerards (2012b), p. 32; and De Búrca (2013), p. 171.

244 Kühling (2009), p. 490; Gerards (2012b); De Búrca (2013), p. 184; and Douglas-Scott (2011), p. 681.

245 Kühling (2009), pp. 482 and 490. See section 7.6.1.

246 Von Bogdandy, Kottmann, Antpöhler, Dickschen, Hentrei & Smrkolj (2012), p. 495; Besson (2011a), p. 114; and Eriksen (2003), p. 356.

247 According to Greer & Williams, therefore, the EU and the ECJ mainly serve a model of 'institutional justice'. By contrast, the ECtHR is seen to serve a model of individual and seemingly also of constitutional justice. See Greer & Williams (2009), pp. 463 and 475–476.

248 Gerards (2012b); and Gerards (2011a).

This could still allow room for the ECJ to give expression to specific characteristics of EU law, while also providing for some clarity.[249] As explained in the previous section, there might be reasons for the ECJ to undertake a different assessment of the limitations of fundamental rights under EU law. In the development of a doctrine of positive obligations, for example, the ECJ could be expected to take into account the limited fundamental rights competences of the EU and the limited scope of application of EU fundamental right, which will be explained in chapters 8 and 9.

Whether and when the ECJ would indeed want to develop its fundamental rights doctrines further may also depend on the types of cases that are brought to the Court. More elaborate reflections on whether the ECJ could be expected to develop a doctrine of positive obligations are, therefore, given in chapter 11. This chapter examines specific examples of judgment of the ECJ on cases giving rise to positive obligations, and evaluating certain problematic aspects of those cases.

7.7. CONCLUSIONS

This chapter has discussed a variety of factors that shape the institutional position and the judicial culture of the ECJ. It has been explained that the ECJ is a court which deals with much wider issues than only fundamental rights protection, and it employs a rather specific style of reasoning, which is relatively formal in nature and which is usually not very elaborate. This by itself means that there is less potential for a development of positive obligations by the ECJ in its case-law. Some of the specific features relating to the institutional position as well as the judicial culture of the ECJ are of particular importance for the potential development of positive obligations by this Court. First, the ECJ is very much dependent on the questions which are referred to by the national courts under the preliminary reference procedure, which forms the main procedure used to ensure the protection of fundamental rights within the context of EU law. Generally, the ECJ is intent on answering only questions which are specifically formulated by the national courts, and the national courts may therefore play an important role in the further development of positive obligations at the EU level by referring relevant questions to the ECJ. Often, the ECJ is also inclined to have regard to the specific choices that have been made by the EU legislature, including in cases on fundamental rights, and it will not easily overturn those choices. The ECJ has different ways of showing a deferential review towards the EU institutions. These include a 'reconciliatory approach' and a procedural type of review. Interestingly, both of these techniques actually provide room for a development of positive obligations, mostly of a procedural nature, which can be directed at the judiciary or the administrative authorities of the member states. In cases where there are important interests of EU law at stake, such as the protection of the free movement provisions as well as when serious

[249] Kühling (2009), pp. 490–491.

interferences with fundamental rights have taken place, it could also be expected that the ECJ would further allow for a development of positive obligations, as it applies a more strict review of the fundamental rights requirements in such cases.

It has been explained in this chapter that the ECJ has not radically altered its judicial style in response to the increase of fundamental rights cases that have been brought since the Charter has become binding. It has, moreover, been slow in developing its own fundamental rights doctrines, even if it has stressed the autonomy of EU law in cases on fundamental rights. The approach of the ECJ in fundamental rights cases has been criticised for that reason. According to the critics, the case-law of the ECJ creates legal uncertainty, and this casts doubts as to whether the ECJ indeed takes fundamental rights protection seriously. This is considered problematic, especially by those who consider that the ECJ should play an important and active role in the protection of fundamental rights within the context of EU law, because of the concerns over the democratic legitimacy of EU law. From this perspective, it would be valuable for the ECJ to clearly show to the national courts that it now takes fundamental rights concerns sufficiently into account.

Finally, it has been explained that if the ECJ, perhaps in response to criticism on its case-law, were to develop fundamental rights doctrines, it has been advised in the literature to take the case-law of the ECtHR as its source of inspiration. The ECtHR has much experience in dealing with fundamental rights matters, and therefore enjoys legitimacy. At the same time, it is expected that in developing its own and autonomous approach, the ECJ will also take into account principles and concerns that are specific to EU law.

CHAPTER 8

EU COMPETENCES AND SUBSIDIARITY IN FUNDAMENTAL RIGHTS PROTECTION

8.1. INTRODUCTION

The limited competences of the EU are often mentioned as a problematic issue in relation to its obligation to protect fundamental rights.[1] The limits related to the competences of the EU are addressed at different places in the Charter, the explanations to the Charter, the EU Treaties as well as in the context of the accession to the Convention, and in the discussions related thereto.[2] The EU does not have a general competence to take action to protect fundamental rights, so how can positive obligations which may require legislative, administrative or judicial measures to be fulfilled actually be accommodated within the context of EU law? Would the ECJ, first, be expanding the competences of the EU institutions if it were to impose positive obligations on them to ensure the protection of fundamental rights in the implementation of certain policy fields of EU law? Secondly, would the ECJ (always) be interfering in the competences of the member states, if it were to impose obligations on them to take additional measures to ensure that fundamental rights are protected within the scope of EU law? Thirdly, would the ECJ leave gaps in the protection of fundamental rights if it decided that there was no scope to accept positive obligations on the basis of the limited competences of the EU? To gauge the potential for the development of positive obligations by the ECJ, the issue of competences is clearly important. This chapter examines whether and within what limits the definition of negative or positive obligations can be reconciled with the principle of limited EU competences. To answer this question, this chapter will address the inherently complicated relationship between the EU's limited competences and its obligation to protect fundamental rights.[3]

As this chapter will show, this thesis takes the principle of attributed powers of the EU as the main starting point for determining the extent to which positive obligations can be incorporated into EU law. An important reason for this is the clear emphasis

1 This has also been discussed in section 1.1.3.

2 See the fifth section of the preamble of the Charter; the second sentence of Article 51(1) of the Charter; the explanations to Article 51(2) of the Charter; the second sentence of Article 6(1) TEU; Declaration No. 1 to the Lisbon Treaty; and Article 1(3) and 9(1) of the Draft Agreement for the Accession of the EU to the European Convention for Human Rights, 47+1(2013)008rev2, Final Report to the CDDH, 10 June 2013.

3 ECJ 28 March 1996, *Opinion 2/94*, paras 26–27.

which has been placed on the principle of limited competences within the context of fundamental rights protection by the EU in various legal provisions and documents. This approach further takes into account that the member states have already provided for mechanisms which secure the protection of fundamental rights, and these can also be used to ensure the effective protection of EU law. As will be explained, however, there are also other viewpoints that can be taken on how the concept of positive obligations can be incorporated into EU law. Several scholars take into account principles of international law and of state responsibility to justify imposing positive obligations on the EU as a whole. These should accordingly be met by all the EU institutions, including the ECJ, which may pass certain obligations on to the member states.

This chapter will first briefly explain what the basic principles governing the division of competences between the EU and the member states entail (section 8.2.). Thereafter, an in-depth discussion will follow on how the competences of the EU to protect fundamental rights can be defined, looking mainly at the academic discussions on this topic (section 8.3.). As there are some fundamental rights competences for the EU, the following section discusses how it may be decided when the EU would have to make use of these competences and undertake certain actions to ensure the effective protection of fundamental rights (section 8.4.). Aside from the principles of subsidiarity and proportionality, other relevant principles and considerations will be discussed, which have been derived from the academic debate on this topic, the case-law of the ECJ, and reports of the European Commission relating to specific EU legislative proposals on the protection of fundamental rights. This section will explain how these principles and considerations interrelate. As a final point, this chapter will examine how it can further be ensured that room is given to the member states to apply their own national standards of fundamental rights and the standards of international human rights treaties (section 8.5.). The chapter ends with some brief conclusions (section 8.6.).

8.2. THE PRINCIPLE OF ATTRIBUTED COMPETENCES AND THE DIVISION OF POWERS BETWEEN THE EU AND ITS MEMBER STATES

The principle of attributed powers means that the EU can only act within the limits of the competences which have been conferred to it by the member states in order to achieve its objectives.[4] This basic definition of the principle of attributed powers, also known as the principle of conferral, is given in Article 5(2) TFEU. In addition, Article 4(1) TFEU explains that the member states retain the competences which they have not conferred to the EU. These principles are at the heart of the existence of the EU and they are of key concern for defining the powers of the EU. Of equal importance is the distinction which has been made between different types of competences. The EU

4 The objectives of the EU are set out in Article 3 TEU, which also includes the promotion of peace, the EU's values and the well-being of its peoples.

has exclusive, shared and complementary competences, and Articles 3 to 6 TFEU list the different areas which fall within each one of these competences.[5] The categorisation of these different competences has important implications for the degree of power which the EU and the member state can exercise in a given area, which is indicated by Article 2 TEU.

Accordingly, in areas of exclusive competences to act, the EU has the exclusive power to legislate and adopt legally binding acts. This applies *inter alia* to the customs union, the establishment of competition rules within the internal market and the conclusion of certain international agreements.[6] The member states in these areas may only act if they have been empowered by the EU or in implementation of EU acts. Thus in areas of exclusive competences, the room for member state action is very limited.

In areas of shared competences, there is generally much more room for member states to take action. Here, both the EU and the member states may adopt legally binding acts. There is no exhaustive list that can be given of the policy fields in which the EU has such shared competences. Instead, Article 4(1) TFEU explains that in areas which have not been indicated by the Treaty provisions as providing an exclusive or supplementary competence, competences are shared. Article 4(2) TFEU mentions the area of social policy, the environment and the area of freedom, security and justice as examples of such areas. The possibilities for use of these competences by the member states may fluctuate, or rather diminish over time, depending on whether or not the EU has adopted any acts. This is because, on the basis of Article 2(2) TFEU, the member states exercise their competences to the extent that the EU has not exercised its competence, or when the EU has decided to cease exercising its competences.[7] As soon as the EU has taken action within an area of shared competences, the area becomes 'pre-empted'. The degree of power of the EU within this category of shared competences may vary widely between the different areas concerned.[8] The EU may have exhaustively regulated a particular area, which then severely restricts the competences of the member states, but the EU also may provide for minimum harmonisation, leaving power to a larger degree at national level.

The third category of EU competences is that of the complementary competences. This implies that the EU is allowed to take action to support, coordinate and supplement the actions of the member states, yet, as determined by Article 2(5) TFEU, without superseding the competences of the member states. Areas in which the EU has complementary competences are health, industry and culture. In these areas, the EU may not go as far as harmonising the member states' laws and regulations.

---

5 Craig (2004).

6 Article 3(2) TFEU further determines when the conclusion of an international agreement falls within this category.

7 The manner in which the EU may cease such competences is determined by Declaration 18 to the Lisbon Treaty.

8 It is stressed by Protocol No. 25 to the Lisbon Treaty that member states are still allowed to take action when the EU has exercised a shared competence because such action does not cover the whole area, but 'only covers those elements governed by the Union act'.

There are a few other areas in which the EU may take action, even though they are not as such indicated as an exclusive, shared or complementary competence by the Treaty. Article 2(3) TFEU determines that the EU has a competence to coordinate the economic, employment and social policies of the member states. According to Article 2(4) TFEU, the EU may also take measures in the field of the common foreign and security policy and the defence policy. These areas used to be part of a separate pillar in the former Community's structure. They remain somewhat different, as the actions of the EU and the jurisdiction of the ECJ to review the lawfulness of those actions are subject to specific limitations.[9]

The different categories of competence show generally which degree of power the EU may exercise in a certain area and, importantly, how the division between the competences ofthe member states and the EU works. Yet, the indication of an area as an exclusive, shared or complementary competence remains, to some extent, merely a starting point. Further indications for determining the degree of power which can be exercised by the EU and the member states are the exact subject matter on which the EU may take action, the type of acts than can be adopted (regulations, directives, minimum or maximum harmonisation etc.), and the type of legislative procedures that must be followed. This is determined by the particular legal bases which have been provided for throughout the Treaty and by other types of EU acts which lay down such rules. Thus, within the different categories of competences generally, there may be varying degrees of power which may be held by the EU.

Despite the fact that there are fairly detailed rules on the division of competences between the EU and the member states and certain restrictions that need to be respected, the expansion of the competences of the EU has given cause for concern.[10] The Lisbon Treaty aimed to address this by laying down further rules and mechanisms to help curb the expansion of EU competences. It also has provided for the categorisation of the different competences, and it has placed further emphasis on the principles of subsidiarity and proportionality, which are explained in section 8.4.3.[11]

The expansion of competences of the EU has been attributed, partly, to the very broad interpretation of the competences by the EU institutions.[12] There are some powers which have been laid down in quite a broad way in the EU Treaties. Of concern here, in particular, are Article 114 TFEU, which allows for the adoption of harmonising measures with the object of the establishment and functioning of the internal market, and Article 352 TFEU, which provides for a residual power to take measures to attain one of the objectives set out in the Treaty. These provisions have been used to justify the adoption of a wide range of actions by the EU.[13]

---

9 See Article 275 TFEU.

10 See e.g. Craig (2004).

11 Cf. Craig (2004), p. 338.

12 Prechal, De Vries & Van Eijken (2011), p. 214.

13 A striking example is provided by the establishment of a directive harmonising patient's rights based on Article 114 TFEU. This legal basis can be used to ensure the establishment of the internal market,

Some scholars also particularly blame the ECJ for the expansion of the EU competences. The ECJ has, for example, accepted, to some extent, the idea of implied powers, which entails that the EU may act if this is necessary to achieve an objective that is in principle to be pursued by an explicit power.[14] The ECJ has also adopted quite a deferential approach in checking whether the EU institutions have made use of the correct legal basis. Lastly, the ECJ has appeared to have allowed for an expansion of the EU's competences by bringing a wide range of matters within the scope of EU law.[15] The ECJ has interpreted, for example, the free movement rules in a particularly extensive manner. As soon as the ECJ decides that such matters fall within the scope of these provisions, the member states must ensure respect for EU law, even when they have not conferred specific powers to the EU to act in such fields.[16]

Thus, to understand the expansion of EU competences, it is of importance to take account of a variety of factors – broad Treaty provisions, the approach of the EU institutions and the approach adopted by the ECJ.[17] This is particularly useful in relation to the potential to identify positive obligations. These factors will help to identify the limits to the competences for imposing such obligations and, in addition, they may help to highlight whether recognition of positive obligations could lead to an unwarranted expansion of competences and, if so, how this could be avoided. In this respect it is important to point out that, while the limits related to the principle of attributed powers are primarily concerned with the legislative powers of the EU and are thus addressed to the EU legislature, it is also considered that the ECJ needs to show respect for these limits.[18]

8.3. EU COMPETENCES TO PROTECT FUNDAMENTAL RIGHTS

8.3.1. SILENCE IN THE EU TREATIES AND THE CASE-LAW OF THE ECJ

The EU Treaty rules do not specifically identify a competence of the EU to undertake action to protect fundamental rights. The question of what kind of competences the EU has, if any, to protect fundamental rights for long formed a topic of academic debate.

but the directive includes various seemingly non-internal market related provisions, such as patients' rights, see Directive 2011/24/EU of 9 March 2011 on the application of patient's rights in cross-border healthcare [2011] OJ L88/45.

14 ECJ 29 November 1956, C-8/55, *Fédération charbonnière de Belgique v. High Authority*.

15 Prechal, De Vries & Van Eijken (2011), p. 242.

16 Cf. also Barents (2008), p. 349.

17 Craig (2004); and Dashwood (2006).

18 Article 51 of the Charter also specifically addresses the limits related to the powers of the EU. In the context of the Charter, it is expected that the ECJ will take these limits into account when applying the Charter's provisions, see Groussot, Pech & Petursson (2013), p. 100.

It is also mostly in these debates that answers to that question may be found, as will be discussed further below.[19]

The 'competence issue' has only briefly been addressed by the ECJ in *Opinion 2/94*.[20] In this opinion, the ECJ was asked to examine the compatibility of the accession of the European Community to the Convention – which was delivered at a time where the Treaties did not yet include a specific legal basis for the EU to do so. The ECJ emphasised the principle that there must be a specific power on the basis of which the Community may act. It clarified that a power may be expressly provided for in the Treaty, but it may also be implied therefrom.[21] The ECJ concluded that 'No Treaty provision confers on the Community institutions any general power to enact rules on human rights or to conclude international conventions in this field'.[22]According to the ECJ there was thus no *general* power for the Community to protect fundamental rights. Several scholars have argued that in the opinion the ECJ did not deny the existence of a competence for the Community in the field of fundamental rights protection altogether, and that it left room for the existence of another type of competence to protect fundamental rights.[23] The ECJ's finding on the existence of a fundamental rights competences in *Opinion 2/94* must further be viewed against the background of this opinion. In *Opinion 2/94*, the ECJ was only asked to figure out whether the Community was competent, at the time, to accede to the Convention. The ECJ explained in the opinion that:

> Respect for human rights is ... a condition for the lawfulness of the Community acts. Accession to the Convention would, however, entail a substantial change in the present Community system for the protection of human rights in that it would entail the entry into of the Community into a distinct international institutional system as well as integration of all the provisions of the Convention into the Community legal order.
>
> Such a modification of the system for the protection of human rights in the Community, with equally fundamental institutional implications for the Community and for the Member States, would be of constitutional significance and would therefore be such as to go beyond the scope of Article 235 [*ex* Article 352 TFEU]. It could be brought about only be way of Treaty amendment.[24]

---

19 Alston & Weiler (1999), pp. 24–25. See also Weiler & Fries (1999), pp. 158–161; Eeckhout (2002), pp. 981–988; and Besson (2011b), pp. 44–55.

20 ECJ 28 March 1996, *Opinion 2-94*. In *Opinion 2/13*, in which the ECJ was asked to determine whether the specific modalities for arranging the accession of the EU to the Convention was compatible with EU law, the EU's competences to protect fundamental rights were only addressed in negative terms, see Opinion 2/13, 18 December 2014, paras 160–161.

21 ECJ 28 March 1996, *Opinion 2/94*, paras 2–26.

22 ECJ 28 March 1996, *Opinion 2/94*, para. 27. The ECJ partly reiterated this in ECJ 17 February 1998, C-249/96, *Grant*, para. 45.

23 Cf. Alston & Weiler (1999), pp. 24–25; and Eeckhout (2002), pp. 982–983.

24 ECJ 28 March 1996, *Opinion 2/94*, paras 34–35. Later, this was partly reiterated in ECJ 17 February 1998, C-249/96, *Grant*, para. 45.

Article 6(2) TEU has now given effect to the requirement for a clear legal basis for the accession of the EU to the Convention. The Treaties have also made clear that the protection of human rights constitutes one of the objectives of the EU. Article 2 TEU indicates that 'respect for human rights' is one of the values upon which the EU has been founded, and Article 3 TEU clarifies that the promotion of such values forms an objective of the EU.[25] The exact competences of the EU to ensure fundamental rights protection are, however, still not as such defined by the Treaties. Instead, the competence issue is mainly addressed in negative terms.[26] Article 6 TEU stipulates that neither the provisions of the Charter nor the accession can affect or extend in any way the competences of the EU as defined in the Treaties. Such limitations appear to be based on the principles which the ECJ developed in *Opinion 2/94* on the competences of the Community to protect fundamental rights, as has been mentioned above.[27] Yet, as discussed, the precise implications of these limitations are not entirely clear.

If the protection of fundamental rights would only require the EU institutions or the member states to refrain from taking action, which means that it would comply with a negative obligation, this does not necessarily give rise to a direct conflict with the limited competences of the EU. After all, in that situation provision of fundamental rights only set limits to action, instead of demanding new action to be taken. Even there, however, some scholars have argued that the compliance with a negative obligation, in situations falling within the scope of EU law, can be considered problematic from the perspective of the principle of attributed powers.[28] In their view, the definition of fundamental rights limits by the ECJ or by the EU legislature can still broaden the scope of EU law in an area where the EU does not have clear competences, because the exercise of the member states' powers at national level are then further restricted.[29]

In relation to the positive measures which may be required to ensure effective respect for fundamental rights, the issue of competences has been considered particularly pressing.[30] There is a wide range of measures that have been envisaged as necessary for the EU to take. This includes institutional measures and practical arrangements to provide for monitoring and reporting mechanisms, as well as legislative measures designed to promote and protect fundamental rights across the many different policy fields of the EU.[31] It is unclear whether there is any scope for the EU to adopt such measures on the basis of its existing competences.

---

25 Specifically in the area of the EU's external policies, it is emphasised further by Articles 3(5) and 21(2) TEU that the value of human rights is to be upheld, promoted and consolidated.

26 Cf. Besson (2011b), p. 40. Besson refers to these provisions as the 'standstill clauses'.

27 There has been some disagreement over whether or not there was already a competence provided under the treaty regime existing at the time which would allow the accession. In particular, Article 351 TFEU has been pointed out as a relevant basis, see Alston & Weiler (1999), pp. 22–27; and Weiler & Fries (1999), pp. 154–165.

28 See in particular Muir (2014a).

29 See Prechal, De Vries & Van Eijken (2011), p. 242.

30 See Besson (2011b), pp. 50–53; Prechal, De Vries & Van Eijken (2011), p. 214; Van der Velde (2009), pp. 74–78; De Schutter (2004), pp. 29–31; and Heringa & Verhey (2001), pp. 19–20.

31 See in particular Alston & Weiler (1999).

Clearly, there is thus a debate on the limited competences of the EU to protect fundamental rights at EU level, although it is more outspoken in relation to positive obligations than in relation to negative obligations. To understand the consequences of this debate for the potential to develop a doctrine of positive obligations for the EU, it is important to further analyse what powers the EU may have in this field. The following subsections therefore discuss the different types of fundamental rights powers which are generally recognised, and it indicates several provisions in the Treaty and in the Charter that are relevant to this debate. This discussion will not pay further attention to the EU's fundamental rights powers in its external relations. This study mostly focuses on the EU's fundamental rights competences based on its internal law, and the examples that can be found in the case-law of the ECJ are also based on that law.[32]

8.3.2. A GENERAL POWER TO PROTECT FUNDAMENTAL RIGHTS

Some scholars believe that there is a certain general power for the EU to protect fundamental rights, even though the ECJ denied the existence of such a power in *Opinion 2/94*. Alston and Weiler have been the most forceful in defending this position.[33] They found that in order to ensure respect for fundamental rights in matters that cut across the different fields of Community law, certain general measures need to be taken, and that appropriate legal bases for doing so were provided by Community law.[34] Such measures could entail monitoring and reporting mechanisms or legislative measures designed to protect the fundamental rights of citizens which could be affected when they exercise the free movement rights.[35] Alston and Weiler pointed to Article 352 TFEU in particular as an appropriate basis to allow for the adoption of certain general measures to protect fundamental rights, which provides for a residual legal basis for EU action.[36] In addition, Article 114 TFEU has been mentioned as a basis that would allow broad measures to be taken in relation to the establishment and the functioning of the internal market.[37] The use of both these legal bases for adopting fundamental rights actions must be approached very carefully, however. In *Opinion 2/94*, the ECJ explained – in respect of the former version of Article 352 TFEU – that it 'cannot be used as a basis for the adoption of provisions whose effect would, in substance, be to

32 On these external fundamental rights competences, see Besson (2011b), pp. 48–50. The discordance between the EU's internal and external powers to protect fundamental rights has briefly been explained in section 7.6.1. The examples of positive obligations in the EU context are discussed in chapter 11.

33 Alston & Weiler (1999), pp. 22–27. See also Weiler & Fries (1999), pp. 159–160; and De Schutter (2004), pp. 17–18.

34 Alston & Weiler (1999), pp. 22–27.

35 Weiler & Fries (1999), pp. 158–159.

36 Alston & Weiler (1999), pp. 26–27.

37 Weiler & Fries (1999), p. 158.

amend the Treaty without following the procedure which it provides for that purpose'.[38] Moreover, as indicated in section 8.2., the use of Articles 114 and 352 TFEU by the EU is especially considered to have contributed to the problem of the expansion of the EU's competences, and for that reason, it is often looked at with some suspicion.

It could further be argued that Article 7 TEU allows the EU to take certain general measures to protect fundamental rights, because this power is not as such restricted to a specific competence field of the EU. This provision allows the Council to take certain actions if 'there is a clear risk of a serious breach by a Member State of the values referred to in Article 2 TEU'. As explained earlier, the respect for human rights is mentioned by Article 2 TEU as one of the key values of the EU. Based on this provision, the Council can make recommendations to the member state and, ultimately, suspend the voting rights of a member state if its response remains insufficient. So far, the far-reaching powers provided by Article 7 TEU to intervene in the area of fundamental rights have not been used.[39] There has been a great lack of political willingness to actually make use of this provision.[40] This could certainly cast some doubt as to whether the EU has a viable general power to protect fundamental rights on the basis of this provision.

Interestingly, however, Article 352 TFEU has been used as a legal basis to adopt certain general measures in the field of fundamental rights. This provision was relied on to establish the Fundamental Rights Agency of the EU, which is mainly entrusted with the task of disseminating and collecting information on fundamental rights problems in Europe.[41]

8.3.3. SPECIFIC POWER TO PROTECT FUNDAMENTAL RIGHTS

In some areas, the member states have attributed a specific power to the EU to protect certain fundamental rights.[42] Article 16(2) TFEU, first, allows the EU to enact rules relating to the protection of personal data by the EU institutions, bodies, offices and agencies and the member states in so far as they carry out activities falling within the scope of EU law and rules relating to the free movement of such data. This provision has, for example, been used to adopt the General Data Protection Regulation.[43] Next,

---

38 Regulation No. 168/2007 of 15 February 2007 establishing a European Union Agency for Fundamental Rights [2007] OJ L53/1. Alston & Weiler mainly rely on the former version Article 308 TEC, see Alston & Weiler (1999), pp. 21–22.

39 However, there are some recent developments in relation to Article 7 TEU, see section 6.4.

40 Cf. Von Bogdandy, Kottmann, Antpöhler, Dickschen, Hentrei & Smrkolj (2012), p. 490.

41 Besson (2011b), p. 47. Initially Article 352 TFEU was used as the relevant basis for adopting Directive 76/207/EEC of 9 February 1976 on the implementation of the principle of equal treatment for men and women as regards access to employment, vocational training and promotion, and working conditions [1976] OJ L39/40.

42 See Besson (2011b), p. 46; and Muir (2014b), p. 33.

43 Directive 2016/80/EU of 27 April 2016 on the protection of natural persons with regard to the processing of personal data and on the free movement of such data [2016] OJ L119/1. See Directive 95/46/EC of 24 October 1995 on the protection of individuals with regard to the processing of personal data and the free movement of such data [1995] OJ L281/31.

Article 19 TFEU allows the EU to take action to combat discrimination based on sex, racial or ethnic origin, religion or belief, disability, age or sexual orientation. This provision has led to the adoption of the Race Equality Directive, as well as the Framework Equality Directive.[44] Thirdly, of importance to mention in this respect is Article 157(3) TFEU, which allows measures to be taken to ensure the application of the principle of equal opportunities and equal treatment of men and women in matters of employment and occupation.

In the areas defined by these provisions, the EU may thus develop policies which aim to protect certain fundamental rights. While these powers relate only to certain, perhaps narrowly defined, fundamental rights issues, they can be of great importance for the EU because their subject matters relate to multiple policy fields of relevance for the EU, such as labour law and free movement law. Since these powers may cut across different fields of EU law, they have been typified as horizontal fundamental rights powers.[45] Moreover, these specific powers of the EU to protect fundamental rights have been interpreted quite broadly by the EU legislature. For example, the Race Equality Directive provides a broad material scope of application. Its provisions apply to matters such as employment and working conditions, but also housing as well as education.[46] Therefore, although the specific competences of the EU are directed to restricted fields, they can have effects in a broad area.

8.3.4. INDIRECT POWER TO PROTECT FUNDAMENTAL RIGHTS

8.3.4.1. *An Indirect, Accessory or Functional Rule-making Power*

Several scholars have argued that the EU has an indirect power to protect fundamental rights, which is sometimes referred to as an accessory or a functional rule making power.[47] This is understood as a power for the EU to adopt rules or measures to protect fundamental rights when exercising its specific competences under the Treaties.[48] When the EU, for example, adopts certain acts on the basis its powers in the area of asylum law, it can be understood to have an accessory power to ensure that relevant

44 Directive 2000/43/EC of 29 June 2000 on implementing the principle of equal treatment between persons irrespective of race or ethnic origin [2000] OJ L180/22; Directive 2000/78 of 27 November 2000 establishing a general framework for equal treatment in employment and occupation [2000] OJ L303/16.

45 Eeckhout (2002), p. 985.

46 See Article 3 of Directive 2000/43/EC.

47 For the use of the term 'indirect power' see Besson (2011b), pp. 44–45; Weiler & Fries (1999), pp. 154–158; and Muir (2014b), p. 33. For the use of the term 'accessory or functional rule making power', see Eeckhout (2002), pp. 984–985. Also cf. Muir (2014a), p. 226; and Ladenburger (2012), p. 23.

48 Cf. the arguments made by Alston & Weiler (1999), p. 20; Weiler & Fries (1999), pp. 154–155; and Eeckhout (2002), pp. 982–983.

fundamental rights are respected in relation to the actions which it undertakes.[49] The EU has, after all, an obligation to ensure that its actions comply with fundamental rights on the basis of Article 6 TEU.[50] Article 51(1) of the Charter also expresses that the Union institutions and the member states (must) respect and 'promote the application' of the rights of the Charter in accordance with their respective powers. In the text of the preamble to the Charter, the EU even is called upon to 'strengthen' the protection of fundamental rights.[51] If the EU is to comply with these obligations or tasks within the exercise of its competences, then it must be implied that it has an indirect competence to protect fundamental rights.[52]

There are various examples from which it appears that the EU makes use of an indirect competence to protect fundamental rights.[53] It has been argued that the establishment of certain minimum standards in the area of asylum law, such as the EU Directive for the reception conditions of asylum seekers in the EU, is based on the indirect competence of the EU to protect fundamental rights in that field.[54] Next, there are various legislative instruments, as well as some that await adoption, in the area of criminal law. This includes a Directive to protect the principle of the presumption of innocence and the right to be present at trial, and a Directive to safeguard the rights of children suspected and accused in criminal proceedings.[55] Further, there is a specific provision to be found in the Audiovisual Media Directive which aims to ensure the

---

49 Eeckhout, e.g., has held that 'the Charter would be a nonsense if the EU institutions did not have the power to ensure, through appropriate rule-making, that human rights are respected in the process of applying the acts which they adopt', see Eeckhout (2002), p. 984.

50 Other bases to be found for this position include that the ECJ has held that 'respect for human rights is a condition for the lawfulness of EU law', see ECJ 28 March 1996, *Opinion 2/94*, para. 34; ECJ 23 April 1983, C-294/83, *Les Verts v. Parliament*, para. 23; and ECJ 18 December 2014, *Opinion 2/13*, para. 169. The ECJ only very incidentally has held that the EU institutions have a (positive) duty to ensure the observance of fundamental rights, see ECJ 26 November 1996, C-68/95, *T. Port v. Bundesanstalt für Landwirtschaft und Ernährung*, para. 40; and ECJ 11 July 1985, C-60/84, *Cinéthèque v. Fédération nationale des cinémas français*, para. 26.

51 Section 8.3.4.4. further discusses some provisions of the Charter that could specifically require certain measures to be taken by the EU. More generally, it can be held that many of the Charter's fundamental rights are phrased as empowering rights ('everyone has the right to …'). Especially in contrast to the provisions of the Convention which are mainly phrased as defensive rights (for example, 'no one shall be deprived of …'), the rights of the Charter seem to give more direct ground for entitlement to governmental action.

52 Besson (2011b), p. 50.

53 It has been explained that the EU also used indirect competences to address several of the fundamental rights challenges in Hungary, see Dawson & Muir (2013), p. 1964; and cf. the 2013 Report on the application of the EU Charter of Fundamental Rights, pp. 13–14. De Schutter has provided a list of areas of EU law where close connections to fundamental rights protection can be found, see De Schutter (2004), pp. 18–19.

54 See Directive 2003/9/EC of 27 January 2003 laying down minimum standards for the reception of asylum seekers [2003] OJ L31/18; and Eeckhout (2002), p. 984.

55 See Articles 82, 83 and 85 TFEU. For some current legislative proposals of the Commission in this field, see <http://ec.europa.eu/justice/criminal/criminal-rights/index_en.htm>.

protection of the right to information and the pluriformity of the media.[56] Moreover, EU Regulations and Directives often include provisions specifically to ensure the right to be heard or the right to an effective judicial remedy, which could be considered to form an expression of the EU's indirect competence to protect those rights.[57]

Also to be mentioned is the former Data Retention Directive which was adopted on the basis of Article 95 of the Treaty establishing the European Community (TEC), the former version of Article 114 TFEU. This Directive laid down important rules regarding the protection of the right to privacy and the protection of personal data in relation to the retention of data by telecommunication providers which could be used for the investigation, detection and prosecution of serious crimes.[58] Article 114 TFEU, which is a legal basis that allows the EU to adopt harmonising measures with the object of the establishment and functioning of the internal market, was thus (necessarily) used to ensure indirectly that certain fundamental rights were protected. This Directive was declared invalid by the ECJ, however, which considered that its provisions provided insufficient protection to the right to privacy and the protection of personal data.[59]

In addition, it can be seen that specific recitals of Directives and Regulations often mention certain fundamental rights which need to be taken into account by the EU institutions or the member states in the implementation of the provisions of such instruments. More recently, it has been noted that fundamental rights are increasingly receiving attention in EU legislation, which can result in such recitals being included in Directives or Regulations.[60] This may also result in the adoption of specific legal provisions, such as those mentioned above.

While the EU could thus take different sorts of measures on the basis of this indirect competence and, in different areas, it would seem that certain limitations apply. The indirect competence to take action to protect fundamental rights is always dependent on the existence of an explicit power for EU authorities to take legislative or other kinds of actions in a certain field. Eeckhout has clarified that this 'is not an autonomous power to legislate on human rights, as it is strictly a function of the other, non-human

---

56 Directive 2010/13/EU of the European Parliament and of the Council of 10 May 2010 on the coordination of certain provisions laying down by law, regulation or administrative action in Member States concerning the provision of audiovisual media services (Audiovisual Media Services Directive). See in particular Article 15 and preambles 48 and 55.

57 Muir (2014a), pp. 226–227. An example is Article 9(1)(c) of Directive 2010/13 of 10 March 2010 on the coordination of certain provisions laid down by law, regulation or administrative action in Member States concerning the provision of audiovisual media services [2010] OJ L95/1) which protects the respect for human dignity and the prohibition of discrimination on various grounds.

58 Directive 2006/24/EC of the European Parliament and the Council of 15 March 2006 on the retention of data generated or processed in connection with the provision of publicly available electronic communications services or public communications networks [2006] OJ L105/54. See also Muir (2014a), p. 226.

59 ECJ 8 April 2014, Joined cases C-293/12 and C-594/12, *Digital Rights Ireland*.

60 Muir (2014a), pp. 226–227. It has become somewhat of a standard practice for the EU institutions to undertake assessments of compliance of their legislative actions on the basis of so-called fundamental rights checklists. See, for example, European Commission, Operational guidance on taking account of fundamental rights in Commission impact assessments, SEC(2011) 567 final.

rights powers which are conferred on the institutions'.[61] Therefore, in the exercise of its indirect competence to protect fundamental rights, the EU is bound by the specific limitations that apply to its explicit power. As a consequence, the EU may only be able to lay down minimum standards of fundamental rights protection, because such a limitation could apply on the basis of the explicit power.[62] Another implication of the accessory character of this indirect competence seems to be that the EU cannot take action if the only or primary aim of its action is to secure fundamental rights protection.

The existence of an indirect competence of EU fundamental rights is thus largely based on academic theories, while its existence also further seems to show in the legislative practices of the EU. It is not clearly expressed in the EU Treaties nor in the case-law of the ECJ. Still, the case-law of the ECJ may provide grounds to believe that the ECJ could (in the future) accept the indirect competence of the EU to protect fundamental rights. The ECJ has accepted in other case-law that the EU legislature uses Article 114 TFEU, the internal market basis, to pursue certain health objectives. The ECJ has been asked to decide about the legality of the use of Article 114 TFEU (and its former versions) as a legal basis to adopt the different Tobacco Directives, which have been contested on various occasions.[63] These Directives have provided rules which restrict the manufacture, presentation and sale of tobacco. The ECJ has found that such measures can be adopted on the basis of Article 114 TFEU, but the measure must 'genuinely have as its object the improvement of the conditions for the establishment and functioning of the internal market'.[64] The ECJ has held that the establishment of rules to ensure the protection of human health is thus not fully prohibited, but it also has found that the legal basis of Article 114 TFEU cannot be used to circumvent this limitation.[65] Here, it is of interest that Article 168(5) TFEU specifically excludes that harmonisation measures can be undertaken by the EU in the area of health protection. More recently, the ECJ has affirmed, in respect of another challenge to the validity of a new EU Regulation laying down rules on tobacco, that 'the EU legislature cannot be prevented from relying on that legal basis on the ground that public health protection is a decisive factor in the choices to be made'.[66] The ECJ specifically noted in this regard that Articles 168(1) and 114(3) TFEU hold that a high level of protection of human health should be guaranteed in the EU's policies and activities.

Potentially, the ECJ could express similar considerations on the use of Article 114 TFEU (or another legal basis) by the EU legislature to ensure the protection of fundamental rights within the context of EU law. An important difference being, of

---

61 Eeckhout (2002), p. 983. Also cf. Dougan (2015), p. 1202.

62 De Schutter (2004), p. 30.

63 See e.g. ECJ 5 October 2000, C-376/98, *Germany v. Parliament and Council*; and ECJ 10 December 2002, C-491/01, *British American Tobacco (Investment) and Imperial Tobacco*. More recently, see ECJ 4 May 2016, C-358/14, *Poland v. Parliament and Council*; and ECJ 4 May 2016, Joined cases C-477/14 and C-547/14, *Pillbox 38*.

64 ECJ 5 October 2000, C-376/98, *Germany v. Parliament and Council*, para. 99.

65 ECJ 5 October 2000, C-376/98, *Germany v. Parliament and Council*, paras 77–83.

66 ECJ 4 May 2016, C-358/14, *Poland v. Parliament and Council*, para. 34.

course, that there is no clause in the Treaty expressly prohibiting the harmonisation of fundamental rights standards, as there is for the harmonisation of laws in the area of health protection, nor does the EU Treaty specifically express that a high level of fundamental rights protection is guaranteed. The ECJ could, however, take other obligations laid down in the EU Treaties or in the Charter into account, such as those generally expressed in Article 6 TEU and Article 51(1) of the Charter.

In addition, there are various other relevant provisions laid down in the EU Treaties and the Charter that can be taken into account by the ECJ in its review of EU legislation. These provisions, which are discussed in the following subsections, indicate more clearly (although some are more general than others) what types of positive measures could be undertaken by the EU legislature, as well as by the member states, to ensure the effective protection of fundamental rights, especially in relation to the exercise of the indirect competence which the EU is considered to have.

8.3.4.2. Article 4(3) TEU: The Principle of Loyal Cooperation

It is of interest to mention the principle of loyal cooperation as laid down in Article 4(3) TEU first. This provision may indirectly serve as a basis to set requirements to protect fundamental rights within the scope of EU law, in particular for the member states. Article 4(3) TEU stipulates that:

> Member States shall take any appropriate measure, general or particular, to ensure fulfilment of the obligations arising out of the Treaties or resulting from the acts of the institutions of the Union. Member States shall facilitate the achievement of the Union's tasks and refrain from any measure which could jeopardise the attainment of the Union's objectives.

While this provision seems to be aimed at the member states only, the ECJ has clarified that the EU institutions are also bound to comply with the obligation of loyal cooperation *vis-à-vis* the member states and among the EU institutions themselves.[67] It could, therefore, be used as a basis for imposing further (positive) obligations on the EU institutions as well as on the member states. Indeed, the ECJ has mentioned the principle of loyal cooperation in its case-law as a foundation for the establishment of some important and seemingly far-reaching principles, such as the principle of supremacy.[68] The ECJ has also clarified that the principle requires the member states to secure that individuals can bring procedures at national level to claim damages as a result of state responsibility for breaches of EU law.[69] The ECJ has moreover used the

---

67 See Article 13(2) TEU; and ECJ 28 February 1991, C-234/89, *Delimitis v. Henninger Bräu*, para. 53. In this judgment, the ECJ clarified that there was an obligation for the Commission to provide information to the national courts.

68 ECJ 15 July 1964, C-6/64, *Costa/E.N.E.L.* (the principle of supremacy); and ECJ 19 June 1990, C-213/89, *Factortame*, paras 19–20 (principle of effectiveness).

69 ECJ 19 November 1990, Joined cases C-6/90 and C-9/90, *Francovich*, paras 33–36.

principle of loyal cooperation as a basis for imposing an obligation on the member states to take all necessary and appropriate measures to prevent violations of the free movement provisions by obstacles committed by private parties.[70]

In some cases, the ECJ has emphasised the importance of the principle of loyal cooperation in the area of fundamental rights protection. In *Opinion 2/13* on the draft agreement for the accession of the EU to the Convention, for example, the ECJ set forth the principle of loyal cooperation among the main principles to be taken into account within the context of the accession of the EU to the Convention.[71] Also, in the case of *Åkerberg Fransson*, the principle of loyal cooperation was used to support the conclusion that the Charter is applicable to member states' measures falling within the scope of EU law.[72] More particularly, the principle of loyal cooperation has been used by the ECJ as a basis to develop the principle that national authorities must interpret national law as far as possible in light of the wording and the purpose of EU law, which includes respect for certain fundamental rights.[73] Lastly, the principle that interim measures must be provided by national courts to secure the effective protection of EU law was based by the ECJ on the principle of loyal cooperation, and has been used to protect fundamental rights.[74]

Yet, the use of the principle of loyal cooperation as a basis to develop far ranging obligations is not uncontested. In particular, Article 4(3) TEU does not give clear directions as to what types of measures must be taken. According to Temple Lang the principle has been invoked especially in cases 'when a new legal issue or a new situation arises, where there is little or no relevant case-law and arguments are being based on general principles'.[75] If only for that reason, the principle must be used very cautiously by the ECJ in the development of fundamental rights obligations, especially in areas where there are no very clear and specific fundamental rights powers.

8.3.4.3. *Article 19(1) TEU: Provision of Remedies at National Level*

Further, in relation to the indirect competences of the EU to protect fundamental rights, it is important to mention Article 19(1) TEU. This provision stipulates that 'Member States shall provide remedies sufficient to ensure effective legal protection in the fields covered by Union law.'

---

70 ECJ 9 December 1997, C-265/95, *Commission v. France*, para. 32. On this topic, see further Stachel (2006).

71 ECJ 18 December 2014, *Opinion 2/13*, para. 173.

72 ECJ 7 May 2013, C-617/10, *Åkerberg Fransson*, para. 25. The ECJ has also mentioned the principle in the context of social security law, see ECJ 16 December 2004, C-293/03, *My*, para. 49; and ECJ 10 September 2015, C-408/14, *Wojchiechowski*.

73 ECJ 13 November 1990, C-106/89, *Marleasing*, para. 8; and see e.g. ECJ 29 January 2008, C-275/06, *Promusicae*, paras 68 and 70. For further examples, see section 11.3.2.

74 ECJ 19 June 1990, C-213/89, *Factortame*, para. 20; and see ECJ 18 December 2014, C-562/13, *Abdida*, paras 59–62.

75 Temple Lang (2008), p. 1526.

This provision has been included in the Lisbon Treaty, and must be read against the background of the discussions on the competence of the EU to establish requirements in relation to the procedural rules at national level.[76] The ECJ has clarified that the principle of national procedural autonomy applies where there are no specific procedural rules that have been established to protect EU law.[77] Thus member states are considered to have retained their competence in the field of procedural law. At the same time, the ECJ has been willing actively to guide the remedies and powers that need to be provided by national courts and administrative authorities to ensure the effective application of EU law.[78] This can include certain positive obligations for the member states, as explained in chapter 11.[79] The formulation of these obligations by the ECJ has created tensions in view of the limited competences of the EU in the field of procedural law. The new Article 19(1) could be seen as providing a clearer basis under EU law for requiring the member states to introduce or amend their procedural rules. It could therefore also provide a basis for certain procedural obligations which are related to the protection of fundamental rights. The ECJ has already used this new provision as a basis for a requirement to introduce a remedy at national level.[80] At the same time, the Court has stressed that it is important not to read too much into Article 19(1), by expressly holding that 'neither the Treaty nor Article 19 TEU intended to create new remedies before the national courts to ensure the observance of European Union law other than those are already laid down by national law' and explaining that remedies would only need to be created incidentally.[81] Indeed, as Van Gerven has held, 'frequently there is no need to create new remedies under national law but just to broaden the scope of existing ones'.[82] It still remains true, however, that Article 19(1) could offer an interesting basis for requiring such an extended reading of existing remedies.

8.3.4.4. *Charter Rights Calling for Positive Measures*

There are several rights and provisions laid down in the Charter itself that could provide a further basis for the EU legislature and the ECJ to derive positive measures, and provide indications of what types of measures would have to be taken to protect those rights.

First, Article 51(1) of the Charter is relevant to identifying when the EU institutions could or should act. This provision stipulates that the EU institutions and the member

---

76 See in particular Dubos (2015), pp. 18–19.

77 ECJ 16 December 1976, C-33/76, *Rewe*, para. 5.

78 Cf. Prechal & Widdershoven (2011); Van Cleynenbreugel (2012b); and Beijer (2015).

79 See in particular section 11.3.1.

80 It has also been relied upon by the Court in ECJ 17 September 2014, C-562/12, *Liivima Lihaveis* para. 68.

81 ECJ 3 October 2013, C-583/11, *Inuit Tapiriit Kanatami and others v. Parliament and Council*, paras 104–105. Also see Dubos (2015), p. 18.

82 Van Gerven (2000), p. 517.

states – in so far as they are implementing EU law – 'shall respect the rights, observe the principles and promote the application' of the provisions of the Charter 'in accordance with their respective power and respecting the limits of the powers of the Union as conferred on it in the Treaties'. This provision thus only provides a very general requirement for the EU institutions, as well as the member states, to take the rights of the Charter into account in the exercise of their powers under EU law. The use of somewhat strong language in this provision – that is, 'the promotion of fundamental rights' – suggests, to some extent, however, that the EU institutions, as well as the member states, are required actively to ensure the protection of fundamental rights which can be affected when they are exercising their powers under EU law.

Secondly, and more specifically, Article 52(1) of the Charter expressly requires that interferences with fundamental rights must be provided for by law as one of the requirements that must be met for interference to be justified under EU law.[83] This provision could, therefore, provide an important basis for taking legislative action. The ECJ has not yet shed much light on how the legality requirement under Article 52(1) is to be interpreted within the context of EU law.[84] It can be important, however, to take into account the case-law of the ECtHR on the requirement of restrictions to be 'prescribed by law'. Article 52(3) of the Charter, which requires that rights of the Charter which correspond to those of the Convention are given the same meaning and scope as is provided for under the Convention, specifically refers to the limitation criteria of the Convention.[85] For this reason, it could be expected that similar principles will be applied in relation to the interferences with fundamental rights on the basis of EU law, while Article 52(3) also allows for a higher level of protection to be provided and the autonomy of EU law to be respected.[86] The Convention's legality requirement for limitations of fundamental rights is construed rather broadly in the ECtHR's case-law. Depending on the subject matter, limitations may be provided for by legal provisions and by case-law.[87] The ECtHR also particularly looks at the 'quality of the law' and requires that states provide adequate legal protection against arbitrariness. According to the ECtHR, the legal framework must indicate with sufficient clarity the scope of the discretion and the way in which it is exercised.[88] This is especially relevant when public authorities have obtained wide discretionary powers to take measures that interfere with an individual's fundamental rights, such as secret surveillance of communications or the storage and use of a person's fingerprints and DNA samples. Interpreted in a similar manner, the legality requirement of Article 52(1) of the Charter could be taken

[83] There are further examples of Charter provisions which require that limitations on specific fundamental rights are provided for by law, see Article 8(2) on the protection of personal data; Article 17(1) on the right to property; and Article 47 on the right to effective remedies and a fair trial.

[84] See further Triantafyllou (2002); and Peers (2014), p. 1470.

[85] See the explanations to the Charter and section 6.9.1.

[86] Further on the meaning of Article 52(3), see sections 6.9.1. and 7.6.2.2.

[87] Cf. ECtHR 26 April 1979, no. 653874, *Sunday Times v. the United Kingdom*, paras 47–49.

[88] See ECtHR 2 August 1984, no. 8691/79, *Malone v. the United Kingdom*, para. 67; and ECtHR 4 December 2008, nos. 30562/04 and 30566/04, *S. and Marper v. the United Kingdom*, paras 95–99.

to include an obligation for the EU institutions to establish procedural or material safeguards to prevent arbitrary interferences with fundamental rights that could be caused by action taken by the EU in the exercise of its competences.[89]

Thirdly, there are several other provisions of the Charter which guarantee specific fundamental rights and indicate in more detail what kind of guarantees would have to be provided to secure those rights.[90] The right to protection of personal data (Article 8), for example, prescribes requirements which must be fulfilled in the processing of data (para. 2) and requires control to be exercised by an independent authority (para. 3). This could imply that such a control system needs to be set up, although it is far from clear who should take action to do so – the member states or the EU institutions. Similarly, but more straightforwardly, the right to good administration (Article 41) provides specific rights and/or obligations which must be protected/fulfilled by the EU administrative authorities, such as the obligation to give reasons for its decisions (para. 2(c)), and to make good any damages (para. 3). Elsewhere, the positive obligation to provide legal aid to ensure an individual's access to justice is specifically listed under the right to an effective remedy and a fair trial (Article 47).

Fourthly, there are various rights which have been included in the Charter that may be looked at as a basis for positive obligations as they require, by their very nature, active measures to be taken for their full realisation.[91] This applies, above all, to the rights contained in the Charter's Chapters on Equality (III) and on Solidarity (IV) which include *inter alia* the rights of the child (Article 24);[92] the entitlement to social security and social assistance (Article 34); and the protection of the environment (Article 37). They also include several work related rights such as the protection in the event of unjustified dismissal (Article 30) and the right to fair and just working conditions (Article 31). The right to education (Article 14) forms a right which depends on measures taken by the government, to be found in another part of the Charter. In relation to some of those and other provisions of the Charter, it is interesting to find that they expressly require protection to be provided in accordance with EU laws and/ or national laws and practices. Some examples thereof include Article 35 on health care and Article 28 on the right of collective bargaining and action. These provisions may not give rise to direct judicial claims for positive action, as they would most probably

---

89 Cf EU Network of independent experts on fundamental rights, Report on the situation of fundamental rights protection in the European Union in 2003, CFR-CDF.repEU.2003, p. 31.

90 See in more detail Jaeckel (2003).

91 In this regard, the right to human dignity as protected by Article 1 of the Charter can also be of importance to take into account as a provision generally giving rise to active measures. It would seem to gain particular importance in relation to the protection of the right to family life of migrants and the protection of the interests of minors, see Dupré (2013), p. 337; and Dupré (2014), pp. 6–7. Case-law of the ECJ which mentions Article 1 of the Charter include ECJ 27 February 2014, C-79/13, *Saciri and others*, para. 35; and ECJ 17 July 2014, C-474/13, *Pham*, para. 20.

92 This provision requires special protection and care to be provided to children, having their interests taken into account and their views to be heard in actions concerning them. Article 24 has already been taken into account in several cases of the Court, see e.g. ECJ 6 June 2013, C-648/11, *MA and others*, paras 57–61; and ECJ 26 April 2012, C-92/12 *PPU Health Service Executive*, para. 127.

constitute 'principles' within the meaning of Article 52(5) of the Charter (see chapter 6), yet they could give rise to certain actions by the EU institutions and the member states in so far as their policies under EU law would affect those specific fundamental rights.[93]

8.3.5. REMAINING TENSIONS: COMPETENCE CREEP OR PROTECTION GAPS?

As concluded in the foregoing subsections, it is plausible that the EU has some fundamental rights competences which could allow it to take (legislative) action to protect fundamental rights, and thereby ensure that certain positive measures which can be related to the protection of fundamental rights are undertaken. Sections 8.3.4.2. to 8.3.4.4. have indicated several relevant legal bases to be taken into account in this regard. It has even been argued that, when all these competences are looked at in combination, it can be maintained that the EU has a complementary or otherwise a shared competence to protect fundamental rights.[94] Even if this were true, the fundamental rights competences are still limited. They are restricted to very specific competence fields (such as non-discrimination and privacy) or they need to be accessory to the actions taken by the EU on an express legal basis. As such, the fundamental rights powers of the EU are not expressly listed by the EU Treaty rules, which creates a certain tension in view of the principle of attributed powers.[95] From the viewpoint of the principle of attributed powers, criticism therefore can still be raised in relation to certain action the EU has taken to protect fundamental rights. At the same time, it is equally possible to criticise the EU for failing to take action for the reason that there is no competence to act.[96] Both lines of criticism will be briefly explained in this section to complete the discussion of the scope and the limits of the fundamental rights powers of the EU.

The first line of criticism is related to the risk of 'competence creep', that is, the risk of silent and surreptitious expansion of the competences of the EU. Such expansion can, for example, be caused by an over-broad interpretation of a legal basis by the EU's institutions.[97] One of prime examples that is often discussed in relation to competence creep is the adoption of the Race Directive, due to its broad scope of application.[98] The Race Directive was adopted on the basis of Article 19(2) TFEU, which forms one of the EU's specific fundamental rights bases. This Directive forbids direct as well as indirect

93 See section 6.10. for an explanation on the distinction between rights and principles.
94 Cf. Muir (2014a), p. 239; and Besson (2011b), p. 47.
95 Dubout (2014), p. 193; and De Schutter (2004), pp. 5–8 and 11–12.
96 Cf. Muir (2014b), p. 33; and De Schutter (2004), pp. 11–12.
97 Cf. section 8.2. for the various factors that can contribute to the expansion of the competence of the EU. Section 9.2.2. specifically discusses criticisms of competence creep in relation to the judgments of the ECJ.
98 Besson (2011b), pp. 54–55.

forms of discrimination on the basis of racial or ethnic origin in a diverse range of areas including access to employment, working conditions, social security, health care, education and housing.[99] In some of these areas the EU has not been attributed any powers at all (housing) or only powers which cannot be used to harmonise the laws of the member states (health care and education). Moreover, as Eeckhout has commented (writing at a time when the Treaty on European Community law was still in force) 'some of those matters come within EC competences which are weak in character (e.g. education), and with respect to others it is difficult to see any link at all with the Community's powers'.[100] Also in relation to the establishment of the Fundamental Rights Agency, it has been noted that this requires a broad interpretation of the EU's powers.[101] The EU's residual legal basis, that is, Article 352 TFEU was used for this, while the ECJ had clearly held in *Opinion 2/94* that this legal basis could not be used as a general basis to enact rules to protect fundamental rights.[102]

Next, the use by the EU of an indirect competence to protect fundamental rights can be criticised. Seeing that there is a broad range of areas where EU law has ramifications for the protection of fundamental rights, Muir finds that (all) EU legislation can in effect easily be used as a 'vehicle for fundamental rights protection'.[103] It can be considered problematic if the EU uses certain legal bases to ensure fundamental rights and that legal bases were conferred for different policy objectives: 'Such a use of legislation giving effect to a policy objective that is initially different from fundamental rights protection may be perceived as a circumvention of limits on EU competences and feed virulent criticisms ...'[104]

It is therefore necessary that a further political debate takes place over whether, and to what extent fundamental rights protection should be provided for in specific policy fields under EU law.[105]

The second line of criticism is related to a totally different risk, which is that of 'underprotection' of fundamental rights. Here, the main concern is that the EU cannot take action in specific situations because of the limited powers of the EU, which could lead to protection gaps. It is especially feared that the limited powers of the EU do not allow it to take action in response to fundamental rights issues that cut across the different policy fields of the EU, especially now that it is not easy to have recourse to one

99 Directive 2000/43/EC of 29 June 2000 implementing the principle of equal treatment between persons irrespective of racial or ethnic origin [2000] OJ L180/22.

100 Eeckhout (2002), p. 986.

101 Besson (2011b), pp. 54–55.

102 Still, however, the powers or rather tasks of the Fundamental Rights Agency are fairly limited as this agency only aims to provide expert advice to the institutions of the EU and the member states, see Article 4 of Council Regulation No 168/2007/EC of 15 February 2007 establishing a European Union Agency for Fundamental Rights [2007] OJ L53/1.

103 Muir (2014a), p. 228.

104 Muir (2014a), p. 233.

105 Muir (2014a), p. 242.

of the broad legal bases which the Treaty provides for.[106] Another possible gap that has been pointed out is that an effective protection of fundamental rights could require a maximum harmonisation of the rules of the member states, while the specific legal bases provided for under EU law may only allow for a minimum harmonisation. This could, in particular, take place with respect to the protection of fundamental rights in the area of asylum law, but also in the area of criminal law, as some scholars have pointed out.[107] In both areas, member states need to cooperate on matters regulated by EU law, while the differences in terms of the substantive and procedural fundamental rights between the member states could provide an obstacle to their cooperation.[108] As such, however, this should not so much give rise to worries over the effective protection of fundamental rights. It must be concluded that a protection gap would only manifest itself in areas of exclusive competences. In areas of shared and complementary competences, (potential) problems could still be solved at national level, where the national authorities can take action (or are obliged to do so under the Convention) to provide for effective protection of fundamental rights.

Importantly, there is an increasing interest in clarifying the division of powers between the EU and the member states in the field of fundamental rights protection.[109] It seems that in the legislative processes more attention is now being paid to the impact of certain EU actions on fundamental rights protection especially after the Lisbon Treaty.[110] This provides potential that the EU legislature will decide whether certain kinds of measures will need to be taken by the EU institutions or by the member states in the implementation of EU law at national level, when this is necessary to effectively protect fundamental rights. If such issues remain undefined, however, the ECJ could instead be asked to clarify and determine how exactly the competences of the EU and the member states in respect of fundamental rights protection must be divided.[111]

Besson has explained that it can be very difficult to determine which powers need to be conferred to the EU to ensure fundamental rights protection in all its policies, since the specific requirements of fundamental rights may only become clear in very concrete circumstances.[112] In respect of the concept of positive obligations, it is indeed clear that they are often revealed only in circumstances which cannot always be foreseen by legislatures, and therefore are also defined by courts on a case-by-case basis.[113] Then,

---

106 Besson notes that the protection of the rights of the child could be an issue where the EU's system might leave a gap, see Besson (2011b), p. 51. Yet for suggestions on the measures that could be envisaged in the relevant competent fields of the EU, see Alston & Weiler (1999), pp. 22–27; and De Schutter (2004).

107 De Schutter (2004), p. 30.

108 De Schutter (2004), p. 31.

109 Cf. however De Schutter who has concluded (in 2004) that 'fundamental rights are not seen as influencing the allocation of powers between the Member States and the Union', see De Schutter (2004), p. 31.

110 See Muir (2014b); and section 8.3.4.1.

111 Besson (2011b), p. 62; Muir (2014a), pp. 219–246; and Muir (2014b), pp. 25–37.

112 Besson (2011b), pp. 52 and 59. Also cf. Dubout (2014), p. 198.

113 See section 4.5.

the theoretical difficulty that would arise is that there is no competence available at EU level that could legitimate certain actions are undertaken by the EU institutions to protect fundamental rights in that particular situation.

Thus a certain risk of competence creep as well as a certain risk of underprotection is perceived and it is of clear importance to take this into account in examining to what extent the EU can actively protect fundamental rights. It is submitted, however, that to be able to assess whether such risks are real, it is also relevant to have a look at the actual reasons and the specific situations in which it becomes necessary for the EU to undertake positive measures to protect fundamental rights. These reasons and more general situations are discussed in the next section. More specific situation types are discussed in chapter 11, where specific case-law examples are provided.

8.4. REASONS FOR ACTIVELY PROTECTING FUNDAMENTAL RIGHTS AT EU LEVEL

8.4.1. DIFFERENT APPROACHES FOR INCORPORATING A THEORY OF POSITIVE OBLIGATIONS WITHIN EU LAW

In order to estimate the potential for the development of positive obligations in the EU context, it must be determined at what point it actually can be expected that the EU will use its powers to protect fundamental rights and impose obligations on the EU institutions and the member states accordingly.

There are diverging views as to when the EU is required to take action to protect fundamental rights, which has to some extent already been discussed in chapter 7.[114] A similar ambiguity can be seen in the literature on the establishment of positive obligations under EU law. De Schutter has held that:

> The question *when* positive obligations may be identified which impose on the institutions of the Union to adopt certain measures for the effective protection of fundamental rights recognized in the Charter is more controversial than *whether* such positive obligations may in principle be derived from the Charter.[115]

It has been argued that the EU has obligations to adopt certain measures to protect fundamental rights and that it needs to perform a more active role in this field. Ahmed and Butler, in particular, have argued that the EU is indeed bound to fulfil certain positive obligations.[116] They have mainly based their argument on principles of international law. In their view, the EU is bound by customary international law, and by several international human rights treaties to which it has acceded itself. These

---

114 See section 7.6.1.

115 De Schutter (2004), p. 20.

116 Ahmed & Butler (2006), in particular pp. 788–792.

instruments can give rise to certain positive obligations for the EU. EU law itself stipulates in Article 351 TFEU that rights and obligations which arise from treaties to which the member states have signed up before they acceded to the EU (or before 1 January 1958) shall not be affected by the EU Treaties. This would imply that EU law cannot override the obligations of the member states under, for example, the Convention or the UN human rights treaties. Ahmed and Butler argue that when the member states are no longer able to protect the rights and obligations provided for under the said treaties autonomously, as a result of the transfer of competences to the EU, the EU itself would be bound to comply with the positive obligations arising from the protection of such treaties. This theory appears especially relevant in areas where the EU enjoys exclusive powers, because national powers in those areas have been pre-empted. However, Ahmed and Butler also find this theory to be relevant in areas of shared or complementary competences.[117]

Stubberfield has also argued that the EU is likely to incur positive obligations on the basis of principles of international law in the specific context of the return of asylum seekers under the Dublin Regulation.[118] Stubberfield holds that, once the EU accedes to the ECHR, the EU could incur some of the positive obligations which have been defined by the ECtHR. The specific criteria which have been formulated by the ECtHR to impose the relevant positive obligations on the states parties are, according to Stubberfield, also to be applied to the EU, because 'insofar as the EU adopts the attributes and powers of a sovereign state, it must assume commensurate obligations'.[119] In Stubberfield's view, it is of importance, first, to determine to what degree an action or omission of the EU contributes to the breach of a fundamental right and, secondly, to what degree the EU should have anticipated the fundamental rights breaches and should have taken action to avoid them.[120] Stubberfield also finds that positive obligations would mainly become relevant in areas where the EU enjoys exclusive powers. In the particular context of the Dublin returns, member states' obligations have not, as such, been pre-empted by the EU. Nevertheless, Stubberfield argues that this area is characterised by a high degree of coercion, and that there is little room left for the member states to exercise the discretion that they have been given.[121] Therefore, there is good reason to attribute responsibility for fulfilling certain positive obligations to the EU. She applies the criteria of causation and the existence of knowledge from the case-law of the ECtHR to arrive at the conclusion *inter alia* that the European Commission is likely to be found responsible for having to take action to investigate fundamental rights infringements in the context of the Dublin Regulation.[122]

---

117 Ahmed & Butler (2006), p. 800.
118 Stubberfield (2012).
119 Stubberfield (2012), p. 141.
120 Stubberfield (2012), pp. 133–134.
121 Stubberfield (2012), p. 127.
122 See section 3.2.6.

Such legal principles and the argumentations of these scholars could form valid reasons for the EU to adopt active measures to protect fundamental rights. However, for several reasons, these approaches also can be considered problematic.[123]

One of the first obvious problems is that the EU is not yet (directly) bound by the obligations which Ahmed and Butler and Stubberfield have derived from international human rights law. Clearly, the EU is not yet bound to the Convention since it has not acceded yet. Also in respect of the other international instruments, it is questionable whether they would directly bind the EU, given the approach the ECJ so far has taken to this.[124] Furthermore, as long as the EU has not acceded to the Convention, the ECtHR will hold the member states accountable for the actions they have taken as a result of transferring powers to international organisations such as the EU.[125] On the basis of its *Bosphorus* doctrine, the ECtHR will only apply a presumption of equivalent protection of fundamental rights provided for by an international organisation in situations where a state is fully bound to comply with its obligations under the law of that international organisation, and where a state does not have discretion to deviate from its international obligations.[126] Once the EU has acceded to the Convention, the ECtHR is expected to deviate from its *Bosphorus* doctrine.[127] It may then be expected that the EU will indeed incur positive obligations following from the judgments of the ECtHR.[128] The finalisation of the accession can still take quite some time.[129] In the meantime, it is difficult to maintain that specific obligations for the EU to protect human rights follow from the Convention or any other international treaties that it is not itself a party to.

In relation to this, it is also relevant to take into account that the approaches of Ahmed and Butler and Stubberfield are mainly focused on fundamental rights protection in areas of exclusive powers of the EU. This seems to disregard that in most situations, the EU enjoys shared or complementary powers with the member states, and it is mostly here that the concerns over the protection of fundamental rights by the EU would seem

---

123 Ahmed & Butler recognise that a different approach is taken under EU law to protect fundamental rights, and of which they are very critical, see Ahmed & Butler (2006), pp. 772–776.

124 The EU is, however, a party to the UN Convention on the Rights of Persons with Disabilities, see Council Decision 2010/48 of 27 January 2010 concerning the conclusion, by the European Community, of the United Nations Convention on the Rights of Persons with Disabilities [2010] OJ L23/35). The ECJ has decided that EU law which implements measures decided at international level do not enjoy immunity from review by the Court, see ECJ 18 July 2013, Joined cases C-584/10 P, C-593/10 P and C-595/10 P, *Commission and others v Kadi*, para. 67.

125 Cf. ECtHR 30 June 2005, no. 45036/98, *Bosphorus v. Ireland*; and ECtHR 6 December 2012, no. 12323/11, *Michaud v. France*.

126 ECtHR 30 June 2005, no. 45036/98, *Bosphorus v. Ireland*, paras 155–158.

127 Cf. Gragl (2014b), p. 19.

128 See further Gragl (2014b).

129 At the same time, different reservations have been built in (the co-respondent mechanism and the procedure of prior involvement) to preclude the ECtHR from deciding whether the EU or its member states can be held accountable for an infringement of fundamental right, and perhaps for fulfilling certain positive obligations. This will still have to be decided on the basis of the EU's internal laws *inter alia* on the basis of the division of powers between the EU and the member states.

to arise.[130] The principle of attributed competences, and the division of competences between the EU and the member states thus are important principles to take into account.[131] Consequently, in most situations, a failure to fulfil (positive) obligations to protect fundamental rights cannot exclusively be attributed to the EU. Seemingly for these reasons, the ECJ itself has very clearly stated in *Opinion 2/13*, that 'the EU is, under international law, precluded by its very nature from being considered a State'.[132]

Principles of state responsibility could also, instead, form valid reasons for relying on the mechanisms provided for at national level to secure the effective protection of fundamental rights in the application of EU law. At national level, it can, in principle be expected that a regulatory and institutional framework to protect fundamental rights is provided for. This framework may be based on the national constitutions as well as on the obligations under the Convention. A similar perspective has been taken by Advocate General Gulmann in the opinion in the case of *Bostock*.[133] This case, which was discussed in chapter 7, was concerned with the adverse consequences of the establishment of a system of milk quotas by Community law for the protection of the right to property of a specific farmer. In the opinion in this case, Advocate General Gulmann argued that:

> The fact that a legal problem has arisen as a result of the adoption of Community rules is, in my view, not in itself sufficient to entail that the solution adopted for that problem by the national authorities must necessarily respect the fundamental rights applying in the Community legal order. The starting point is that such problems can and should be resolved within the framework of the national legal systems in accordance with the solutions which apply in the Member States to corresponding legal problems that have arisen on the basis of national legislation. The most natural solution in a situation such as this is that individuals have their rights protected within the framework of the respective national legal system. There is no reason to believe that the Member States' legal systems cannot perform that task adequately. It is not insignificant in this respect that the Member States of the Community are all States that are governed by the rule of law and are obliged to respect the fundamental rights as laid down in the European Convention on Human Rights.[134]

This argumentation makes clear that it is instructive to think about the arrangements that may already have been made at national level to ensure the protection of fundamental rights and the fufilment of positive obligations.[135] Yet, this argumentation cannot always be validly applied, as will be discussed in more detail later.

---

130 See EU Network of independent experts on fundamental rights, Report on the situation of fundamental rights protection in the European Union in 2003, CFR-CDF.repEU.2003, p. 30.

131 See Article 2 of Protocol No. 8 relating to Article 6(2) of the Treaty on European Union on the accession of the Union to the European Convention on the protection of human rights.

132 ECJ 18 December 2014, *Opinion 2/13*, para. 156. See also Stubberfield (2012), p. 141.

133 Section 7.2.1.

134 See the opinion of AG Gulmann in C-2/92, *Bostock*, para. 33.

135 Cf. the criticism which has been raised by Weiler & Lockhart on the approach of the Advocate General, as well as on the outcome of the case in the judgment of the Court of Justice, see Weiler & Lockhart (1995), pp. 605–617.

In sum, it is difficult to hold that there is a broad competence for the EU to protect fundamental rights and a concomitant power to impose positive obligations on the EU institutions and the member states, although certainly there are sound arguments for doing so. Moreover, even if it is accepted that the EU should take on stronger responsibility in this field, account should be taken of the powers and responsibilities of the member states to protect fundamental rights.

8.4.2. AN APPROACH BASED ON THE DIVISION OF POWERS BETWEEN THE EU AND THE MEMBER STATES

In determining whether and to what extent the EU may be required to adopt positive measures to protect fundamental rights, this study uses an approach which is different from that of scholars such as Ahmed and Butler and Stubberfield, who base their views on the need to respect international and European human rights obligations. The approach taken in this study is based on the internal rules relating to the protection of fundamental rights within EU law. It is grounded in the protection of fundamental rights under the rules laid down in the EU's own Charter and its Treaties, and it has regard to the existing mechanisms within the member states for the protection of fundamental rights. It is thus very sensitive towards the specific competences which have been attributed to the EU. It also accepts that a deliberate choice has been made by the drafters of the Treaty and the Charter to limit the protection of fundamental rights by the EU to the specific actions that may be undertaken on the basis of its competences (Article 51(1) of the Charter) and to prohibit the EU institutions from going beyond these existing powers (Article 51(2) of the Charter). This approach may continue to be relevant for determining the positive obligations even after the accession of the EU to the Convention, since the accession stipulates that the competences of the EU must continue to be respected.[136]

Compared to the arguments discussed in section 8.4.1., the approach envisaged here presents a much more modest account of the obligations which the EU could incur on the basis of fundamental rights. It is not likely to give rise to the creation of a certain institutional framework or other structural obligations, such as, for example, Alston and Weiler have proposed. It is more concerned with the regulatory framework that must be provided for by the EU to ensure fundamental rights protection.[137]

Taking this particular internal perspective into account, the following subsections dicuss a range of different reasons which could indicate at what point the EU is required to undertake certain action to protect fundamental rights and potentially fulfill certain positive obligations. Evidently, the principles of subsidiarity and proportionality are discussed first, as they form the main set of principles within EU law for determining

136 Final report of Working Group II on the incorporation of the Charter and the accession to the Convention of 22 October 2002, CONV 354/02, p. 13.

137 Alston & Weiler (1999).

when the EU must use its powers to protect fundamental rights in areas of shared and complementary competences (section 8.4.3.). As will be explained, they provide for a very broad ground to determine whether any action by the EU in the field of fundamental rights is necessary, and more specific grounds are needed to substantiate such claims. In academic debates as well as in the preparatory documents for legislative proposals of the European Commission, such grounds can be found. They reveal that it can be necessary to establish a connection between EU acts and fundamental rights infringements (section 8.4.4.); a certain risk of a race to the bottom in fundamental rights standards (section 8.4.5.); and/or adverse effects for the primacy, unity and effectiveness of EU law (section 8.4.6.). Depending on the actual circumstances, several of these grounds may be relevant for determining the need for any action by the EU. The different grounds discussed in sections 8.4.3. to 8.4.6. mostly play a role in situations where the EU enjoys shared or complementary competences with the member states. They may also be relevant in areas of exclusive powers, but it is important to recognise that the member state may not be given any room to ensure fundamental rights protection on their own.[138]

8.4.3. SUBSIDIARITY AND PROPORTIONALITY

The principles of subsidiarity and proportionality are of key importance in general to determine whether the EU has a competence to act. Within the context of fundamental rights protection, the principle of subsidiarity is also particularly stressed by Article 51(1) of the Charter. This provision, which relates to the scope of application of the EU Charter, stipulates that 'The provisions of this Charter are addressed to the institutions, bodies, offices and agencies of the Union with due regard for the principle of subsidiarity …'. As a clarification, the explanations relating to the provisions of the Charter state that this refers to the 'logical consequences of the principle of subsidiarity and … the fact that the Union only has those powers which have been conferred upon it'.[139]

The principle of subsidiarity is defined generally in Article 5 TEU as follows:

> in areas which do not fall within its exclusive competences, the Union shall act only if and in so far as the objectives of the proposed action cannot be sufficiently achieved by the member state, either at central level or at regional and local level, but can rather, by reason of the scale or effects of the proposed action, be better achieved at Union level.

This principle is therefore mainly relevant for actions which fall outside the EU's exclusive competences. Article 5(3) TEU requires a two-pronged test to be undertaken to determine whether the requirements of subsidiarity are met. It must first be ascertained whether action may be sufficiently undertaken at national level to achieve

138 See Article 2(1) TEU. Cf. De Schutter & Butler (2008); andAhmed & Butler (2006), pp. 788–789.
139 Explanations relating to the Charter of Fundamental Rights (2007/C 303/32).

the envisaged objective and, second, whether the scale or effects of the proposed action constitute a reason for the EU to undertake action.[140]

The underlying general rationale of the principle of subsidiarity is that action is taken as closely as possible to the citizens of the EU.[141] Applying this principle to matters concerning fundamental rights protection, it seems most logical to assume that it is at national level where the interests of fundamental rights protection could be served best.[142] Here a parallel can be drawn to the meaning of the subsidiarity principle in the case-law of the ECtHR, which equally implies that fundamental rights protection preferably is provided for at the national level.[143] The principle could be applied to the EU in much the same vein. The application of fundamental rights standards as laid down in the national constitutions by the national authorities would generally be held to cater best for the needs of individuals.[144]

Nevertheless, the principle of subsidiarity may still justify action to be taken at EU level to protect fundamental rights.[145] In line with the principle of subsidiarity, fundamental rights protection would have to be secured by the EU where such protection cannot adequately be achieved by the member states alone and the scale or effects of EU action also provide a beneficial outcome. Especially where matters have a transnational dimension or member states need to fulfil (international) treaty obligations, there would be valid reasons for the EU itself to undertake action to protect fundamental rights. Relevant fundamental rights matters to be addressed at the EU level could, for example, be related to protection of the environment or combating terrorism.[146]

The application of the principle of subsidiarity in the context of fundamental rights protection may not always be straightforward. In practice, it can appear quite difficult to apply this principle in a consistent manner.[147] To what extent, for example, does the second criterion of Article 5(3) TEU (scale or effects of EU action) have an independent meaning, if according to the first criterion it is already established that actions can not sufficiently be achieved at national level? Aside from that, how can it really be determined that uniform standards are necessary to develop an effective EU policy?

Specifically in relation to the protection of fundamental rights by the EU, Muir has pointed out that measuring fundamental rights protection in terms of effectiveness is

---

140 Cf. Barents (2008), p. 388; and Opinion of A-G Kokott in C-358/14, *Poland v. Parliament and Council*, paras 142, 149–154 and 161–166.

141 See the preamble to Protocol (No 2) on the application of the principles of proportionality and subsidiarity.

142 Cf. Von Bogdandy (2000), pp. 1316–1318.

143 See section 2.4.

144 Muir (2014a), p. 239. Muir argues that as soon as the EU undertakes action, the scope for the application of national fundamental rights standards becomes limited on the basis of Article 53 of the Charter and the *Melloni* case-law.

145 Alston & Weiler (1999), p. 27. Also cf. Butler & De Schutter (2008), pp. 313–319.

146 Suerbaum (2013), p. 391.

147 Davies (2006); and Jančić (2015), pp. 953–956. Jančić argues that attention should be shifted away from the principle of subsidiarity towards the principle of conferral as a way of curbing the expansion of EU competences.

inherently difficult.[148] Fundamental rights have a specific function and are of a specific nature, which generally sets them apart from any other EU law.[149] Fundamental rights function to regulate the relationship within states and it may, for that reason, be difficult to measure their cross-border effects. Also, it may not make sense to undertake a comparative efficiency test with regard to the impact of the establishment of fundamental rights standards on the national or the EU level, because fundamental rights always require some prioritising or a balancing exercise to be undertaken.[150] Muir therefore finds that the principle of subsidiarity cannot provide a useful yardstick for determining whether action must be undertaken by the EU to protect fundamental rights. There are thus some doubts as to whether the principle of subsidiarity is suitable for determining whether the EU needs to take action to protect fundamental rights.

The principle of proportionality is described in Article 5(4) TEU in relation to the division of competences between the EU and the member states. It requires that 'the content and form of Union action shall not exceed what is necessary to achieve the objectives of the Treaties'. This reflects the general meaning that is to be given to the proportionality principle.[151] If a choice can be made between several means, then the least onerous one must be chosen, and the disadvantages thereof must not be disproportionate to the aims pursued. This principle is perhaps more straightforward than the subsidiarity principle and could imply, for example, that Directives would have to be adopted instead of regulations.

Both the principles of subsidiarity and proportionality are considered as important instruments to limit the expansion of the powers of the EU.[152] Certain formal mechanisms have been introduced with the Lisbon Treaty to ensure compliance with these principles. A separate protocol, for example, has been added to the EU Treaties on subsidiarity and proportionality, requiring the European Commission when preparing new legislative acts to adopt a 'detailed statement making it possible to appraise compliance with the principles of subsidiarity and proportionality'.[153] Also, the role of the national parliaments has increased, as they are now allowed to block legislative proposals by the European Commission if they consider that the principle of subsidiarity is not complied with.[154] There is thus quite some interest in the application

148 Muir (2014a), pp. 240–241.
149 Cf. De Schutter (2004), p. 12; and Muir (2014a), p. 222.
150 Muir (2014a), p. 239.
151 See e.g. ECJ 4 May 2016, C-358/14, *Poland v. Parliament and Council*, para. 78.
152 See generally De Búrca (2001a); Davies (2006); and Craig (2012), pp. 72–87. It has been shown that the national parliaments have made use of their powers to strike down the EU's initiatives to legislate on worker's rights to strike, see the Proposal for a Council Regulation on the exercise of the right to take collective action within the context of the freedom of establishment and the freedom to provide services, COM(2012) 130 final.
153 According to Article 9 of the Protocol on subsidiarity and proportionality, the Commission must further submit an annual report on the application of Article 5 TFEU.
154 See Articles 6 and 7 of the Protocol on subsidiarity and proportionality.

of the principles of subsidiarity and proportionality by the political institutions at EU and at national level.[155]

Since there is increasing interest in compliance with the principles of subsidiarity and proportionality of the legislative proposals of the EU, it is possible to explore how these principles are actually applied in respect of the actions taken by the EU to protect fundamental rights. A few reports that have been drafted on the legislative proposals of the EU have been examined in this study in order to find how such principles are applied. The explanatory memorandum on the proposal for the General Data Protection Regulation, for example, shows that cross-border flows of personal information was an important factor which contributed to the decision of the EU to further harmonise the standards of the member states on privacy and personal data protection. The explanatory memorandum shows that the increasing cross-border flows of personal information pose specific challenges for the enforcement of data protection legislation by the member states.[156] There are divergent levels of data protection in the different member states, and therefore uniform rules on protection of personal data would be needed. In the explanatory memorandum it is held that such rules could best be provided by adopting legislation in the form of a Regulation.[157]

Similarly, the increasing cross-border movement of individuals proves to be an important consideration in adopting minimum (procedural) fundamental rights standards in the area of criminal law. In the impact assessment on the proposal for a Directive protecting the rights of children suspected or accused of criminal proceedings, it is explained that the increasing numbers of individuals travelling across borders require that proper and effective action is undertaken at EU level to protect the rights of those who become involved in criminal proceedings.[158] Member states are not considered to be well able to deal with these actions alone, especially when they concern vulnerable persons such as children.[159] For that reason, certain minimum standards are adopted to secure the right to a fair trial, inter alia, in a Directive on the right to the interpretation and translation of criminal proceedings, a Directive on the

155 While the ECJ is willing to examine the compliance with the principle of subsidiarity, it is generally considered to apply only a very deferential assessment, see De Búrca (1998), p. 225. For examples of recent such examinations by the ECJ, see ECJ 18 June 2015, C-508/13, *Estonia v. Parliament and Council*; and ECJ 4 May 2016, C-358/14, *Poland v. Parliament and Council.*

156 Proposal for a Regulation on the protection of individuals with regard to the processing of personal data and on the free movement of such data (General Data Protection Regulation), COM (2012) 11, 25 January 2012.

157 Proposal for a Regulation on the protection of individuals with regard to the processing of personal data and on the free movement of such data (General Data Protection Regulation), COM (2012) 11, 25 January 2012, pp. 5–6.

158 Impact Assessment for a Commission proposal for a Directive on procedural safeguards for children suspected or accused in criminal proceedings, SWD (2013) 480, 27 November 2013, p. 32.

159 Impact Assessment for a Commission proposal for a Directive on procedural safeguards for children suspected or accused in criminal proceedings, SWD (2013) 480, 27 November 2013, p. 33.

right to information in criminal proceedings, and a Directive on the right of access to a lawyer and communication with a third party in cases of deprivation of liberty.[160]

These examples show that the principles of subsidiarity and proportionality can provide important and helpful considerations when deciding the type and degree of action that the EU needs to take in the area of fundamental rights protection. They can be especially helpful in respect of the cooperation between the authorities of the member states, and in situations where the rights of vulnerable persons are at stake. At the same time, as discussed earlier, the principles of subsidiarity and proportionality often merely provide for a very general starting point for determining whether EU action is required. In other situations it can still be difficult to measure the effects of EU action in relation to fundamental rights protection and the need to take action. Indeed, an equally strong argument can be made for the protection of certain rights by the national authorities. Hence, although the principles of subsidiarity and proportionality are important in deciding whether there is a competence for the EU to take action to protect fundamental rights, and to impose obligations on the EU intitutions and on the member states, it will not be sufficient to look only at these principles when making that decision.

8.4.4. CONNECTIONS BETWEEN EU ACTS AND FUNDAMENTAL RIGHTS INFRINGEMENTS

If it appears that certain actions of the EU interfere with certain fundamental rights, it could be expected that the EU takes action to protect those rights or compensate for the (potential) harm done. The EU could, for example, adopt preventive and remedial measures and define the restricted circumstances in which such interference may legitimately be made by the EU institutions or the member states. Indeed, one primary justification for the EU to take measures in the field of fundamental rights protection would actually be to secure that its own acts do not as such cause an unjustified interference with fundamental rights. For example, if the EU were to intervene in the internal market by adopting certain trading rules, which could directly interfere with the fundamental rights of individuals or undertakings such as the right to property, it could be reasoned that the EU would need to adopt rules on arrangements for compensation. Likewise, if the European Commission were to interfere with the rights to privacy during an inspection on the basis of competition rules, it would be necessary for certain remedies to be provided at EU level so that individuals are able to complain about infringements and, if appropriate, to enable the act that led to the breach to be

---

[160] Directive 2014/64/EU of 20 October 2010 on the right to the interpretation and translation of criminal proceedings [2010] OJ L280/1; Directive 2012/13/EU of 22 May 2012 on the right to information in criminal proceedings [2012] OJ L142/1; and Directive 2013/48/EU of 22 October 2013 on the right of access to a lawyer and communication with a third party in cases of deprivation of liberty [2013] OJ L294/1.

declared void. Such 'corrective measures' may be necessary to ensure compliance with the negative obligation not to violate fundamental rights as such and/or to prevent interferences with fundamental rights by public (administrative) authorities.[161] Especially in situations where a direct causal connection between EU acts or decisions and fundamental rights infringements can be made, it seems logical that the EU will undertake certain actions to ensure that unjustified interferences do not take place. As such, this also follows from the principles of international law underlying the attribution of state responsibility, and from the system for justifying restrictions on the basis of the Convention.[162]

The competence for the EU to protect fundamental rights in this context is clearly an indirect competence, which follows from and is accessory to the express and direct competences granted to it under the EU Treaties. The specific legal bases which have been discussed in sections 8.3.4.2. to 8.3.4.4., such as the principle of loyal cooperation and the legality requirement under Article 52(1) of the Charter, are relevant here to define the measures that may need to be taken by the EU. If the EU were to exercise such an indirect competence in an area of EU law where it has exclusive powers, it would be logical to assume that the EU also secures that the relevant measures are taken to secure compliance with (negative) fundamental rights obligations. This is because the member states would not enjoy any discretion to ensure protection. However, in areas of shared and supportive competences, discretion could, in particular, have been given to the member states to adopt (detailed) rules on preventive and remedial measures.[163] The member states may be required to apply their own national regimes for protection of fundamental rights to their actions taken under EU law.[164] There is good reason for setting such requirements, which has been explained by the EU independent network of experts on fundamental rights as follows:

> with few exceptions, the violations of the Charter may result not directly from the activities of the Union – as would be the case in particular if secondary law of the EU were to impose to the Member States to commit violations of fundamental rights – but could rather originate from the margin of appreciation which is left to the Member States by EU instruments.[165]

It may thus be difficult to construe a clear causal connection between the acts of the EU and the fundamental rights infringements under EU law. Nonetheless, the margin of appreciation that was provided for to the member states under EU secondary legislation has been addressed in several cases which have been brought before the ECJ. One such

---

161 See EU Network of independent experts on fundamental rights, Report on the situation of fundamental rights protection in the European Union in 2003, CFR-CDF.repEU.2003, p. 31.

162 Cf. Ahmed & Butler (2006).

163 Cf. Butler & De Schutter (2008), pp. 316–317.

164 Also cf. the opinion of AG Gulmann in C-2/92, *Bostock*, para. 33 discussed in section 8.4.1.

165 See EU Network of independent experts on fundamental rights, Report on the situation of fundamental rights protection in the European Union in 2003, CFR-CDF.repEU.2003, CFR-CDF.repEU.2003, p. 30.

case is *Parliament v. Council*, which concerned the protection provided for under the Family Reunification Directive.[166] The Directive expressly allowed member states to apply integration criteria to children over the age of 12 before authorising their entry and residence.[167] The Directive did not further clarify what kinds of safeguards would need to be provided at national level to prevent unjustified and arbitrary interferences with the right to respect for private and family life in that case. In its judgment on this particular case, the ECJ explained that 'A provision of a Community act could, in itself, not respect fundamental rights if it required, or expressly or impliedly authorised, the Member States to adopt or retain national legislation not respecting those rights'.[168] However, the ECJ still concluded in this case that 'the Directive leaves the Member States a margin of appreciation, it is sufficiently wide to enable them to apply the Directive's rules in a manner consistent with the requirements flowing from the protection of fundamental rights'.[169]

The ECJ thus found that member states are required to ensure the protection of fundamental rights within the exercise of EU law provisions, but it also trusted them to be able and competent to do so on the basis of their national legislation. In other cases, the ECJ has clarified that the member states must 'ensure that they do not rely on an interpretation of an instrument of secondary legislation which would be in conflict with the fundamental rights or with the other general principles of EU law'.[170] Therefore, EU secondary legislation does not always need to spell out all the detailed rules to ensure that restrictions are provided for by law, which may be required by Article 52(1) of the Charter.

So the question remains at what point, then, it could be expected that legislative action is undertaken at EU level to secure the protection of fundamental rights in areas of shared or complementary competences. Is there a certain responsibility that could be attributed to the EU to take such action?

It seems that the existence of serious interferences with fundamental rights in the implementation of EU law at national level would provide an important justification for the EU legislature to adopt provisions laying down substantive and procedural safeguards to prevent arbitrary interferences with fundamental rights. This conclusion can be reached on the basis of the case of *Digital Rights Ireland*.[171] However, other cases of the ECJ also demonstrate that serious interferences with fundamental rights can provide an important reason to ensure fundamental rights protection at EU level.[172]

---

166 ECJ 27 June 2006, C-540/03, *Parliament v. Council*.

167 Article 4(1) of Directive 2003/86/EC of 22 September 2003 on the right to family reunification [2003] OJ L251/21.

168 ECJ 27 June 2006, C-540/03, *Parliament v. Council*, para. 23. Also cf. ECJ 6 November 2003, C-101/01, *Lindqvist*, paras 83–84.

169 ECJ 27 June 2006, C-540/03, *Parliament v. Council*, para. 104.

170 ECJ 21 December 2011, Joined cases C-411/10 and C-493/10, *N.S. and others*, para. 77; and ECJ 15 February 2016, C-601/15, *J.N.*, para. 60.

171 ECJ 8 April 2014, Joined cases C-293/12 and C-594/12, *Digital Rights Ireland*.

172 See sections 7.5.2. and 7.6.2.3.

The case of *Digital Rights* was about the former Data Retention Directive, which required the member states to ensure that certain metadata gathered by telecommunication providers was retained for the purpose of the prevention, investigation, detection and prosecution of serious crimes.[173] The Directive formulated some safeguards, such as demanding a minimum and a maximum period to be set for the retention of the data. For the most part, however, it left considerable discretion to the national authorities in providing for further arrangements, such as those related to the access of public authorities to those data. Did the EU legislature thereby fail to secure adequate protection of fundamental rights? In answering this question, the Advocate General reasoned as follows:

> It is necessary in that regard, first of all, to explain that a situation in which the European Union restricts itself to adopting legislation harmonising provisions invariably adopted by the majority of the Member States is not comparable to a situation in which the European Union decides, additionally, to make such legislation applicable generally.
>
> In the first case, the European Union can … essentially leave to the national legislatures the task of ensuring that the legislation adopted on their own initiative and entailing a limitation on fundamental rights contains all the guarantees necessary to ensure that the limitations and their application ('access') comply with all the quality of law requirements and the principle of proportionality.
>
> In the second case, on the other hand, where the limitation on fundamental rights stems from the legislation of the European Union itself and is therefore attributable to it, the European Union legislature's share of the responsibility is quite different. In the case of directives, it is clear that it will be for the Member States to set out in detail the guarantees necessary to regulate the limitation on fundamental rights in an instance such as the present one. However, the European Union legislature must play a leading role in defining those guarantees. It is from this perspective that it is necessary to examine compliance with the quality of the law requirement.[174]

According to the Advocate General, therefore, it makes a difference whether EU law has merely harmonised the provisions of national law, or whether it has imposed a new obligation on the member states which could interfere with fundamental rights. Because the Data Retention Directive did not establish an optional regime for the member states to take measures in respect of the retention of data, and instead imposed obligations on the member states which could interfere with fundamental rights, the Directive 'should have been accompanied by a simultaneous development as regards guarantees and therefore have led the European legislature to regulate in outline the very broad

---

173 Directive 2006/24/EC of the European Parliament and of the Council of 15 March 2006 on the retention of data generated or processed in connection with the provision of publicly available electronic communications services or of public communications networks [2006] OJ L105/54.

174 Opinion of AG Cruz Villalón in Joined cases C-293/12 and C-594/12, *Digital Rights Ireland*, paras 115–117.

authority conferred on the Member States with regard to access to the data and their use, by the adoption of specifications in the form of principles'.[175] The Advocate General further argued that:

> The European Union legislature cannot, when adopting an act imposing obligations which constitute serious interference with the fundamental rights of citizens of the Union, entirely leave to the Member States the task of defining the guarantees capable of justifying that interference. It cannot content itself either with assigning the task of defining and establishing those guarantees to the competent legislative and/or administrative authorities of the Member States called upon, where appropriate, to adopt national measures implementing such an act or with relying entirely on the judicial authorities responsible for reviewing its practical application. It must, if it is not to render the provisions of Article 51(1) of the Charter meaningless, fully assume its share of responsibility by defining at the very least the principles which must govern the definition, establishment, application and review of observance of those guarantees.[176]

Thus, according to the Advocate General, in case of serious interferences with fundamental rights on the basis of EU law, there is a greater responsibility for the EU to ensure that appropriate measures are taken to prevent or remedy fundamental rights infringements, and less discretion can be given to the member states. The ECJ, to a certain extent, agreed. It decided in its judgment on the *Digital Rights* case that the EU legislature had failed to secure sufficient respect for fundamental rights because the Directive lacked clear substantive and procedural safeguards in relation to a serious interference with the right to privacy and the protection of personal data.[177]

In deciding who is to regulate fundamental rights issues in relation to secondary EU law, it thus could be of particular importance to look at whether EU legislation imposes new obligations on the member states, and whether they may cause a serious infringement of fundamental rights when further (corrective) measures may be needed to effectively secure those fundamental rights.[178]

---

175 Opinion of AG Cruz Villalón in *Digital Rights Ireland*, para. 118.

176 Opinion of AG Cruz Villalón in *Digital Rights Ireland*, para. 120.

177 ECJ 8 April 2014, Joined cases C-293/12 and C-594/12, *Digital Rights Ireland*, paras 60–61.

178 Further support for this argument could also be found in the case of *Parliament v. Council*, see ECJ 5 September 2012, C-355/10 *Parliament v. Council*. This specific case was brought by the European Parliament against the adoption of EU measures in the context of see border surveillance measures. At para. 77, the ECJ held that 'it is important to point out that provisions conferring powers of public authority on border guards – such as the powers conferred in the contested decision, which include stopping persons apprehended, seizing vessels and conducting persons apprehended to a specific location – mean that the fundamental rights of the persons concerned may be interfered with to such an extent that the involvement of the European Union legislature is required'. The ECJ seems to indicate in this judgment that because of the seriousness of the interferences that could take place, the EU legislature needs to be involved to spell out the further conditions and safeguards that would have to be provided.

8.4.5. PREVENTING A RACE TO THE BOTTOM

Because free movement of individuals and of undertakings can take place throughout the EU, it has been argued that there is a certain risk that member states are tempted to lower their level of fundamental rights standards. This risk of a 'race to the bottom' forms an important ground, according to De Schutter, for the EU to introduce measures to prevent the downgrading of the standards of fundamental rights within the EU.[179]

A race to the bottom was feared early on, in relation to the protection of the social rights of workers under Community law.[180] It was argued that the free movement of undertakings and the free movement of workers within the Community would create a risk that undertakings would be attracted to doing business mostly with and within member states with a relatively low standard of fundamental rights. The necessity to comply with a high standard of fundamental rights protection could have been seen as a disadvantage for undertakings. Member states could, for that reason, be tempted to lower their standards to attract foreign investments. Potentially, undertakings could also decide to relocate to member states where the fundamental rights standards were lower than elsewhere. Action at EU level was therefore considered necessary to address the lowering of the social rights standards. It was for this reason, according to De Schutter, that the member states decided to confer competences to the European Community to take legislative action in relation to the right to equal pay for men and women and in relation to the right to paid leave.[181]

This 'race to the bottom' argument still seems to be relevant in present circumstances. It has been suggested that there is a risk that the member states may lower their standards of privacy rights because of the important role played by the free movement of information and data on a world-wide scale.[182] It is common knowledge that the business models of social media giants such as Facebook and Google is based, to a considerable extent, on the free flow of information and of personal data. Compliance with high standards of fundamental rights would form an obstacle to their business models and thus discourage their establishment in member states which have high standards on privacy rights. Therefore, there is a good reason for high standards of privacy standards to be established at EU level.

Outside the sphere of the internal market, De Schutter has also found that there is a similar risk for a race to the bottom in the standards of fundamental rights protection

179 See De Schutter (2004), pp. 18–19. Also cf. EU Network of independent experts on fundamental rights, Report on the situation of fundamental rights protection in the European Union in 2003, CFR-CDF.repEU.2003, pp. 31–32; and Barnard (2011), pp. 648–649.

180 This was recognised in ECJ 8 April 1976, C-43/75, *Defrenne v. Sabena (No 2)*, paras 8–9: 'Article 119 pursues a double aim. First, in light of the different stages of the development of social legislation in various member states, the aim of Article 119 is to avoid a situation in which undertakings established in States which have actually implemented the principle of equal pay suffer a competitive disadvantage in intra-community competition as compared with undertakings established in States which have not yet eliminated discrimination against women workers as regards pay.'

181 De Schutter (2004), pp. 5–7.

182 Benett & Raab (2006).

in the area of asylum law.[183] In the absence of border controls within the EU, asylum seekers could decide to go forum shopping for the most favourable standards within the EU.[184] In response, member states might also want to restrict the rights of these asylum seekers to prevent high numbers of asylum applications. Again, the establishment of common standards at EU level could prevent this race to the bottom. De Schutter has argued that:

> although the Member States are recognized the possibility to fully respect fundamental rights under their jurisdiction, whichever accommodations this requires from the Union …, States are neither encouraged, nor do they have incentives to, *develop* human rights beyond the minimal obligation to respect them.[185]

Thus, in areas of shared (and potentially also complementary) competences, the EU would be best placed to secure a high level of fundamental rights protection. De Schutter has further explained that it is necessary for the EU to go beyond providing for only minimum standards of fundamental rights protection to prevent a race to the bottom, because the member states do not have an incentive to provide for higher levels themselves in certain areas of EU law.[186]

In relation to this, Stubberfield has also argued that states could be tempted to 'hide behind the organisational veil' and even try to escape their fundamental rights obligations under international law in areas falling within the scope of EU law if they only need to comply with minimum standards of fundamental rights.[187] In some areas of EU law, this is difficult to achieve, because it has been determined that only minimum standards and rules can be established on the EU level. For example, in the area of criminal law, only minimum standards may be established to improve the judicial cooperation in criminal matters having a cross-border dimension and to define certain serious criminal sanctions and offences.[188] The competences of the EU to take certain actions in the area of asylum law are, however, no longer restricted to adopting minimum rules. It could, therefore, develop a Common European Asylum System on the basis of its competences.[189] Based on the argument of the risk of the 'race to the bottom', such competences could then indeed be used to the fullest extent possible.

While the justification for adopting EU action to ensure fundamental rights protection on the basis of the aim to prevent a 'race to the bottom' seems compelling, it must be admitted that it can in fact be quite difficult to establish that a downgrading of fundamental rights standards actually takes place as a result of the free movement of

183 De Schutter (2004), pp. 20–21.

184 The risk of forum shopping in the context of asylum applications is also indicated by the Court in ECJ 21 December 2011, Joined cases C-411/10 and C-493/10, *N.S. and others*, para. 79.

185 De Schutter (2004), pp. 3–4.

186 De Schutter (2004), pp. 21–22.

187 Stubberfield (2012), p. 127.

188 Article 82(2) and 83(1)–(2) (criminal law), Article 153(2)(a) (social rights in the labour area).

189 Cf. Article 78 and 79 TFEU.

individuals and undertakings within the EU. So far, no statistical data showing this has been provided.[190] For that reason, it still may be useful to rely also on other arguments when seeking to establish a sound basis for taking EU action.

8.4.6. ENSURING THE PRIMACY, UNITY AND EFFECTIVENESS OF EU LAW

The protection of the primacy, unity and effectiveness of EU law constitutes an important consideration in the case-law of the ECJ on fundamental rights.[191] It can be argued that it may also provide the EU with an important ground for justification of the adoption of rules to protect fundamental rights in areas of shared or complementary competences.

The establishment of uniform rules by the EU legislature may become necessary when there exists a variety of fundamental rights standards throughout the member states that actually hampers the effectiveness of EU law itself. According to Barnard, this particular reason formed an important ground for the decision of European Community to adopt rules to ensure the protection of workers' social rights within the internal market.[192] Barnard discusses that it was expected that the divergence of fundamental rights standards in the different member states could create obstacles to the free movement of workers and the free movement of undertakings. Such obstacles and distortions to the market needed to be removed in order to secure integration and the effective functioning of the market. Therefore, rather than serving as a correction to the destructive effects of the market leading to a race to the bottom, as discussed in section 8.4.5., the adoption of certain standards in the field of social rights of workers at EU level could be justified as ensuring a level playing field to the benefit of economic operators active within the internal market.

Similarly, in the area of data protection, the protection of the effectiveness of EU law also seems to form an important driver behind the establishment of uniform standards on fundamental rights.[193] The explanatory memorandum to the proposal for the EU's General Data Protection Regulation shows that the fragmentation of privacy standards was considered an important rationale for further harmonisation of the rules of the member states on that issue.[194] The differences between the member states

---

190 Barnard explained that there was little evidence on the basis of statistical information showing that a race to the bottom of social rights standards was likely to take place within the EU, see Barnard (2011), p. 649.

191 See in particular section 6.3. for an explanation of this rationale for the EU system of fundamental rights protection.

192 Barnard (2011), p. 645.

193 De Schutter (2008), p. 550.

194 See e.g. preambles 2, 7 and 11 of the Proposal for a Regulation of the European Parliament and of the Council on the protection of individuals with regard to the processing of personal data and on the free movement of such data (General Data Protection Directive) COM(2011) 11 final.

constitute obstacles to the pursuit of economic activities within the EU and they could distort competition. In the absence of common rules, practical challenges arise for the enforcement of data protection legislation and, for that reason, uniform rules need to be established at EU level.[195]

In some areas, such as the area of freedom, security and justice, it has, instead, been decided that the judicial and administrative authorities of the member states must cooperate on the basis of the principle of mutual recognition.[196] This basically implies that they must cooperate on the basis of divergences in the fundamental rights standards of the different member states. In relation to some topics, it has been decided that certain minimum standards related to such areas are to be established at EU level to secure the effective application of such cooperation mechanisms, as illustrated by the directives in the area of criminal law pointed out earlier.[197]

Thus to address the risks for the protection of the primacy, unity and effectiveness of EU law, the EU could also decide to intervene in a certain area by harmonising the standards of fundamental rights.

8.5. PROVIDING ROOM FOR THE APPLICATION OF NATIONAL OR INTERNATIONAL FUNDAMENTAL RIGHTS STANDARDS

As alluded to in sections 8.4.1. and 8.4.2., there remain important arguments that fundamental rights protection should be provided at national level in situations that are related to EU law. It may be preferable that national authorities, which are closest to the individuals whose fundamental right are affected, make the appropriate arrangements. In this situation it can, however, be important that EU law expressly clarifies that the member states have discretion to apply their national standards of fundamental rights law, and the human rights standards under international treaties.

It has sometimes been argued that EU law does not sufficiently address this issue of the desirability of regulation of fundamental rights matters on the national rather than the EU level. There are some general provisions which aim to regulate such conflicts, such as Article 351 TFEU and Article 53 of the Charter, yet in practice these provisions do not appear to be readily applied.[198] Article 351 TFEU clarifies that the (human

---

[195] Proposal for a Regulation of the European Parliament and of the Council on the protection of individuals with regard to the processing of personal data and on the free movement of such data (General Data Protection Directive) COM(2011) 11 final, p. 6.

[196] See also section 6.8.

[197] Impact Assessment for a Commission proposal for a Directive on procedural safeguards for children suspected or accused in criminal proceedings, SWD (2013) 480, 27 November 2013, p. 32. Further cf. De Schutter (2008), pp. 550–555.

[198] Besson (2011b), p. 56.

rights) treaties or agreements which member states have signed up to before their accession to the EU are not affected by the EU Treaties. Yet, in the second paragraph of this provision, member states are required to 'take all appropriate steps to eliminate the incompatibilities established'. What exactly is expected of member states in this respect, and what room are they afforded to comply with those treaties? This remains unclear.[199] With respect to the application of Article 53 of the Charter, which allows member states to apply higher standards of fundamental rights, there appear to be even more worries, especially since the ECJ clarified in the judgment of *Melloni* that higher standards of national fundamental rights may be applied by national authorities and courts in respect of obligations stemming from EU law, as long as this does not compromise 'the primacy, unity and effectiveness of EU law'.[200]

The EU legislature could secure that rules of EU law more 'harmoniously' co-exist with the standards of national or international fundamental rights by clarifying the scope available to the member states to apply those standards.[201] In Directives and Regulations, specific derogation clauses could be included, or they could determine that the rules of EU law would have to be interpreted in line with the relevant standards of international law. De Schutter finds that Article 52(3) of the Charter provides helpful inspiration for drawing up such clauses.[202] This provision demonstrates a specific link between the interpretation of the Charter's rights and the rights of the Convention.[203] With respect to norms coming from other European or international sources of fundamental rights law, which are relevant for the protection of fundamental rights in a certain area of EU law, such links could also be established. One way of providing such protection is by inserting so-called 'optioning rules' in EU secondary legislation, which allow the member states to make their own choices on the protection of fundamental rights.[204]

In areas which are, to a large degree, exhaustively regulated by EU law, it could even be highly desirable to include such clauses. This does not necessarily and only apply to areas of exclusive competences, however. Stubberfield has explained, for example, that the area of asylum law is de facto highly regulated by EU law and there is a fairly prescriptive relationship between the EU and the member states which, in effect, creates the impression that the member states enjoy very little discretion.[205] It also

199 De Schutter & Butler (2008).
200 ECJ 26 February 2013, C-399/11, *Melloni*, para. 60. See also section 6.8.
201 De Schutter (2004), p. 32.
202 De Schutter (2004), p. 33.
203 On Article 52(3) of the Charter, see section 6.9.1.
204 See further section 9.3.2.3.
205 Stubberfield (2012), p. 127. See also Besselink (1998). In *Opinion 2/13*, the ECJ has held that 'the Member States have, by reason of their membership of the EU, accepted that relations between them as regards the matters covered by the transfer of powers from the Member States to the EU are governed by EU law to the exclusion, if EU law so requires, of any other law', see ECJ 18 December 2014, *Opinion 2/13*, para. 193.

seems necessary to include specific clauses on the scope for application of national and international fundamental rights areas where there are many different legal regimes that could be applied to a specific area of EU law, such as the area of asylum law.[206]

8.6. CONCLUSIONS

The scope for the adoption of measures by the EU to ensure the protection of fundamental rights and the imposition of positive obligations has raised many questions, given that the EU has not been conferred a clear and general competence to protect fundamental rights under the EU Treaty. This chapter has explained that the EU arguably does have some powers to protect fundamental rights. The EU can be said to have specific fundamental rights powers relating to certain concrete topics (section 8.3.3.), as well as a more indirect power to protect fundamental rights in other areas where it has been given explicit powers to undertake its different policies (section 8.3.4.). The indirect competence to protect fundamental rights must be understood as an accessory competence that is based on, and limited to, the explicit powers the EU has been given in several policy fields. This indirect competence can be used to ensure that the EU does respect fundamental rights in the exercise of its explicit powers. It is less certain whether there exists a more general power to protect fundamental rights, which could allow the EU to take action in areas where it does not have an explicit and concrete competence. At the least, it could be argued that the EU must be very careful in relying on this more general power.

There are several reasons why the EU may want to adopt measures to ensure fundamental rights protection (section 8.4.). The principle of subsidiarity provides a very general argument or justification as to why action would be needed. It can be necessary for the EU legislature to take action when very clear connections can be made between EU acts and fundamental rights infringements, when there is a risk of a 'race to the bottom' in the protection of fundamental rights standards, and where the primacy, unity and effectiveness of EU law itself is at stake. Which of these may provide relevant grounds for EU action is very much dependent on the specific circumstances, the specific area of law, and the (fundamental rights) interests that must be taken into account. These different grounds may also apply simultaneously.

There are various legal bases to be found in the EU Treaties and in the Charter that contain clearer indications on some of the types of measures which can be undertaken by the EU legislature, or by the member state in the implementation of EU law at the national level, to ensure the effective protection of fundamental rights (see sections 8.3.4.2. to 8.3.4.4.). These legal bases are useful to help the EU institutions decide how and to what degree they could exercise their indirect competence to protect

206 Cf. Muir (2014a), p. 227. See further Besselink (1998).

fundamental rights. This *inter alia* includes the principle of loyal cooperation and the legality requirement in relation to fundamental rights interferences.

These legal bases will also be especially relevant for the ECJ to take into account if cases are brought which reveal that the EU institutions and the member states, in the implementation of EU law at national level, have failed to secure the effective protection of fundamental rights, even though a relevant competence for the EU to take actions in that field could have been construed. These legal bases, in combination with the reasons for taking action at EU level discussed in this chapter may provide important arguments for the ECJ to allow it to formulate positive obligations in its case-law. Such specific cases are discussed in chapter 11.

CHAPTER 9

THE LIMITED SCOPE OF APPLICATION OF EU FUNDAMENTAL RIGHTS

9.1. INTRODUCTION

The scope of application of EU fundamental rights is of great significance. It is of importance to determine at what point fundamental rights matters fall within the scope of Union law, because then the ECJ becomes competent to exercise judicial review and to set fundamental rights standards. This has implications for the powers that can be exercised by the EU institutions and the member states in the respective areas.[1] Moreover, if the ECJ were to apply EU fundamental rights to situations where there are no rules of EU law, and therefore no powers for the EU, this would have the effect of unacceptably extending the EU's powers. The scope of application of EU fundamental rights is also of particular importance for exploring the (potential) development of positive obligations on the basis of EU law. The main question to be asked in that respect is to what degree it can be expected that positive obligations could indeed fall within, or rather outside, the scope of application of EU law.

In answering this question, the meaning of Article 51 of the Charter is of central concern. This chapter discusses, first, how scholars have interpreted the meaning of this provision (section 9.2.). What scope and what limits do they derive from this provision for the protection of fundamental rights by the ECJ, and how do they expect the ECJ to accommodate a notion of positive obligations into EU law on the basis of this provision? By finding answers to those questions, a theoretical framework for a development of positive obligations is set out which aims to respect the limits laid down in Article 51. Next, it is examined how the ECJ itself has interpreted and applied Article 51 of the Charter (section 9.3.). In this regard, three types of situations which the ECJ has found to fall within the scope of application of EU fundamental rights will be discussed. It is submitted that the EU in fact enjoys different types of powers in these three types of situations. The existence of these different types of powers needs to be acknowledged when assessing whether it would be possible for the ECJ to develop positive obligations in its case-law. This chapter is rounded up by some final conclusions on the scope which Article 51 seems to allow for the development of positive obligations, and the limits that need to be taken into account (section 9.4.).

---

1 See Prechal, De Vries & Van Eijken (2011), pp. 214–215 and 234–235.

9.2. ARTICLE 51 OF THE CHARTER AND ITS EFFECTS ON A DEVELOPMENT OF POSITIVE OBLIGATIONS BY THE ECJ

9.2.1. BACKGROUND TO ARTICLE 51 OF THE CHARTER AND ITS MAIN EFFECTS ON THE DEVELOPMENT OF POSITIVE OBLIGATIONS

Chapter 6 already discussed, to some extent, the meaning of Article 51(1) on the scope of application of the Charter.[2] It should be noted that Article 51 of the Charter is comprised of the following two paragraphs:

> 1. The provisions of the Charter are addressed to the institutions, bodies, offices and agencies of the Union with due regard for the principle of subsidiarity and to the Member States only when they are implementing Union law. They shall therefore respect the rights, observe the principles and promote the application thereof in accordance with their respective powers and respecting the limits of the powers of the Union as conferred on it in the Treaties.
>
> 2. The Charter does not extend the field of application of Union law beyond the powers of the Union or establish any new power or task for the Union, or modify powers and tasks as defined in the Treaties.

This provision limits the scope of application of the rights of the Charter to actions taken by the EU institutions and agencies and to the member states. The Charter only applies to the actions of the member states when they are 'implementing Union law'.

Several scholars have argued that the limits laid down in Article 51 were intentionally included to prevent a federalising effect,[3] which could potentially be brought about by an activist approach of the ECJ towards the application of the fundamental rights guaranteed by the Charter. Such effects have been experienced in the United States, where the Supreme Court started reviewing measures of the states on the basis of the federal Bill of Rights, even in contexts where states were exercising their own competences. It was feared that, if the ECJ were to adopt a similar approach, the application of the Charter would further encroach on the member states' powers and the protection of their national constitutional rights.[4]

The first and the second paragraph of Article 51 clearly aim to preserve the limitations to the competences of the EU. This means that the powers of the member states to pursue their sovereign policies and to apply their national standards of fundamental rights may not be unduly limited on the basis of EU fundamental rights standards.

---

2 See section 6.7.

3 See in particular Eeckhout (2002); and Groussot, Pech & Petursson (2013).

4 Groussot, Pech & Petursson (2013), pp. 99–101.

From the perspective of the principle of attributed powers, as discussed in chapter 8, it would be problematic if an interpretation of fundamental rights given by the ECJ were to lead to a harmonisation of national law if there were no specific powers for the EU to adopt legislative measures in a certain field.[5] It is therefore necessary that the ECJ has regard to the limited scope of application of the Charter and respects the division of competences between the EU and the member states.[6]

More specifically, in relation to the development of positive obligations, Heringa and Verhey have argued that 'Article 51 necessarily reduces to a great extent the consequences which might otherwise flow from fully accepting the meaning and scope of the ECHR. That meaning and scope include positive obligations, but these can only be imposed upon the Community or the Union within their already existing powers.'

Other scholars have also submitted that Article 51 was specifically included in the Charter to prevent the ECJ from following the example of the ECtHR in expanding the reach of the fundamental rights by means of developing positive obligations.[7] For that reason, they argue, Article 51 now clearly stipulates that the limited powers of the EU preclude that 'any new power or task' is established.

It is thus clear that the ECJ cannot, like the ECtHR, reason, in an abstract fashion and purely based on a fundamental rights provision, what state action may be required to ensure the effective protection of those rights and, if necessary, formulate positive obligations.[8] Instead, the ECJ must always pay close attention to the scope of EU law and it must make sure not to set requirements that fall outside that scope.

As a consequence, it is to be expected that the ECJ will only establish positive obligations which relate to a specific field in which the EU is entitled to exercise powers and where a specific rule of EU law provides the basis for the EU institutions and the member states to take certain measures. Article 51 clearly precludes the ECJ from developing any self-standing positive obligations, that is, obligations which have no basis in EU law at all. The ECJ is thus, in principle, expected to formulate supportive positive obligations only. This is a type of obligation which, as explained in chapter 3, is inextricably linked to the negative obligation to protect fundamental rights and which is necessary to prevent violations of such a negative obligation.[9] Examples of such supportive positive obligations include procedural and remedial positive obligations. Chapter 11 will demonstrate that these kinds of obligations have indeed been developed in the case-law of the ECJ.[10]

5 Craig (2011b), p. 424. See section 8.2.
6 Dougan (2015), pp. 129–1210.
7 Van der Velde (2009), pp. 74–75.
8 Groussot, Pech & Petursson (2013), p. 100.
9 See further section 3.3.2. Cf. Van Kempen (2008), pp. 16–20; and Heringa & Verhey (2001), p. 19.
10 See sections 11.3. and 11.44.

9.2.2. GAPS IN PROTECTION OR COMPETENCE CREEP?

Concern has been expressed that, given the limitations of Article 51 of the Charter, the ECJ will lack sufficient powers to ensure the effective protection of fundamental rights and to recognise positive obligations. Heringa and Verhey, for example, noted that:

> It is feasible that a situation could occur in which the Community or the Union infringes one of the rights laid down in the Charter. At the same time it could happen that under the Court's case-law this infringement could give rise to a corresponding positive obligation. If the Union does not have the power to meet such an obligation it could happen that the infringement (of the negative obligation) could and would be remedied, whereas the violation of the positive obligation (the substance of the right is *de facto* illusory) would remain. This would create a potential situation of conflicts and confusion, which would not contribute to the transparency and effectiveness of human rights protection.[11]

Heringa and Verhey thus envisaged that situations might arise in which the specific powers needed to provide fundamental rights protection had not been conferred by the member states to the EU. Indeed, it must be recognised that the specific requirements of fundamental rights can sometimes only become clear in concrete circumstances and they cannot therefore always be foreseen in the process of conferring competences.[12] Heringa and Verhey concluded that Article 51 of the Charter limits the possibility of providing effective protection of fundamental rights, and could create gaps in the protection of fundamental rights. They specifically noted that the ECJ may not be able to ensure, on the basis of Article 52(3) of the Charter, that the rights of the Charter are given the same meaning and scope as the rights of the Convention, because they require positive obligations to be met.[13]

Such concerns could be dismissed if a broader reading were to be given to the scope of application of the rights of the Charter. Advocate General Sharpston has famously argued that the ECJ needs to interpret the scope of application of EU law broadly so that it can be ensured that the fundamental rights of EU citizens are effectively protected.[14] Sharpston has held that the protection of fundamental rights can be made dependent on 'the existence and scope of a material EU competence'.[15] This would not require that there is a specific provision of EU law which applies to a situation at hand, nor that secondary legislation is actually enacted in that field of competence. On the basis of this approach, a broad range of situations could be brought within the scope of application of EU fundamental rights.[16] Some scholars have further suggested that, in exceptional

11 Heringa & Verhey (2001), pp. 19–20.
12 See also the discussion in section 8.3.5.
13 Heringa & Verhey (2001), p. 20.
14 Opinion A-G Sharspton in C-34/09, *Zambrano*.
15 Opinion A-G Sharspton in C-34/09, *Zambrano*, para. 163.
16 These would rather clearly seem to create a federalising effect, which Article 51 of the Charter was aimed at preventing. See further Groussot, Pech & Petursson (2013), pp. 99–101; Besson (2011b), pp. 37–39; and Eeckhout (2002).

situations, there should be room for the ECJ to ensure fundamental rights protection in areas where the EU does not, as such, enjoy any powers. Von Bogdandy and others argued that this would be necessary in situations where the protection of the essence of the fundamental rights of EU citizens is at stake.[17] In their view, there is a presumption under EU law that member states retain sovereign powers to protect fundamental rights only as long as they can indeed ensure that the essence of fundamental rights is protected. The ECJ could accept jurisdiction in such cases on the basis of Article 20 TFEU, which protects EU citizenship.[18]

So far, the ECJ has showed itself ready to accept quite a broad scope of application for EU fundamental rights.[19] The ECJ has extended the scope of application of the Charter in some cases to situations where the connection with EU law was, in fact, rather weak.[20] The ECJ has also applied the Charter in situations where the EU was not given a specific power to take legislative action in the relevant area.[21] In other situations it has not been clear (at least from the viewpoint of national law) whether the power to take certain measures really derived from EU law. Scholars have concluded that the resulting scope of application of the Charter is wider than the legislative scope of application of EU law.[22] As a result of this broad reading of the scope of application of EU fundamental rights, there would perhaps be room to allow for the acceptance of positive obligations, indeed more than would be expected by Heringa and Verhey, and effective protection of fundamental rights could be realised more easily.

It has also been suggested that an over-broad scope of application of EU fundamental rights can give rise to conflicts with the principle of attributed powers, especially in light of the potential creation of positive obligations. Prechal, De Vries and Van Eijken stated that:

> at the very moment when a matter is within the scope of the Treaty, the Member States competences to act are limited by the relevant Treaty provisions, general principles of law or fundamental rights. Yet this form of what is primarily considered a negative intervention may imply, upon second analysis, positive obligations – that is to say, obligations for the Member States to act. This, however, is often believed to be primarily a matter of implementation of EU legislation. Unsurprisingly, this shift from negative to positive obligations raises questions in relation to the principle of attributed powers.[23]

---

17 See further for their views, section 7.6.1.; and Von Bogdandy, Kottmann, Antpöhler, Dickschen, Hentrei & Smrkolj (2012).

18 Von Bogdandy and others also pointed out, as further support for their viewpoints, that the ECJ already accepted in the *Zambrano* case that 'Article 20 TFEU precludes national measures which have the effect of depriving citizens of the Union of the genuine enjoyment of the substance of the rights conferred by virtue of their status as citizens of the Union', see ECJ 8 March 2011, C-34/09, *Zambrano*, para. 42; and Von Bogdandy, Kottmann, Antpöhler, Dickschen, Hentrei & Smrkolj (2012), p. 491.

19 See section 6.7.1.; and section 9.3.2.

20 Eeckhout (2002), p. 970.

21 These cases are further discussed in section 9.3.2.

22 See Groussot, Pech & Petursson (2013), p. 100; and Prechal, De Vries & Van Eijk (2011), pp. 213–215 ff. Also see De Búrca (1998), p. 221; and Dubout (2014), p. 195.

23 Prechal, De Vries & Van Eijken (2011), p. 235.

Prechal, De Vries and Van Eijken have explained that when specific matters are brought within the scope of EU law by the ECJ, the EU institutions might too easily be triggered to take legislative action. They argue that this directly and possibly unduly expands the competences of the EU.[24] In their view, this would be problematic in light of the principle of attributed powers.[25] It would also be problematic if the ECJ were to define certain actions for the EU institutions and for the member states while the procedural guarantees that are inherent to the legal basis for EU actions as such had not been ensured.[26] Some concerns thus also stem from the political nature of positive obligations. As was noted in chapter 4, similar concerns have been expressed with respect to the development of positive obligations by the ECtHR.[27] Again, that might be a reason for the ECJ to be wary of defining such obligations, especially when there is no clear connection to EU law. Prechal, De Vries and Van Eijken conclude that the principle of attributed powers does not provide for a helpful framework that could be applied if positive obligations were to arise under EU law. This actually puts the ECJ in a very difficult position in responding to relevant cases that could potentially be brought. Prechal, de Vries and Van Eijken call upon the EU legislature instead to further clarify what limits need to be taken into account by the ECJ, and they further call upon the ECJ to apply judicial wisdom in dealing with these situations.[28]

Perhaps it may be replied to this that the principle of attributed powers, as discussed in the previous chapter, can already help to delimit the Court's powers to impose such positive obligations. Article 51 of the Charter requires the ECJ to take into account that the limited powers of the EU must be respected, that the division of the power between the EU and the member states may not be affected, and that the powers of the EU may not be expanded. These specific limits follow from the general Treaty rules on the limited powers of the EU, which have been discussed in detail in the previous chapter. The explanations on the Charter also mention in relation to Article 51 that account must be taken of the 'logical consequences of the principle of subsidiarity and of the fact that the Union only has those powers which have been conferred upon it'. Thus, the limits on the powers of the EU, as well as the specific interpretation of the principle of subsidiarity in the context of fundamental rights protection, could provide a relevant framework to be taken into account by the ECJ in deciding what obligations follow from the Charter.[29] This particular framework is set out in the conclusios of chapter 10.[30]

---

24 See Prechal & Corthaut (2010), p. 5; and Prechal, De Vries & Van Eijken (2011), pp. 214–215, 235 and 244–245. The prime example being the adoption of the Patients' Rights Directive. First, the ECJ brought medical activities within the scope of the free movement provisions, and developed further principles in its case-law under that heading. Thereafter, a Directive on patients' rights was enacted to codify the Court's case-law and lay down even further guarantees and rights that need to be provided to patients receiving cross-border medical care.

25 Prechal, De Vries & Van Eijken (2011), pp. 235–236.

26 Prechal, De Vries & Van Eijken (2011), p. 241.

27 See section 4.4.

28 Prechal, de Vries & Van Eijken (2011), p. 246.

29 Cf. Van Eijken (2015), p. 42.

30 See in particular section 10.4.

9.2.3. RESPONDING TO GAPS IN THE PROTECTION OF FUNDAMENTAL RIGHTS: FLEXIBILITY IN THE INTERPRETATION OF THE SCOPE OF APPLICATION OF EU FUNDAMENTAL RIGHTS LAW

Positive obligations are, in principle, established in situations of omissions of the state. Often it concerns certain gaps in the policies and laws of the state which reveal that insufficient protection is provided for the fundamental rights of some, potentially vulnerable, indiviuals.[31] In relation to the situation of gaps in the protection of EU law, some scholars have thought of ways in which the ECJ could respond to ensure protection particularly on the basis of general principles of law (which include fundamental rights).[32] This is particularly interesting for the purposes of this study, since gap-filling in the sphere of fundamental rights protection may require positive measures to be taken by the national authorities or the EU institutions.

First, Lenaerts and Guitiérrez-Fons have looked more generally at how the ECJ could respond to certain gaps in EU law on the basis of general principles of EU law.[33] They find that general principles of law can have three functions under EU law: they can be a ground for judicial review, an aid to interpretation, or a basis for gap-filling.[34] According to Lenaerts and Guitiérrez-Fons:

> the gap-filling function of general principles, which is grounded in the Treaties themselves, ensures the coherence of the EU legal order without encroaching upon the choices made by the authors of the Treaties or by the EU legislature. It follows that such gap-filling function is consistent with the principle of separation of powers. Vertically, when engaging in gap-filling, the ECJ endeavours to find a comprise guaranteeing that the project of European integration is not put at risk, whilst making sure that its decisions are sufficiently close to the practice and values to national courts to enjoy recognition and credibility in the Member States. In deploying a comparative analysis, the ECJ will seek the solution that does not risk encountering incomprehension or resistance in some Member States.[35]

The use of general principles in gap-filling thus prevents the scope of application of EU law from being interpreted too rigidly. It could be argued that a similar use could be made of fundamental rights as general principles in relation to cases on positive obligations. According to Lenaerts and Gutiérrez, in order to find out whether a positive obligation can be imposed in response to a certain gap that has been left by the EU legislature and/ or the national legislature, the ECJ needs to look at the current practices and values of the member states. The judgment of the ECJ in the case of *Köbler* is taken as an example

31 See section 3.2.3.2.
32 See Lenaerts & Gutiérrez-Fons (2010); and Van der Velde (2009).
33 Lenaerts & Gutiérrez-Fons (2010), p. 1635.
34 Lenaerts & Gutiérrez-Fons (2010), p. 1629.
35 Lenaerts & Guitérrez-Fons (2010), p. 1636.

to illustrate this.[36] In this judgment, the ECJ established that individuals should be given a remedy before their national courts, to enable them to claim compensation as a result of an incorrect interpretation of EU law by their national court of last instance.[37] In determing this, the ECJ specifically paid attention to the fact that the member states already applied principles of state liability to decisions of national courts in one way or other, so it could also require the member states to ensure that individuals can claim compensation where there has been an incorrect interpretation of EU law by the national courts.[38] The member states would only need to extend their existing remedies to apply to situations concerned with EU law and for most member states, apparently, there would be no need to create entirely new remedies.[39] A positive obligation that might seem to be imposed by the ECJ in this case, that is, the creation of a remedy, could also potentially be fulfilled by the member states on the basis of their national laws and their existing judicial frameworks.

Van der Velde has also discussed how the ECJ could respond to any gaps in the protection of EU law, specifically those that require positive obligations to be formulated to ensure protection of fundamental rights.[40] In his response to other scholars who have held that the limited scope of application of fundamental rights precludes the ECJ from accepting positive obligations, Van der Velde has suggested that the ECJ could use the concept of 'indirect competences' to enable it to recognise positive obligations under EU law. The concept of an 'indirect competence' is explained in chapter 8.[41] In short, it entails that the EU has competence to protect fundamental rights when it is exercising its explicit legal powers, for example those which it has in the area of the internal market or in the area of freedom, security and justice. The ECJ may be required to define positive obligations that have not yet been recognised under national law or by the ECtHR. There are some difficulties related to this solution, as explained in chapter 8. The existence of an indirect competence of the EU to protect fundamental rights remains accessory to the explicit powers of the EU, and the restrictions which apply to the exercise of such explicit powers must be taken into account. There are thus limits to be mindful of, however, the notion of gap-filling can provide some room for the ECJ to accept positive obligations if the EU legislative framework shows certain gaps.

In developing positive obligations on the basis of an indirect or a specific competence to protect fundamental rights and/or in gap-filling, the ECJ must not only ensure that it respects the vertical division of powers, but also, as Prechal, De Vries and Van Eijken have explained, the horizontal division of powers.[42] The horizontal division of

36 ECJ 30 September 2003, C-224/01, *Köbler*.
37 Lenaerts & Gutiérrez-Fons (2010), p. 1634.
38 ECJ 30 September 2003, C-224/01, *Köbler*, para. 48.
39 In practice, the creation of this remedy has appeared to be difficult, however, and it appears to be barely used.
40 Van der Velde (2009), pp. 74–78.
41 See further section 8.3.4.
42 Prechal, De Vries & Van Eijken (2011), pp. 213–214.

powers is concerned with the relation between the ECJ and the other institutions of the EU.[43] Article 13(2) TEU specifically determines that 'Each institution shall act within the limits of the powers conferred on it in the Treaties, and in conformity with the procedures, conditions and objectives set out in them' and that 'the institutions shall practice mutual sincere cooperation'.[44] This requires that the ECJ, when interpreting EU law, must take into account the specific Treaty provision on the basis of which the relevant rule of EU law had been enacted. These legal bases determine more specifically what the EU institutions and what the member states are entitled to do under EU law.

The main example that is put forward as an illustration of how the interpretation of fundamental rights by the ECJ could lead to conflicts with the horizontal division of powers, are the judgments of the ECJ in the cases of *Mangold* and *Kücückdeveci*.[45] In those cases, discussed in some detail in chapter 6, the ECJ decided that individuals can rely on the principle of non-discrimination on grounds of age in a case before the national court, even though the provisions of an EU Directive have not yet or not yet correctly been implemented in national law.[46] The ECJ requires that the national court sets aside a provision of national law to ensure the protection of the principle of non-discrimination in these cases between private parties. However, such an effect was precluded by the provisions of EU secondary law that were considered applicable to the case. For that reason, Prechal, De Vries and Van Eijken have stated that the judgments of the ECJ in *Mangold* and *Kücükdeveci* can be regarded as examples of 'judicial competence creep'.[47] They have held that the ECJ ruled in contravention of the horizontal limits of the powers of the EU, because the EU legislature had explicitly wanted to grant discretion to the member states in the implementation of the Directive.[48] In order to prevent such competence creep, the ECJ is thus advised to be careful to take the vertical and horizontal dimensions of its limited powers into account, which would also apply to cases on positive obligations. It may be difficult, however, for the ECJ to determine the exact scope of the powers of the EU. Chapter 8 explained that there are different views on the extent of the fundamental rights competences of the EU. Moreover, in some areas there may have been no clear political debate over whether fundamental rights protection should be provided for at supranational level, and this may leave the ECJ in a difficult position.[49] It is thus essential for the ECJ to still show 'judicial wisdom' in this area.

---

43 Onn the institutional position of the ECJ *vis-à-vis* the EU institutions, see also section 7.5.2.

44 Prechal, De Vries & Van Eijken (2011), pp. 213–214.

45 ECJ 22 November 2005, C-144/04, *Mangold*; and ECJ 19 January 2010, C-555/07, *Kücükdeveci*. Also see Craig (2011b), p. 418–422; Prechal, De Vries & Van Eijken (2011); and Opinion of AG Mazák in C-411/05, *Palacios de la Villa*, para. 95.

46 See section 6.7.2.

47 Prechal, De Vries & Van Eijken (2011), p. 244.

48 Prechal, De Vries & Van Eijken (2011), p. 244.

49 Muir (2014a), p. 242.

9.3. THE INTERPRETATION OF ARTICLE 51 BY THE ECJ

This section will discuss how broadly the ECJ has indeed interpreted Article 51 of the Charter, and where it finds that the limits of the scope of application should be placed. The underlying reasoning that has guided the ECJ's interpretation of the scope of application of EU fundamental rights under the Charter has not been made very clear in its case-law. However, it has on some occasions stated that the scope of application of EU fundamental rights is restricted on the basis of the limited powers of the EU (section 9.3.1.). A look is taken at three different types of situations which have been recognised by the ECJ as falling within the scope of application of EU fundamental rights, in order to see the potential for a development of positive obligations in those different situations (section 9.3.2.). Further, it is clarified that the ECJ has also decided in some situations that the member states enjoy sovereign powers under EU law so that, generally, EU fundamental rights cannot be applied in those situations (section 9.3.3.). Lastly, attention is drawn to the scope which the ECJ allows for member states to apply their own standards of fundamental rights on the basis of national law (section 9.3.4.).

9.3.1. THE RELATION BETWEEN THE LIMITED SCOPE OF APPLICATION OF EU FUNDAMENTAL RIGHTS AND THE LIMITED POWERS OF THE EU

As explained in chapter 6, the ECJ held in its seminal judgment in the *Åkerberg Fransson* case that EU fundamental rights apply to the actions of the member states where 'national legislation falls within the scope of European Union law'. This seems to be broader than the limitation which is laid down in Article 51 of the Charter itself, which is that member states must be 'implementing Union law'. In *Åkerberg Fransson*, the ECJ explained the scope of application of the Charter in relation to the principle of the limited competences of the EU in the following way:

> Where ... a legal situation does not come within the scope of European Union law, the Court does not have jurisdiction to rule on it and any provision of the Charter relied upon cannot, of themselves, form the basis for such jurisdiction ...
>
> The considerations correspond to those underlying Article 6(1) TEU, according to which the provisions of the Charter are not to extend in any way the competences of the European Union as defined in the Treaties. Likewise, the Charter, pursuant to Article 51(2) thereof, does not extend the field of application of European Union law beyond the powers of the European Union or to establish any new power or task for the European Union, or modify powers and tasks as defined in the Treaties ...[50]

[50] ECJ 26 February 2013, C-617/10, *Åkerberg Fransson*, paras 22–23.

Similar considerations have been put forward by the ECJ in other judgments on the scope of application of EU fundamental rights, notably in *Pfleger*, which is discussed further below.[51] The ECJ has emphasised these limits in cases that were brought before it on situations which had only a very faint connection to EU law, and in which it decided that EU fundamental rights could, for that reason, not be applied.[52] There are also several examples of cases in which national courts had referred questions to the ECJ on the protection of fundamental rights in relation to the areas of social security and immigration law.[53] In these cases the ECJ decided that it manifestly lacked jurisdiction to rule on the questions that were referred to it by the national courts.[54] These matters in principle fall within the competences of the member states; and the ECJ also found that the referring courts had provided little guidance as to why those specific situations that were at issue would (otherwise) fall within the scope of the EU Charter. Considering athis, the ECJ thus generally aims to respect the limited powers of the EU by restricting the scope of application of EU fundamental rights.

On some recent occasions, the ECJ has expressly drawn attention to the existence of a specific obligation that needs to be laid in EU law as a requirement for EU fundamental rights to be applied. The absence of such a specific obligation of EU law has provided a reason for the ECJ to find that EU fundamental rights could not be applied to the actions of the member states.[55] In the *Julian Hernández* case, the ECJ held that:

> ... fundamental European-Union rights could not be applied in relation to national legislation because the provisions of EU law in the area concerned did not impose any specific obligation on Member States with regard to the situation at issue in the main proceedings.
>
> ... the mere fact that a national measure comes within an area in which the European Union has power cannot bind it within the scope of EU law, and, therefore, cannot render the Charter applicable.[56]

Here, the ECJ explains that it is not sufficient to only point out in general that a situation falls within an area in which the EU happens to have a competence to act. The same point also seems to have been made by the ECJ in the cases of *Iida* and *Siragusa*. In these cases the ECJ clarified that 'the concept of "implementing Union law" requires

51 ECJ 30 April 2014, C-390/12, *Pfleger*, para. 33.

52 ECJ 8 May 2014, C-483/12, *Pelckmans Turnhout*, para. 21; ECJ 6 March 2014, C-206/13, *Siragusa*, para. 20; ECJ 15 November 2011, C-256/11, *Dereci and others*, para. 70; and ECJ 11 November 2014, C-333/13, *Dano*, para. 88. Interestingly, the ECJ used the same line of reasoning in *McB*, where it did decide that the Charter could be applied. See further section 9.3.3.

53 See e.g. ECJ 7 May 2015, C-608/14, *Pondiche*; and ECJ 7 May 2015, C-496/14, *Vǎraru*.

54 See e.g. ECJ 7 May 2015, C-608/14, *Pondiche*, para. 20; and ECJ 7 May 2015, C-496/14, *Vǎraru*, para. 17.

55 ECJ 10 July 2014, C-198/13, *Julian Hernández*, paras 35–36 and 44–46; and ECJ 22 May 2014, C-56/13, Érsekcsanádi Mezögazdasagi, para. 56.

56 ECJ 10 July 2014, C-198/13, *Julian Hernández*, paras 35–36.

a certain degree of connection above and beyond the matters covered being closely related or one of those matters having an indirect impact on the other'.[57]

Overall, therefore, it seems that the ECJ is well aware of the need to limit the scope of application of the EU Charter. Nevertheless, as the next section will show, matters are slightly more complicated in relation to some of the case-law of the ECJ. In some of its judgments, the ECJ has chosen to provide protection of fundamental rights, even though there was no clear obligation laid down in EU law and/or the EU did not actually seem to enjoy any power in the area concerned.

9.3.2. THE SPECIFIC SITUATIONS WITHIN THE MEANING OF 'IMPLEMENTING UNION LAW'

In exploring how the limited scope of application of the EU relates to the limited powers of the EU, it is useful to distinguish three types of situations which show a different relation to the principle of attributed powers.[58] These three situations, briefly mentioned in chapter 6, are the agency situation, the situation of measures derogating from the EU fundamental freedoms, and optioning rules.[59] As will be explained, in each of these situations the EU exercises a different type of competence, which has important implications for the extent to which the ECJ can develop fundamental rights standards. It is argued that this also impacts on the extent to which the ECJ can develop positive obligations in these different situations.

9.3.2.1. *The Agency Situation*

The first type of situation that has been distinguished by the ECJ with respect to the actions of the member states, concerns the classic agency situations, or the *Wachauf* situation.[60] In this situation, member states take measures to implement specific provisions of secondary EU law. Here, the competence of the member states to take measures emanates from EU law, and it could therefore be rationalised that EU law must also ensure that the member states exercise these powers with respect for fundamental rights. The application of EU fundamental rights standards to this agency situation

---

57 ECJ 6 March 2014, C-206/13, *Siragusa*, para. 24; and cf. ECJ 8 November 2012, C-40/11, *Iida*, para. 77.

58 See section 6.7.

59 Scholars often recognise the *Wachauf* or 'agency situation' as one type of situation, and the *ERT*-situation, or the situation where member states derogate from the free movement rules, as a second type. See most recently Dougan (2015); Sarmiento (2013); and Groussot, Pech & Petursson (2013). Some scholars further distinguish a third type of situation, that is, where for other reasons a connection to EU law can be found and EU fundamental rights need to be complied with. See Prechal & Corthaut (2010), p. 19; and Opinion of AG Sharpston in C-427/06, *Bartsch*. Since these situations are relatively rare, this situation is not discussed further in this study.

60 See section 6.7.1.

seems clearly in harmony with the division of powers between the EU and the member states.[61] Even when the member states enjoy discretion in implementing provisions of EU law, it would still be logical to assume that the EU standards of fundamental rights are applied, because the member states continue to act as 'agents' of EU law.[62] Negative as well as positive obligations could thus be imposed on the member states in such situations to ensure that fundamental rights are protected

As held already, there are also examples of cases in which the member states seemingly were acting as agents of EU law and were for that reason brought within the scope of application of EU fundamental rights, even though the connection to EU law was somewhat weak. The specific situation in the case of *Åkerberg Fransson* can be taken as an example to explain this.[63] In *Åkerberg Fransson*, the ECJ examined the application of a Swedish rule that allowed a criminal sanction to be imposed on an individual for tax evasion even though an administrative sanction had already been imposed. This raised questions in light of the principle of *ne bis in idem*. The ECJ held that the tax penalties and criminal proceedings which were instituted by the national authorities against the applicant for tax evasion formed an implementation of obligations laid down in EU law.[64] The ECJ explained that several provisions of the applicable Directives and Article 4(3) TEU imposed a (general) obligation on the member states to take all legislative and administrative measures to ensure the collection of VAT that was due on its territory and to prevent the evasion thereof.[65] The ECJ further pointed to Article 325 TFEU as a relevant provision, since this provision requires the member states to take measures to counter illegal activities affecting the financial interests of the EU through effective deterrent measures.[66] The ECJ recognised in its judgment that the national legislation upon which the tax penalties and criminal proceedings were found had not actually been adopted to transpose the said provisions of EU law. It held, however, that this did not imply that EU fundamental rights standards could not be applied. After all, the application of the criminal and administrative proceedings in this case were, in the end, imposed as effective penalties for conduct prejudicial to financial interests of the European Union.[67]

It can be contested whether the member state in such a case really acts as an agent of EU law. In the case of *Åkerberg Fransson*, it could just as easily have been decided that the measures that were taken did not constitute implementation of EU law, as it was not obvious that the power to take those measures had been conferred on the

---

61 Cf. Dubout (2014), pp. 198–199.

62 At the same time, there should be room for the application of the national standards of fundamental rights, see section 9.3.4. as well as section 8.3.5.

63 Muir (2014a), p. 238.

64 ECJ 26 February 2013, C-617/10, *Åkerberg Fransson*, para. 27.

65 ECJ 26 February 2013, C-617/10, *Åkerberg Fransson*, para. 25.

66 ECJ 26 February 2013, C-617/10, *Åkerberg Fransson*, paras 25–27. According to Sarmiento *Åkerberg Fransson* was 'at the fringes of Article 51(1) of the Charter', see Sarmiento (2013), pp. 1267–1277.

67 ECJ 26 February 2013, C-617/10, *Åkerberg Fransson*, para. 28.

member state under EU law.[68] In fact, it could have been argued that the principle of national procedural autonomy applied in this case.[69] The choice made by the Court can, arguably, only be explained by its rather functional approach to the application of EU fundamental rights standards.[70] On the basis of this approach 'it is not the intention of the *State*, but the *function* of the State act regarding the implementation of EU law which matters'.[71] From the viewpoint of EU law, it could be argued that the member states were mandated to take certain actions in the case of *Åkerberg Fransson*.[72] These mandates were laid down in the provisions that were indicated by the ECJ, even though they gave broad discretion as regards the choice for certain implementing measures. From the national law perspective, however, it can be difficult to accept that such matters are also governed by EU law. Therefore, there are also cases, albeit exceptional ones, in which the Court did expressly take into account that national legislation was not adopted to give effect to EU law, in particular in the context of EU citizenship law, where the member states clearly still enjoy certain sovereign powers.[73] In the case of *Iida*, the ECJ also expressly took into account whether the national legislation at issue was actually intended to implement provisions of EU law.[74]

Most of the agency-type situations show that certain arrangements may already have been made at the national level to secure the protection of fundamental rights. They may form part of the member states' own legal and administrative structures, as the example of *Åkerberg Fransson* shows. Nevertheless, complying with EU fundamental rights standards could, if necessary, require the member states to further amend certain laws or policies. The case of *DEB* shows an example where member states would need to make such adjustments.[75] This case was about a German undertaking that had suffered financial loss as a result of the fact that the German government was too late with the implementation of EU Directives establishing an internal market in natural gas.[76] The undertaking involved wanted to lodge a complaint to establish state liability and to claim compensation, but it did not fulfil the criteria for the grant of legal aid to be able to start the court proceedings on the basis of national law. The ECJ held that the principle of effective judicial protection needed to be ensured in this situation, and that it could require the German authorities to grant legal aid (based also on the specific circumstances of the case).[77] Amendments would therefore specifically need to be

---

68 The Advocate General had also concluded differently from the ECJ, see A-G Cruz Villalón, C-617/10, *Åkerberg Fransson*.

69 Similarly, in the case of *DEB*, the ECJ held that national measures which provided legal aid, but were not as such intended as measures to strictly implement EU law, needed to be applied to a Directive, see ECJ 22 December 2010, C-279/09, *DEB*.

70 Cf. Sarmiento (2013), p. 1279; and Muir (2014a), p. 238.

71 Sarmiento (2013), p. 1279.

72 Sarmiento (2013), pp. 1280–1281.

73 Cf. Van Eijken (2015), pp. 71–73.

74 ECJ 8 November 2012, C-40/11, *Iida*, para. 79.

75 See also section 7.5.3.

76 ECJ 22 December 2010, C-279/09, *DEB*.

77 ECJ 22 December 2010, C-279/09, *DEB*, paras 52 and 59.

made to protect the fundamental right of legal persons such as *DEB*, which could in particular be affected by the establishment of rules at EU level in the internal market.

If, moreover, the protection of fundamental rights at the national level in these agency situations would show certain omissions, it would seem legitimate for the ECJ to impose a positive obligation on the member states. After all, it needs to be secured that the exercise of powers emanating from EU law at the national level are in compliance with negative as well as positive fundamental rights standards. As chapter 8 explains, the ECJ would then need to have regard to the existence of a certain fundamental rights competence for the EU, such as a specific or an indirect fundamental rights competence, to be able to impose a positive obligation.

9.3.2.2. The Situation of Derogation from the Free Movement Rules

The second situation where EU fundamental rights standards have been accepted as applying to the actions of the member states is when they derogate from the Treaty rules on free movement.[78] The ECJ has defined this type of situation in the case of *ERT* and, more recently, in the case of *Pfleger*. In the *Pfleger* case, Austria had introduced a new law on games of chance which meant that gaming machines which were operated without a licence could be confiscated and destroyed.[79] In addition, administrative or criminal penalties could be imposed on persons involved in the organisation of unlicensed games. The ECJ held that the freedom to choose an occupation, the freedom to conduct a business, and the right to property (Articles 15 to 17 of the Charter) needed to be protected by Austria in order to justify its restriction of the freedom to provide services (Article 56 TFEU).[80]

The application of the EU standards of fundamental rights to this situation type leads to some disagreement among scholars. In particular, it can be questioned whether in this situation the measures that are taken by the member states actually find their basis in EU law (that is, on the basis of the derogation clause in the free movement provision).[81] Member states could find that such measures are, in fact, taken on the basis of powers granted to them by national law, so the EU institutions should not intervene.[82] In the case of *Pfleger*, for example, the area of games of chance is not harmonised under EU law.[83] With regard to this type of situation, Besselink has, for example, explained that: 'they [the member states] engage in an act which does not have

---

78 See e.g. Kühling (2009), pp. 497–498; and Groussot, Pech & Petursson (2013).

79 ECJ 18 June 1991, C-260/89, *ERT*; ECJ 30 April 2014, C-390/12, *Pfleger*.

80 ECJ 30 April 2014, C-390/12, *Pfleger*, paras 30–36 and 57–60.

81 Cf. Weiler & Fries (1999), pp. 163–164.

82 Dubout (2014), p. 200.

83 Cf. the arguments made by several governments of the member states in ECJ 30 April 2014, C-390/12, *Pfleger*, para. 30.

the EC as its efficient cause and yet is governed by EC law. In this case, EC law is not constitutive or attributive, but merely regulative with regard to Member State action.'[84]

Craig explained the application of EU fundamental rights in these types of cases in, seemingly, quite a different way, that is, one which is more closely geared to the principle of attributed powers. Craig found that:

> The Member State in a case such as *ERT* is prima facie caught by a violation of free movement law, and is then seeking to act on a power given by EU law to provide a defence to that violation. It is in that sense implementing a power of defence or derogation provided by EU law, which only operates within certain conditions, including compliance with rights, are satisfied.[85]

While this may be considered as a reasonable explanation, it is still unclear exactly how the ECJ rationalises the application of EU fundamental rights standards in this situation. In the case of *Pfleger*, which is more recent than the *ERT* case, the ECJ merely explained that 'The use by a Member State of exceptions provided for by EU law in order to justify an obstruction of a fundamental freedom guaranteed by the Treaty must ... be regarded ... as "implementing Union law" within the meaning of Article 51(1) of the Charter'.[86] This does not provide much clarity as to whether the Court would thus find that the situation is in fact similar to the one where the member states are acting as agents of EU law.

It is generally accepted that the ECJ scrutinises measures taken by the member states that restrict the free movement provisions. The ECJ has clearly been given a power to do so.[87] The member states' justifications for such restrictions need to be in conformity with EU law, and this includes respect for fundamental rights. Nonetheless, there is a certain difference as compared to the agency situation discussed in the previous section, because there are no specific obligations that have been laid down by the EU legislature in secondary EU law. When derogating from the free movement rules, member states are often exercising their own, to a large extent, sovereign policies. It has been seen that derogations from the free movement law are taken in policy areas that can be quite sensitive, such as the area of gambling.[88] The way in which the member states pursue such policies may greatly differ. In such areas, the EU may expressly have been excluded from having power to take legislative measures. If the ECJ were to actively intervene in such an area where there are no legislative powers for the EU, a certain tension arises in view of the principle of attributed powers. Some criticism as to the application of EU fundamental rights standards is thus possible. However, it is also generally accepted that the member states need to comply with EU standards of fundamental rights when they seek to justify a restriction of the free movement provisions.

---

84 Besselink (2001), p. 77.
85 Craig (2011b), p. 431.
86 ECJ 30 April 2014, C-390/12, *Pfleger*, para. 36.
87 Cf. Azoulai (2008), pp. 1341–1342; and Prechal, De Vries & Van Eijken (2011), p. 245.
88 Avbelj (2004). See Sarmiento (2013), p. 1297; Dubout (2014), p. 200; and Besselink (2001), p. 77.

It has been argued that in the situation of derogating from the free movement rules, the ECJ should adopt a different approach to fundamental rights, or, at the least, it should apply different standards. Some scholars have suggested that the Court should leave it up to the national courts to determine whether fundamental rights have been complied with, and restrict itself to examining whether the principles of proportionality and non discrimination have been respected.[89] Others have submitted that the ECJ should restrict itself to applying the standards which must be complied with under the Convention.[90] Most in fact seem to argue that the ECJ should grant much discretion to the member states seeing that there is a great diversity between the member states as to how they pursue their national policies which are subject to the review of the ECJ in the *ERT* situation.[91] The ECJ could, further, clarify more generally that the member states have some leeway in applying their own national fundamental rights standards beyond the standards which they need to comply with under EU law.[92] Also, it has been found that the ECJ should differentiate the strictness of its review on the basis of the specific fundamental right which is under review. A less deferential review could, for example, be applied when it concerns fundamental rights of a more economic nature, when it concerns a violation of a 'core human rights', or where a 'serious or persistent breach of a fundamental right' takes place in a member state.[93]

As discussed earlier, the ECJ has not, in general, made clear what standard of review it applies in these cases. In some cases, the ECJ seems to have recognised the limited legislative powers of the EU without clarifying what effect that would have on its own standards of review. In the *Viking Line* case, for example, the ECJ examined the justification given for a restriction of the freedom of establishment in the light of the protection of the right to strike.[94] A Finnish shipping company wanted to establish itself in Estonia as the wages paid in Estonia were lower those that had to be paid in Finland. The company was then confronted by the Finish trade union which threatened to strike against its plans. In the case that was brought before the Court, the Danish and the Swedish government argued that the conditions for exercising the right to strike were governed by national law, and that since the Community does not have a competence to regulate the right to strike on the basis of Article 137(5) TEC (now Article 153 TFEU),

89 Jacobs (2001), pp. 336–341.

90 Weiler & Fries (1999), pp. 164–165.

91 See Avbelj (2004), p. 72. See also Weiler & Fries (1999), p. 165; Kühling (2014), pp. 498–499; and Dubout (2014), p. 203.

92 Sarmiento (2013), pp. 1297–1298.

93 See Avblej (2004), p. 74; Weiler & Fries (1999), p. 165; and Opinion AG Maduro in C-380/05, *Centro Europa*, paras 21–22.

94 ECJ 11 December 2007, C-438/05, *Viking Line*, para. 40. Cf. further the references made by the ECJ in the case of *Viking* in para. 40, and cf. ECJ 11 September 2007, Joined cases C-76/05 and C-318/05, *Schwarz and Gootjes* (on education); ECJ 11 November 2004, C-372/04, *Watts*, para. 147 (on social security); and ECJ 1 April 2008, C-267/06, *Maruko* (on same-sex relations), para. 59.

the measures taken with regard to collective action fell outside the scope of Community law.[95] The ECJ held, in response to these objections, that:

> even if, in the areas which fall outside the scope of the Community's competence, the Member States are still free, in principle to lay down the conditions governing the existence and exercise of the rights in question, the fact remains that, when exercising that competence, the Member States must nevertheless comply with Community law ...
>
> Consequently, the fact that Article 137 EC does not apply to the right to strike or to the right to impose lock-outs is not such as to exclude collective action such as that at issue in the main proceedings from the application of Article 43 EC.[96]

Thus, the ECJ recognises the competence of the member state to regulate the right to strike, while it also finds that in the same context requirements can be imposed on the basis of the free movement provisions under Community law. In its examination of the restriction of the free movement of services, the ECJ held that the right to take collective action and the right to strike are guaranteed as general principles under Community law, but that they are also subject to certain restrictions.[97] Article 28 of the Charter, for example, states that it is to be protected in accordance with Community law and national law and practices. The ECJ found that the right to take collective action for the protection of workers can provide a legitimate interest that can justify a restriction of the Treaty's free movement provisions.[98] The ECJ further noted that the Community has an economic as well as a social purpose based on the objectives listed in the Treaty, which means that the rights of free movement need to be balanced against objectives pursued by social policy. Nonetheless, in its proportionality assessment of the measures that had been taken by the member state, the ECJ mainly set out several strict conditions that needed to be fulfilled to protect the free movement of services. It held, for example, that it would need to be assessed by the national court whether the collective action taken could reasonably be considered to fall within the objective of protecting workers.[99] This would not be the case if it were established that the jobs or conditions of employment at issue were not seriously threatened. The national court also needed to examine whether there were less restrictive means that could be taken to protect the right to collective action than a strike.[100]

The approach of the ECJ in this case has been criticised because the Court did not seem intent on further strengthening the protection of the fundamental right at issue.[101]

95 ECJ 11 December 2007, C-438/05, *Viking Line*, paras 39 and 42.

96 ECJ 11 December 2007, C-438/05, *Viking Line*, paras 40–41. Cf. further the references made by the ECJ in the case of *Viking* in para. 40; and cf. ECJ 11 September 2007, Joined cases C-76/05 and C-318/05, *Schwarz and Gootjes* (on education); ECJ 11 November 2004, C-372/04, *Watts*, para. 147 (on social security); and ECJ 1 April 2008, C-267/06, *Maruko*, para. 59.

97 ECJ 11 December 2007, C-438/05, *Viking Line*, para. 44.

98 ECJ 11 December 2007, C-438/05, *Viking Line*, paras 77–79.

99 ECJ 11 December 2007, C-438/05, *Viking Line*, para. 81.

100 ECJ 11 December 2007, C-438/05, *Viking Line*, para. 87.

101 Barnard (2011), pp. 673–675.

This could be explained because of the clear lack of a regulatory competence of the EU to protect the right to strike, as was mentioned earlier. At the same time, the Court could also have taken a different approach to show respect for the choices made by the member states in their own, sensitive, policy fields, such as it did in the case of *Omega* and *Sayn-Witgenstein*, where it affirmed the discretion that the member states enjoyed in making their own assessment in cases showing a conflict between the free movement provisions and fundamental rights.[102] Moreover, the ECJ could have set requirements for the assessment of the proportionality of the restriction of the fundamental rights, aside from those that related to the restriction of the free movement provision. It had clearly done so in the case of *Schmidberger*.[103] Seeing the different approaches in these cases, the Court does not yet seem to have a single solution yet for the assessment that needs to be made in this type of situation, and it thus unclear what standard it will impose and for what reason.

The question for the purpose of this research is whether the ECJ would also be willing to impose further positive obligations on the member states in this type of situation. It could be argued that if a strict review of the measures taken by the member states cannot be undertaken because of the tension that this would create in light of the division of powers between the EU and the member states, there also is not much room to 'interfere' by imposing strict positive obligations. The ECJ could, rather, be expected to grant considerable discretion to the member states in deciding on the meaures they would take in this area, provided that these measures meet the requirements of the protection of the free movement provisions as such. Moreover, in this type of situation it is difficult to find out what kind of fundamental rights competence the EU is given, and thus whether the EU can be held to have been given an indirect competence to protect fundamental rights, which could further justify the imposition of positive obligations (see chapter 8).

Because of this particular tension in view of the principle of attributed powers, it is submitted that the ECJ needs to be very careful when recognising positive obligations under these specific circumstances.

9.3.2.3. *The Situation of Optioning Rules*

As chapter 6 briefly mentioned, the ECJ has also applied EU fundamental rights standards in situations where the member states are given a clear discretionary power under EU law.[104] In particular, in the case of *N.S. and others*, the ECJ decided that when member states exercise a discretionary power that is granted to them under EU law, the member states are implementing EU law within the meaning of Article 51(1) of the

---

102 ECJ 14 October 2004, C-36/02, *Omega*, paras 30 and 37; and ECJ 22 December 2010, C-208/09, *Sayn-Wittgenstein*, paras 86–87. See further section 7.5.3. and De Vries (2013).

103 ECJ 12 June 2003, C-112/00, *Schmidberger*, para. 51.

104 See section 6.7.1.

Charter, and they must comply with EU fundamental rights standards.[105] Sarmiento has argued that in this type of situation, the member states are applying an optioning rule under EU law.[106] This is different from a situation where the member states are given discretion in the implementation of EU law when they are acting as agents of EU law. This distinction can be explained by looking in more detail at the specific rules which brought the circumstances of the case of *N.S. and others* within the scope of application of the Charter. This case was about the Dublin Regulation which, as explained earlier, lays down an obligation for member states to return asylum seekers to the country of first arrival within the EU which is responsible for dealing with an asylum application.[107] The Dublin Regulation also provides that member states may decide to deal with the asylum application themselves. The ECJ held in relation to this rule, what Sarmiento thus calls an 'optioning rule', that it 'grants member states a discretionary power which forms an integral part of the Common European Asylum System provided for by the FEU Treaty and developed by the European Union legislature' and that it:

> forms part of the mechanisms for determining the Member State responsible for an asylum application provided for under that regulation and, therefore, merely an element of the Common European Asylum System. Thus, a member state which exercises that discretionary power must be considered as implementing European Union law within the meaning of Article 51(1) of the Charter.[108]

In this situation, EU law is thus constitutive for the exercise of a specific power by the member states – without a provision of EU law being in place, the member states could not take regulatory action. At the same time, the member states are not placed under an obligation to exercise the specific powers granted to them. Rather, as in the case of *N.S. and others*, the member states can use the discretionary power to apply their own policies, based on their sovereign powers and in accordance with international human rights law. Sarmiento has defined the type of provisions of *N.S. and others* as an 'optioning rule', because it grants the member states a choice or an option to take a variety of actions in an area governed by EU law.[109] Sarmiento has further explained the difference from the agency situation discussed above, and finds that there can be discretion for the member states in both situations to exercise the power. In the case of optioning rules, however, the member states have been given the choice to make use of the specific power under EU law, whereas in the case of mandating rules, the member states are, from the start, under an obligation to exercise the specific power. Thus by

---

105 ECJ 21 December 2011, Joined cases C-411/10 and 493/10, *N.S. and others*, paras 64–66.

106 Sarmiento (2013), pp. 1281–1282.

107 Article 3(2) of Regulation No. 343/2003/EC of 18 February 2003 establishing the criteria and mechanisms for determining the Member State responsible for examining an asylum application lodged in one of the Member States by a third-country national [2003] OJ L50/1. See also sections 6.8., 7.5.2. and 11.5.3.

108 ECJ 21 December 2011, Joined cases C-411/10 and 493/10, *N.S. and others*, paras 65 and 68.

109 Sarmiento (2013), pp. 1281–1282.

contrast, in the case of *Åkerberg Fransson*, the member states were under an obligation under EU law, on the basis of a mandating rule, to undertake a specific activity.[110]

In the situation where optioning rules are applied, there seems to be limited power for the EU to regulate the protection of fundamental rights as well. Since the EU specifically grants these discretionary powers to the member states, it could be argued that there is room for the ECJ to assess whether the member states have complied with EU standards of fundamental rights. Yet, in comparison to the *ERT* situation, the review that can be undertaken by the ECJ in the application of the EU fundamental rights standards by the member states could be expected to be even more restricted, because of the deliberate choice that has been made under EU law not to regulate these standards. Therefore, to impose positive obligations on the member states would again be difficult since the member states have 'deliberately' been granted a discretion to use these powers. The ECJ can thus be expected to impose positive obligations only in a very limited form.

9.3.3. THE SOVEREIGN POWERS OF THE MEMBER STATES

The ECJ has explained that, in some cases, the member states still enjoy sovereign powers, even if there is a clear substantive connection to EU law. The case of *Dano* is an example of such a case.[111] In its judgment, the ECJ established that the conditions for receiving social benefits do not fall within the scope of application of EU fundamental rights even though there are EU rules which coordinate the social security systems of the member states. The ECJ explained that the specific EU Regulation at issue had not intended to lay down the conditions creating the right to 'special non-contributory benefits' – which is an important term that is used in the provisions of the Regulation – and that therefore the member states had retained their competence to lay down the conditions for the grant of such benefits.[112] Thus, the Court had regard to the fact that the member states had expressly aimed to exclude a certain area from the scope of application of EU law. Therefore, it decided that member states are not implementing EU law within the meaning of Article 51(1) of the Charter when they are determining the conditions for granting social benefits. Consequently, the ECJ could not review the specific refusal at issue, which was the grant of such benefits to two Romanian nationals, in light of the principle of non-discrimination.

The Court has shown a similar approach in the case of *Willems and others*.[113] In this case, the question at issue was whether the use and storage of biometric data for purposes other than the issuing of passports and identity cards was precluded by EU

---

110 See also De Mol (2013), pp. 32–33.

111 ECJ 11 November 2014, C-333/13, *Dano*.

112 ECJ 11 November 2014, C-333/13, *Dano*, paras 87–91.

113 ECJ 16 April 2015, Joined cases C-446/12 and C-449/12, *Willems and others*. Also cf. some of the recent orders of the ECJ which were discussed in section 9.3.1.

law. Under the EU Regulation, member states incurred an obligation to store such data for the purpose of issuing passports and identity cards.[114] In its judgment in the case that was referred by the national court, the ECJ pointed out that a recital and a provision had been included in the said Regulation, which made it clear that the use and storage of the biometric data for other purposes than those stated under the Regulation was to be governed by national law and not by EU law.[115] On that note, the ECJ decided that it did not need to determine the compatibility of the storage and use of biometric data for other purposes, such as for the detection and prosecution of criminal offences, in light of the fundamental rights to privacy and the protection of personal data as guaranteed by Articles 7 and 8 of the Charter. The Regulation was not applicable to those issues.[116]

The ECJ may thus take into account, in particular, the choices that have been made by the EU legislature with regard to application of EU law to certain situations that might have some connection to EU law. In the cases of *Dano* and *Willems and others*, it was, to some extent, clearly indicated by the EU legislature that the specific areas fell outside the scope of application of EU fundamental rights, because they had been mentioned in EU secondary law. Sometimes, such indications are not very clearly provided in secondary EU legislation. The case of *Julian Hernández*, for example, concerned a specific Spanish rule that restricted entitlement to remuneration of employees who were dismissed by an employer that had become insolvent, to a limited period. The ECJ decided that this matter fell outside the scope of application of EU law.[117] It pointed out that the relevant Directive (on the protection of employees in the event of the insolvency of the employer) had stated that it 'shall not affect the option of the Member State to apply or introduce laws, regulations or administrative provisions which are more favourable to employees'.[118] According to the ECJ, this meant that this 'does not grant the Member States an option of legislation by virtue of EU law, but merely … recognises the power which the Member States enjoy under national law to provide for … more favourable provisions outside the framework of the regime established by that directive'.[119] Thus, if EU legislation provides for a rule that allows for more favourable protection at the national level, the ECJ may decide that such a situation falls outside the scope of application of EU law.

---

114 See also 7.5.3 for a further discussion of this case.

115 ECJ 16 April 2015, Joined cases C-446/12 and C-449/12, *Willems and others*, para. 47. See Regulation No. 444/2009/EEC of 28 May 2009 on standards for security and features and biometrics in passports and travel documents issued by Member States, recital 5 and article 4(3). In particular, recital 5 holds that 'Regulation (EC) No 2252/2004 requires biometric data to be collected and stored in the storage medium of passports and travel documents with a view to issuing such documents. This is without prejudice to any other use or storage of these data in accordance with national legislation of Member States. Regulation (EC) No 2252/2004 does not provide a legal base for setting up or maintaining databases for storage of those data in Member States, which is strictly a matter of national law.'

116 ECJ 16 April 2015, Joined cases C-446/12 and C-449/12, *Willems and others*, para. 50.

117 ECJ 10 July 2014, C-198/13, *Julian Hernández*.

118 ECJ 10 July 2014, C-198/13, *Julian Hernández*, para. 44.

119 ECJ 10 July 2014, C-198/13, *Julian Hernández*, para. 44.

In some cases where the ECJ has recognised that member states enjoy certain sovereign powers, it has also decided that EU fundamental rights may still be applied, albeit to a limited extent, that is, merely as aids to interpretation. In its judgment on the *McB.* case, the ECJ recognised that the questions that were raised by the national court concerned an area where the member states enjoy sovereign powers.[120] This case was about the removal of a child by its mother to another member state. The father of the child claimed custody rights before the national court, which had to apply certain rules laid down in the Brussels IIbis Regulation on the jurisdiction, recognition and enforcement of certain matters related to family law.[121] The ECJ, mindful of the fact that the questions raised were also concerned with the rights to custody of a child, affirmed that there are limited competences of the EU in this field and held that 'there should be no assessment of national law as such'. It held that the Charter should be interpreted solely for the purpose of the interpretation of the Brussels IIbis Regulation.[122] Thus, in such cases the ECJ still applies a very careful approach in developing fundamental rights standards.

All in all, in these situations where, according to the ECJ, the member states enjoy sovereign powers, it can be expected that the ECJ will not scrutinise the compliance by the member states of their respect for fundamental rights, or as in the case of *McB.*, only in a very limited way. Therefore, the ECJ would also not be expected to develop positive obligations in this type of situation.

9.3.4. THE DISCRETION FOR THE MEMBER STATES TO APPLY THEIR OWN FUNDAMENTAL RIGHTS STANDARDS

As has been alluded to in section 9.3.2.1., the ECJ has clarified that the member states still have room to apply their own standards of fundamental rights in situations which fall within the scope of EU fundamental rights. The ECJ has interpreted Article 53 of the Charter – which more broadly addresses the application of fundamental or human rights stemming from the national constitutions or from international treaties in fields where EU law also applies – to mean that:

> where an EU legal act calls for national implementing measures, national authorities and courts remain free to apply national standards of protection of fundamental rights, provided that the level of protection provided for by the Charter, as interpreted by the Court, and the primacy, unity and effectiveness of EU law are thereby not compromised.[123]

---

120 ECJ 5 October 2010, C-400/10, *McB.*

121 Regulation No. 2201/2003/EC of 27 November 2003 concerning jurisdiction and the recognition and enforcement of judgments in matrimonial matters and the matters of parental responsibility, repealing Regulation No. 1347/2000/EC [2003] OJ L338/1.

122 ECJ 5 October 2010, C-400/10, *McB.*, paras 51–52.

123 ECJ 26 February 2013, C-399/11, *Melloni*, para. 60; and ECJ 26 February 2013, C-617/10, *Åkerberg Fransson*, para. 29.

Some scholars have interpreted this as a further form of intrusion by the ECJ into the powers of the national authorities to apply the fundamental rights laid down in their own constitutions.[124] The protection of the 'primacy, unity and effectiveness' is in that respect regarded mainly as a limitation to the protection of national standards. It is also possible to give a rather different reading to the judgment, which is more friendly towards the preservation of the national powers. Indeed, Sarmiento has argued that by its rulings in the *Melloni* and *Åkerberg Fransson* the ECJ may have aimed to address the division of competences between the EU and the member states in the field of fundamental rights. Sarmiento has noted that:

> In *Melloni* and *Åkerberg Fransson* the ECJ has confirmed the shared nature of fundamental rights protection, guaranteeing Member State action in areas not previously pre-empted by EU law. Recognizing the relevance of national fundamental rights when EU rules grant discretionary choice to Member States, but imposing strict primacy once a domain is completely determined by EU rules, the ECJ emphasizes the importance of a coordinated separation of tasks between the Union and the Member States in the area of fundamental rights protection.[125]

According to Sarmiento, the ECJ had actually aimed to clarify how the standards of EU law and national law interact in areas of EU law depending on the competences that are exercised.[126] It could concern exclusive, shared or complementary powers, as discussed in chapter 8.[127] Sarmiento explains that areas could either be completely determined by EU law, in which case there is no discretion for the member states and, accordingly, the EU standard of fundamental rights does not only apply, but also must prevail over the national standard of fundamental rights. By contrast, when an area is only partially determined by EU law, the member states enjoy discretion in implementing EU law. This means that they may apply their national standard of fundamental rights if these go beyond the EU standard of fundamental rights.[128]

From this perspective, when the member states enjoy considerable discretion under EU law, there could be an important reason for the ECJ to refrain from formulating very specific positive obligations that would need to be complied to protect fundamental rights within the context of EU law.

9.4. CONCLUSIONS

On the basis of the analysis conducted in this chapter, it can be held that there is room for the ECJ to accept that positive obligations to protect fundamental rights fall within

124 See section 6.8.
125 Sarmiento (2013), p. 1291.
126 Sarmiento (2013), p. 1291–1298.
127 See section 8.2.
128 Sarmiento (2013), p. 1289.

the scope of application of EU law. Article 51 of the Charter clearly poses constraints on the ECJ in this regard, because it requires the ECJ to pay attention to the specific fields in which the EU is entitled to exercise powers and to specific rules laid down in EU primary and secondary law. It is therefore to be expected that the ECJ would primarily define a supportive type of positive obligation to protect fundamental rights within the scope of EU law. This concerns an obligation that is necessary to secure that the EU institutions and the member states, in their implementation of EU law, comply with the negative obligation not to violate fundamental rights. In responding to certain gaps that may still have been left in the legislative frameworks of the EU, and in the implementation thereof by the member states, the ECJ could be asked to determine whether certain (regulatory) actions on the EU institutions and the member states would need to be undertaken. In that regard, the ECJ may seek to secure that its solutions comply with the current practices and values of the member states and prevent a too rigid application of the scope of application of EU fundamental rights.

The analysis of the case-law of the ECJ on the interpretation of Article 51(1) of the Charter has further shown that it is, to some extent, still difficult to find the specific viewpoint of the ECJ on the reach of the EU fundamental rights obligations, especially towards the actions of the member states. Generally, it seems straightforward: when the EU has exercised certain competences and the national authorities act in implementation of EU law, EU fundamental rights apply. In this classic agency situation on the application of EU fundamental rights to the member states, there is room for the ECJ to formulate negative as well as positive obligations to ensure the protection of fundamental rights. The complexity is, however, that there are various areas where the member states have retained their sovereign powers, even though EU law and EU fundamental rights still may play a role. In particular, this may apply in relation to the situation of national derogations from the EU fundamental freedoms or the exercise of fully discretionary powers. This may result in a situation where the member states are asked to comply with EU fundamental rights standards, while they are conducting certain policies, such as protecting the right to strike, which clearly fall outside of the sphere of the legislative competences of the EU. In that respect, the ECJ may need to be very careful if imposing positive obligations of a legislative kind on the member states. Moreover, now that EU law itself does not provide a clear mandate on the member states to ensure the protection of fundamental rights, the ECJ would not be expected actively to interfere in the fundamental rights policies, which member states mostly base on their own national laws. The ECJ would thus not be expected to impose positive obligations in those situations.

CHAPTER 10

PART II – CONCLUSIONS

10.1. THE SPECIFIC PARAMETERS OF EU LAW DEFINING THE SCOPE AND THE LIMITS FOR THE DEVELOPMENT OF POSITIVE OBLIGATIONS

In this chapter, the main findings of the analysis undertaken in part II are presented. This part has studied the specific system of fundamental rights protection in the EU to find out whether it allows for any development of positive obligations by the ECJ. The Charter provides some potential for the recognition of positive obligations. It contains a great variety of fundamental rights which could require active measures to be taken by the EU institutions as well as by the member states. The Charter also, however, lays down some important conditions for protecting such fundamental rights in the EU context. It determines *inter alia* that the Charter only applies to the actions of the EU institutions and the member states in so far as they are implementing EU law. This important condition necessarily limits the scope for a development of positive obligations. However, as has also been explained, it does not exclude such development altogether. There are various other conditions that can be expected to be of influence in the development of positive obligations in the context of EU law.

In this chapter, it is first of all explained that the use of the preliminary reference procedure plays an important role in the (potential) development of positive obligations by the ECJ (section 10.2.). After that, the main relevant legal bases for a development of positive obligations on the basis of EU law are indicated (section 10.3.). Then it is explained how the limited competences of the EU, in combination with the limited scope of application of EU fundamental rights, can allow for the recognition of a concept of positive obligation by the ECJ, albeit to a limited extent (section 10.4.). In this section in particular, the conclusions following from chapters 8 and 9 are drawn together. Lastly, a few other, more specific factors that can influence the degree to which the ECJ could be expected to further develop positive obligations in its case-law are addressed. These mainly concern the specific institutional position of the ECJ and the role it can be expected to play in protecting fundamental rights (section 10.5.).

The conclusions on the scope and the limits for a development of positive obligations are used in chapter 11 to further assess their application in specific case-law examples, and they form the basis for the final conclusions in chapter 12.

10.2. THE DEVELOPMENT OF POSITIVE OBLIGATIONS UNDER THE PRELIMINARY REFERENCE PROCEDURE

Within the EU context, claims relevant to fundamental rights protection are generally not brought to the ECJ directly by individuals. As has been discussed in chapter 7, the preliminary reference procedure by national courts constitutes the most important procedural avenue that is used to clarify how fundamental rights must be protected under EU law.[1] This is the result, partly, of the restrictive interpretation of the standing requirements for individuals to bring direct actions to the ECJ that would allow them to address fundamental rights violations. It also has to do, however, with the fact that in most circumstances, national authorities rather than the EU institutions are responsible for the protection of EU law and the implementation and enforcement of EU law. Thus, it is mostly before the national courts that issues concerning the protection of EU fundamental rights will arise. Hence, national courts play a very important role for the potential (further) development of positive obligations under EU law, and the development of positive obligations is, to a certain extent, dependent on the willingness of national courts to refer questions on the protection of fundamental rights to the ECJ. They may be encouraged by the parties in a particular case to make such preliminary references, but ultimately it is the national court's prerogative to decide on the referral. The national court also decides on the formulation of the question as well as on the level of detail with which it formulates the inquiry into the relevant measures.

Under the preliminary reference procedure, the ECJ may decide to leave quite some discretion to the national authorities. The national courts and authorities are then relatively free to determine how to apply the ECJ's requirements and how to accommodate for the new interpretations in their national laws and practices. National courts can then potentially decide to formulate positive obligations on the basis of their own constitutions and they may especially look at the case-law of the ECtHR to find the positive obligations they need to comply with under the Convention.

It can thus, overall, be concluded that there are some procedural limitations to the development of positive obligations in the EU context. The process depends on the national courts to referring relevant cases to the ECJ. In addition, there is little room for individuals to raise questions over potential gaps in the protection of their fundamental rights. Finally, the national courts may be given considerable some leeway when implementing the ECJ's judgments in their own case-law.

---

1 See section 7.4.

10.3. THE RELEVANT LEGAL FRAMEWORK FOR THE DEVELOPMENT OF POSITIVE OBLIGATIONS UNDER EU LAW

The findings of part II have also shown that the Charter contains important provisions for a development of positive obligations. The Charter, which only became binding in 2009, for the most part contains a codification of the rights which were already guaranteed by the ECJ as general principles of EU law in its case-law, supplemented by rights which were to be found in other national and international instruments of fundamental rights. Consequently, it mainly concerns rights that the member states were already bound to respect. Moreover, it may be noted that, in its case-law, the ECJ had developed several crucial principles regarding the scope of application of EU fundamental rights and the interrelationship with other sources of fundamental rights. Nevertheless, the advantage of the Charter is that it provides greater clarity as to which fundamental rights are guaranteed and how this should be done. Since 2009 it has become the main point of reference in the case-law of the ECJ to determine the application and the interpretation of the fundamental rights that are guaranteed by the EU. In addition, it has led to an increase in the number of ECJ judgments that deal with fundamental rights protection. Seeing this, the Charter could also potentially encourage the ECJ to further develop principles on how fundamental rights are to be protected within the context of EU law, including those which relate to a concept of positive obligations.

In general terms, the Charter requires the EU institutions and the member states, in so far as they act within the scope of EU law, to 'respect the rights, observe the principles and promote the application' of the Charter's provisions. It has been argued that this could be taken to mean that there is room for the EU institutions and the member states to take positive measures to protect fundamental rights within the context of EU law. Chapter 8 has also indicated various other provisions of the Charter which can provide a more specific basis to determine what types of measures could be relevant to be undertaken by the EU legislature as well as by the member states to effectively secure those rights.[2] Of the fundamental rights that have been included in the Charter, several, by their very nature, require active measures to be taken, such as the social and economic types of fundamental rights. So far, the ECJ has not engaged in the interpretation of such rights, however, and it can be held that there is a limited basis for the ECJ to develop positive obligations in relation to those rights. Moreover, Article 52(5) of the Charter implies a specific limitation to the judicial development of positive obligations if a provision contains a 'principle' instead of a 'right'. The ECJ still has to decide which particular provisions include such 'principles' instead of 'rights', as

---

2 See section 8.3.4.4. See, for example, Article 8 of the Charter on the protection of personal data, which refers to the establishment of a data protection institution and could thus require institutional measures to be taken.

only few indications on this issue have been given in the explanations to the Charter. It is expected, however, that the notion of principles mainly relates to social and economic rights, or perhaps more generally most of the provisions which have been headed under the 'solidarity' chapter of the Charter.[3]

Article 52(3) of the Charter could further provide an especially important basis for a development of positive obligations. This provision requires that the provisions of the Charter which correspond to the rights of the Convention – that is, most of the civil and political rights – are to be given the same scope and meaning as the Convention rights. The Convention has, indeed, always formed an important source of inspiration for the interpretation of fundamental rights by the ECJ. The ECJ has often used the provisions of the Convention as well as the case-law of the ECtHR as a basis for interpreting fundamental rights within the context of EU law. It is in the interest of consistency that it should do so. It has been explained that in recent years the ECJ has shown to be intent on developing an autonomous interpretation of fundamental rights on the basis of the Charter. Seemingly for that reason, it is now less frequently making references to relevant provisions of the Convention and judgments of the ECtHR. Therefore, it is possible that the ECJ could also decide to provide for an autonomous interpretation of the positive obligations that need to be respected within the context of EU law. The ECJ has, however, continued to refer to the case-law of the ECtHR, and there are several examples in which the ECJ has also relied on specific examples of positive obligations that were developed the ECtHR.[4] Thus, it would seem that the ECJ is generally willing to accept the (relevant) positive obligations that have been formulated by the ECtHR.

Another potential legal basis for the development of positive obligations that is of interest is Article 52(1) of the Charter. As part of the proportionality requirement for fundamental rights interferences, this provision determines that interferences of fundamental rights must be provided for by law. In relation to the interferences that might take place because of certain acts taken on the basis of EU law, this could require a certain legislative framework to be set up in order to prevent or further limit such interferences.

In addition to the Charter, the EU Treaties also contain some general legal bases for the development of positive obligations. In particular, the principle of loyal cooperation (Article 4(3) TEU) and the requirement to provide for remedies at the national level to secure the protection of EU law (Article 19(1) TEU) could be of interest.[5] These provisions require the member states to adopt general and procedural measures, and have been used by the ECJ to establish some important principles of EU law and to impose obligations on the member states to ensure the effective protection of EU law at the national level. These principles can therefore also be expected to play an important ground which the ECJ would use to formulate positive obligations, especially if it is seen that gaps have been left in the protection of fundamental rights in the EU context.

3 See section 6.10.

4 See section 7.6.2.2.

5 See sections 8.3.4.2. and 8.3.4.3.

Thus, there are several legal bases and sources available under EU law, which could be used by the ECJ when developing positive obligations in its case-law. Indeed, when it is clear that certain actions are necessary in relation to the policies and the acts that the EU institutions are competent to adopt, the ECJ may be expected to require that the EU legislature and policy-making bodies ensure that certain positive measures are taken (see section 10.4.).[6] Furthermore, in the implementation of EU law at the national level, it could be expected that certain procedures and regulations will be adopted to secure fundamental rights if the existing legal and administrative framework at national level would not already ensure sufficient protection. If gaps nonetheless are found in EU legislation or in their implementation at national level, the national courts and the ECJ may be asked to define whether certain actions need to be taken by the EU institutions or by the member states to effectively secure fundamental rights. It may, after all, not always be possible for the EU legislature to predict how the policies and actions of the EU in practice will affect the protection of fundamental rights of individuals or a specific group of individuals and what measures will be required to safeguard these rights in an effective manner. Thus, the national courts and the ECJ may still need to play an important role.

10.4. THE LIMITED COMPETENCES OF THE EU IN COMBINATION WITH THE LIMITED SCOPE OF APPLICATION OF EU FUNDAMENTAL RIGHTS

Article 51 of the Charter recalls that EU fundamental rights apply only in limited situations, and that the EU has limited competences, which must not be affected by the application of the Charter. *Prima facie* the scope for a development of positive obligations thus seems to be very much restricted, since the EU has not been given clear competences to protect fundamental rights. As discussed in chapters 8 and 9, various scholars have argued that Article 51 of the Charter to some extent stands in the way of a recognition of positive obligations by the ECJ. Some scholars therefore have looked for other justifications for the acceptance of positive obligations. They have, for instance, pointed to principles relating to state responsibility for the protection of fundamental rights under international law as a possible ground that could be used to develop positive obligations within the context of EU law.[7] In chapter 8, it has been explained, however, that such approaches do not take sufficient account of the rules relating to the division of competences between the EU and the member states, nor do they provide sufficiently strong reasons to be able to conclude that it is indeed at EU

6 It was explained in part II that, in addition to the ECJ, the EU's political institutions themselves are nowadays also more closely checking whether the policies of the EU are in accordance with the requirements of the Charter, see sections 6.4. and 8.3.4.

7 See section 8.4.1.

level that fundamental rights are best protected. In most situations, the EU does not enjoy exclusive powers to take measures, and EU law provides much discretion for the member states to provide for protection. The approach developed in this study is thus based on the internal rules of the EU on the division of powers between the EU and the member states. This aims to meet the concern expressed in the Charter itself, as well as elsewhere, that the competences of the EU should not be unwarrantedly expanded.

It has been argued in part II of this study that the ECJ can accept positive obligations if they meet the requirements of Article 51(1) of the Charter. This means that positive obligations need to relate to a specific field in which the EU is entitled to exercise powers as well as to certain rules of primary and/or secondary EU law. Since the ECJ needs to pay attention to the specific field in which the EU is entitled to exercise a power and to any specific rules of EU law that apply to a given situation, it is expected that the ECJ will, primarily, formulate a supportive type of positive obligation. This type of positive obligation could be necessary to ensure that the EU does not fail to comply with its negative obligations in the sphere of fundamental rights protection, as well as to ensure that it provides for remedial measures when interferences do take place.

Given these conditions, in deciding whether it could accept a positive obligation, the ECJ would first need to have regard to the degree to which and the way in which the EU has chosen to protect fundamental rights in a given situation. For example, rules laid down in an EU Directive on equal treatment law would clearly bring a situation within the scope of application of EU fundamental rights. However, some specific rules may not yet be clear from the text of the Directive. EU secondary law may, for example, not have established what kinds of procedural requirements must be met by the EU institutions or by the member states to effectively protect the relevant fundamental rights (for example, the prohibition of discrimination) within that framework. Where this seems to leave a gap in the protection of fundamental rights, the ECJ could consider imposing a positive obligation to close this gap. To be able to impose a positive obligation on the member states or the EU institution on the basis of fundamental rights in that situation, however, there needs to be a certain competence under EU law to do so. Article 51(1) of the Charter specifically requires that the limitations on the competences of the EU are respected, and this also follows from Article 5 TEU which holds that the EU can only take action if it is conferred with a specific competence. This means that the ECJ could only impose a positive obligation on the EU institutions (or on the member states) to act if the legal basis in the EU Treaties allows for this. In the case of non-discrimination, such a competence can possibly be found in Article 19 TFEU. For positive obligations related to other fundamental rights, however, such as socio-economic rights, it may be much more difficult to find such an express legal basis. In that case, it could be argued that the member states retain the freedom to fill any gaps themselves, and it is not up to the ECJ to determine how they should use this freedom.

Surely, this means that the ECJ has to establish whether there is a concrete competence for the EU to act in all cases where it might consider imposing positive obligations. In this respect, it is relevant to reiterate that there is no general fundamental rights power that is not related to specific competence fields of the EU. The ECJ has acknowledged this, and there is no basis under the Treaties to be able to argue differently. Beyond this limitation, however, it is generally agreed that the EU still has certain specific as well as indirect competences to be able to protect the fundamental rights when it exercises one of its competences that is explicitly indicated by the EU Treaty.[8] When such specific competences exist, as in non-discrimination law, for example, it is relatively obvious that the ECJ might decide to impose some positive obligations. For the development of positive obligations in other areas, however, the indirect competences of the EU to protect fundamental rights are especially important. The notion of indirect competences basically entails that when the EU has explicit competences to act, such as in the field of the internal market or in the area of freedom, security and justice, it also, implicitly or indirectly, has the power to protect fundamental rights, because it needs to ensure that its actions respect and perhaps even promote fundamental rights. At the same time, as discussed in chapter 8, there are two important conditions that must be met in this respect. First, any type of action that is established to ensure the protection of fundamental rights by the EU, needs to be shown to be accessory to the exercise of the explicit competences on which such action is based. Secondly, the form of such action must remain within the boundaries that have been established by the drafters of the Treaty concerning the explicit power. This may entail, for example, that maximum harmonisation of national law is excluded, or that only supportive actions can be taken. Still, this would mean that there is room to adopt supportive positive obligations on the basis of an indirect competence to protect fundamental rights.

As mentioned above, however, it is not enough for a certain topic to fall within the (explicit or indirect) competences of the EU for the ECJ to be allowed to impose a positive obligation. Just as important is to determine whether and to what degree a specific positive obligation would fall within the scope of application of EU fundamental rights. After all, Article 51(1) of the Charter stipulates that fundamental rights need only be respected (and, consequently, positive obligations may only be imposed) when EU law is applicable. Therefore, as argued in chapter 9, some EU action would already need to have been undertaken to allow for further imposition of any positive obligations. Consequently, if there is a competence to act for the EU institutions, but it has not yet been used to draft secondary legislation, or if a Directive leaves a certain matter entirely to the discretion of the member states, a particular issue may not yet fall within the scope of EU law and, consequently, of the EU Charter. In that case, there is clearly no room for the ECJ to oblige the member states or the EU institutions to protect such fundamental rights in a particular manner.

Again, however, this limitation to the potential for the development of positive obligation by the ECJ must be put into perspective. Chapter 9 has explained that the ECJ has accepted a broad reading of the scope of application of EU fundamental rights. In fact, the scope of application of EU fundamental rights may even be broader than that of the EU's legislative competences as such. The broad scope of application could

8 See sections 8.3.3. and 8.3.4.

be useful to reason that obligations may be imposed on the EU institutions or on the member states to protect fundamental rights. The ECJ may need to apply a flexible interpretation to the scope of application to be able to respond to the gap-filling function of fundamental rights that can give rise to positive obligations.[9]

More specifically in relation to member states' action (or inaction), three different types of situations have been discussed in which the ECJ has decided to hold the EU fundamental rights applicable. The potential for development of positive obligations is closely related to these three situations.

First, EU fundamental rights apply when the member states act as agents of EU law. This is the case where the member states take measures to implement specific provisions of secondary EU law, such as Directives and Regulations. In the agency situation, there seems to be scope for the ECJ to accept positive obligations, since it needs to be ensured that the actions taken by the EU institutions comply with fundamental rights guarantees, both negative and positive. Such compliance then also needs to be ensured if the actions are implemented by the member states at the national level. In determining the form that positive obligations can take in this type of situation, the ECJ needs to have regard to the kind of fundamental rights competences enjoyed by the EU. It may either concern a field where the member states are applying provisions of EU law that derive from the specific fundamental rights competences of the EU, or a field in which the member states are applying provisions of EU law in which the EU is considered to enjoy an indirect competence to protect fundamental rights, and where the two conditions mentioned earlier have been met (that is, the positive obligation must be accessory, and it must respect the degree to which harmonising measures can be taken).

In the other two types of situations that have been defined by the ECJ, that is, where member states derogate from EU law, and where they make use of optioning powers – it would be less logical to accept that the ECJ could develop positive obligations. It has been argued that in these situations, it is far less obvious that the actions taken by the member states directly derive from EU law; quite to the contrary.[10] Member states are instead developing their own policies based on national law, and these can concern quite sensitive policy areas for which there is no legislative competence for the EU to take action. Therefore, it would be more difficult to find that the EU enjoys an indirect competence to protect fundamental rights which it could use to actively protect fundamental rights. It would be very difficult to accept that the ECJ could require legislative positive obligations to be taken if the EU does not enjoy any competence to take such action.

Thus, when the ECJ wishes to develop positive obligations on the basis of EU law, it needs to be aware of an intricate combination and interrelatedness of the limited competences of the EU and the scope of protection of fundamental rights. It constantly

---

9 See section 9.2.3.

10 See sections 9.3.2.2. and 9.3.2.3.

needs to check both whether the EU would be competent to act to protect a certain fundamental right (even if this competence may be an indirect one), and to what extent the EU fundamental rights can be held to apply to the actual situation at hand. Clearly, this implies that the potential for development of such positive obligations is rather limited, but it also has been argued that this is not necessarily problematic from the viewpoint of fundamental rights protection. In most situations the national authorities retain the power to provide fundamental rights protection on the basis of their own laws.

10.5. WHY AND WHEN COULD THE ECJ ACCEPT POSITIVE OBLIGATIONS?

The ECJ can thus accept positive obligations to protect fundamental rights on the basis of EU law based on the existing judicial procedures and the limited competences of the EU in combination with the limited scope of application of EU fundamental rights. In most situations, however, there is no clear obligation for it to do so, especially as many fundamental rights can also be protected on the national level. Nonetheless, as explained in chapters 7 and 8 in particular, there can be important arguments as to why fundamental rights protection needs to be ensured at the EU level. These are addressed below.

10.5.1. REASONS FOR ACTIVE PROTECTION OF FUNDAMENTAL RIGHTS AT THE EU LEVEL

In determining whether and when the EU legislator could use its fundamental rights competences, there are various considerations that could play a role. It is suggested that the considerations which have been set out in chapter 8 also should be taken into account by the ECJ when considering to accept positive obligations.

First, the principle of subsidiarity can provide a helpful standard in determining whether it is necessary to take action under EU law. Article 51(1) of the Charter even expressly requires the ECJ to take into account the principle of subsidiarity.[11] The principle of subsidiarity requires an effectiveness test to be undertaken within the meaning of Article 5(3) TEU. This means, as explained in chapter 8, that action is secured best by the EU when certain objectives cannot adequately be achieved by the member states and the scale or effects of EU action also provide a beneficial outcome. In many situations, fundamental rights would not appear to have any cross-border

[11] Several scholars have held that the ECJ specifically aimed to ensure respect for the principle of subsidiarity in its case-law by adjusting the intensity of its review, see e.g. De Búrca (1998), p. 225. However, Muir has explained that this is not the correct interpretation of the subsidiarity principle under Article 51(1) of the Charter, see Muir (2014a), p. 243.

effect as they apply to the relations within states only. Generally, therefore, the principle of subsidiarity often could provide a good reason to argue that action to ensure the protection of fundamental rights must be taken at the national level, since the national authorities are closest to the individuals whose interests must be protected. Nonetheless, there are specific examples that can be taken from EU legislative practices (for example, the impact assessments or the explanatory memorandums to legislative proposals), which explain that there may be certain cross-border dimensions to the protection of fundamental rights. This is especially true, for example, in relation to the enforcement of privacy rights. Since there clearly are cross-border flows of information, it may be necessary to establish uniform rules on the protection of personal data at the EU level to be able to effectively enforce the relevant privacy rights. The principle of subsidiarity can point towards acceptance or positive obligations by the ECJ, but also, as mentioned earlier, towards rejection thereof.

Secondly, the degree of the connection between EU acts and fundamental rights infringements could provide an important consideration arguing for preventive and remedial measures to be established, or for certain compensation to be made for the harm that is caused by the adoption of certain policies by the EU. In particular, it could be considered necessary to take such action if EU legislation has not harmonised certain laws and practices that were already in place at the national level but, rather, introduced new obligations for the member states that could interfere with fundamental rights. Also, it could be expected that certain preventive or remedial measures will be formulated at EU level where EU legislation or decisions could lead to serious fundamental rights interferences.[12] It may be expected that the ECJ would want to establish such relevant positive obligations, since it has been willing to establish important principles in the area of freedom, security and justice in order to prevent serious interference with fundamental rights from taking place.

Thirdly, the ECJ could take into account that fundamental rights are best secured at EU level in circumstances where there is a risk that EU free movement law might indirectly lead to a lowering of the fundamental rights standards of the member states. For example, in the area of privacy law, it has been argued that there is a risk that member states would lower their standard of protection in order to attract certain undertakings whose business models rely on the use of personal data. Member states could start to compete with each other and entice such undertakings to establish themselves in their jurisdiction, by offering the least possible number of 'obstacles' in terms of the privacy standards which must be applied. In those circumstances, action would be needed at EU level to prevent the member states from deciding to provide for a lower level of fundamental rights standards. Also, in the area of asylum law, it could be argued that a high level of fundamental rights standards is best secured under EU law, since the member states may not be willing to go beyond the minimum level of protection of

[12] See further section 8.4.4.

fundamental rights that they are required to provide on the basis of their international human rights obligations.[13]

Fourthly, the argument could be used that the establishment of standards of protection of fundamental rights at the EU level is in the interest of securing the primacy, unity and effectiveness of EU law itself. In areas where the national authorities need to cooperate on the basis of EU law, for example in areas where the principle of mutual recognition applies, a certain level of uniformity in the standards of fundamental rights protection applied by the member states may be needed.[14] Provided that there is a competence for the EU to take action in this field, it can be expected that the ECJ would formulate relevant positive obligations from this perspective.

In some situations, these considerations may not be of any great assistance, or they may be outweighed by the concerns of the member states, which wish to retain their own standards of fundamental rights protection. The ECJ may then specifically want to explain that the member states should be left sufficient scope to apply their own fundamental rights standards, and there are specific techniques allowing it to do so.[15] Nevertheless, it is suggested that these factors may be at least of some assistance in determining when the indirect competence to impose positive obligations can be actually used. It is thus suggested that the ECJ could take these considerations into account in actively shaping the positive obligations that need to be complied with by the EU institutions and its member states. It is clear, moreover, that in areas of exclusive competences, that is, in areas where there is no discretion for the member states to apply their own rules to ensure the protection of fundamental rights, the ECJ will need to formulate relevant positive obligation at the EU level.

10.5.2. THE ROLE OF THE ECJ IN THE FIELD OF FUNDAMENTAL RIGHTS

In general, it is still quite difficult to conclude exactly what role the ECJ aims to play in the field of fundamental rights, and thus whether it would be willing to avail itself of the existing competences and other factors as discussed above. Neither the EU Treaties nor the Charter provide very clear indications as to its particular role. On the one hand, fundamental rights have acquired an important place in the EU's legal order yet, on the other hand, there remains much emphasis on the limited competences of the EU. Seeing the emphasis on the limited competences, it could be expected that the ECJ would be wary of developing positive obligations in its case-law. As discussed earlier, the ECJ can choose to apply quite deferential review, especially where it concerns sensitive economic and social choices that need to be taken by the EU legislature, and it may wait for the national courts to raise relevant questions. Even in cases where the

13 See further section 8.4.5.
14 See further section 8.4.6.
15 See section 7.5.3.

ECJ deals with fundamental rights issues, it appears to cherish its formal style and does not elaborate much on how fundamental rights are to be protected, nor which fundamental rights doctrines are of relevance to take into account. Indeed, it can be concluded that, so far, the ECJ has been rather slow to develop fundamental rights doctrines in its case-law.

Based on the findings in chapter 7, it may be argued that the ECJ could do more to protect fundamental rights in an effective manner. Especially in some areas, there are fears that the ECJ too easily lets the interests of EU law prevail. From this perspective it could be of importance for the ECJ to respond in more detail to the questions raised by the national courts over potential positive obligations that need to be complied with, within the scope of application of fundamental rights. It may also wish to meet the concerns raised over the uncertainty and unpredictability of how fundamental rights are to be protected as well as those over the effective and genuine protection of fundamental rights by the EU. It could do so by developing fundamental rights doctrines – such as a positive obligations doctrine – which could be specifically geared to the particular characteristics and features of the EU legal system.

In developing such fundamental rights doctrines in its case-law, the ECJ does not necessarily need to 'invent' such doctrines, and it could rely on how other courts have dealt with various fundamental rights theories. In particular. the ECtHR is considered to provide for useful priciples for protection of fundamental rights which could be taken into account by the ECJ. The ECtHR has set forth a doctrine of positive obligations which was explained in part I of this study. At the same time, as already mentioned, the ECJ needs to interpret fundamental rights autonomously, and protect important interests of EU law. In the development of a positive obligations doctrine, the ECJ therefore could, in particular, be expected to pay attention to the limited competences of the EU and the limited scope of application of EU fundamental rights, as explained earlier.

10.5.3. THE JUDICIAL STYLE OF THE ECJ

Lastly, in developing positive obligations in its case-law, it is important to remember that it might not fit with the judicial culture of the ECJ as such to clearly determine what actions the EU institutions or the member states are to take to ensure an effective protection of fundamental rights. The ECJ is known for its brevity in answering the questions which are referred to it by national courts and for leaving them much leeway to implement such answers, as discussed in chapter 7. In some areas of EU law in particular (such as asylum law), where national courts often have requested guidance from the ECJ on the interpretation of fundamental rights, the reasoning of the ECJ has, so far, been terse. The ECJ may, therefore, develop positive obligations in its case-law in a rather less elaborate and precise manner than the ECtHR.

The ECJ might also find that it is not well-placed, for example given its position *vis-à-vis* another particular political institution, to establish what measures need to be taken by public authorities to effectively protect fundamental rights. The ECJ generally prefers to answer the questions of the national courts on the basis of available legal basis under the EU Treaties and under EU secondary law, rather than on the basis of the provisions of fundamental rights. Indeed, if the ECJ were to indicate specifically what measures are required to be taken by public authorities, it could become subject to claims of judicial activism. Arguably, by indicating such specific measures, it could be seen to be overstepping the boundaries of its mandate. Again, in developing a doctrine of positive obligations specific to the EU context, this should be accommodated.

PART III

SYNTHESIS

CHAPTER 11

THE DEVELOPMENT OF POSITIVE OBLIGATIONS WITHIN THE CONTEXT OF EU LAW: OVERVIEW AND EVALUATION OF THE CASE-LAW OF THE ECJ

11.1. INTRODUCTION

This chapter aims to portray and further discuss the examples of positive obligations that are present in the case-law of the ECJ. Some of these examples have already been addressed in the discussions in part II. Here, an overview is given of these and other examples of positive obligations so that some further insight can be given into the kinds of positive obligations that can be recognised within the context of EU law. In addition, a selection of five case are reviewed further and assessed in light of the conclusions reached in part II on the scope of, and the limits on, the development of positive obligations under EU law (see chapter 10). This analysis aims to establish whether (if at all) the development of positive obligations by the ECJ raises conflict with the specific principles of EU law.

The following section first briefly explains how the distinction between the concepts of positive and negative obligations can be made within the context of EU law and for what specific reasons it is relevant to make this distinction (section 11.2.). After that, an overview of the different examples of positive obligations from the case-law of the ECJ is given (section 11.3.). On the basis of this overview, the types of positive obligations that can so far be recognised within the current case-law of the ECJ are identified (section 11.4.). A further examination is then made of some specific judgments of the ECJ to find out whether or not the ECJ has overstepped the specific limits of EU law, or whether the approach adopted is too restrictive (section 11.5.). The chapter is rounded up by a conclusion (section 11.6.).

11.2. THE DISTINCTION BETWEEN POSITIVE AND NEGATIVE OBLIGATIONS WITHIN THE CONTEXT OF EU LAW

The ECtHR also has contrasted the recognition of negative obligations which, more traditionally, follow from the protection of fundamental rights, with the recognition of positive obligations.[1] The ECtHR in principle adopts a different approach when examining whether states have complied with their negative or positive fundamental rights obligations. The ECtHR has further stated that the scope for positive obligations under the Convention is limited. This evidently raises the question what exactly is the difference between positive and negative obligations. As explained in part I, the way in which the ECtHR has made the distinction between positive and negative obligations in its case-law has been debated and criticised.[2] This distinction can be difficult to make.[3] Therefore, it is of interest to clarify how the distinction is actually to be made within the context of EU law.

First of all, it should be recalled that the concept of positive obligations within the context of EU law was defined in the introductory chapter as follows: 'An obligation to take active measures which is based on the protection of fundamental rights and which is not already specified by EU (secondary or primary) law.'[4]

As this definition shows, and as explained in the introductory chapter, it is important to take into account the role that is played by provisions of secondary and primary EU law. Such provisions may already lay down the conditions and the actions which EU institutions or member states must take to ensure fundamental rights protection, so that there is no need to formulate positive obligations on the basis of fundamental rights provisions.

In the particular context of EU law, the positive obligations that may be accepted by the ECJ can be expected to be closely linked to negative obligations. This is because necessarily there will always be a certain act or a certain provision that needs to bring the situation within the scope of application of EU fundamental rights. The example of the case of *T. Port*, which was also used in the introductory chapter of this study, can further illustrate this.[5] In that case, the ECJ established that the Community institutions were under the obligation to take measures to protect the fundamental rights of traders in the transition to the common market. Ahmed and Butler have argued that the imposition of this positive obligation by the ECJ concerned a 'corrective' measure that needed to be taken to repair the damages suffered by the violation of a certain fundamental right.[6] Therefore, to their mind, this case would in fact not illustrate a 'true example' of a positive obligation.[7] Ahmed and Butler are correct in pointing out that in the case of *T. Port*, the measures which the ECJ imposed on the Community institutions were related to a positive act that was already established by Community law. Nevertheless, this makes it no less a positive obligation. The case-law of the ECtHR also shows several examples of such positive obligations, that is, obligations which have

1 See in particular section 3.5.
2 See section 3.2.3.
3 See section 3.2.3.
4 See section 1.4.
5 ECJ 26 November 1996, C-68/95, *T. Port.*
6 Ahmed & Butler (2006), pp. 794–795.
7 Ahmed & Butler (2006), p. 795.

a strong connection to positive measures which had previously been taken by the states.[8] In the case of *Marckx v. Belgium*, for example, the ECtHR imposed a positive obligation on the states parties to ensure the legal recognition of the family rights of children born out of wedlock.[9] In that case, the state had also taken a certain positive act, by establishing a legislative and administrative framework for the recognition of family rights, and it could have been argued that the state violated its negative obligation in respect of children born out of wedlock.

There are several features discussed in part I that explain what sets positive obligations apart from negative obligations.[10] These features are also relevant in the EU context. These are that positive obligations, contrary to negative obligations, (i) do not follow (directly) from provisions on fundamental rights and their structure, but need to be implied in individual cases; (ii) require states to take active measures which can (only) relate to certain gaps in their policies; (iii) and have an 'alternative' structure, which means that they leave a choice as to the measures which need to be taken by states.

Applying these conceptual differences to the, arguably, positive obligation by the ECJ in the case of *T. Port*, it can first be seen that the obligation for Community institutions to take active measures to protect the right to property of the undertaking also did not follow directly from the specific provision on the right to property. Instead, it was formulated by the ECJ in an individual case and it appeared in individual circumstances of hardship for the particular undertaking. Secondly, as indicated by the Court, it appeared that the EU institutions would have to take certain positive measures to protect fundamental rights. Thirdly, there was a choice of different measures that could be taken by the Community institutions to ensure that the right to property is effectively protected. These could be of a more practical nature or of a legal nature. Perhaps, certain rules would have to be established by the EU institutions to deal with these kinds of cases.

A further explanation of how the distinction between positive and negative obligations can be made has been given by several scholars in the specific context of the case-law of the ECJ on national procedural rules.[11] In this context, the principle of effective judicial protection has provided an important basis for the ECJ to impose either negative or positive obligations on the member states. Prechal and Widdershoven explained that:

> the principle of effective judicial protection implies both a *negative* and a *positive* obligation. Here a 'negative obligation' means that national provisions which fail to satisfy the requirements of the principle of effectiveness or effective judicial protection must be set aside. In other words, they are eliminated. The positive obligation, on the other hand, is that new national powers or remedies have to be created.[12]

---

8 See sections 3.2.3. and 3.3.2.

9 ECtHR 13 June 1979, no. 6833/74, *Marckx v. Belgium*.

10 See, again, section 3.5.

11 See Prechal, De Vries & Van Eijken (2011); Prechal & Widdershoven (2011); Van Cleynenbreugel (2012a); and Van Cleynenbreugel (2012b).

12 Prechal & Widdershoven (2011), p. 41. Cf. Van Cleynenbreugel (2012b), p. 89.

Thus in EU law as much as in the Convention system, the difference is that certain active measures must be taken by states in order to ensure the protection of fundamental rights, such as granting certain powers to public authorities or creating new remedies. Prechal and Widdershoven further explain this by looking at the judgments of the ECJ in *Factortame* and *Unibet*. In the case of *Factortame*, the ECJ specifically required national courts to grant interim relief to ensure the effective protection of EU law, while under the domestic laws of the United Kingdom (where the case originated), this particular remedy could not be provided.[13] 'New national powers or remedies' would need to be created, requiring the member states to take certain actions, potentially of a legislative kind. This, therefore, could be said to amount to the establishment of a positive obligation by the ECJ.[14] Likewise in the case of *Unibet*, the ECJ also specifically indicated that interim measures needed to be provided to ensure the protection of the principle of effective judicial protection.[15]

Often in the context of these national procedural rules, the ECJ, holds that member states only need to respect the requirements of effectiveness and equivalence.[16] Within these 'negative' limitations, member states are, in principle, free to apply their own procedural standards and rules if EU (secondary) law does not prescribe particular procedural standards which must be provided for at national level. In this approach, the member states would primarily appear to incur a negative type of obligation. Hence, Van Cleynenbreugel has explained that the ECJ could often decide to take this 'negative obligations' approach when examining the procedural standards at national level. This would imply that the ECJ simply declares that EU law precludes certain procedural rules at the national level. The ECJ then leaves it to the member states to provide for the appropriate arrangements. This would be different when a positive obligations approach is used. In such an approach the ECJ would itself define which type of arrangement needs to be made at the national level. The ECJ limits the discretion given to the member states and, as a consequence, 'taking the positive actions then becomes a matter of EU law instead of national law'.[17] Taking this approach thus has a clear bearing on the allocation of a specific power at either national level or at EU level. In that respect, making the distinction between positive and negative obligations is of importance in view of the division of competences between the EU and the member states.

Also in the EU context, there can thus be a fine line between imposing a negative or a positive obligation on the member states. The member states could in both contexts be required to take certain actions to comply with the judgment of the Court. The main

---

13 ECJ 19 June 1990, C-213/89, *Factortame*, paras 18–22.

14 Prechal & Widdershoven (2011), p. 41. Cf. Van Cleynenbreugel (2012b), p. 89. Prechal & Widdershoven and Van Cleynenbreugel have concluded, in respect of other similar cases, that the ECJ has in fact imposed positive obligations on the member states, see Prechal & Widdershoven (2011), pp. 31–50, 40–43 and 47–49; Van Cleynenbreugel (2012a), pp. 90–100; and Van Cleynenbreugel (2012b), pp. 81–100.

15 ECJ 13 March 2007, C-432/05, *Unibet*, para. 67. The case of *Abdida* is relevant here too, which is discussed in section 11.5.4.

16 ECJ 16 December 1976, C-33/76, *Rewe*.

17 Van Cleynenbreugel (2012b), pp. 89–91.

difference between positive and negative obligations then is that positive obligations are actually and specifically formulated by the ECJ itself, while in case of negative obligations it merely assesses whether the member states have not as such violated the negative obligations which already follow from EU fundamental principles or from primary or secondary EU law. In addition, the defining features of positive and positive obligations in relation to the case-law of the ECtHR, as provided above, can be helpful too. Positive obligations are generally about individual cases that show that the EU and the member states have been inactive in response to individual circumstances.

11.3. EXAMPLES OF POSITIVE OBLIGATIONS IN THE CASE-LAW OF THE ECJ

Taking into account the definition of positive obligations, as well as the specific distinction between positive and negative obligations that applies within the EU context, this section sets out various examples of positive obligations that may be found in the case-law of the ECJ. These examples have been derived from a study of literature on this subject; they also follow from an analysis of the more recent case-law of the ECJ, which covers the period of the entry into force of the Charter until mid 2016.[18] A categorisation is made of the obligations which the Court has set for the EU institutions (section 11.3.1.); and for the member states when they take measures as agents of the EU (section 11.3.2.); where they derogate from the free movement rules (section 11.3.3.); and when they make use of optioning rules under EU law (section 11.3.4.). This distinction on the different situations of application of fundamental rights has also been made in previous chapters.[19] There, it has been explained that the scope for a development of positive obligations differs on the basis of the specific type of situation that applies.

11.3.1. POSITIVE OBLIGATIONS FOR THE EU INSTITUTIONS

Aside from the specific case of *T. Port* discussed earlier, so far, there only appear to be positive obligations for the EU institutions at the procedural level. The ECJ has developed some positive procedural obligations for the EU institutions in its judgments in the *Kadi* cases, where several actions had been brought first before the General Court and later before the ECJ by individuals seeking annulment of certain EU Regulations implementing the UN sanctioning regimes.[20] These regimes had listed Kadi (and

---

18 The analysis was finalised on 1 June 2016.

19 See chapter 9 on the limited scope of application of fundamental rights and chapter 10 on the conclusions of part II.

20 See ECJ 3 September 2008, Joined cases C-402/05 P and C-415/05 P, *Kadi and Al Barakaat International Foundation/ Council and Commission*; and ECJ 18 July 2013, C-584/10, *Commission and others v. Kadi.* See further on these cases Cuyvers (2014).

others) on the list of persons and entities that were associated with Usama Bin Laden, the Al-Qaeda network and the Taliban, so that their assets could be frozen and travel bans imposed. In its judgments on these cases, the ECJ has spelled out quite clearly that the EU authorities needed to inform the persons and entities subject to such sanctions of the grounds for their placement on that list and that they needed to ensure that the persons and entities involved were able to make their views known within a reasonable time after placement on the list.[21] These positive procedural obligations had clearly not been provided for under the applicable EU Regulations, nor were they at the time met by the competent authorities.[22] As a result of the interpretation of the ECJ of the rights of defence, clear changes have needed to be made in order to make up for the procedural shortcomings related to these sanction decisions.

There also is a procedural obligation to be found in the judgment of the General Court in the case of *LTTE v. Council*.[23] This case was about the decision of the Council to freeze the funds of a terrorist organisation on the basis of a decision to that effect of a third country. The General Court made clear in the case of *LTTE v. Council* that when the Council adopts this kind of decision, it must thoroughly verify whether the protection of the rights of the defence and the right to effective judicial protection in that third-country is indeed equivalent to the level of fundamental rights guaranteed by the EU. The Council would thus have to undertake certain investigations into the compliance with fundamental rights in third countries to ensure that it protects fundamental rights effectively. More recently, the ECJ also has held that the Commission is under an obligation to check for the compliance with fundamental rights by third countries in the case of *Schrems*.[24] In this case, the ECJ had to review the validity of a decision that had been taken by the Commission on the basis of Directive 95/46.[25] This decision involved the United States providing an adequate level of protection of personal data for the purpose of the transfer of data and the free movement of data of EU citizens to the United States. In its judgment, the ECJ explained that it had serious concerns as to whether there were any rules adopted in the United States intended to limit interference with the fundamental rights of persons whose data was transferred from the EU to the United States.[26] It appeared that access to such data could easily be obtained by the authorities in the United States with the objective of the protection of national security. Moreover, it was unclear whether there were remedies available for persons whose privacy rights would be interfered with by those measures. The ECJ thus

---

21 See ECJ 3 September 2008, Joined cases C-402/05 P and C-415/05 P, *Kadi and Al Barakaat International Foundation/ Council and Commission*, paras 336–337 and 348.

22 See ECJ 3 September 2008, Joined cases C-402/05 P and C-415/05 P, *Kadi and Al Barakaat International Foundation/ Council and Commission*, para. 325.

23 GC 16 October 2014, T-208/11, *LTTE v. Council*, paras 138–139 and 201–212.

24 ECJ 6 October 2015, C-362/14, *Schrems*.

25 See Directive 95/46/EC of 24 October 1995 on the protection of individuals with regard to the processing of personal data and the free movement of such data [1995] OJ L281/31.

26 ECJ 6 October 2015, C-362/14, *Schrems*, paras 87–98.

decided to annul the Commission's decision. The ECJ also clarified, potentially with a view to a new decision that would have to be taken by the Commission, that it needs to periodically check whether the level of protection in a third country is liable to change, and also when evidence is provided to that effect.[27]

The obligations which are formulated in these types of cases thus require particular procedures to be followed and to be established by the EU institutions. The judgments of the ECJ (and of the General Court) also provide a specification of how the rights of defence and the principle of effective judicial protection are to be guaranteed.

Another positive procedural obligation which was formulated by the ECJ can be found in the case of *Gascogne*.[28] The ECJ held that a remedy needed to be provided to allow undertakings to bring a complaint for damages as a result of lengthy competition law procedures. The ECJ directly formulated this obligation on the basis of the judgment of the ECtHR in the case of *Kudla v. Poland*, which holds that states must take measures to ensure that the right to a fair trial under Article 6 ECHR is guaranteed within a reasonable time.[29] In the case of *Gascogne*, the ECJ specifically found that, to ensure respect for Article 47 of the Charter, a remedy should be made available before the General Court to claim for damages if the procedure that challenges a decision of the European Commission in the field of competition law is not completed within a reasonable time.[30]

11.3.2. POSITIVE OBLIGATIONS FOR THE MEMBER STATES IN THE AGENCY SITUATION

As compared to the previous section, a wider variety of positive obligations can be found with respect to the fundamental rights obligations that must be fulfilled by the member states when they are acting as agents of EU law. As shown below, a range of positive obligations can be found which mainly require the national courts to ensure the enforcement, sanctioning and effective application of EU law at national level. Next, some positive obligations for the administrative authorities and for the legislature at national level will be discussed.

---

27 ECJ 6 October 2015, C-362/14, *Schrems*, para. 76.

28 ECJ 26 November 2013, C-58/12, *Group Gascogne v. Commission*.

29 ECtHR 26 October 2000, no. 30210/96, *Kudla v. Poland*, para. 156. In other cases, the ECtHR has clarified that states could take different types of measures to ensure the right to a fair trial within a reasonable time. States could, for example, adopt structural measures to prevent excessive duration of legal proceedings, or they could take measures to expedite the procedures itself by fixating time limits and imposing corresponding sanctions. See ECtHR 29 March 2006, no. 36813/97, *Scordino v. Italy (No. 1)*, paras 183 and 186–188; and ECtHR 26 June 2001, no. 26390/95, *Beck v. Norway*, para. 27. See also the dissenting opinion of Judge Cassedeval to ECtHR, *Kudla v. Poland*.

30 ECJ 26 November 2013, C-58/12, *Group Gascogne v. Commission*, para. 83.

11.3.2.1. Positive Obligations for the Member States' Judiciaries

There are several examples where the ECJ established that judicial remedies need to be made available to allow individuals to challenge infringements of the rights they have under EU secondary law. This has been held necessary, for example, in a case to protect the rights of an employee under EU law *vis-à-vis* an employer, and in a case to enable an individual to challenge decisions on the grant of certain EU subsidies.[31] As a basis for inferring this type of procedural obligation, the ECJ referred to Articles 6 and 13 ECHR, as well as Article 47 of the Charter, which all enshrine principles of effective judicial protection.[32] Such procedural obligations may also be based on different grounds, however. In the case of *UPC Telekabel Wien*, for example, the Court used the right of individuals to freedom of information under Article 11 of the Charter as a basis for imposing an obligation on the member states to provide a remedy.[33] This was necessary to allow internet users to claim their rights of information before their national courts in a situation where an injunction was imposed on internet service providers to end infringments of intellectual property rights, which could result in interference with the right of information.

Furthermore, according to the case-law of the ECJ, national courts must be able to exercise several far-reaching powers to ensure that fundamental rights are protected in cases on EU law. The ECJ has established that national courts have an obligation to interpret national law in conformity with certain fundamental rights which must be protected under EU law, such as the right to intellectual property, the right to privacy and the right to the protection of personal data.[34] If necessary, national courts may also need to set national provisions aside if they conflict with such fundamental rights, in particular the principle of non-discrimination on grounds of age.[35] In this context, the ECJ has also required national courts to have available special techniques and special rules that enable them to review the legality of removal decisions in situations where information on the reasons for the removal are not made public for reasons of state security.[36] Following the case-law of the ECJ, national courts must, further, be able to

---

31 ECJ 15 October 1987, C-222/86, *Heylens* (free movement of workers), para. 14; ECJ 27 March 2014, C-314/12, *UPC Telekabel Wien* (freedom of information of internet users), para. 57; and ECJ 17 September 2014, C-562/12, *Liivimaa Lihaveis* (refusal to grant EU subsidies, para. 67).

32 ECJ 15 May 1986, C-222/84, *Johnston*, paras 17–19; and ECJ 15 October 1987, C-222/86, *Heylens*, para. 14; ECJ 17 September 2014, C-562/12, *Liivimaa Lihaveis*, paras 67 and 75.

33 ECJ 27 March 2014, C-314/12, *UPC Telekabel Wien*, para. 57.

34 ECJ 26 June 2007, C-305/05, *Ordre des barreaux francophone and germanophone and others*, para. 28; and ECJ 29 January 2008, C-275/06, *Promusicae*, paras 68 and 70; and ECJ 6 December 2012, Joined cases C-356/11 and C-357/11, *O and others*, para. 78.

35 Cf. ECJ 19 November 1991, C-6/90, *Francovich*, paras 31–37; ECJ 25 July 1991, C-208/90, *Emmott*, paras 21–23; ECJ 16 February 2012, C-182/10, *Solvay*, para. 49; ECJ 22 November 2005, C-144/04, *Mangold*, para. 77; and ECJ 19 January 2010, C-555/07, *Kücükdeveci*, para. 51; and ECJ 19 April 2016, C-441/14, *Danski Industri*, para. 37.

36 See ECJ 4 June 2013, C-300/11, *ZZ*, paras 57–58; and ECJ 5 June 2014, C-146/14 PPU, *Mahdi*, para. 62.

set aside an administrative decision and substitute that decision by ordering alternative measures. All these requirements could require judicial powers to be amended or new ones to be introduced. In some of these cases, the ECJ clearly makes the national courts responsible for the protection of certain fundamental rights between private parties. Similarly, the ECtHR has imposed positive obligations on the national courts to ensure such protection in horizontal situations.[37]

Next, the case of *Léger* shows that the national court can incur an obligation to undertake certain (small) investigations to secure the protection of fundamental rights.[38] In this case, the ECJ was asked to determine whether homosexual men could be permanently excluded from taking part in voluntary blood donation on the basis of the health risk they posed due to their sexual behaviour. The ECJ held that the national court was required to examine whether this group did indeed experience a heightened risk of acquiring an infectious disease on the basis of current medical, scientific and epidemiological knowledge, in order to avoid unwarranted discrimination on grounds of sexual orientation.[39]

Lastly, the ECJ has established that individuals must be able to claim compensation in their national courts for damages caused by Member States' failure to implement EU law correctly, which is necessary to secure the effectiveness of EU law.[40] The ECJ has clarified that this obligation also applies when national courts have failed to secure the correct application and interpretation of fundamental rights in the application of EU law to cases between private parties.[41] Again, certain remedies would need to be made available, or specific rules established, to allow such claims to be brought at national level.

11.3.2.2. Positive Obligations for the Member States' Administrative Authorities

Increasingly, the ECJ is determining the procedural standards that must be met by the national administrative authorities if they adopt such decisions on the basis of EU law.[42] In areas such as tax law, customs law, asylum and immigration law, the ECJ has established that individuals must be heard by the national authorities before decisions are taken that may adversely affect their interests, and that such decisions must be sufficiently

37 Such similar positive obligations for the national courts have been established by the ECtHR in ECtHR 24 June 2004, no. 59320/00, *Von Hannover*, para. 57; and ECtHR 13 July 2004, no. 69498/01, *Pla and Puncernau*. Further cf. Besson (2011a), p. 116; and Kühling (2009), p. 493.

38 ECJ 29 April 2015, C-528/13, *Léger*.

39 ECJ 29 April 2015, C-528/13, *Léger*, paras 63–66.

40 See also section 8.3.4.2.

41 See ECJ 19 November 1991, Joined cases C-6/90 and C-9/90, *Francovich and Bonifaci v. Italy*; ECJ 24 January 2012, C-282/10, *Dominguez*, para. 43; and 15 January 2014, C-176/12, *Association de médiation sociale*, para. 50.

42 See Beijer (2015), pp. 133–134.

reasoned so to allow those individuals to challenge those decisions.[43] Sometimes, the ECJ leaves little discretion to the member states and it may even expressly prescribe the new procedures that need to be created to comply with the announced positive obligations.[44] The ECJ has, moreover, determined in the case of *Abdida* that member states may need to make provision for the basic needs of a third-country national who suffers from a particularly serious illness while awaiting the appeal of a transfer decision (see also section 11.5.4.). All these obligations in the examples mentioned were not expressly provided for by the applicable EU legislation.[45]

11.3.2.3. Positive Obligations for the Member States' Legislatures

Very exceptionally, the ECJ has imposed an obligation of a legislative nature on the member states. In the case of *Chatzi*, the ECJ established that the national legislature was required to take measures to ensure that due account is taken of the particular needs of parents of twins within the parental leave regime.[46] This obligation was not specifically provided for under the applicable EU Parental Leave Directive, which only required Member States to meet certain minimum standards. Instead, it was imposed by the ECJ on the basis of the protection of the principle of equal treatment (see also section 11.5.2.).[47]

11.3.3. POSITIVE OBLIGATIONS FOR THE MEMBER STATES WHEN DEROGATING FROM THE FREE MOVEMENT RULES

The situation where member states derogate from EU (free movement) law forms a rather special category in which member states are protecting fundamental rights within the scope of EU law, as discussed in chapter 9.[48] Here, the member states are advancing the obligation to protect fundamental rights as part of their justification for restricting a free movement provision. In some cases that have been brought before the ECJ it is clear that the member states are acting on the basis of their (own) positive

---

43 On the right to be heard, see ECJ 22 November 2012, C-277/11, *M.*, para. 81; ECJ 18 December 2008, C-349/07, *Sopropé*, paras 36–37; and ECJ 3 July 2014, C-129/13, *Kamino International Logistics*, paras 31–34. On the obligation for courts to motivate their decisions, see ECJ 15 October 1987, C-222/86 *Heylens*, para. 15; ECJ C-300/11, *ZZ*, para. 65; ECJ 17 July 2014, Joined cases C-141/12 and C-372/12, *YS. and others*, paras 66–67; and ECJ 22 November 2012, C-277/11, *M.*, para. 88.

44 ECJ 5 November 2014, C-166/13, *Mukarubega*, para. 62; and ECJ 11 December 2014, C-249/13, *Boudjlida*, paras 55–56.

45 See ECJ 18 December 2014, C-562/13, *Abdida*, paras 59–62.

46 See ECJ 16 September 2010, C-149/10, *Chatzi*, paras 68 and 75. Cf. De Mol (2012), pp. 27–28.

47 Clause 2(1) of the annex to Council Directive 96/34/EC of 3 June 1996 on the framework agreement on parental leave concluded by UNICE, CEEP and the ETUC [1996] OJ L145/24.

48 See section 9.3.2.2.

obligation to protect fundamental rights. In the case of *Schmidberger*, for example, the member state at issue was taking legal as well as practical measures to ensure that a demonstration could take place at a polluting motorway.[49] This case was brought to the ECJ because it caused interference with the free movement of goods. Also in the case of *Familiapress*, the ECJ examined measures that had been taken on a member states' initiative to ensure the right to freedom of expression which seemed to restrict the free movement of goods.[50] In this latter case, a specific law had been adopted by Austria prohibiting prize competitions. This was likely to obstruct the exercise of the free movement of goods, in this case for a German magazine containing puzzle prize competitions. In its judgment, the ECJ recognised that the maintenance of press diversity aimed to help safeguard freedom of expression which is protected by Article 10 ECHR.[51] However, the ECJ also required the national court to undertake a study of the Austrian press market, to determine whether the Austrian law indeed aimed to ensure the maintenance of the press.[52] In that respect, it has been argued by scholars that the ECJ also imposed a positive obligation on the national court.[53]

The cases of *Schmidberger* and *Familiapress*, however, primarily appear to provide examples of where a positive obligation of the member state that is based on national law or on the Convention creates a conflict with the EU free movement rules. The case of *Berlington* shows a different example.[54] This case was about the introduction of a new licensing system for the operation of slot machines in Hungary as part of a new policy of games of chance. The ECJ found that this system caused a restriction on the free movement of services. It clarified that in revoking the licences of operators which did not comply with the requirements under the new policy, the national legislature was under an obligation to either allow the holders of those licences a transitional period of sufficient length to adapt to the new licensing system or otherwise provide reasonable compensation.[55] In formulating this obligation, the ECJ referred to the case-law of the ECtHR which contains such requirements in relation to the protection of the right to property.[56] The ECJ thus may establish a certain remedial or corrective positive obligation on the basis of the protection of fundamental rights, which member states need to fulfil when they seek to justify the EU free movement rules.

49 See ECJ 12 June 2003, C-112/00, *Schmidberger*; and cf. Morijn (2006), pp. 29–33.
50 ECJ 26 June 1997, C-368/95, *Familiapress*.
51 ECJ 26 June 1997, C-368/95, *Familiapress*, para. 18.
52 ECJ 26 June 1997, C-368/95, *Familiapress*, para. 29.
53 Prechal, De Vries & Van Eijken (2011), p. 241.
54 ECJ 11 June 2005, C-98/14, *Berlington*.
55 ECJ 11 June 2005, C-98/14, *Berlington*, para. 85.
56 ECtHR 13 January 2015, no. 65681/13, *Vékony v. Hungary*, paras 34–35. The Court of Justice addressed the protection of the right to property as guaranteed by Article 17 of the Charter in ECJ 11 June 2005, C-98/14, *Berlington*, paras 90–91.

11.3.4. POSITIVE OBLIGATIONS FOR THE MEMBER STATES WHEN APPLYING OPTIONING RULES

In the specific case of *N.S. and Others* the ECJ formulated a positive obligation in relation to the member states' so-called optioning rules. The ECJ held that the member states were responsible for ensuring that asylum seekers were not sent back to another member state under the Dublin Regulation if there were substantial grounds for believing that the asylum seeker would face a real risk of treatment contrary to Article 4 ECHR.[57] This case is discussed in more detail below, so it does not need to be examined in any great detail here (see section 11.5.3.).[58]

11.4. THE TYPES OF POSITIVE OBLIGATION WITHIN THE CONTEXT OF EU LAW

The analysis of the case-law of the ECJ shown above demonstrates that only certain types of positive obligations are, so far, to be found. The case-law in particular demonstrates the recognition of a range of procedural types of positive obligations. Many such obligations have been developed by the ECJ for the national authorities, and mostly for the national courts. Often, in fact, the national court incurs responsibility that fundamental rights are indeed actively protected within the context of EU law.

It is also notable that the obligations which the ECJ has formulated in its case-law can mainly be classified as obligations of an intrinsic and of a supportive nature.[59] Intrinsic types of positive obligations require measures to be taken so that fundamental rights can actually be enjoyed by individuals. Looking at the case-law of the ECJ, there are many examples of where procedures and remedies need to made available so that individuals can enjoy the rights which are granted to them under EU law. Supportive positive obligations are necessary to secure that public authorities do in fact comply with the negative obligation to protect fundamental rights. Often, the establishment of the judicial powers and necessary are also necessary to ensure that fundamental rights are protected within the relations between an individual and an EU institution or a member state.

There are, however, also some examples of positive obligations in the case-law of the ECtHR that aim to ensure the protection of fundamental rights in private relations. Some of the procedural obligations that have been established are, in particular, applied in disputes between two private parties. Most clearly, in the case of *UPC Telekabel Wien*,

---

57 See ECJ 21 December 2011, Joined cases C-411/10 and C-493/10, *N.S. and others*, para. 94. The notion of positive obligation is further discussed in the context of the Dublin Regulation in the Opinion of AG Trstenjak in C-245/11, *K*, paras 70–71; and in the Opinion of AG Jääskinen in C-4/11, *Puid*, paras 60–64.

58 See section 11.5.2.

59 See section 3.3.2. on the different types of positive obligations in the case-law of the ECtHR.

the requirement to provide for a remedy at national level was imposed to ensure that an individual could claim his or her right to the protection of information *vis-à-vis* an internet service provider. Also in the case of *Chatzi*, on the right to parental leave for twins, the imposition of the positive obligation was relevant to secure the protection of the fundamental rights of an employee *vis-à-vis* and employer, thus between two private parties.

Moreover, the case of *Abdida* seems to show that there also can be a social dimension related to positive obligations under EU law. The provision of basic needs seemed to be warranted on the basis of the clear vulnerability of a seriously ill individual, especially while awaiting for a decision on an asylum application.

11.5. RESPECTING THE LIMITS OF EU LAW?

In this section, five selected judgments of the ECJ are examined in more detail to assess how far the ECJ can go in developing positive obligations, keeping in mind the theoretical and legal framework that has been set out in part II. The cases discussed here have been subjected to academic debate and academic criticism. Discussion of these particular five cases allows an evaluation of whether such critiques are justified from the perspectives presented in part II. The discussion starts with one example in which the ECJ decided not to recognise a positive obligation (the *Grant* case), followed by four other examples where the ECJ decided differently, which have already been mentioned in earlier chapters (the cases of *Chatzi*, *N.S. and others*, *Abdida* and *T. Port*).

11.5.1. THE *GRANT* CASE

In the Court's judgment on the *Grant* case, which was delivered in the late 1990s, the ECJ decided that discrimination based on sexual orientation was not specifically prohibited under Community law.[60] Some scholars have criticised this judgment,[61] stating that the ECJ unwarrantedly denied the recognition of a positive obligation of a legislative kind for the Community to protect discrimination based on sexual orientation.[62] It is thus of interest to determine whether or not there was indeed scope for the ECJ to accept this positive obligation.

In the case of *Grant* a female employee of South-West Trains Ltd had asked for the grant of travel concessions for her female partner. South-West Trains refused to grant the concession, because it only allowed such concessions in the case of unmarried partners if the partner was of the opposite sex. The ECJ was asked about the lawfulness of this discrimination by the national court, as Community law had specifically

---

60 ECJ 17 February 1998, C-249/96, *Grant v. South-West Trains*.

61 Cf. the case-note of McInnes (1999).

62 Ahmed & Butler (2006), p. 795.

prohibited discrimination on the basis of sex as regards pay under Article 119 TEC (now Article 157 TFEU). Also, a Directive had been adopted to implement the principle of equal treatment more generally in the context of access to employment, vocational training and promotion and working conditions.[63] The ECJ decided, however, that the situation in the *Grant* case fell outside the scope of application of Community law.[64] In its judgment, the ECJ explained that it did not concern a case of sex discrimination. It held that 'travel concessions are refused to a male worker if he is living with a person of the same sex, just as they are to a female worker if she is living with a person of the same sex'.[65] The ECJ further looked into how the EU's member states had treated same-sex relationships as regards opposite-sex relationships and marriages. In that regard, the ECJ took into account the case-law of the ECtHR, from which it derived that relationships of same sex and of opposite sex and marriages could not yet generally be treated alike throughout the different states parties.[66] The ECJ therefore concluded that an interpretation of discrimination on the basis of sex that would include sexual orientation 'does not in any event appear to reflect the interpretation so far generally accepted of the concept of discrimination based on sex which appears in various international instruments concerning the protection of fundamental rights'.[67] In addition, it held that:

> although respect for the fundamental rights which form an integral part of those general principles of law is a condition of legality of Community acts those rights cannot in themselves have the effect of extending the scope of the Treaty provisions beyond the competences of the Community.[68]

According to the ECJ, to include the situation of Ms Grant within the scope of application of EU law, would mean that a conflict with the limited competences would arise. Fundamental rights protection could therefore not be granted on the basis of Community law. If the Court had accepted a broader reading of the scope of application of EU law, which means that it would have needed to accept that the situation did fall within the scope of Community law, then this could, implicitly, have given rise to a certain positive obligation for the member states.[69] Considering that they did not yet prohibit discrimination based on sexual orientation, the member states would have had to bring their national laws in line with the judgment of the ECJ, seeing that they were

---

63 Directive No. 76/207/EEC of 9 February 1976 on the implementation of the principle of equal treatment for men and women as regards access to employment, vocational training and promotion, and working conditions [1976] OJ L39/40.

64 ECJ 17 February 1998, C-249/96, *Grant v. South-West Trains* para. 47.

65 ECJ 30 April 1996, C-13/94, *P. v. S. and Cornwall County Council*, para. 27.

66 ECJ 17 February 1998, C-249/96, *Grant v. South-West Trains*, paras 31–35.

67 ECJ 17 February 1998, C-249/96, *Grant v. South-West Trains*, para. 47.

68 ECJ 17 February 1998, C-249/96, *Grant v. South-West Trains*, para. 45.

69 Cf. Ahmed & Butler (2006), p. 795.

also under an obligation to prevent sex discrimination under their national laws on the basis of Treaty provision and the Directive.

The decision of the ECJ not to recognise a positive obligation has been heavily criticised. Ahmed and Butler have held with respect to the judgment of the ECJ in the *Grant* case that:

> The ECJ made clear that even if it had interpreted discrimination based on sex to include discrimination based on sexual orientation, the absence of a positive act of the EU which in fact did so discriminate meant that the directives implementing former Article 119 were not breaching human rights standards binding upon the EU. Even if Article 119 failed to prohibit discrimination on all those grounds mandated by human rights standards, there would be no breach of or remedy under, the EU's internal law, because Article 119 expressed the limits of EU competences. If, on the other hand, Article 119 had mandated discriminatory treatment in a way that was inconsistent with human rights standards, then there would have been a violation of its obligations to respect human rights and the EU would be under an obligation to correct that. Thus the EU's internal human rights obligations would seem to be insufficient in general to impose positive obligations. The EU's internal human rights regime is interpreted only to curtail positive acts by the EU institutions, not to mandate positive acts by them.[70]

Ahmed and Butler concluded that this judgment shows that the EU's system of fundamental rights protection is fundamentally flawed. Seeing that fundamental rights protection is constrained by the principle of limited powers, the ECJ would be precluded from imposing any type of positive obligations on the EU institutions or on the member states. Other scholars have also found that the ECJ's interpretation of the term 'sex' was too narrow and have argued that the ECJ should indeed have reached an opposite conclusion to ensure that the fundamental rights of Ms Grant were effectively protected.[71]

The ECJ had shown in a previous judgment in the case of *P. v. S.* that it was willing to take a more flexible approach to the interpretation of sex discrimination, seemingly to prevent any gaps in the protection.[72] Advocate General Elmer referred to this particular judgment in his opinion in the case of *Grant*. It showed, according to the Advocate General, that the ECJ did allow for an interpretation of the principle of equal treatment in a way that would work for gender discrimination in present-day society, and which could also be applied to prohibit the particular form of discrimination found in the case of *Grant*.[73] In the case of *P. v. S.* the ECJ had decided that the dismissal of an employee who was undergoing gender reassignment constituted a form of discrimination which was prohibited by the applicable equal treatment Directive. The ECJ had reasoned that 'the right not to be discriminated against on grounds of sex is one of the fundamental human rights whose observance the Court has a duty to ensure' and that therefore 'the

70 Ahmed & Butler (2006), p. 795.
71 Cf. the case-note of McInnes (1999).
72 ECJ 30 April 1996, C-13/94, *P. v. S. and Cornwall County Council*. See also section 9.2.3.
73 Opinion of AG Elmer in C-249/96, *Grant v. South-West Trains*.

scope of the Directive cannot be confined simply to discrimination based on the fact that a person is of one or the other sex'.[74] The ECJ decided that if 'such discrimination is based, essentially if not exclusively, on the sex of the person concerned', it would be contrary to the prohibition of discrimination on grounds of sex.[75]

Apparently, however, the ECJ found that declaring the case of *Grant* to be within the scope of application of Community law would be a bridge too far. Although a more flexible interpretation of Community law would have given a more effective protection of fundamental rights, this would have given rise to clear tensions with the principle of attributed powers. In its judgment in the case of *Grant*, the ECJ specifically pointed out that including sexual orientation as a form of sex discrimination was not yet accepted by (all) the member states. The ECJ thus clearly took note of the fact that there was not sufficient consensus among the member states as to what discrimination on grounds of sex would mean.[76] It could for that reason also not be accepted that a power to prohibit discrimination on grounds of sex, as well as sexual orientation, had indeed been conferred to the Community or could be interpreted in that way on the basis of an interpretation based on the current standards of the member states. The ECJ seemed to have wanted to protect the horizontal division of powers towards the EU institutions as well.[77] In its judgment, it took particular note of the fact that the EU legislature had, in the meantime, been given a power to take certain legislative actions to respond to cases on discrimination based on sexual orientation.[78] It would thus be more respectful of the division of tasks between the ECJ and the EU legislature, if this issue was either addressed by the member states themselves or if the EU legislature undertook a particular form of action.

Thus the division of competences between the EU and the member states, as well as between the ECJ and the EU legislature, would have been directly affected if the ECJ had concluded in the case of *Grant* that discrimination based on sexual orientation was at the time prohibited by Community law.[79] From the viewpoint of the principle of attributed powers, this judgment of the ECJ thus seems reasonable, especially as there did not appear to be any real consensus throughout the member states on this issue at that time.

11.5.2. THE *CHATZI* CASE

The judgment of the ECJ in *Chatzi* shows an exceptional example of the formulation of the establishment by the ECJ of a legislative positive obligation for the member states to

---

74 ECJ 30 April 1996, C-13/94, *P. v. S. and Cornwall County Council*, para. 19.
75 ECJ 30 April 1996, C-13/94, *P. v. S. and Cornwall County Council*, para. 21.
76 See section 9.2.3. for the conditions on the gap-filling function of fundamental rights.
77 This has been discussed in section 9.2.3.
78 ECJ 17 February 1998, C-249/96, *Grant v. South-West Trains*, para. 48.
79 In a more recent case, the Court was able to respond to a case of discrimination based on sexual orientation, see ECJ 1 April 2008, C-267/06, *Maruko*.

ensure compliance with the principle of equal treatment.[80] The acceptance of a positive obligation in the *Chatzi* case has been criticised, as discussed in chapter 7.[81] Here, it is further assessed to what extent such criticism was justified.

To recall, and further explain, the *Chatzi* case was concerned with the implementation by the Greek government of a specific provision laid down in the EU's Parental Leave Directive. Under this Directive member states are required to ensure that employees have a right to parental leave of at least three months.[82] It was, however, unclear how the minimum obligation of parental leave would be calculated in the case of parents of twins. Ms Chatzi, who had become the parent of twins, applied for a first term of parental leave, which in Greece had been set at nine months. Her application for a second term was refused by her employer. It was questioned by the national court whether this treatment complied with the principle of equal treatment, and it referred a preliminary question to the ECJ on this matter.

The ECJ found that the specific provision of EU law needed to be interpreted as far as possible in light of the principle of equal treatment.[83] It held that parents of twins find themselves in a special situation.[84] Raising twins requires greater effort than raising a single child, but raising twins is not necessarily the same as raising two children of different ages, according to the Court. This must as such be taken into account by the national legislature when implementing the obligations laid down in the Directive.[85] The ECJ noted that the national legislature had a wide freedom to ensure the protection of the rights of parents of twins, and that measures could be envisaged such as allowing the parents of twins flexibility as to when they would take leave on the basis of the age of the child, to provide for flexible ways of organising work, material assistance in the form of access to childcare centres or financial aid.[86] It was, the ECJ held, further for the national court to examine whether the national rules in fact did meet the specific needs of twins. The ECJ concluded its judgment by holding that:

> read in the light of the principle of equal treatment, this clause obliges the national legislature to establish a parental leave regime which, according to the situation obtaining in the Member

---

80 Also cf. ECJ 18 March 2014, C-167/12, *D.*, in which the ECJ determined that the member states were competent to regulate the right to parental leave specifically for surrogate mothers. The Advocate General had argued, however, that ECJ needed to take into account that the EU legislature had at the time not taken into account the specific situation of surrogate mothers, and that it should be secured by EU law that parental leave would be provided, see A-G Kokott in the opinion to C-167/12, *D.*, paras 39 and 41.

81 See the discussion in sections 7.2.2. and 7.5.2.

82 Clause 2.1 of the framework Agreement on 14 December 1995 parental leave, set out in the annex to Directive 96/34/EC of 3 June 1996 on the framework agreement on parental leave concluded by UNICE, CEEP and the ETUC [1996] OJ L145/4.

83 ECJ 16 September 2010, C-149/10, *Chatzi*, para. 73.

84 ECJ 16 September 2010, C-149/10, *Chatzi*, paras 67–68.

85 ECJ 16 September 2010, C-149/10, *Chatzi*, para. 75.

86 ECJ 16 September 2010, C-149/10, *Chatzi*, paras 72–73.

State concerned, ensures that the parents of twins receive treatment that takes due account of their particular needs.[87]

It was concluded in chapter 7 that it is rare for the ECJ to explicitly hold that the national legislature is required to ensure compliance with principles of fundamental rights. The ECJ is usually expected to hold that a certain provision is to be interpreted in light of a fundamental right in a certain way without clarifying what actions need to be taken by the different branches of the state.[88] The imposition of this positive obligation by the ECJ in the case of *Chatzi*, however, has received very critical reactions for other reasons.[89] It has, for example, been questioned whether the ECJ did in fact draw the right conclusion by finding that the parents of twins find themselves in a different situation compared to other parents, and it is unclear what comparator the ECJ has actually used in reaching that decision. More particularly, it has been questioned whether the ECJ was competent to impose the said positive obligations from the viewpoint of the division of powers between the EU and the member states. The Directive had only laid down an obligation for the member states to provide for a minimum period for parental leave of three months. Therefore, it was argued, any type of protection that went further than this minimal obligation, that is, any situation in which the member states decided to provide a longer term of parental leave than strictly required, would fall outside the scope of application of EU law.[90] In that respect, it has been found problematic that the ECJ provided some particular suggestions as to the type of measures which the member states could take.[91] The ECJ indicated that, generally, a longer period of parental leave as well as a certain degree of flexibility to take leave on the basis of the age of the child could be an option. The ECJ also suggested that flexible ways of organising work could accommodate the needs of the parents of twins.[92] Such measures are clearly not demanded by the Directive and they would, indeed, still seem to belong to the policy areas of the member states.[93]

On the basis of the conclusions reached in part II, it is nonetheless logical to argue, as the ECJ did, that the member states incur a positive obligation, as such, to ensure compliance with the principle of equal treatment as regards the period of parental leave from the perspective of the division of powers. In defining the period of parental leave, the member states are implementing an obligation of EU law, and they are therefore acting in that situation as agents of EU law, which clearly falls within the scope of EU

87 ECJ 16 September 2010, C-149/10, *Chatzi*, para. 75.

88 See sections 7.3. and 7.4.

89 Muir (2013); and De Mol (2012), pp. 27–28.

90 Muir (2013), p. 89–90. In other cases, the ECJ has taken a more careful approach when it concerned the more favourable measures that member states could adopt on the basis of their own national rules, see ECJ 10 July 2014, C-198/13, *Julian Hernández and others*; and ECJ 22 May 2014, C-56/13, *Érsekcsanádi Mezögazdasagi*.

91 De Mol (2013), pp. 95–97.

92 ECJ 16 September 2011, C-149/10, *Chatzi*, para. 72.

93 Muir (2013), p. 89–90; and De Mol (2013), pp. 95–97.

law.[94] In implementing this obligation, the ECJ could thus require the member states to ensure respect for the principle of equal treatment. In doing so, the ECJ seems to have attempted to close a gap that had been left in the protection of fundamental rights by the EU legislature, as well as the national legislature. It may be argued that the regulation of parental leave for parents of twins had escaped the attention of the EU as well as the national legislature.[95] The ECJ in its judgment highlighted the fundamental nature of the principle of equal treatment as well as the right to parental leave, as they are both recognised by Articles 20 and 33(2) of the Charter.[96] Potentially, these provisions form important bases for formulating the said positive obligation. Still, however, the ECJ also acknowledged that the Parental Leave Directive had only provided for minimum harmonisation, and that the national legislature was given discretion in this area.[97]

Perhaps in the *Chatzi* case the ECJ further also specifically took into account that the protection of fundamental rights could have been secured best by the national legislature, to solve criticism that could be raised in relation to a more direct horizontal effect of fundamental rights in this case.[98] In this case, the ECJ was faced with questions raised by a national court on the protection of fundamental rights in a dispute between two private parties. The national court inquired what period for parental leave needed to be granted in the case of twins, with a view to that particular case. If the ECJ itself had determined the specific period that would be appropriate for the case of twins, this would have had a serious impact on the horizontal dispute. The employer could have incurred the additional burden of having to grant an extra term of leave. Seen from this perspective, perhaps, the approach of the ECJ in the case of *Chatzi* should be welcomed. It will create greater legal certainty if the national legislature instead of the national courts provide solutions to the protection of fundamental rights. The ECtHR also has developed the concept of positive obligations in its case-law in order to secure the protection of fundamental rights between private parties indirectly. This way, the state itself is rendered responsible for the failure to provide protection of fundamental rights.[99]

It is interesting to note that in other cases on the direct horizontal effects of fundamental rights, several Advocates General have taken the doctrine of positive obligations into account in their opinions. They have discussed the concept of positive obligations as an alternative to imposing obligations directly on individuals in order to ensure the protection of the fundamental rights of other individuals.[100] On the basis of the case-law of the ECJ in the cases of *Mangold* and *Kücückdeveci*, national courts have

---

94 Cf. De Mol (2013), p. 95.

95 Cf. the arguments made by A-G Kokott in the opinion to C-167/12, *D.*, paras 39 and 41.

96 ECJ 16 September 2011, C-149/10, *Chatzi*, para. 63.

97 ECJ 16 September 2011, C-149/10, *Chatzi*, paras 69–71.

98 See section 6.7.2.

99 See section 2.8.

100 Cf. Opinion of AG Cruz Villalón in C-176/12, *AMS*, paras 36–37; and Opinion of AG Jääskinen in C-131/12, *Google Spain*, para. 119. Cf. further Groussot & Gill-Pedor (2013), pp. 242–243; De Vries & Van Mastrigt (2013), p. 274; Hartkamp (2013), pp. 195–196; and De Mol (2013), p. 270.

been required to ensure a certain type of direct horizontal effect of the principle of non-discrimination in relations between private parties. The ECJ has been heavily criticised for this case-law, because the direct horizontal effect of fundamental rights is not yet accepted in all member states.[101] Thus the development of a positive obligation by the ECJ could, in fact, be seen as a helpful response to such criticism.[102]

The judgment of the ECJ may, nevertheless, be criticised because the Court did not seem to respect the vertical division of powers when indicating all the specific measures that the member states could take to be able to fulfil their positive obligation as mentioned above. The ECJ may have wanted to secure a more uniform interpretation in this context; that is, to secure the effective protection of EU law. This gives rise to difficulties, however, when certain measures fall within areas where the EU does not enjoy any powers. From the reasoning provided in its judgment in this case, it is unclear whether these measures were prescribed by the Court with the aim of protecting the uniformity and effectiveness of EU law.

The *Chatzi* case clearly shows that although the ECJ may legitimately impose positive obligations on the basis of EU law, a certain tension with its limited powers can arise as soon as it gives more detailed guidance on how such a positive obligation could be fulfilled.

11.5.3. THE *N.S. AND OTHERS* CASE

The case of *N.S. and others* was discussed in chapter 9 as one of the clear examples where the ECJ has accepted that the member states are required to make use of their discretionary power under EU law to ensure fundamental rights protection. In this case, the member states were required to accept responsibility for dealing with an asylum application.[103] As argued in chapter 9, this case was concerned the application of an 'optioning rule' under EU law by the member states, that is, Article 3(2) of the Dublin Regulation.[104] This provision gives the member state a choice of whether or not to make use of a specific power granted to them by EU law to ensure the protection of fundamental rights on the basis of national law or on the basis of the Convention.

---

101 See also section 9.2.3.

102 De Mol (2013), p. 270.

103 See section 9.3.2.3.

104 Article 3(2) of Regulation No. 343/2003/EC of 18 February 2003 establishing the criteria and mechanisms for determining the Member State responsible for examining an asylum application lodged in one of the Member States by a third-country national [2003] OJ L50/1. This provision holds: 'By way of derogation from paragraph 1, each Member State may examine an application for asylum lodged with it by a third-country national, even if such examination is not its responsibility under the criteria laid down in this Regulation. In such an event, that Member State shall become the Member State responsible within the meaning of this Regulation and shall assume the obligations associated with that responsibility. Where appropriate, it shall inform the Member State previously responsible, the Member State conducting a procedure for determining the Member State responsible or the Member State which has been requested to take charge of or take back the applicant.'

For that reason, it was concluded in chapter 9 that there was only a limited scope for a development of positive obligations in this type of situation.

The ECJ decided in *N.S. and others* that the member states and their national courts are under an obligation to prevent the transfer of an asylum seeker to a specific member state if this is necessary to secure the protection of the prohibition of inhuman and degrading treatment.[105] The ECJ thereby imposed a positive obligation on the member states to prevent asylum seekers from being exposed to a serious risk of a violation of a fundamental right in another member state.[106]

In arriving at its decision, the ECJ expressly took into account the judgment of the ECtHR in the case of *M.S.S. v. Belgium and Greece*, which was very relevant to the *N.S. and others* case. In *M.S.S. v. Belgium and Greece*, the ECtHR decided that Belgium had violated Article 3 ECHR by sending asylum seekers back to Greece as this knowingly exposed them to conditions of detention and living conditions that amounted to degrading treatment contrary to Article 3.[107] Serious concerns had arisen at the time over the reception of asylum seekers in Greece and over their access to the asylum procedure. In the case of *N.S. and others*, the ECJ was given the opportunity to decide whether the member states would still be required, under the Dublin Regulation, to comply with the general obligation to transfer asylum seekers to the member state of first arrival.[108] The national courts of the United Kingdom and of Ireland had inquired whether the member states were under an obligation to use their power under Article 3(2) of the Regulation if an asylum seeker would be exposed to a serious risk of treatment in the member states of first arrival which was contrary to fundamental rights, such as the prohibition of inhuman and degrading treatment guaranteed under Article 4 of the Charter.

The ECJ explained in *N.S. and others* that where the member states exercise the power granted to them under Article 3(2), they are implementing EU law within the meaning of Article 51(1) of the Charter, and they must therefore comply with the EU standards of fundamental rights. Taking into account, *inter alia*, the case-law of the ECtHR on this subject matter, the ECJ held that:

> to ensure compliance by the European Union and the Member States with their obligations concerning the protection of fundamental rights of asylum seekers, the Member States, including the national courts, may not transfer an asylum seeker to the 'Member State responsible' within the meaning of Regulation No 343/2003 where they cannot be unaware that systemic deficiencies in the asylum procedure and in the reception conditions of asylum seekers in that Member State amount to substantial grounds for believing that the asylum seeker would

105 Cf. Opinion of A-G Jääskinen in C-4/11, *Puid*, paras 60–64.

106 See for this conclusion also Opinion AG Jääskinen in C-4/11, *Puid*, paras 60–63; Opinion AG Trstenjak in C-245/11, *K*, para. 70; and *Fontanelli* (2011), E-39.

107 ECtHR 21 January 2011, no. 30696/09, *M.S.S. v. Belgium and Greece*, para. 367.

108 Article 3(1) of the Dublin Regulation establishes that the member state of first arrival is responsible for examining the asylum application.

> face a real risk of being subjected to inhuman and degrading treatment within the meaning of Article 4 of the Charter.[109]

This interpretation seems wholly justifiable in light of the effective protection of fundamental rights, and it also follows, to a certain degree at least, from the interpretation of fundamental rights given by the ECtHR on this issue. Rather than providing constraints on the use of the member states' discretionary powers, however, the ECJ thereby obliged the member states to make use of their discretionary power under EU law to ensure that fundamental rights would be protected.[110]

Arguably, given the conclusions reached in chapters 8 and 9, there seems only limited scope for the ECJ to actively shape the positive obligations which the member states need to fulfil in this respect because of the division of powers between the EU and the member states in this case.[111] The Dublin Regulation only regulates the procedures that member states need to follow in order to prevent forum shopping by asylum seekers throughout Europe and to ensure rapid and effective procedures for asylum seekers.[112] More substantive protection of asylum seekers' fundamental rights is in principle left outside the scope of this Regulation. The Dublin Regulation applies the principle of mutual recognition.[113] The member states would therefore have to observe fundamental rights protection on the basis of national law and relevant international (human rights) law instruments. If required by those laws, member states could make use of the discretionary power that is granted to them under the Regulation to be able to derogate from this general rule.[114] This discretionary power has become known as the 'sovereignty clause'; one that thus seems to fall outside the regulatory competence of the EU.[115] The ECJ therefore was not expected to be able to give concrete and active direction on the policies which the member states pursued in this field, and also it was not able to require the member states to make use of their powers in specific circumstances.[116]

Surely, it could be argued that EU law, which in some respects had to a large degree harmonised the procedural obligations of the member states, had actually caused the interference with the fundamental rights to take place. The EU Regulation had, after all, provided a basis to send asylum seekers back to the member state of first arrival. For that reason, it could be argued that there was an indirect competence for the EU

---

109 ECJ 21 December 2011, Joined cases C-411/10 and C-493/10, *N.S. and others*, para. 94.

110 Canor (2013), pp. 391–394; Muir (2014a), p. 236. Conversely De Mol (2012), p. 34; Opinion AG Trstenjak in C-245-11, *K*, paras 63–77; and Opinion AG Trstenjak in Joined cases C-411/10 and C-493/10, *N.S. and others*.

111 See in particular sections 9.3.2.3. and 10.4.

112 Cf. recital 4 and Article 1 of Regulation No. 343/2003/EC.

113 See section 6.8. on the principle of mutual recognition.

114 Articles 6 to 8 and 15 of the Regulation No. 343/2003/EC further allow the member states to take up responsibility in order to take into account particular circumstances, such as the presence of family members in another member state or the minority, disability or old age of the asylum seeker.

115 Canor (2013), p. 391.

116 Sarmiento (2013), p. 1281.

to compensate for this. There is a certain connection to be made here between the acts of the EU and potential fundamental rights infringements. It could therefore be argued, as suggested in chapter 8, that, because of the serious nature of the violation of fundamental rights in this case, the ECJ could apply the protection of EU fundamental rights and impose a positive obligation on the member states.[117] Potentially, a version of the 'reverse Solange' doctrine could also be applied, which allows the ECJ to scrutinise fundamental rights protection in areas where the EU does not enjoy power, when the essence of the protection of fundamental rights is at stake.[118] The application of this doctrine, which suggests that there is a more general power of the EU to protect fundamental rights in the member states is controversial, however.[119] It has also been suggested in chapter 8 that there is little scope for a development of positive obligations on the basis of this power.[120]

Another approach, which has been suggested by Canor, perhaps would fit better with the division of powers between the EU and the member states. Canor argued that in the case of *N.S. and others*, the ECJ actually re-interpreted the obligations laid down under the Regulation in light of fundamental rights to ensure that the mechanism of the Dublin transfers was valid.[121] The system established by EU law was clearly flawed, and needed to be declared invalid, or as happened in this case, be repaired. By formulating the obligation for the member states to check whether other member states complied with fundamental rights, the ECJ actually 'rescued' the validity of the Regulation.[122] This technique of 'reconciliatory interpretation' can be considered to be respectful of the subsidiary position of the ECJ *vis-à-vis* the EU legislature, as discussed in chapter 7.[123] If this reasoning were to be be applied, the ECJ would have needed to review the situation in *N.S. and others* as one where the member state acts as an agent of EU law. EU law in principle mandates the member states (under Article 3(1) of the Regulation) to send asylum seekers back to the member state of first arrival. When a member state decides to return an asylum seeker to the member state of first arrival, they are clearly applying a specific obligation laid down in EU law, and they can be expected to comply with EU fundamental rights protection. As submitted earlier, when member states actually act as agents of EU law, positive obligations could be imposed in line with the indirect competence to protect fundamental rights.

Nonetheless, it would still seem that this solution must be used carefully. Muir has held in response to the decision of the ECJ in the case of *N.S. and others* that:

> a significant consequence is that the existence of EU legislation on a matter closely intertwined with fundamental rights matters, but not specifically designed to regulate fundamental rights

---

117 See section 8.4.4.
118 Cf. Von Bogdandy, Kottmann, Antpöhler, Dickschen, Hentrei & Smrkolj (2012).
119 Canor (2013), p. 384.
120 See section 8.3.2.
121 Canor (2013), p. 389.
122 Canor (2013), p. 389.
123 See section 7.5.2.

> protection, becomes a vehicle to create an EU obligation (supervised by EU institutions and national courts) for the Member States to be alert to the fundamental rights records of their peers.[124]

In a substantive sense, compliance with fundamental rights is not intended to be harmonised by the Dublin Regulation. Therefore, the obligation to comply with fundamental rights should remain accessory to the specific obligation laid down in EU law. In the judgment of *N.S. and others*, the ECJ also seemed keenly aware of the fact that it was entering into an area for the most part belonging to the sovereign powers of the member states. The ECJ attempted to limit as much as possible the impact that its judgment would have in respect of the extension of the powers of the EU. The ECJ stressed that the obligation only arose in the exceptional situation of 'systemic deficiencies' of the other member states.[125] This entails that 'there are substantial grounds for believing that there are systemic flaws in the asylum procedure and reception conditions for asylum applicants in the Member State responsible, resulting in inhuman or degrading treatment, within the meaning of Article 4 of the Charter ...'.[126]

While the ECJ thus had decided in the *N.S. and other* case to provide for fundamental rights protection by imposing a positive obligation on the member states and their national courts, it would have been more in line with the principle of attributed powers if it had applied a different approach to interpreting the powers of the member states under EU law in line with fundamental rights standards. As argued earlier, there is a clearer basis for imposing the positive obligation within the scope of the application of EU law by member states when they act as agents of EU law, and within the limits of an indirect competence to protect fundamental rights in that situation.

11.5.4. THE *ABDIDA* CASE

In the *Abdida* case, the ECJ has decided that member states need to adopt interim measures as well as provide for the basic needs of a third-country national who is seriously ill and is awaiting the results of an appeal to a decision that he or she must return.[127] The ECJ has developed these positive obligations on the basis of the principle of *non-refoulement*, and the right to effective judicial protection. As will be explained, the provisions of the Directive, which brought this situation within the scope of EU law, did not specify that such obligations needed to be fulfilled by the member states on the basis of EU law.[128] It is interesting to explore how the ECJ went about developing these obligations, since the formulation of procedural positive obligations by the ECJ in its

124 Muir (2014a), p. 236.
125 ECJ 21 December 2011, Joined cases C-411/10 and C-493/10, *N.S. and others*, paras 86 and 106.
126 ECJ 21 December 2011, Joined cases C-411/10 and 493/10, *N.S. and others*, para. 86.
127 ECJ 18 December 2014, C-562/13, *Abdida*, paras 52 and 59–62.
128 See also Beijer (2015), pp. 132–133.

case-law is generally received critically because the EU only enjoys limited powers in this area.[129]

In the *Abdida* case, there is a clear connection between the positive obligations that were defined by the ECJ on the basis of fundamental rights provisions and the obligations of the member states which were already defined by the applicable Directive. The Directive on the common standards and procedures in Member States for returning illegally staying third-country nationals, required member states to provide for effective remedies to appeal a return decision, and for corresponding powers to be given to the authority or body responsible for reviewing the return decisions, including the possibility to temporarily suspend the enforcement of the return decision.[130] The ECJ held that this meant that the Directive did not necessarily require a return decision to be suspended as soon as an appeal was lodged.[131] The Directive also required the member states to take into account as far as possible the principle that 'emergency health care and essential treatment of illness are provided' when a removal was postponed because the removal would violate the principle of *non-refoulement*.[132] The ECJ admitted that the Directive does not specifically say that basic needs would have to be provided by the member states if an appeal is made. In both situations, however, where interim mesures are provided a well as where basic needs are provided, it clearly could be argued that the member states were acting as agents of EU law, because they were acting on the basis of more general obligations laid down by the Directive which applied to that situation.

In developing procedural obligations for the member states in its case-law, the ECJ generally holds that when EU law does not provide detailed rules for the procedural protection of rights which individuals derive from EU law, the principle of national procedural autonomy applies and it is for the member states to apply their own procedural rules.[133] Member states are required to ensure, on the basis of the principle of loyal cooperation as contained in Article 4(3) TEU, that their procedural rules comply with the principle of equivalence and effectiveness. These principles mean that the procedural rules may not be less favourable than those relating to similar actions of a domestic nature, and also that the procedural rules may not make it impossible in practice to exercise rights which individuals derive from EU law. In some cases, the ECJ has stressed that EU law does not, in principle, require member states to provide for new remedies other than those that already exist at national level.[134] It has been held that by using this approach, the ECJ intends to develop only negative obligations

129 See section 8.3.4.3.
130 Article 13 of Directive 2008/115/EC of 16 December 2008 on common standards and procedures in Member States for returning illegally staying third-country nationals ('the Returns Directive') [2008] OJ L348/98.
131 ECJ 18 December 2014, C-562/13, *Abdida*, para. 44.
132 Article 14(1)(2) of the Returns Directive.
133 ECJ 16 December 1976, C-33/76, *Rewe*, para. 5.
134 ECJ 13 March 2007, C-432/05, *Unibet*, para. 40.

for the member states, while it is only in exceptional cases that the member states may need to make available new procedures and/or new procedural rules in this context.[135] Therefore, when, as in the example of *Abdida*, the ECJ clarifies that member states incur an obligation to provide for interim measures, such an approach can be considered rather intrusive, given the limited powers which the EU enjoys in that area.

It is interesting to find that the ECJ did not in fact express clear concern for the division of powers of the EU in its judgment in *Abdida*. The ECJ specifically established that the provisions of the Directive were, as stated in the recital, to be interpreted with respect for the fundamental rights and dignity of the person concerned.[136] Indeed, perhaps for that reason, the ECJ considered that the EU enjoyed an indirect competence to protect fundamental rights in the context of the Directive, which should be used to protect procedural rights as well. It may have used the concept of an indirect competence to fill the specific gaps that appeared to have been left by the EU legislature and the national legislature, in order to be able to provide fundamental rights protection in circumstances that might not have been foreseen.

Some scholars have held that fundamental rights provide a stronger basis than the principle of the effective protection of EU law to allow for positive procedural obligations to be established.[137] At the same time, EU law provides a clear basis in Article 19 TEU, which requires member states to provide remedies sufficient to ensure effective legal protection in fields covered by EU law.[138] Therefore, some scholars have discussed whether the EU already enjoys a broader power to be able to establish positive procedural obligations for the member states.[139]

In the *Abdida* case, the ECJ specifically found support for the development of positive procedural obligations on the basis of the case-law of the ECtHR.[140] The ECJ referred to the judgment of the ECtHR in the case of *Hirsi Jamaa and others v. Italy* which contains a requirement for the states parties to take positive measures in the form of interim measures to ensure respect for the right to an effective remedy.[141] Therefore, the case of *Abdida* shows that the rights of the Charter, in combination with the positive

---

135 See Prechal & Widdershoven (2011), pp. 31–50, 40–43 and 47–49; and Van Cleynenbreugel (2012a); and Van Cleynenbreugel (2012b). See further section 11.2.

136 ECJ 18 December 2014, C-562/13, *Abdida*, para. 42.

137 Prechal & Widdershoven (2011), p. 47. However, the use of fundamental rights in an instrumental way must be prevented and the rights of other individuals must not be affected. It can be seen, for example, that in the case of *Tele2 Sverige* the argument was made, by one of the intervening governments, that there is a positive obligation for states to secure the right to security of persons within their territory, and this entails that data retention measures must be taken. This could result in an oppressive effect resulting from the imposition of a positive obligation. See the argument made in Opinion A-G Saugmandsgaard Øe in Joined cases C-203/15 and C-698/15, *Tele2 Sverige*, para. 183.

138 See section 8.3.4.3.

139 Van Gerven (2000), p. 502.

140 Cf. Prechal & Widddershoven (2011), p. 48.

141 See ECJ 18 December 2014, C-562/13, *Abdida*, paras 52 and 61; and cf. ECtHR 26 April 2007, no. 25389/05, *Gebremedhin v. France*, para. 67; and ECtHR 23 February 2012, no. 27765/09, *Hirsi Jamaa and others v. Italy*, para. 200.

obligations developed in the case-law of the ECtHR, provide an important basis for the imposition of a positive (procedural) obligation on the member states, even though the ECJ could also have referred to a Treaty provision (Article 19(1) TEU) that provides for a limited competence of the EU to impose positive procedural obligations.[142]

The ECJ in *Abdida* also imposed an obligation on the member state to provide for the basic needs of a third country national who is seriously ill and awaits the outcome of an appeal to a decision for return. It could be argued that the development of this type of obligation is problematic, because the EU does not really as such enjoy a power to regulate these kind of social needs, which in organisational and financial terms, could be of a burdensome nature.

It could, however, be argued that there may also be a clear indirect competence in this case to provide such protection in relation to obligations which the member states must fulfil as agents of EU law. This is, as held earlier, clearly the case in the situation of *Abdida*. It would then be necessary that such obligations remain accessory to the obligation that was defined in the Directive itself, however. Interestingly, in this regard, the ECJ also explained certain limits on the obligation imposed:

> The requirement to provide emergency health care and essential treatment of illness under Article 14(1)(b) of Directive 2008/115 may, in such a situation, be rendered meaningless if there were not also concomitant requirement to make provision for the basic needs of the third country national concerned. It should be noted, however, that it is for the Member States to determine the form in which such provision for the basic needs of the third country national concerned is to be made.[143]

Thus, the ECJ expressed clear awareness of the discretion which the member states enjoy in this area. The approach developed by the ECJ in the case of *Abdida* therefore seems fully respectful of the principle of attributed powers, while the Court was also able to secure an effective protection of fundamental rights in an area where the member states act as agents of EU law.

11.5.5. THE *T. PORT* CASE

The *T. Port* case is one of the rare examples where the ECJ has clearly defined a positive obligation for the EU institutions.[144] For that reason, it is relevant to the discussion in this chapter. It is also of interest, as will be explained, because it seems that the ECJ actually restricted the power of the member states to provide protection of fundamental rights, and potentially fulfil their own positive obligations.

---

142 See ECJ 18 December 2014, C-562/13, *Abdida*, paras 47 and 52. Cf ECtHR 26 April 2007, no. 25389/05, *Gebremedhin v. France*, para. 67; ECtHR 23 February 2012, no. 27765/09, *Hirsi Jamaa and others v. Italy*, para. 200; and ECtHR 27 May 2008, no. 26565/05, *N. v. the United Kingdom*, para. 42.

143 ECJ 18 December 2014, C-562/13, *Abdida*, paras 59–60.

144 ECJ 26 November 1996, C–68/95, *T. Port*.

The *T. Port* case was explained to some extent in the first section of this chapter, in particular to be able to clarify the distinction between positive and negative obligations in the context of EU law.[145] To recall, in this case the ECJ held that the Community institutions were required to take measures to protect the fundamental rights of a trader in the transition to the common market (in bananas).[146] A specific regulation was established, namely Regulation 404/93 to replace various national arrangements. It introduced a particular system of tariff quotas for the import of bananas differentiated for ACP bananas (from African, Caribbean and Pacific Countries) and third-country bananas.[147] The quota system was exhaustively regulated by the Community Regulation. Only the European Commission was given powers to take measures 'to assist the transition from arrangements existing before the entry into force of this Regulation to those laid down by this Regulation, and in particular to overcome difficulties of a sensitive nature'.[148] This left no room for the national authorities to grant further licences or relief. Port, an undertaking which imported third-country bananas faced particular hardship as a result of the Regulation, which established a strict regime for the import of those bananas. Port had obtained its licences based on an unusually low quantity of bananas imported, due to a breach of contract by a Colombian supplier in previous years. As a result of the limited licence, Port was unable to meet future (financial) obligations concluded under long-term contracts. Initially, Port's requests for additional licences were refused by the national authorities and the national courts did not provide for interim relief. The German *Bundesverfassungsgericht* (Federal Constitutional Court) concluded that Port's constitutional right to property was irreparably infringed and the *Verwaltungsgericht* (administrative court) imposed interim measures. At the same time the *Verwaltungsgericht* referred a preliminary question to the ECJ addressing the failure of the European Commission to exercise its own powers under Article 30 of the Regulation to take measures regarding the transition from national arrangements to the Regulation's measures which were intended 'in particular to overcome difficulties of a sensitive nature', as this could have satisfied the needs of Port.

The ECJ concluded that the Community institutions were under a positive obligation to act in protection of Community fundamental rights.[149] The Commission had, however, been given broad discretion under the Regulation to take such transitional

145 See section 1.4.

146 ECJ 26 November 1996, C-68/95, *T. Port*, para. 40. See also De Witte, p. 882 and Weiler & Fries (1999), pp. 155–156.

147 Council Regulation No. 404/93/EEC of 13 February on the common organisation of the market in bananas (the 'Banana' Regulation) [1993] OJ L47/1. Earlier Germany had sought to annul the regulation before the Court, but failed, see ECJ 5 October 1994, C-280/93, *Germany v. Council*. For a further background to these 'banana' cases, see Everling (1996).

148 Article 30 of Regulation No. 404/93/EEC.

149 ECJ 26 November 1996, C-68/95, *T. Port*, para. 40. See also De Witte, p. 882 and Weiler & Fries (1999), pp. 155–156.

measures. It was therefore required, according to the Court, to take transitional measures in derogation of the general rules under the Regulation to accommodate individual traders who could not predict the consequences of their actions after the establishment of the common market in bananas.[150]

From a fundamental rights perspective and a perspective of indirect competences, it is logical in this case that the EU institutions incurred a duty to take measures to protect fundamental rights if their actions breached the fundamental rights of particular individuals. In the case of *T. Port*, it could be held that the Community had caused infringements of the fundamental rights of traders by taking measures to organise a common market in bananas. Moreover, with a view to the transitional period, the Community legislature expressly allowed the Commission to act in cases of hardship if it was considered necessary to protect fundamental rights. The Court, as a protector of fundamental rights of undertakings, transposed this seemingly discretionary competence into a positive obligation. The effective protection of fundamental rights was in this way ensured at the supranational level.

From a perspective of subsidiarity, however, it would seem far less logical to impose on the Commission a requirement to provide protection of fundamental rights.[151] Even though this concerned an area of exclusive powers of the EU, it still could be relevant to take national arrangements into account. As a supranational institution, the Commission is not directly aware of individual cases of fundamental rights infringements. The national authorities are placed much closer to the undertakings and can (more quickly) take certain actions that would cater to their specific needs. If the national courts had decided to grant additional licences to the undertaking, this would seem to have directly affected the protection of the principles of supremacy and the principle of effectiveness of EU law, however. The national courts could only adopt interim measures under the specific circumstances which the ECJ defined in its judgment on the basis of previous case-law.[152]

Therefore, in this specific case, it appeared that the only option to fill the gap in the protection of fundamental rights was to impose an obligation on the Commission to adopt transitional measures which would offer relief to Port. This would also provide for the protection of the primacy and effectiveness of EU law. It could be held that in these circumstances, the member states no longer enjoyed any fundamental rights powers, because all their powers in this area had been succeeded to the Community. The approach of the ECJ could, from that point of view, be held to be in line with the division of powers between the EU and the member states. At the same time, this

[150] ECJ 26 November 1996, C-68/95, *T. Port*, paras 34–38 and 42.
[151] See section 8.4.3. for a discussion of the principle of subsidiarity.
[152] ECJ 26 November 1996, C-68/95, paras 56–62. The conditions have been established by the Court in ECJ 21 February 1991, Joined cases C-143/88 and C-92/89, *Zuckerfabrik Suederdithmarschen and Zuckerfabrik Soest*; and ECJ 9 November 1995, C-465/93, *Atlanta Fruchthandelsgesellschaft and others (I) v. Budensansalt fuer Landwirtschaft.*

example shows that, from the more general perspective of subsidiarity, protection of fundamental rights protection would perhaps have been better offered at the national level.

11.6. CONCLUSIONS

This chapter has shown that the case-law of the ECJ includes a small variety of judicial, administrative and legislative positive obligations which must be complied with by the member states, and a few procedural positive obligations that must be met by the EU institutions. Such positive obligations were clearly formulated by the ECJ in relation to specific obligations or acts that were defined by EU secondary or primary law. Moreover, the measures which the ECJ required to be fulfilled in the cases discussed could also be derived from the fundamental rights provisions which the ECJ mentioned in its judgments. It is clear from the outset, moreover, that the positive obligations discussed in this chapter often concern a supportive type of positive obligation, and are mostly of a remedial nature. Apparently, there must always be a connection to certain obligations which must be fulfilled by the member states under EU (secondary or primary) law.

The examination of some specific and controversial cases by the ECJ has shown that the ECJ may need to be careful in accepting positive obligations in its case-law. As explained in this chapter, by indicating that certain measures need to be taken to ensure the protection of fundamental rights, the ECJ may directly shift the power to take measures from the national level to the EU level. This could raise questions if the EU does not enjoy clear powers in the specific area at issue. First, a development of positive obligations by the ECJ may be limited because the specific legal basis for taking legislative actions under the EU Treaties applies only to certain actions (see the *Grant* case). In other cases, it may be agreed that there is a sufficient basis under EU law to impose a legislative positive obligation on the member states, but that the ECJ would still be interfering in the member states' sovereign powers if it indicates too clearly what kinds of measures the member states should take to fulfil such a positive obligation (see the *Chatzi* case). In two of the cases discussed (the *N.S. and others* case and the *Abdida* case), the ECJ found clear support for the development of positive obligations on the basis of the judgments of the ECtHR even though, as has been argued, there was actually quite some tension because of the limited powers of the EU in those areas. As explained, the ECJ could possibly solve such tension by explaining under what circumstances the member states indeed incurred the respective obligations, as well as by clarifying that the member states could actually still enjoy either their sovereign or discretionary powers under EU law.

One specific case (the *T. Port* case) has shown that it can also become necessary for the ECJ to impose a positive obligation on the EU institutions, because the EU enjoys an exclusive power in a certain area. This example, however, showed that, because of the principle of subsidiarity, there can be good reason to ensure the protection of fundamental rights at national level instead.

If the ECJ wishes to further legitimise the development of positive obligations, it may need to pay attention to the limited powers of the EU in its judgments. At the same time, the ECJ may also want to ensure in its judgments that fundamental rights are protected in an effective manner. The ECJ does not always clearly show the underlying rationales in its judgments. The ECJ could in the future express such reasons more clearly, especially if it receives further criticism for lack of a clear justification of developing positive obligations under EU law.

CHAPTER 12
CONCLUSIONS AND RECOMMENDATIONS

12.1. INCORPORATING POSITIVE OBLIGATIONS TO PROTECT FUNDAMENTAL RIGHTS IN EU LAW?

The main purpose of this study was to establish whether there is scope for recognition of a concept of positive obligations to protect fundamental rights under EU law and, if so, in what manner the ECJ could develop a doctrine of positive obligations in its case-law. To find answers to these questions, this study, first, has drawn inspiration from the case-law of the ECtHR. Part I of this study has explained in what way states can incur positive obligations to protect fundamental rights under the Convention, and what the effects are of the recognition of such positive obligations by the ECtHR. In addition, part I has dealt with the criticisms related to this development. It has *inter alia* explained that states' obligations in relation to the protection of fundamental rights have been expanded on the basis of the recognition of positive obligations; these obligations may require burdensome measures to be taken by states; the development of positive obligations creates a certain amount of legal uncertainty; and the establishment of positive obligations by the ECtHR may come close to political decision-making. These types of criticism have (partially) been overcome by the principles that have been established by the ECtHR in its case-law. The ECtHR has explained that positive obligations form part of the effective protection of fundamental rights, and that states nowadays have the power to influence the enjoyment of individual's fundamental rights. The ECtHR also recognises that states are given discretion when choosing the measures to provide protection, and that certain limits apply to the scope for positive obligations under the Convention. These principles, as well as their more specific elaborations, have been held to be of special interest if the ECJ were to recognise similar kinds of positive obligations.

Part II of this study has explored the system of EU fundamental rights protection and some of its specific limitations, in order to find out whether, and to what extent, this allows for a similar development of positive obligations to take place. Specific attention was paid to the ECJ's own institutional characteristics and its judicial culture; to the issue of the limited competences of the EU; and to the limited scope of application of EU fundamental rights.

On the basis of the review of the relevant legal provisions, case-law and legal theory, this study has shown that, under certain conditions, there is scope for the development of positive obligations under EU law. This development implies that the ECJ will define certain actions that need to be taken by the EU institutions or the member states to protect certain fundamental rights if such actions have not already been specified by secondary EU law. Several examples provided in the case-law of the ECJ show that the ECJ has already been willing to formulate certain kinds of positive obligations. Such positive obligations appear to be directed mainly at the member states, and they are often of a procedural nature. The member states have, for example, been required to introduce certain procedural requirements to ensure the effective protection of EU law at national level, and to take certain preventive measures to comply with the prohibition of inhuman and degrading treatment of individuals within and outside of the EU. Such a development is necessary and inevitable. Gaps could appear in the protection of fundamental rights in situations falling within the scope of EU law, which might not, or even could not, have been foreseen by the EU legislature or in the implementation of EU legislation at the national level. It has been argued that provisions on EU fundamental rights, especially those laid down in the Charter – in combination with provisions of primary and of secondary law which bring such situations within the scope of application of EU law – can provide a relevant basis for the ECJ to impose positive obligations on the EU institutions and on the member states. It was concluded in chapter 10, however, that this 'gap-filling' through imposing positive obligations can only be accepted if it is acknowledged that the EU has an indirect competence to protect fundamental rights in relation to the explicit powers which have been conferred on it by the member states.

Surely, this implies a rather modest development of positive obligations in comparison to the case-law of the ECtHR. As a result of the limited competences of the EU, the protection of fundamental rights by the EU authorities remains accessory to the regulatory activities for which the EU has been conferred specific powers. The analysis of several specific examples of positive obligations in the case-law of the ECJ has shown that criticism may be raised over this development in view of the limited competences of the EU to protect fundamental rights. In some areas and situations, the EU enjoys no, or very limited, powers, which will influence the degree to which the ECJ can formulate positive obligations, as well as the kinds of positive obligations it might accept. Moreover, there are limited procedural possibilities for the ECJ to establish certain positive obligations for the EU institutions or the member states. Generally, the initiative is taken by national courts to refer relevant questions to the ECJ, instead of by individual claimants bringing procedures directly before this Court.

These main conclusions and answers to the main questions of this study are explained in more detail in the following sections of this chapter. First, a more detailed explanation is given of how the specific legal system of the EU allows for a development of positive obligations, especially taking into account the findings that have followed from the analysis of specific case-law examples in chapter 11 (section 12.2.). After that, several contrasts are shown to the development of positive obligations by the ECtHR to further clarify what kind of development of positive obligations could take place under EU law (section 12.3.). Next, special attention is paid to the different types of positive obligations that exist (section 12.3.1.); the procedural limitations that apply within the context of EU law (section 12.3.2.); the political character of positive obligations under EU law (section 12.3.3.); and the specific judicial style of the ECJ (section 12.3.4.). After this, some recommendations are made as to how the ECJ could further develop a doctrine of positive obligations in its case-law (section 12.4.). Lastly, this chapter reflects on a question that has often been raised in the literature, that is, whether the development of positive obligations within the context of EU law can be expected to give rise to competence creep or whether, in view of the limits of EU law, certain gaps in protection can be expected to arise (section 12.5.).

12.2. A LIMITED SCOPE FOR THE DEVELOPMENT OF POSITIVE OBLIGATIONS UNDER EU LAW

12.2.1. THE RELEVANCE OF SECONDARY EU LAW AS A FRAMEWORK FOR THE PROTECTION OF FUNDAMENTAL RIGHTS

Development of 'positive obligations' within the context of EU law can be said to take place only if the ECJ were to define an obligation for an EU institution or for the member states to take measures to protect fundamental rights which are not already specified by EU (secondary or primary) law. This is the basic definition of positive obligations, explained in the introductory chapter of this study.[1] Within the context of EU law, in general, provisions of secondary EU law spell out the specific rights which individuals may invoke and the corresponding obligations which states could incur. Therefore, in contrast to the Convention, there is less need for defining positive obligations on the basis of general fundamental rights. In that respect, the legal framework for the protection of fundamental rights under EU law is clearly very different from that created by the Convention. To illustrate this further, it must be recognised that the EU has been given specific competences to adopt legislation which it could use to ensure the protection of some fundamental rights. In the area of privacy protection, for example, a fairly detailed regulative framework has been adopted defining what rights individuals may invoke under EU law and what legislative and procedural obligations the member states must comply with. In that area, the national courts and the ECJ can therefore generally turn to secondary EU law to determine the scope and the meaning of the protection of fundamental rights which can be provided on the basis of EU law. Seeing that general fundamental rights provisions play a much less important role within the context of EU law than they do in the Convention context, there is less urgency for the judicial development of positive obligations. When adopting certain policies, the EU legislature may have already settled for certain solutions that could be used to secure

1 See section 1.4.

the protection of fundamental rights effectively. This also explains why only a very limited development of positive obligations under EU law has taken place.

Still, fundamental rights can have an important role to play in EU law, that is, as tools to interpret provisions of secondary EU law, to determine the validity of those provisions, and to fill certain gaps. Chapter 11 has shown various examples in the case-law of the ECJ of situations in which EU secondary law did not provide sufficient clarity regarding the measures that needed to be adopted to ensure fundamental rights compliance. In those situations, certain gaps appeared, because specific procedures or regulations had not been provided at the EU level, nor by means of implementation at the national level.[2] One of the clearest examples is that the ECJ has needed to clarify that national courts must be able to adopt interim measures to effectively secure the application of EU law at national level and to protect the principle of effective judicial protection.[3] The ECJ has also held that such interim measures need to be provided by national courts in the specific situation of a third-country national who is seriously ill, and is awaiting the results of an appeal against a decision that he must return to his country of origin. Then, such interim measures are necessary to secure the principle of effective judicial protection as well as the principle of *non-refoulement*.[4] In addition, the ECJ has defined that the member states must further provide for the basic needs of the individual in such a situation. Secondary EU law did not impose such specific obligations on the member states, but they needed to be formulated by the ECJ on the basis of fundamental rights provisions. Such cases show that the EU legislature, and the national legislature, may not always be able to fully foresee what actions, remedies and judicial powers will be necessary to ensure the protection of fundamental rights in relation to the tasks that must be executed on the basis of EU law. In particular, the needs of certain vulnerable individuals might not be foreseen. As a consequence, gaps can appear in the protection of fundamental rights in situations that can fall within the scope of EU law.

The Charter and the EU Treaties provide various legal bases that could be used to determine what actions are necessary to protect fundamental rights. Such legal bases have been set out in chapter 8 and are especially relevant for the EU in the exercise of its indirect competence to protect those rights (see further below).[5] The EU may need to ensure, for example, that remedies are provided for by the member states on the basis of Article 19(1) TEU in fields covered by EU law. Also, any interferences with the fundamental rights under the Charter must be provided for by law on the basis of Article 52(1) of the Charter. These are obligations that need to be met by the EU institutions in the exercise of their explicit competences, and by the member states in

---

2 See in particular section 11.3.

3 ECJ 19 June 1990, C-213/89, *Factortame*, paras 18–22; and ECJ 13 March 2007, C-432/05, *Unibet*, para. 67.

4 See ECJ 18 December 2014, C-562/13, *Abdida*, paras 52 and 59–62; and the analysis provided of this case in section 11.5.4.

5 See in particular section 8.3.4.4.

the implementation of EU law at the national level, and could thus give rise to actions of a procedural or of a legislative nature. These legal bases are also especially relevant for the ECJ to take into account if gaps in the protection are discovered.

However, even in these situations of gap-filling, the ECJ must still carefully take the specific framework of secondary EU law into account to be able to determine the scope of the rights and the obligations which it may establish. Often (the preambles to) Directives and Regulations will specify which fundamental rights must be taken into account by the competent public authorities. Directives and Regulation may also include provisions or recitals that help to clarify that there is no scope for such action at the EU level. The power to take certain actions may then have been retained at the national level.[6]

12.2.2. THE DEVELOPMENT OF POSITIVE OBLIGATIONS ON THE BASIS OF AN INDIRECT POWER TO PROTECT FUNDAMENTAL RIGHTS

The question of the EU's fundamental rights competences is of clear importance in relation to the development of positive obligations by the ECJ. Based on the principle of attributed powers, the EU can only take action in fields for which it has specifically been conferred competences to do so. Article 51 of the Charter also specifically requires that the competences of the EU are not affected or expanded on the basis of the protection of fundamental rights. When defining positive obligations under EU law, it is therefore necessary that a certain competence to adopt measures can be construed under EU law.

The EU clearly does not have a general competence to take action to protect fundamental rights, and many scholars have therefore expressed fear that a development of positive obligations within the context of EU law would either lead to competence creep or to gaps in protection.[7] It has been explained in chapter 8, however, that there is sufficient ground to argue that the EU enjoys both a specific and an indirect competence to protect fundamental rights, and that those competences need to be taken into account by the ECJ in formulating positive obligations.[8] Indeed, in some specific areas, such as privacy protection and non-discrimination, the EU has been conferred a specific competence to take action. Moreover, in areas where the EU has been conferred explicit competences to take (legislative) action, for example in the area of asylum law or in the area of free movement law, it can be argued that there also is an indirect competence for the EU to secure the protection of fundamental rights. On the basis of Article 6 TEU, and in particular Article 51(1), there is a general requirement for the EU institutions and the member states, in so far as they act within the scope of EU law, to respect

6 See section 9.3.3.

7 See sections 1.1.3., 8.3.5. and 9.2.2. Final conclusions on the potential for competence creep or gaps in protection are given in section 12.5.

8 See sections 8.3. and 10.4.

and even promote the fundamental rights in relation to their actions. Therefore, some competences can be construed to incorporate positive obligations into EU law.

The indirect competence for the EU to ensure active protection of fundamental rights must be construed narrowly, however. Given the principle of attributed powers, the actions which can be taken on the basis of such an indirect competence must be seen as accessory to the actions for which there is an explicit basis in the EU treaties. Also, certain limits in relation to the explicit competences of the EU must be respected. For example, the full harmonisation of national law is excluded in the areas of asylum law and privacy law. Hence, in defining positive obligations, the ECJ must take into consideration that the general competence to protect fundamental rights remains at national level and that the national authorities remain competent to make their own choices as to how to provide protection of fundamental rights.

These limitations further became apparent from the analysis that was undertaken in chapter 11 on the establishment of several kinds of positive obligations by the ECJ in its case-law. When certain types of actions are not defined by provisions of secondary and primary EU law, such as in the area of national procedural law, then it may also be concluded that they do not form part of the competences of the EU. The ECJ thus needs to pay attention to the division of powers between the EU and the member states in defining positive obligations. The ECJ could, for example, decide to formulate a procedural positive obligations for the member states because the EU enjoys an indirect competence that needs to be used to ensure that the actions of the EU effectively protect fundamental rights. However, the ECJ may then still need to clarify that the member states enjoy a great deal of discretion in the area of national procedural law.

12.2.3. THE DIVISION OF COMPETENCES BETWEEN THE EU AND THE MEMBER STATES

Chapter 8 has explained that in most cases where fundamental rights could be affected under EU law, the EU enjoys shared or complementary competences.[9] This means that additional reasons are needed to be able to decide why certain actions need to be taken at EU level rather than at the national level.

First and foremost, the principle of subsidiarity provides a relevant consideration. This principle intimates that by reason of scale or effects, action is better taken at the EU level than at the national level. It can be difficult to apply this criterion to fundamental rights cases, since in most cases it would seem that action is taken best at national level by the national authorities, as they are closest to the individual, the circumstances of a case, and the specificities and demands of their societies and legal systems. Transnational dimensions to the protection of fundamental rights are not always readily apparent. One clear example that can be mentioned here, however, is the area of privacy protection, where personal data may 'physically' cross borders.

9 See section 8.4.

However, there are also other arguments that can be made to show that fundamental rights are protected more effectively at the EU level. The degree of interconnectedness of EU acts and fundamental rights infringements could provide an important consideration arguing for preventive and remedial measures to be established by the EU, or for compensation to be made for the harm that is caused by the adoption of certain policies. It may also be argued that fundamental rights are best secured at EU level if there is a risk that EU free movement law will indirectly lead to a lowering of the fundamental rights standards of the member states. The establishment of fundamental rights standards at the EU level might further be explained, because it is also in the interest of securing the primacy, unity and effectiveness of EU law itself. These different arguments are relevant for the EU legislature in deciding when to take action, and they could also provide further support if the ECJ were to formulate a relevant positive obligation on the basis of EU law.

Although the arguments outlined above are often raised, some scholars have, instead, looked at other principles and arguments. In particular, as addressed in chapter 8, they have referred to principles of state responsibility under international law and the principles developed in the case-law of the ECtHR.[10] It is argued that the EU itself is bound to comply with the obligations arising from the protection of international human rights treaties to the extent that the member states are no longer able to protect those rights and obligations autonomously as a result of the transfer of competences to the EU. In that situation, the EU must incur positive obligations if, in a similar way to states, it can be considered to have the means to provide protection and to have knowledge of an actual risk of fundamental rights infringements taking place. It has been explained in this study that such arguments can be relevant mainly and only in areas where the EU enjoys exclusive powers. In those situations, there is generally no discretion at the national level to ensure the protection of fundamental rights. The ECJ must therefore also take this into account when deciding whether to accept positive obligations in such areas.

Even in cases on exclusive competences, it may still be most useful to look at principles which are relevant in areas of shared and complementary competences to determine whether and at what point positive obligations need to be developed under EU law. The member states may already have a specific legal and administrative framework that could be used to effectively secure fundamental rights. The ECJ would thus not always have to formulate 'new' positive obligations. In cases of exclusive competences, the ECJ may have to make sure, however, that the member states indeed use their regulatory frameworks and procedures to secure protection of fundamental rights. They would have to be put under an obligation, because they might otherwise find that they do not have discretion to apply those rules and procedures under EU law. If the application of such national rules and procedures were to be considered to undermine the effectiveness and unity of EU law, however, the ECJ would have to decide to impose new positive obligations on the member states or on the EU institutions.

---

10 These arguments have further been set out in section 8.4.1.

12.2.4. LIMITED SCOPE OF APPLICATION OF EU FUNDAMENTAL RIGHTS

Chapter 9 of part II has specifically looked into the question of the limited scope of application of EU fundamental rights. Article 51(1) of the Charter importantly requires that EU fundamental rights only apply to the member states when they implement Union law. The ECJ therefore can only accept positive obligations which can be held to fall within the scope of EU law. For positive obligations to be recognised, there needs to be a connection that can be made between a certain type of positive obligation and a provision of EU law. The development of positive obligations under EU law thus generally requires that a specific right or obligation has already been recognised in the EU Treaties and/or in secondary EU law. As has been explained above, this provision of EU law is also very much relevant in determining to what extent there is a competence for the EU institutions or the member states to take certain actions to ensure the effective protection of fundamental rights. The ECJ cannot recognise positive obligations which have no clear connection to rights and obligations that have been laid down in EU law, because this would mean that the ECJ would be over-extending the powers of the EU.

The ECJ has developed a broad scope of application of EU fundamental rights which could be considered useful where positive obligations need to be formulated. It has been explained that three types of situations can be distinguished in this regard. The member states are either acting as agents of EU law, they are derogating from the free movement rules, or they are applying so-called optioning rules, which means that they have a choice to adopt their own sovereign policies within the framework of EU law obligations. It is foremost in the first type of situation, thus in the agency situation, that several kinds of positive obligations could legitimately be developed by the ECJ. In this type of situation, most logically either a specific fundamental rights competence or an indirect fundamental rights competence of the EU applies. However, in the situation where member states are derogating from the free movement rules or where they are applying their optioning rules, it is far less logical to impose positive obligations, because it is more difficult to construe that an indirect competence has been given to the EU to protect fundamental rights. The ECJ would easily be interfering in the sovereign powers of the member states, and it must therefore be very careful in formulating positive obligations, especially if they are of a legislative kind. This point has further been proven by the analysis undertaken in chapter 11 of the *N.S. and others* case.[11] The ECJ formulated a positive obligation for the member states in this case to prevent inhuman and degrading treatment of asylum seekers who are sent back to another member state on the basis of the Dublin Regulation. It could arguably do so on the basis of the indirect competence under EU law to protect fundamental rights, however, there is limited scope for a development of the positive obligation on the basis of the member states' discretionary powers that have been granted to them under EU

[11] See section 11.5.3.

law to apply their own sovereign policies. The ECJ could also decide to refer, again, to the member states own policies and regulations as a means of ensuring effective fundamental rights protection.

12.3. CONTRASTS WITH THE DEVELOPMENT OF POSITIVE OBLIGATIONS BY THE ECtHR

The conclusions provided in the foregoing sections have already revealed that the scope for a development of positive obligations under EU law is much more limited than that under the Convention. This section aims to further clarify some contrasts between the development of positive obligations by the ECtHR and the ECJ. In turn, this will help to identify what can, and what cannot, be expected in terms of a development of positive obligations by the ECJ.

12.3.1. A WIDE VARIETY OF TYPES OF POSITIVE OBLIGATIONS

Part I has discussed the various types of positive obligations that can be recognised within the case-law of the ECtHR.[12] In addition to the main distinction between procedural and material kinds of positive obligations made by the ECtHR, several typologies developed by scholars have been discussed. These typologies help to clarify the different effects of some types of positive obligations, as well as their potentially problematic nature, and they can be of interest for the EU context as well. Only a few types of these positive obligations would be expected to be developed by the ECJ to protect fundamental rights on the basis of EU law.

Chapter 11 has shown that the case-law of the ECJ has mainly defined procedural obligations, which often need to be complied with by the national courts.[13] The ECJ rarely defines obligations of a legislative kind.[14] It can, however, be concluded that there is a basis under EU law that allows the ECJ to further develop positive obligations, including those of a legislative kind. This basis is provided by the specific fundamental rights competences of the EU and the scope of application of EU fundamental rights as discussed above. However, it may be difficult for the ECJ to develop positive obligations to legislate, mainly because of the specific procedural context in which it can provide fundamental rights protection. The ECJ is mainly engaged in a dialogue with the national courts, and it is therefore logical that the ECJ will primarily impose obligation on the national courts to ensure the effective protection of fundamental rights.

---

12 See section 3.3. in particular.

13 See sections 11.3. and 11.4.

14 For an exception, see section 11.5.2.

Also, of the types of obligations found in the ECtHR's case-law, it can be seen that mainly intrinsic and supportive types of positive obligation are accepted in the case-law of the ECJ. The intrinsic type of positive obligation requires states to set up certain institutional and organisational measures, such as a court system, so that fundamental rights can be enjoyed by individuals. Indeed, the case-law of the ECJ provides various examples of where procedures and/or legal provisions had to be introduced to provide protection of rights falling within the scope of EU law. The supportive type of positive obligation essentially requires states to ensure that they comply with their (negative) obligation not to interfere with an individual's fundamental rights. The case-law of the ECJ on positive obligations also often shows a relationship with certain positive acts of the EU institutions or the member states. The obligations were imposed with the aim of preventing fundamental rights infringements in relation to such acts, or to provide for compensation. The recognition of both types of positive obligations can be explained because there must be a certain competence that is already defined within the EU Treaties and/or in legislative instruments of secondary EU law. Fundamental rights provisions cannot by themselves constitute a basis for action to be taken by the EU. Instead, based on the principle of attributed powers, actions undertaken by the EU institutions and the member states are in principle defined in primary or secondary EU law. Therefore, any positive obligation which may arise on the basis of fundamental rights protection in relation to those situations, do so in addition to and within the scope of certain legislative, administrative or executive obligations that have already been defined by EU law. The actions of the EU are often not primarily oriented towards the protection of fundamental rights, but rather towards fulfilling certain objectives in areas, such as the internal market, in which the EU has specifically been conferred competences to undertake actions. If there is no clear connection to EU law, active measures to protect fundamental rights would instead have to be based on national law, potentially in combination with the Convention. Such measures could then be expected to fall outside the scope of EU law.

Therefore, as a result of the limitation that fundamental rights protection can be based on EU law only if there is a clear connection to an obligation or a right that is already defined under EU law, various kinds of positive obligations are precluded from being developed within the EU context.

The case-law of the ECtHR recognises a wider variety of types of positive obligations.[15] Aside from procedural types of positive obligations, the ECtHR has imposed obligations of a material type, which could involve legislative measures (for example to ensure the legal recognition of rights of same-sex couples) or more practical measures (for example to ensure that demonstrations can proceed safely). These obligations, furthermore, may not only be supportive or intrinsic in nature, but they even may be autonomous, which means that states may incur them without there being a very clear connection between the Convention provisions and the positive obligation concerned.

15 See sections 3.3. and 5.3.

The ECtHR's case-law also clearly shows horizontal types of positive obligations. These types of positive obligations aim to protect fundamental rights in the relations between private parties, instead of vertical positive obligations, which are obligations that aim to protect the fundamental rights in the relation between the state and the individual.

There seems little scope for a development of positive obligations of a more horizontal kind within the EU context. Vertical types of positive obligations are more likely to be recognised in the case-law of the ECJ, because fundamental rights provisions generally either aim to prevent the EU institutions' actions and the member states actions in the implementation of EU law negatively interfering with fundamental rights, or to ensure that remedies are provided and compensation can be given for the harm that is caused by the policies of the EU.

However, it must be recognised that the distinction between vertical and horizontal types of positive obligations can be quite difficult to make.[16] Often, there are positive acts of the state involved in the case-law of the ECtHR on positive obligations, even when the underlying conflict appears to be one between private parties. Conversely, some of the positive obligations in the case-law of the ECJ may appear to have a horizontal dimension as well. There are some examples that demonstrate that obligations are imposed to protect the rights of internet users *vis-à-vis* an internet service provider, or the rights of an employee *vis-à-vis* an employer. Moreover, it can be argued that some of the case-law of the ECJ shows that obligations are imposed to protect the rights of certain vulnerable individuals, such as homosexual men or asylum seekers, not only against state action, but also against acts by other private individuals.

Nevertheless, even in those cases where the ECJ imposes positive obligations with a clearly horizontal effect or even of a directly horizontal nature, they can be imposed only in relation to concrete measures which states must already adopt in a certain area on the basis of EU law. Thus, horizontal types of positive obligations could be developed within the EU context only in relation to concrete legal norms that are laid down in EU legislation.

Thus, while there appears to be little scope for a development of horizontal positive obligations, it is relevant to take into account that, in comparison to the ECtHR, the ECJ more clearly requires a certain direct horizontal effect to be given to EU law and to fundamental rights at the national level.[17] Also, concrete norms established in EU Directives and Regulations may have a clear impact on the obligations which private parties need to fulfil in their relations with other private parties. The case of *Google Spain* is a good example that illustrates that a private corporation (*Google*) can be confronted with an obligation on the basis of EU law, in this case to secure the rights to privacy of an individual when certain search results are generated.[18] By contrast, the

---

16 This is also explained in section 3.3.2.

17 See section 6.7.2.

18 ECJ 13 May 2014, C-131/12, *Google Spain and Google*.

ECtHR has always imposed positive obligations on states to secure the protection of fundamental rights in horizontal situations.

Overall, it must be concluded that there is limited room for the acceptance of a wide variety of types of positive obligations on the basis of EU law. Before any type of fundamental rights requirement can be imposed, there must be a connection to rights or obligations that have already been laid down by EU law. Only then a development of positive obligations could be expected, which are most likely to be of a supportive or an intrinsic nature. This also means that there is little scope for a development of autonomous positive obligations, that is, obligations which are not clearly related to states' negative obligations following from the fundamental rights that it protects. After all, there must always be a relevant connection to EU law to allow the EU institutions or the member states to take certain actions on the basis of which (active) fundamental rights requirement can be imposed. This also explains that the ECJ might impose some positive obligations with horizontal effect, but only in limited circumstances.

12.3.2. PROCEDURAL LIMITATIONS

Within the context of EU law, the development of positive obligations can be primarily expected to take place under the preliminary reference procedure.[19] National courts play a very important role in the protection of EU fundamental rights and there is only limited room for individuals to actively bring procedures before the ECJ to challenge the omissions in the protection of fundamental rights within the context of EU law. In comparison, positive obligations are developed by the ECtHR in relation to the complaints which individuals directly bring before the ECtHR, albeit, of course, after having exhausted the domestic remedies.

This shows that the development of positive obligations in the EU context is to an important extent dependent on the willingness of the national courts to refer cases to the ECJ. National courts may decide to provide for the protection of fundamental rights on the basis of their own national laws and/or on the basis of the case-law of the ECtHR rather than on the basis of EU fundamental rights. They could refrain from sending questions to the ECJ as regards the interpretation of fundamental right that are guaranteed by EU law if they were to consider that such questions fall outside the scope of application of EU law.

Secondly, this explains that most of the positive obligations that have been developed in the case-law of the ECJ are directed at the national courts. As mentioned above, the ECJ does not seem inclined to directly develop any legislative obligation but it is instead there to provide answers to the questions that are raised by the national courts. Moreover, it appears that the ECJ often still leaves room for the national courts and the national authorities to decide how they could ensure an effective protection of fundamental rights.

---

19 This has been explained in section 7.4., in particular.

There are thus some procedural limitations for the development of positive obligations in the context of EU law. If these procedural limitations would raise a significant barrier for the rights of individuals to be addressed and positive obligations to be imposed, it might nonetheless still be possible to bring a complaint before the ECtHR. The ECtHR accepts complaints that are brought against one of the member states of the EU and it will exercise review if the member states have discretion in their implementation of EU law at the national law. In that respect, there may be some potential for the ECtHR to further develop positive obligations that are relevant for the member states to comply with, even in the context of EU law. This development might affect the autonomous interpretation of EU law and it might not be in the interest of individuals who seek protection, because the procedures before the ECtHR can be long and cumbersome. It is therefore important that the ECJ uses the opportunities available to develop fundamental rights. Here, it can be recognised that compared to the ECtHR, the EU system of fundamental rights protection provides for some potentially swift procedures to ensure the protection of fundamental rights. If certain measures of the states or the EU institutions must be taken to ensure effective protection of fundamental rights, individual litigants and courts may therefore look at EU law as a source of such protection. As EU law nowadays penetrates into various areas of law, such as asylum law, environmental law and privacy law, EU law might further be regarded as a relevant framework to take into account regarding a development of positive obligations.

12.3.3. THE POLITICAL CHARACTER OF THE DEVELOPMENT OF POSITIVE OBLIGATIONS

One of the main criticisms that has been expressed towards the development of positive obligation by the ECtHR is that it would interfere with political decision-making.[20] The question as to what actions need to be taken by public authorities must, in principle, be answered by democratically elected and politically accountable bodies. This is, in particular, important when it involves high (financially) burdensome measures, or when it concerns very sensitive or complex economic, social or technical affairs. For that reason, the political nature of positive obligations is of continuing concern to the ECtHR, and requires it to tread very carefully. It could be expected that the ECJ would be criticised in a similar way if it were to determine the concrete actions which should be taken by the EU institutions or by the member states on the basis of provisions of fundamental rights. Generally, such actions would need to be determined by means of secondary EU law or by national authorities based on the discretion explicitly given. By establishing positive obligations, the ECJ could be criticised for interfering in the political decision-making process of the EU institutions and/or the member states. Just like the ECtHR, after all, the ECJ is not democratically elected, nor is it politically

---

[20] See in more detail sections 4.4. and 4.5.

accountable. Moreover, it is similar to the ECtHR in that it is placed at the supranational level, and may therefore not be in the best position to make decisions on the actions that need to be taken by national authorities.

Yet, the ECJ operates in some respects in a rather different political sphere as compared to the ECtHR. The ECJ is, for example, directly empowered to review the legislation which has been adopted by the EU institutions and it may directly provide interpretations of EU primary law and secondary legislation.[21] This may mean that it could go further in developing specific positive obligations for the EU institutions.

So far, the ECJ has developed very few positive obligations for the EU institutions, and to the extent that it has done so, such obligations are only of a procedural kind. This may be because EU law must often be further implemented at national level. It may also be because the ECJ aims to be respectful of the choices that have already been made by the EU legislature and does not easily overturn those choices. The ECJ has, in comparison, formulated many more positive obligations for the member states. Although this may have to do with the procedural limitations within the EU context for a development of positive obligations, as has been explained in the previous subsection, this may also be explained by the deference that the ECJ affords to the EU legislature. National courts may indeed also inquire about the validity of EU legislation and perhaps the omissions of the EU legislature in certain areas.

The ECJ could decide to apply a technique of reconciliatory interpretation in reviewing the legislative acts of the EU institutions. This technique aims to re-interpret EU legislation to ensure that it is valid in light of principles of EU law, such as fundamental rights. This technique has been used by the ECJ in several cases that have been discussed in this study, and it has the effect of imposing positive obligations for the member states.[22] It is expected, therefore, that positive obligations that might be politically sensitive will only be formulated for the member states and not for the EU institutions.

Also, the specific EU legal framework can guide the ECJ in determining the scope and the meaning of the rights of individuals, the obligations of states, and the division of powers between the EU and the member states. Some political choices may already have been made, for example that certain powers which should be used to protect fundamental rights should remain at the national level (see section 12.2.).

For the ECJ, it is of special interest that the Charter has been drafted much more recently than the Convention. The ECJ can therefore be expected to use the provisions of the Charter, in combination with EU primary and secondary law, as important guidance when determining the scope and the limits for accepting a certain positive obligation. The horizontal provisions of the Charter are especially relevant, for example Article 51(1) which has been mentioned earlier. These horizontal provisions determine the scope of application and lay down important principles for determining the interpretation of the rights laid down in the Charter. Article 52(5) of the Charter also,

21 Cf. the jurisdiction of the ECtHR given in Article 32 ECHR.

22 See section 7.5.2.

for example, provides for an important limitation to the scope for a judicial development of positive obligations of the 'principles' that are guaranteed in several provisions of the Charter. Although it is still somewhat unclear which provisions contain principles instead of rights, it can be expected that the social and economic rights of the Charter contain principles, and therefore require actions to be taken first by the political bodies of the EU and/or the member states. Thus, contrary to the Convention, the Charter provides more guidance for the ECJ as to which interventions and obligations would or would not be acceptable. On the basis of this legal framework, the development of positive obligations by the ECJ would seem to raise less difficulties as compared to the development of positive obligations by the ECtHR.

As mentioned above, the ECJ has also developed only a limited type of positive obligation for the member states, that is, mostly of a procedural kind or of an intrinsic and supportive kind (see section 12.3.1.). The latter types of positive obligations very closely and logically relate to the fundamental right itself. A supportive obligation is rather directly related to the negative obligation not to interfere with fundamental rights. Seeing that the negative obligation traditionally follows from the protection of fundamental rights, it could be argued that it would often be legitimate for the ECJ to recognise such positive obligations as compared to positive obligations which have a much more autonomous nature.[23]

Still, the ECJ must, just like any other court, be very careful in imposing positive obligations, because certain legal or procedural requirements may not directly follow (textually) from the specific provision that guarantees the fundamental right in question. The ECJ may for that reason be advised to clearly indicate all the relevant legal bases and provide for careful reasoning to explain why a certain obligation can reasonably be imposed. To ensure the imposition of positive obligations on the member states, the ECJ may need to consider whether there is sufficient acceptance of a certain interpretation of fundamental rights. It could have regard to whether a certain type of action is already undertaken at the national level and it could in particular have resort to the case-law of the ECtHR, which may contain a relevant positive obligation. Moreover, as with all positive obligations that could be imposed by the ECJ, it must be taken into account that, in contrast to negative obligations, there are in principle various ways which can be used to comply with positive obligations. Considering that positive obligations lead to active undertakings for states, they can, although not necessarily, lead to considerable organisational and/or financial burdens. The ECtHR has therefore often recognised that positive obligations are obligations of means rather than obligations of result.

The ECJ, thus, just like the ECtHR, needs to be careful in formulating positive obligations because of the political nature these obligations can have, as well as their potential political and financial impact. Here, it can seen that the ECJ is in a less difficult position than the ECtHR, because the ECJ can rely on a comprehensive legal framework

---

23 Cf. the discussion on this in section 4.2.2.

of primary and secondary EU law to underpin its choices, as well as on the case-law of the ECtHR. However, the ECJ must clearly pay attention to the limited competences of the EU in the field of fundamental rights protection to avoid criticism over the potential effects of some positive obligations.

12.3.4. THE SPECIFIC ROLE AND THE JUDICIAL STYLE OF THE ECJ

The ECJ and ECtHR each define positive obligations in rather different ways. As already explained, the ECJ often interprets fundamental rights in the framework of the preliminary reference procedure. This means that it primarily focuses on answering the specific questions that have been presented by the national courts. In its preliminary rulings, the ECJ often provides for only rather formal and terse reasoning, especially so where it concerns the protection of fundamental rights. It may, therefore, not very clearly reveal if and how positive obligations are established within the context of EU law. Also, the ECJ often reasons on a case-by-case basis and usually does not provide very elaborate explanations of its judgments. The judgments of the ECJ may, therefore, bring little clarity over the specific rights which individuals are entitled to on the basis of fundamental rights under EU law, and they may not claify to the competent authorities what specific obligations they need to comply with and which limitations will apply. In comparison, the ECtHR much more clearly indicates in its case-law that it imposes either negative or positive obligations on states parties. It has developed a clear doctrine of positive obligations in its case-law and, as a result, it can refer to several lines of case-law on the concept of positive obligations which it has developed and refined over the years.

The style used by the ECJ and the ECtHR in their case-law is thus very different. This may also be related to the very different roles played by these courts. The ECtHR must respond to complaints of individuals on the violation of their fundamental rights in relation to very specific circumstances. The ECtHR thereby aims to deliver judgments which provide for individual justice, while it also aims to play a broader role in developing certain minimum standards that can be taken into account by states and their courts. In contrast, the ECJ must secure the correct interpretation and application of EU law in many different areas. The protection of fundamental rights is only one subject which is dealt with by the ECJ. The EU Treaties and the various instruments of secondary law, such as Directives and Regulations, contribute to the functioning of the EU internal market or the area of freedom of security and justice without internal frontiers. The primary subjects of the judgments of the ECJ are the EU institutions and the EU member states and their courts; they concern individual persons to a much lesser extent and much less directly. The ECJ has mainly chosen to apply the same style of (formal) reasoning in fundamental rights cases as it applies in other cases, and it has been slow in developing clear fundamental rights doctrines, such as a positive obligations doctrine.

There are, however, concerns over the legitimacy of the decisions of the ECJ in the field of fundamental rights.[24] The ECJ has often been criticised for not taking fundamental rights sufficiently seriously. Some of the decisions it has taken in the field of fundamental rights, on the basis of very formal and brief reasoning, are criticised for not sufficiently addressing the concerns that are related to the protection of fundamental rights. Many scholars have criticised the role the ECJ has played in the field of fundamental rights, finding that the ECJ has done too little. Especially in more recent times, the ECJ has received criticism because it has decided to make less reference to the judgments of the ECtHR in its case-law and has started to focus on an autonomous interpretation of the Charter. The analysis of several cases in chapter 11 has, in particular, shown that the ECJ can be criticised for the way that it imposes a positive obligation.[25] It has been criticised for rejecting certain positive obligations in its case-law, as well as for the way in which it has decided to accept some positive obligations.

In balancing the various demands made and finding a way out, chapter 7 concluded that the ECJ would have to focus, in particular, on the concerns that are raised by the national (constitutional) courts on the protection of fundamental rights within the EU context. It would need to respond more elaborately to the questions raised by the national courts, also if they were to refer questions on positive obligations. After all, the national courts of the member states are important in securing that questions are brought to the ECJ, allowing the ECJ to interpret EU law in a uniform and effective manner. The analysis in chapter 11 has shown, moreover, that considerations of attribution of power are of the utmost importance in positive obligations cases. It has been shown there that by imposing active requirements on the member states to ensure the protection of fundamental rights, the ECJ could shift the power to take measures from the national level to the EU level and it can, therefore, be criticised. The division of competences may need to be addressed by the ECJ if it is to further develop positive obligations in its case-law, and it should pay special and express attention to this in its reasoning.

12.4. RECOMMENDATIONS FOR THE DEVELOPMENT OF A DOCTRINE OF POSITIVE OBLIGATIONS BY THE ECJ

To the extent that the ECJ actually has the opportunity to further develop the scope of positive obligations under EU law, this section aims to provide some suggestions which the ECJ could incorporate. It has already been argued that the ECJ should pay more visible attention to the limits related to the competences of the EU when it defines positive obligations. Questions could otherwise be raised as soon as the ECJ were to define certain types of obligations for the EU institutions or the member states on

24 See for a further discussion sections 7.6.2.2. and 7.6.2.3.

25 See the examples discussed in section 11.5.

the basis of fundamental rights. As discussed in section 12.2., the EU enjoys specific fundamental rights competences, as well as an indirect fundamental rights competence. In respect of the latter, it has been argued that this competence must be explained narrowly. The actions which can be taken on the basis of such an indirect competence must be accessory to the actions for which there is an explicit basis in the EU treaties. Also, limits apply because of the character of the explicit competence to which such a positive obligation is related. The ECJ could make clear that the general competence to protect fundamental rights remains at national level. If the ECJ were to find that there is no basis to accept a positive obligation on the basis of EU law, it could make clear that the member states are still free to provide fundamental rights protection on the basis of their own national law, as well as on the basis of the standards developed under the Convention.[26] This would avoid it being criticised for not paying sufficient attention to the effective protection of fundamental rights, and it could also prevent the member states from 'hiding' behind the obligations they have been given under EU law in a particular field.[27] The protection of fundamental rights can indeed be seen as complicated by the fact that in some areas of EU law rules apply which derive from various sources of international law.

This study holds that ECJ can draw inspiration from the case-law of the ECtHR in developing a positive obligations doctrine.[28] It contains some important principles for determining as well as limiting the scope of positive obligations.[29] The case-law of the ECtHR may arguably include more far-reaching positive obligations for states than the ECJ could ever develop, as has been explained above. However, the principles developed therein could help the ECJ to provide for more clarity and certainty, as well as stronger legitimacy for the development of positive obligations. In particular, the legitimacy of a development of positive obligations would benefit from more elaborate explanations as to the existence of the legal basis, the scope and the limits concerning certain specific positive obligations. The ECtHR's doctrine of positive obligations may provide useful inspiration here.

The ECJ could first of all rely on specific judgments of the ECtHR that are relevant to justify a particular kind of positive obligation and that can be translated to the specific context of EU law. The Convention as well as the case-law of the ECtHR are considered to provide important sources that must be taken into account by the ECJ in interpreting fundamental rights on the basis of Article 52(3) of the Charter.[30] It is also in the interest of consistency that the ECJ secures that fundamental rights are interpreted in the same way under the Charter as they have been interpreted under the Convention. If the

26 See section 7.5.3. where the 'fundamental rights-friendly' approach of the ECJ in the case of *Willems and others* is explained.

27 This fear is particularly raised by Stubberfield (2012).

28 The following is partly based on Beijer (2015).

29 See sections 3.2.6. (on the methodology used by the ECtHR to discover positive obligations) and 3.5. (on the limitations to the scope for the development of positive obligations).

30 See further section 6.9.1. on this point.

ECJ wanted to provide for a different or a more specific interpretation of a positive obligation, it could do so on the basis of the autonomy of EU law, but it would then need to further justify its choices.

The doctrine of positive obligations of the ECtHR contains (at least) two relevant approaches that would further be useful for the ECJ. First, the ECJ may want to take into account that the ECtHR generally grants member states a margin of appreciation in fulfilling positive obligations.[31] Fundamental rights provisions are naturally phrased very broadly and therefore they generally leave choices to be made with regard to the measures that can be taken. Moreover, it is evident that there are many possible ways to comply with positive obligations, which may be more or less resource-demanding or politically sensitive. A supranational authority may not be in the best position to decide on a particular form of protection at the national level, and it is mainly for that reason that the ECtHR has given considerable leeway to the states to determine how they want to comply with their obligations under the Convention. Similarly, the ECJ may want to adopt an approach to expressly make clear that it grants member states discretion in finding appropriate measures at the national level to comply with the fundamental rights obligations that need to be fulfilled on the basis of EU law. At the same time, however, the ECJ's position is somewhat different than that of the ECtHR, as has been discussed in section 12.3. In particular, because of the judicial set up of the EU system, the ECJ may be asked to provide quite clear indications as to the obligations which member states need to fulfil. National courts sometimes refer very specific questions to the ECJ and thus expect clear indications. Also, the ECJ may itself want to provide quite clear indications as to the measures which member states must take to protect EU law to ensure that EU law is applied uniformly. Again, the ECJ could then be expected to further clarify why one specific type of measure would be better than another. Insofar as there are different possibilities to meet the aims of a certain positive obligation, however, it could be expected that the ECJ would leave sufficient room for making choices at national level.

Secondly, in dealing with concerns over the burdens that may be imposed on member states in securing fundamental rights protection, the ECJ may especially want to take into consideration the limitations which apply to the scope of positive obligations. The ECtHR generally does not require states to incur 'impossible or disproportionate burdens' in the protection of fundamental rights.[32] Positive obligations are in principle obligations of best efforts rather than of result. The ECtHR understands that the effective protection of fundamental rights may give rise to measures which have financial implications, especially where social and economic measures need to be taken. There is obviously a limit to what states can achieve. The ECtHR has acknowledged this by

[31] See e.g. ECtHR 19 February 1998, no. 22729/93, *Kaya v. Turkey*, para. 106.

[32] The ECtHR has even expressed that the scope of states' positive obligations is inherently limited under the Convention, see e.g. ECtHR (adm. dec.) 14 May 2002, no. 38621/97, *Zehnalova and Zehnal v. the Czech Republic*.

requiring states only to take 'reasonable measures'.[33] States parties must actually provide the organisational and financial means to allow effective protection.[34] Furthermore, the ECtHR only accepts positive obligations when public authorities have knowledge, or should have had knowledge, of the infringement of the fundamental rights of certain individuals, or groups of individuals, and their causes.[35] The ECJ could express such principles in cases where it enjoys only limited competences and where it enjoys only shared or complementary competences.

12.5. EXPANSION OF COMPETENCES OR GAPS IN THE PROTECTION OF FUNDAMENTAL RIGHTS?

It has been argued that a development of positive obligations within the context of EU law could lead to an expansion of the competences of the EU. This means that if the ECJ were to impose certain active obligations on the EU institutions or the member states on the basis of the provisions of fundamental rights, the competences of the EU would be over-extended. If the ECJ were, however, to consider that there would be no competence to accept positive obligations, this could instead lead to gaps in the protection of fundamental rights. These fears, which have been expressed by different scholars, have been discussed in several places in this study, especially in the introductory chapter.[36] It has even been suggested by some scholars that the accession of the EU to the Convention would be necessary, so that the ECtHR could start establishing the positive obligations that would be relevant for the EU context. In view of the conclusions that have been reached on the basis of this study, some final remarks will be made here on the discussions over the expansion of competences and the gaps in the protection of EU fundamental rights protection.

Starting with the potential extension of the EU's competences, first, reference can be made to the conclusions that have been reached regarding the scope for a development of positive obligations by the ECJ as explained in section 12.2. This has shown that there is room for positive obligations to be established on the basis of the competences that have been given to the EU. The EU has some specific as well as indirect competences which can be used to justify a development of positive obligations within the context of EU law, so that it can be ensured that the policies of the EU comply with the relevant negative and positive obligations to protect fundamental rights. This implies that an extension of the competences of the EU does not necessarily need to take place. Surely, now that that the EU Treaties do not bring great clarity over the limits that apply, and the expansion of the EU competences generally remains an issue of concern, there is

33 See e.g. ECtHR 20 March 2008, nos. 15339/02 to 15343/02, *Budayeva and others v. Russia*, para. 175; and ECtHR 9 December 1994, no. 16798/80, *López Ostra v. Spain*, para. 51. See further section 3.5.3.

34 See Xenos (2012), pp. 100–107.

35 See section 3.5.1.

36 See sections 1.1.3., 8.3.5. and 9.2.2.

indeed a risk that EU law can provide a basis for interference in areas which fall outside the sphere of direct competence of the EU.[37] This does not mean, however, that positive obligations could never be imposed. Instead, it demands additional awareness by the ECJ of the limits relating to the fundamental rights competences of the EU, in particular those that concern the indirect competences for the EU to protect fundamental rights. Also, the ECJ needs to be very careful in developing positive obligations for the member states in situations where they derogate from the free movement rules, and where they apply their optioning rules under EU law. Of particular importance is the principle of loyal or sincere cooperation, laid down in Article 4(3) TEU, which requires the member states to take 'all appropriate measures to fulfil the obligations arising out of the Treaty'. These obligations may extend to areas where the EU does not enjoy any legislative powers and, again, it may be expected that the ECJ would generally be careful in developing far-reaching obligations there.

Looking at the cases which have so far reached the ECJ, it has been shown that the ECJ is usually very careful in imposing (potentially burdensome) obligations on the member states. It has defined a legislative obligation for the member states in very few cases. In the particular context of the development of positive procedural obligations at national level, the ECJ has even stressed that it is only in exceptional situations that the member states are required to introduce new remedies at national level to ensure the protection of fundamental rights. In principle, the ECJ thus relies on the procedural arrangements that have already been provided for at national level. In respect of the situation where the member states derogate from EU law, and when they apply their optioning rules, the ECJ has also been very careful in imposing obligations. Such cases may raise questions in view of the division of powers between the EU and the member states; however, since the ECJ has only developed some small positive obligations of a procedural kind, at the momet, there does not seem to be a reason for much concern here.

More generally, it can be seen that the ECJ has been paying attention to the limited competences of the EU to protect fundamental rights, by clarifying that there are limits to the scope of application of EU fundamental rights which relate to the limited competences of the EU, and also by determining in some cases that the member states still enjoy certain sovereign powers under EU law.[38] Thus, the ECJ seems intent in guarding the limited competences of the EU in the field of fundamental rights protection and, so far, an expansion of competences on the basis of a development of positive obligations does not seem to have taken place.

Next, there is the risk of gaps in the protection of fundamental rights which could be the consequence of the limited scope for accepting positive obligations under EU law. Again, it is submitted that such fears are not necessarily well-founded. On the one hand, indeed, it must be admitted that there are various kinds of positive obligations which cannot be established on the basis of EU law. Seeing especially that there is no general

[37] See sections 8.3.4.2. to 8.3.4.4.

[38] See sections 9.3.1. and 9.3.

competence for the EU to take action, there is no basis to accept positive obligations to respond to certain issues that require a concerted action across the different policy fields of the EU. There is limited scope, for example, to take more comprehensive action to protect the rights of minorities in Europe, which may cut across the different policy fields of the EU. However, the EU would really need to be conferred with a specific competence by the member states to take such actions.

Also, to the extent that EU law does not provide for a full or exhaustive harmonisation of national law, there is in principle scope for the protection of fundamental rights on the basis of national law. In most situations where EU fundamental rights apply, the EU enjoys a shared competence or a complementary competence, which generally leaves discretion for the member states to provide for (farther-reaching) protection of fundamental rights. It has already been concluded that there are few situations where EU law exclusively applies, so in many cases national laws still apply.[39] The primary responsibility for the protection of fundamental rights thus still lies at the national level. It must be held in mind that the member states have already developed a legal framework and (procedural) mechanisms and institutions to provide for such protection. They can, therefore, also be required to respond to the positive obligations that are developed by the ECtHR in relation to the rights that are guaranteed under EU law.

Specific problems can, however, arise in the context of EU law if the member states fail to provide sufficient protection of fundamental rights on the basis of national law. This especially applies in several areas of EU law where the member states need to cooperate on civil and criminal matters and asylum and immigration matters, on the basis of the principle of mutual recognition. This means that the member states must cooperate on the basis of the presumption that other member states provide a sufficient level of fundamental rights protection. There may therefore not be any harmonisation of the applicable fundamental rights standards.[40] Cases have been brought before the ECJ as well as the ECtHR on situations which revealed serious concerns over the adequacy of the protection of fundamental rights in some member states. The cases of *N.S. and others* as well as *Aranyosi and Căldăru* of the ECJ have revealed serious problems regarding, respectively, the reception of asylum seekers as well as access to asylum procedures, and the conditions of detention.[41] In these areas, some member states seem to have failed to comply fully with the positive obligations they have incurred under the Convention. Because of the lack of EU competences on such matters and because of the principle of mutual recognition, there can be little room for the ECJ to interfere in the compliance with such obligations by the member states. Instead, the ECJ could, perhaps, only decide to point out that the member states have positive obligations that they need to comply with within the framework of the Convention. The ECJ could

---

39 It can be important to take into account that the scope for the application of national fundamental rights standards cannot undermine the unity, primacy and effectiveness of EU law on the basis of the *Melloni* ruling of the ECJ, see section 6.8.

40 See section 6.8.

41 For a further explanation of these cases, see section 6.8. and 11.5.3.

reinforce the obligations which the member states need to comply with in their own respective competence spheres, however. If necessary, the ECJ may also decide to make exceptions to the principle of mutual recognition so that it can be ensured by the national courts that the effective protection of fundamental rights is not put at risk. This particular area thus gives rise to certain complications on how the standards of EU law, national law and the Convention interrelate and there are different competence spheres of the EU and the member states to take into account. It is an especially important area that is of continuing concern for the ECJ as well as for the ECtHR, and it is unclear whether the principle of mutual recognition can be applied and an effective protection of fundamental rights can still be secured in those situations.

As a final and last point then, what does all of this say about the desirability of the accession of the EU to the Convention? It can generally be held, on the basis of the conclusions that have been provided, that the accession of the EU to the Convention is not strictly currently necessary because the system of fundamental rights protection at EU level provides certain legal basis and procedural mechanisms that could be used to ensure the recognition of positive obligations at EU level. There continue to be doubts, however, over the adequacy of the protection of fundamental rights provided by the EU institutions (including the EU Courts), seeing that they also have other interests to protect, and because of the fact that there are very limited standing rights for individuals, which forces them to rely on the national courts to address gaps in the protection of fundamental rights under EU law. Especially in the area of criminal law, where legislative instruments are increasingly adopted, there are concerns over the adequacy of the remedies that are provided under EU law for individuals and for the national courts. So if, in future years, specific cases show that such fears over the genuine protection of fundamental rights by the EU and the ECJ are justified, it could become necessary for cases to be brought directly by individuals before the ECtHR to complain about the protection of fundamental rights by the EU institutions.

BIBLIOGRAPHY

Ahmed & Butler (2006)

T. Ahmed and I. Butler, 'The European Union and Human Rights Review: An International Law Perspective', 17 *European Journal of International Law* (2006), pp. 771–801.

Akandji-Kombé (2007)

J.F. Akandji-Kombé, *Positive Obligations under the European Convention on Human Rights: A Guide to the Implementation of the European Convention on Human Rights* (Strasbourg, Council of Europe 2007).

Alexy (2002)

R. Alexy, *A Theory of Constitutional Rights* (Oxford University Press, Oxford 2002).

Alkema (2000)

E.A. Alkema, 'The European Convention as a constitution and its Court as a constitutional court', in: P. Mahoney (ed.), *Protecting human rights: the European perspective: studies in memory of Rolv Ryssdal* (Köln, Carl Heymanns Verlag 2000), pp. 41–63.

Alston & Weiler (1999)

P. Alston and J. Weiler, 'An "Ever Closer Union" in Need of a Human Rights Policy: The European Union and Human Rights', in: P. Alston (ed.), *The EU and Human Rights* (Oxford, Oxford University Press 1999), pp. 3–66.

Arai-Takahashi (2002)

Y. Arai-Takahashi, *The Margin of Appreciation Doctrine and the Principle of Proportionality in the Jurisprudence of the ECHR* (Antwerp, Intersentia 2002).

Augenstein (2013)

D. Augenstein, 'Engaging Fundamental Rights: On the Autonomous Substance of EU Fundamental Rights Law', 14 *German Law Journal* (2013), pp. 1917–1938.

Avbelj (2004)

M. Avbelj, 'European Court of Justice and the Question of Value Choices: Fundamental Human Rights as an Exception to the Freedom of Movement of Goods', Jean Monnet Working Paper 06/04.

Azoulai (2008)

L. Azoulai, 'The Court of Justice and the Social Market Economy: The Emergence of an Ideal and the Conditions for Its Realization', 45 *Common Market Law Review* (2008), pp. 1335–1355.

Barents (2008)

R. Barents, *Het Verdrag van Lissabon: Achtergronden en commentaar* [The Lisbon Treaty: Background and comments] (Deventer, Kluwer 2008).

Barkhuysen (2004)

T. Barkhuysen, *Het EVRM als integraal onderdeel van het Nederlandse materieele bestuursrecht* [The ECHR as an integral part of Dutch substantive administrative law] (Preadviezen (2004): De betekenis van het EVRM voor het materiële bestuursrecht 2004).

Barkhuysen & Van Emmerik (2005)

T. Barkhuysen and M.L. van Emmerik, 'A Comparative View on the Execution of Judgments of the European Court of Human Rights', in: T. Christou and E.P. Raymond (eds.), *European Court of Human Rights: Remedies and Execution of Judgments* (London, British Institute of International and Comparative Law 2005), pp. 1–23.

Barnard (2011)

C. Barnard, 'EU 'Social' Policy: From Employment Law to Labour Market Reform', in: P. Craig and G. de Búrca, *The Evolution of EU Law* (Oxford, Oxford University Press 2011), pp. 641–686.

Bates (2010)

E. Bates, *The Evolution of the European Convention on Human Rights* (Oxford, Oxford University Press 2010).

Beck (2012)

G. Beck, *The Legal Reasoning of the Court of Justice* (Oxford, Hart Publishing 2012).

Beijer (2017)

M.P. Beijer, 'Procedural Fundamental Rights Review by the Court of Justice of the European Union', in: J. Gerards and Eva Brems (eds.), *Procedural Review in European Fundamental Rights Cases* (Cambridge Unversity Press 2017 forthcoming).

Beijer (2015)

M.P. Beijer, 'Active Guidance of Fundamental Rights Protection by the Court of Justice of the European Union: Exploring the Possibilities of a Positive Obligations Doctrine', 2 *Review of European Administrative Law* (2015), pp. 127–150.

Bell (2011)

M. Bell, 'The Principle of Equal Treatment: Widening and Deepening', in: P. Craig and G. de Búrca, *The Evolution of EU Law* (Oxford, Oxford University Press 2011), pp. 611–639.

Bennett & Raab (2006)

C. Bennett and C. Raab, *The Governance of Privacy* (Cambridge, MIT Press 2006).

Besslink (2001)

L. Besselink, 'The Member States, the National Constitutions and the Scope of the Charter', 1 *Maastricht Journal of European and Comparative Law* (2001), pp. 68–80.

Besselink (1998)

L. Besselink, 'Entrapped by the Maximum Standard: On Fundamental Rights, Pluralism and Subsidiarity in the European Union', 35 *Common Market Law Review* (1998), pp. 631–680.

Besson (2011a)

S. Besson, 'European Human Rights, Supranational Judicial Review and Democracy: Thinking outside the judicial box', in: P. Populier and C. van de Heijning (eds.), *Human Rights Protection in the European Legal Order: The Interaction Between the European and National Courts* (Cambridge, Intersentia 2011), pp. 97–145.

Besson (2011b)

S. Besson, 'Chapter 1: The Human Rights Competences in the EU – The State of the Question after Lisbon', in: G. Kofler, M. Poiares Maduro and P. Pistone (eds.), *Human Rights and Taxation in Europe and the World* (IBFD 2011), pp. 37–63.

Besson (2006)

S. Besson, 'The European Union and Human Rights: Towards a Post-National Human Rights Institution'?, 6 *Human Rights Law Review* (2006), pp. 323–360.

Biondi (2004)

A. Biondi, 'Free Trade, A Mountain Road and the Right to Protest: European Economic Freedoms and Fundamental Individual Rights' 51 *European Human Rights Law Review* (2004), pp. 51–61.

Bobek (2014)

M. Bobek, 'Legal Reasoning of the Court of Justice of the EU', 39 *European Law Review* (2014), pp. 418–428.

Bobek (2013)

M. Bobek, 'Of Feasability and Silent Elephants: The Legitimacy of the European Court of Justice Through the Eyes of National Courts', in: M. Adams, J. Meeusen, G. Straetmans, H. De Waele (eds.), *Judging Europe's Judges: The Legitimacy of the Case-law of the European Court of Justice Examined* (Oxford: Hart Publishing 2013), pp. 197–234.

Bobek (2012)

M. Bobek, 'A Fourth in the Court: Why are there Advocates-General in the Court of Justice?', *Cambridge Yearbook of European Legal Studies* 14 (2011–2012), pp. 529–561.

De Boer (2013)

N. de Boer, 'Addressing Rights Divergences Under the Charter: *Melloni*', 50 *Common Market Law Review* (2013), pp. 1083–1103.

Von Bogdandy (2000)

A. von Bogdandy, 'The European Union as a Human Rights Organization? Human Rights and the Core of the European Union', 37 *Common Market Law Review* (2000), pp. 1307–1338.

Von Bogdandy, Kottmann, Antpöhler, Dickschen, Hentrei & Smrkolj (2012)

A. von Bogdandy, M. Kottmann, C. Antpöhler, J. Dickschen, S. Hentrei, M. Smrkolj, 'Reverse Solange – Protecting the Essence of Fundamental Rights Against EU Member States', 49 *Common Market Law Review* (2012), pp. 489–519.

Brems (2013)

E. Brems, 'Procedural Protection: An Examination of Procedural Safeguards Read into Substantive Convention Rights', in: E Brems and J.H. Gerards (eds.), *Shaping Rights in the ECHR* (Cambridge, Cambridge University Press 2013), pp. 137–161.

Brems & Gerards (2016)

J. Gerards and Eva Brems (eds.), *Procedural Review in European Fundamental Rights Cases* (Cambridge, Cambridge University Press 2017 forthcoming).

Brittain (2015)

S. Brittain, 'The Relationship Between the EU Charter of Fundamental Rights and the European Convention on Human Rights: an Originalist Analysis', 11 *European Constitutional Law Review* (2015), pp. 482–511.

Broberg & Fenger (2014)

M. Broberg and N. Fenger, *Preliminary References to the European Court of Justice* (Oxford, Oxford University Press 2014).

Bröllmann (2005)

C. Bröllmann, 'Law-making Treaties: Form and Function in International Law', 74 *Nordic Journal of International Law* (2005), pp. 383–403.

De Búrca (2013)

G. de Búrca, 'After the EU Charter of Fundamental Rights: The Court of Justice as a Human Rights adjudicator?', 20 *Maastricht Journal of European and Comparative Law* (2013), pp. 168–184.

De Búrca (2011)

G. De Búrca, 'The Evolution of EU Human Rights Law', in: P. Craig and G. De Búrca (eds.), *The Evolution of EU Law*, (New York, Oxford University Press 2011), pp. 465–497.

De Búrca (2003)

G. de Búrca, 'Fundamental Rights and Citizenship', in: B. de Witte (ed.), *Ten Reflections on the Constitutional Treaty for Europe* (European University Institute, Robert Schuman Centre for Advanced Studies and Academy of European Law 2003), pp. 11–44.

De Búrca (2001a)

G. de Búrca, 'Setting Constitutional Limits to EU Competences', Francisco Luca Pires Working Paper Series on European Constitutionalism, Working Paper 2001/02.

De Búrca (2001b)

G. De Búrca, 'Human Rights: The Charter and Beyond', Jean Monnet Working Paper No. 10/01.

De Búrca (1998)

G. de Búrca, 'The Principle of Subsidiarity and the Court of Justice as an Institutional Actor', 36 *Journal of Common Market Studies* (1998), pp. 217–236

De Búrca (1993)

G. de Búrca, 'The principle of proportionality and its application in EC Law', 13 *Yearbook of European Law* (1993), pp. 105–150

Butler (2012)

I. Butler, 'Ensuring Compliance with the Charter of Fundamental Rights in Legislative Drafting: the practice of the European Commission', 37 *European Law Review* (2012), pp. 397–419

Butler & De Schutter (2008)

I. Butler and O. de Schutter, 'Binding the EU to International Human Rights Law', 40 *Yearbook of European Law* (2008), pp. 277–320.

Campbell (2006)

A.I.L. Campbell, 'Positive Obligations Under the ECHR: Deprivation of Liberty by Private Actors', 10 *Edinburgh Law Review* (2006), pp. 399–412.

Canor (2013)

I. Canor, '*My Brother's Keeper?* Horizontal *Solange*: "An Ever Closer *Distrust* Among the Peoples of Europe"', 50 *Common Market Law Review* (2013), pp. 383–422.

Carrera & Petkova (2013)

S. Carrera and B. Petkova, 'The Potential of Civil Society and Human Rights Organizations Through Third-Party Interventions Before the European Courts: The EU's Area of Freedom, Security and Justice', in: M. Dawson, B. de Witte and E. Muir, *Judicial Activism at the European Court of Justice* (Cheltenham, Edward Elgar Publishing Limited 2013), p. 233–263.

Christoffersen (2009)

J. Christoffersen, 'Impact on General Principles of Treaty Interpretation', in: M.T. Kamminga and M. Scheinin (eds.), *The Impact of Human Rights Law on General International Law* (Oxford, Oxford University Press 2009), pp. 37–61.

Van Cleynenbreugel (2012a)

P. van Cleynenbreugel, 'Judge-made Standards of National Procedure in the Post-Lisbon Constitutional Framework', 37 *European Law Review* (2012), pp. 90–100.

Van Cleynenbreugel (2012b)

P. van Cleynenbreugel, 'The Confusing Constitutional Status of Positive Procedural Obligations in EU law', 5 *Review of European Administrative Law* (2012), pp. 81–100.

Connelly (1986)

A.M. Connelly, 'Problems of Interpretation of Article 8 of the European Convention on Human Rights', 35 *The International and Comparitive Law Quarterly* (1986), pp. 567–593.

Coppel & O'Neill (1992)

J. Coppel and A. O'Neill, 'The European Court of Justice: Taking Rights Seriously?', 29 *Common Market Law Review* (1992), pp. 669–692.

Craig (2012)

P. Craig, *EU Administrative Law* (Oxford, Oxford University Press 2012).

Craig (2011a)

P. Craig, *The Lisbon Treaty: Laws, Politics and Treaty Reform* (Oxford, Oxford University Press 2011).

Craig (2011b)

P. Craig, 'The ECJ and *Ultra Vires* Action: A Conceptual Analysis', 48 *Common Market Law Review* (2011), pp. 395–437.

Craig (2004)

P. Craig, 'Competence: Clarity, Conferral, Containment and Consideration', 29 *European Law Review* (2004), pp. 323–344.

Craig & De Búrca (2015)

P. Craig and G. De Búrca, *EU Law: Texts, Cases and Materials* (Oxford, Oxford University Press 2015).

Cuyvers (2014)

A. Cuyvers, '"Give Me One Good Reason": The Unified Standards of Review for Sanctions After *Kadi II*', 51 *Common Market Law Review* (2014), pp. 1759–1788.

Dashwood (2006)

A. Dashwood, 'The Limits of the European Community Powers', 21 *European Law Review* (2006), pp. 113–128.

Dauses (1985)

M. Dauses, 'The Protection of Fundamental Rights in the Community Legal Order', 10 *European Law Review* (1985), pp. 398–419.

Davies (2006)

G. Davies, 'Subsidiarity: The Wrong Idea in the Wrong Place, at the Wrong Time', 43 *Common Market Law Review* (2006), pp. 63–84.

Dawson & Muir (2013)

M. Dawson and E. Muir, 'Hungary and the *Indirect* Protection of EU Fundamental Rights and the Rule of Law', 14 *German Law Journal* (2013), pp. 1959–1980.

Van Dijk (1998)

P. van Dijk, '"Positive Obligations" Implied in the European Convention on Human Rights: Are the States Still the "Masters" of the Convention?', in: M. Castermans-Holleman, F. van Hoof and J. Smith (eds.), *The Role of the Nation-State in the 21st Century: Human Rights, International Organisations and Foreign Policy: Essays in Honour of Peter Baehr* (The Hague, Kluwer Law International 1998), pp. 17–33.

Van Dijk & Arai-Takahashi (2006)

P. van Dijk and Y. Arai-Takahashi, *Theory and Practice of the European Convention on Human Rights* (Antwerpen, Intersentia 2006).

Dougan (2015)

M. Dougan, 'Judicial Review of Member State Action Under the General Principles and the Charter', 52 *Common Market Law Review* (2015), pp. 1201–1245.

Douglas-Scott (2011)

S. Douglas-Scott, 'The European Union and Human Rights After the Treaty of Lisbon', 11 *Human Rights Law Review* (2011), pp. 645–682.

Douglas-Scott (2006)

S. Douglas-Scott, 'A tale of two courts: Luxembourg, Strasbourg and the growing European human rights *acquis*', 43 *Common Market Law Review* (2006), pp. 629–665.

Dröge (2003)

C. Dröge, *Positive Verpflichtungen der Staaten in der Europäischen Menschenrechtskonvention* (Berlin, Springer 2003).

Dubos (2015)

O. Dubos, 'The Origins of Proceduralisation of EU Law: A Grey Area of European Federalism', 8 *Review of European Administrative Law* (2015), pp. 7–26.

Dubout (2014)

E. Dubout, 'The Protection of Fundamental Rights and the Allocation of Competences in the EU : a Clash of Constitutional Logics', in: L. Azoulai (ed.), *The Question of Competences in the European Union* (Oxford, Oxford University Press 2014), pp. 193–211.

Dubout (2007)

E. Dubout, 'La Procéduralisation des Obligations Relatives aux Droits Fondamentaux Substantiels par la Cour Européenne des Droits de l'Homme', 70 *Revue trimestrielle de droits de l'homme* (2007), pp. 397–425.

Dupré (2014)

C. Dupré, 'Article 1' in S. Peers *et alia* (eds.), *The EU Charter of Fundamental Rights – A commentary* (Oxford, Hart Publishing 2014), pp. 3–24.

Dupré (2013)

C. Dupré, 'Human Dignity in Europe: A Foundational Constitutional Principle', 19 *European Public Law* (2013), pp. 341–367.

Editorial Comments (2016)

'The Rule of Law in the Union, the Rule of Union Law and the Rule of Law by the Union: Three Interrelated Problems', *Common Market Law Review*, 53, pp. 597–605.

Editorial Comments (2015)

'Safeguarding EU Values in the Member States: Is Something Finally Happening?', *Common Market Law Review*, 52, pp. 619–628.

Editorial Comments (2012)

'Hungary's New Constitutional Order and "European Unity"', *Common Market Law Review*, 49, pp. 871–884.

Eeckhout (2002)

P. Eeckhout, 'The EU Charter of Fundamental Rights and the Federal Question', 39 *Common Market Law Review* (2002), pp. 945–994.

Van Eijken (2015)

H. van Eijken, *EU Citizenship and the Constitutionalisation of the European Union* (Groningen, Europa Law Publishing 2015).

Erikson (2003)

E. Eriksen, 'Why a Charter of Fundamental Rights?', 16 *Ratio Juris* (2003), pp. 352–372.

Everling (1996)

U. Everling, 'Will Europe Slip on Bananas? The Bananas Judgment of the Court of Justice and National Courts', 33 *Common Market Law Review* (1996), pp. 401–438.

Fontanelli (2011)

F. Fontanelli, 'The European Union's Charter of Fundamental Rights Two Years Later', 3 *Perspective on Federalism* (2011), E- 22–47.

Forder (1992)

C.J. Forder, 'Positieve verplichtingen in het kader van het Europees Verdrag tot Bescherming van de Rechten van de Mens en de Fundamentele Vrijheden [Positive obligations within the context of the ECHR]', 17 *NJCM-Bulletin* (1992), pp. 611–637.

Fredman (2008)

S. Fredman, *Human Rights Transformed: Positive Rights and Positive Duties* (Oxford, Oxford University Press 2008).

Frowein (1990)

J.A. Frowein, 'The European Convention on Human Rights as the Public Order of Europe 1 (Bd 2)', Collected Courses of the Academy of European Law (1990), pp. 267–358.

Gerards (2016)

J.H. Gerards, 'The Human Rights Jurisprudence of the European Court of Justice', in: S. Greer, J. Gerards and R. Slowe, *Human Rights in the Council of Europe and European Union* (Cambridge, Cambridge University Press 2016), forthcoming.

Gerards (2015)

J.H. Gerards, 'Who Decides on Fundamental Rights Issues in Europe?: Towards a Mechanism to Coordinate the Roles of the National Courts, the ECJ and the ECtHR', in: S. de Vries, U. Bernitz and S. Weatherill, *The EU Charter of Fundamental Rights as a binding instrument* (Oxford, Hart Publishing 2015), pp. 47–74.

Gerards (2013)

J.H. Gerards, 'Judicial Minimalism and 'Dependency': Interpretation of the European Convention in a Pluralist Europe', in: M. van Roosmalen, B. Vermeulen, F. van Hoof and M. Oosting (eds.) *Fundamental Rights and Principles: liber amicorum Pieter van Dijk* (Intersentia, Cambridge 2013), pp. 73–91

Gerards (2012a)

J. Gerards, 'The Prism of Fundamental Rights', 8 *European Constitutional Law Review* (2012), pp. 173–202.

Gerards (2012b)

J. Gerards, 'Judicial Argumentation in Fundamental Rights Cases – the EU Courts' Challenge' in U. Neergaard and R. Nielsen, *European Legal Method – in a Multi-Level EU Legal Order* (Copenhagen, DJØF Publishing 2012), pp. 27–69.

Gerards (2012c)

J. Gerards, 'The Pilot Judgment Procedure Before the European Court of Human Rights as an Instrument for Dialogue', in: M. Claes and P. Popelier (eds.), *Constitutional Conversations In Europe: Actors, Topics and Procedures* (Antwerp, Intersentia 2012), pp. 371–397.

Gerards (2011a)

J. Gerards, 'Pluralism, Deference and the Margin of Appreciation Doctrine', 17 *European Law Journal* (2011), p. 80–120.

Gerards (2011b)

J.H. Gerards, *EVRM: Algemene beginselen* [*ECHR: General principles*] (Sdu Uitgevers, Den Haag 2011).

Gerards (2009)

J.H. Gerards, 'Judicial Deliberations in the European Court of Human Rights', in: N.J.H. Huls and M. Adams (eds.), *The Legitimacy of Highest Courts' Rulings: Judicial Deliberations and Beyond* (The Hague, T.M.C. Asser Press 2009), pp. 407–436.

Gerards & Fleuren (2013)

J.H. Gerards and J.W.A. Fleuren, *Implementatie van het EVRM en de uitspraken van het EHRM in de nationale rechtspraak: een rechtsvergelijkend onderzoek* [Implementation of the ECHR and the judgments of the ECtHR in national case-law: a comparitive research] (Nijmegen, WODC 2013).

Gerards & Senden (2009)

J.H. Gerards and H. Senden, 'The Structure of Fundamental Rights and the European Court of Human Rights', 7 *International Journal of Constitutional Law* (2009), pp. 619–653.

Gersdorf (1994)

H. Gersdorf, 'Funktionen der Gemeinschaftsgrundrechte im Lichte des Solange II-Beschlusses des Bundesverfassungsgerichts', 119 *Archiv des öffentlichen Rechts* (1994), pp. 400–426.

Van Gerven (2000)

W. van Gerven, 'Of Rights, Remedies and Procedures', 37 *Common Market Law Review* (2000), pp. 501–536.

Gragl (2014a)

P. Gragl, 'Agreement on the Accession of the European Union to the European Convention on Human Rights', in: S. Peers et alia (eds.), *The EU Charter of Fundamental Rights – A Commentary* (Oxford, Hart Publishing 2014), pp. 1727–1823.

Gragl (2014b)

P. Gragl, 'A Giant Leap for European Human Rights? The Final Agreement on the European Union's Accession to the European Convention on Human Rights', 51 *Common Market Law Review* (2014), pp. 13–58.

Greer & Williams (2009)

S. Greer and A. Williams, 'Human Rights in the Council of Europe and the EU: Towards "Individual", "Constitutional" or "Institutional" Justice?', 15 *European Law Journal* (2009), pp. 462–481.

Groussot, Pech & Petursson (2013)

X. Groussot, L. Pech and G.T. Petursson, 'The Reach of EU Fundamental Rights on EU Member States Action after Lisbon', in: S. de Vries, U. Bernitz and S. Weatherill (eds.), *The Protection of Fundamental Rights After Lisbon* (Oxford, Hart 2013), pp. 97–118.

Groussot & Gill-Pedro (2013)

X. Groussot and E. Gill-Pedro, 'Old and New Human Rights in Europe: The Scope of EU Rights *Versus* that of ECHR Rights', in: E. Brems and J. Gerards, *Shaping Rights in the ECHR: The Role of the European Court of Human Rights in Determining the Scope of Human Rights* (Cambridge, Cambridge University Press 2013), pp. 232–258.

Harris, O'Boyle, Bates & Warbrick (2014)

D.J. Harris, M. O'Boyle, E.P. Bates and C. Warbrick, *Law of the European Convention on Human Rights Law of the European Convention on Human Rights* (Oxford, Oxford University Press 2014).

Van Harten & Grootelaar (2014)

H. Van Harten and H. Grootelaar, 'Doorwerking van het Handvest van de Grondrechten van de Europese Unie in de Nederlandse rechtspraak: een kwantitatieve analyse [Effects of the Charter of Fundamental Rights of the EU in the Dutch case-law: a quantitative analysis]', 39 *Nederland Tijdschrift voor de Mensenrechten/NJCM-Bulletin* (2014), pp. 182–200.

Hartkamp (2013)

A. Hartkamp, 'The Concept of (Indirect and Direct) Horizontal Effect of EU Law: The Terminology of European Legal Scholars and of Private Law Scholars', in: U. Bernitz, X. Groussot and F. Schulyok (eds.), *General Principles of EU law and European Private Law* (Alphen aan den Rijn, Wolters Kluwer, Law & Business 2013), pp. 189–197.

Helfer (2008)

L.R. Helfer, 'Redesigning the European Court of Human Rights: Embeddedness as a Deep Structural Principle of the European Human Rights Regime', 19 *European Journal of International Law* (2008), pp. 125–159.

Heringa & Verhey (2001)

A. Heringa and L. Verhey, 'The EU Charter: Text and Structure', 8 *Maastricht Journal of European and Comparative Law* (2001), pp. 11–20.

Hofman & Mihaescu (2013)

H. Hofman and B. Mihaescu, 'The Relation between the Charter's Fundamental Rights and the Unwritten General Principles of EU Law: Good Administration as the Test Case', 9 *European Constitutional law Review* (2013), pp. 73–101.

Jaeckel (2003)

L. Jaeckel, 'The Duty to Protect Fundamental Rights in the European Community', 28 *European Law Review* (2003), pp. 508–527.

Jacobs (2001)

F.G. Jacobs, 'Human Rights in the European Union', *European Law Review* 26 (2001), p. 331–341.

Jančić (2015)

D. Jančić, 'The Game of Cards: National Parliaments in the EU and the Future of the Early Warning Mechanism and the Political Dialogue', 52 *Common Market Law Review* (2015), pp. 939–976.

Keller & Sweet (2008)

H. Keller and A.S. Sweet, *A Europe of Rights: The Impact of the ECHR on National Legal Systems* (Oxford, Oxford University Press 2008).

Van Kempen (2008)

P.H.P.H.M.C. van Kempen, *Repressie door mensenrechten: over positieve verplichtingen tot aanwending van strafrecht ter bescherming van fundamentele rechten* [*Repression by human rights. on positive obligations to apply criminal law to ensure fundamental rights*] (Wolf Legal Publishers, Nijmegen 2008).

Klamert (2014)

M. Klamert, *The Principle of Loyalty in EU Law* (Oxford, Oxford University Press 2014).

Klatt (2015)

M. Klatt, 'Positive Rights: Who Decides? Judicial Review in Balance', 13 *International Journal of Constitutional Law* (2015), pp. 354–382.

Klatt (2011)

M. Klatt, 'Positive Obligations Under the European Convention on Human Rights', 71 *Zeitschrift für ausländisches öffentliches Recht und Völkerrecht* (2011), pp. 691–718.

Klein & Mitchell (2010)

D. Klein and G. Mitchell (eds.), *The Psychology of Judicial Decision Making* (Oxford, Oxford University Press 2010).

Koch (2005)

I.E. Koch, 'Dichotomies, Trichotomies or Waves of Duties?', 5 *Human Rights Law Review* (2005), pp. 81–103.

Krommendijk (2015)

J. Krommendijk, 'The Use of Ecthr Case-Law by the Court of Justice After Lisbon: The View of Luxembourg Insiders', 6 *Maastricht Journal of European and Comparative Law* (2015), pp. 812–835.

Kühling (2009)

J. Kühling, 'Fundamental rights', in: A. von Bogdandy and J. Bast (eds.), *Principles of European Constitutional Law* (Oxford, Hart Publishing 2009), pp. 479–514.

Lacchi (2016)

C. Lacchi, 'Multilevel Judicial Protection in the EU and Preliminary References', 53 *Common Market Law Review* (2016), pp. 679–708.

Ladenburger (2012)

C. Ladenburger, *Protection of Fundamental Rights Post-Lisbon – The Interaction Between the Charter of Fundamental Rights, the European Convention of Human Rights and National Constitutions* (FIDE Institutional Report, 2012).

Vande Lanotte & Haeck (2005)

J. Vande Lanotte and Y. Haeck, *Handboek EVRM* [Handbook ECHR] (Antwerpen, Intersentia 2005).

Lasser (2004)

M. Lasser, *Judicial Deliberations: A Comparative Analysis of Judicial Transparency* (Oxford, Oxford University Press 2004).

Lavrysen (2016)

L. Lavrysen, *Human Rights in a Positive State: Rethinking the Relationship between Positive and Negative Obligations under the European Convention on Human Rights* (Cambridge, Intersentia 2016).

Lavrysen (2013)

L. Lavrysen, 'The Scope of Rights and the Scope of Obligations: Positive Obligations', in: E. Brems and J. Gerards (eds.), *Shaping Rights in the ECtHR: The Role of the European Court of Human Rights in Determining the Scope of Human Rights* (Cambridge, Cambridge University Press 2013), pp. 162–182.

Lawson (2005)

R. Lawson, 'Human Rights: The Best is Yet to Come', 1 *European Constitutional Law Review* (2005), pp. 27–37.

Lawson (1995a)

R.A. Lawson, 'Positieve verplichtingen onder het EVRM: opkomst en ondergang van de "fair balance"-test – Deel I [Positive obligations under the ECHR: rise and fall of the "fair balance"-test – Part I]', 20 *NJCM-bulletin* (1995), pp. 558–573.

Lawson (1995b)

R.A. Lawson, 'Positieve verplichtingen onder het EVRM: opkomst en ondergang van de "fair balance"-test – Deel II [Positive obligations under the ECHR: rise and fall of the "fair balance"-test – Part II]', 20 *NJCM-bulletin* (1995), pp. 727–750.

Leach (2006)

P. Leach, 'Positive Obligations from Strasbourg – Where do the Boundaries Lie?', 15 *Interights Bulletin* (2006), pp. 123–126.

Leach (2005)

P. Leach, 'Beyond the Bug River: A New Dawn for Redress Before the European Court of Human Rights', 10 *European Human Rights Law Review* (2005), pp. 148–164.

Leijten (2015)

A.E.M. Leijten, *Core Rights and the Protection of Socio-Economic Interests by the European Court of Human Rights* (Dissertation, Meijers serie no. 252, 2015).

Lenaerts (2013)

K. Lenaerts, 'The Court's Outer and Inner Selves: Exploring the External and Internal Legitimacy of the European Court of Justice', in: M. Adams, H. De Waele, J. Meeusen and G. Straetmans (eds.), *The Legitimacy of the Case-law of the European Court of Justice* (Oxford, Hart Publishing 2013), pp. 13–60.

Lenaerts (2012a)

K. Lenaerts, 'Exploring the Limits of the EU Charter of Fundamental Rights', 8 *European Constitutional Law Review* (2012), pp. 375–403.

Lenaerts (2012b)

K. Lenaerts, 'The European Court of Justice and Process-oriented Review', Research Paper in Law European Legal Studies 01/2012O (2012).

Lenaerts & Gutiérrez-Fons (2010)

K. Lenaerts and J.A. Gutiérrez-Fons, 'The Constitutional Allocation of Powers and General Principles of EU Law', 47 *Common Market Law Review* (2010), pp. 1629–1669.

Lock (2011)

T. Lock, 'Walking on a tightrope: the draft ECHR accession agreement and the autonomy of the EU legal order', 30 *Common Market Law Review* (2011), pp. 1025–1055.

Lock (2009)

T. Lock, 'The ECJ and the ECtHR: The Future Relationship Between the Two Courts', 8 *International Courts and Tribunals* (2009), pp. 383–385.

Martin (2013)

C. Martin, 'European Exceptionalism in International Law? the European Union and the System of International Responsibility' in M. Ragazzi (ed.), *Responsibility of International Organisations: Essays in Memory of Sir Ian Brownlie* (Leiden, Martinus Nijhoff 2013), pp. 189–100.

Martinico & Pollicino (2010)

G. Martinico and O. Pollicino, *The National Judicial Treatment of the ECHR and EU Laws: A Comparative Constitutional Perspective* (Groningen, Europa Law Publishing 2010).

McCrudden (2001)

C. McCrudden, 'The Future of the EU Charter of Fundamental Rights', Jean Monnet Working Paper 10/01.

McInnes (1999)

J. McInnes, (Case-note:) Case C-249/96, Lisa Jacqueline Grant v. South-West Trains ltd, 36 *Common Market Law Review* (1999), pp. 1043–1058.

De Meyer (1973)

J. De Meyer, 'The Right to Respect for Private and Family Life, Home and Communications in Relations Between Individuals, and the Resulting Obligations for States Parties to the Convention', in: A.H. Robertson (ed.), *Privacy and Human Rights* (Machester, Manchester University Press 1973), pp. 255–283.

De Mol (2013)

M. de Mol, *De Directe Werking van de Grondrechten van de Europese Unie* [dissertation: The Direct Effect of the Fundamental Rights of the EU] (Oisterwijk, Wolf Legal Publishers 2013).

De Mol (2012)

M. de Mol, 'Het toepassingsgebied van Unierechtelijke grondrechten & het beginsel van de allocatie van bevoegdheden [The scope of application of EU fundamental rights and the principle of allocation of competences]', Maastricht Faculty of Law Working Paper 2012/6.

De Mol (2011)

M. de Mol, 'The Novel Approach of the CJEU on the Horizontal Application of the EU Principle of Non-Discrimination: (Unbridled) Expansionism of EU Law?', 18 *Maastricht Journal of European and Comparative Law* (2011), pp. 109–134.

Morijn (2014)

J. Morijn, 'Kissing Awake a Sleeping Beauty? The Charter of Fundamental Rights in EU and Member States' Policy Practice', in: V. Kosta, N. Skoutaris and V. Tzevelekos (eds.), *The EU Accession to the ECHR* (Oxford, Hart Publishing 2014), pp. 123–139.

Morijn (2006)

J. Morijn, 'Balancing Fundamental Rights and Common Market Freedoms in Union Law: Schmidberger and Omega in Light of the European Constitution', 12 *European Law Journal* (2006), pp. 15–40.

Morijn & Van Sasse van Ysselt (2012)

J. Morijn and P.B.C.D.F. van Sasse van Ysselt, 'Niet rechterlijke handhaving van het EU-Grondrechtenhandvest: een analyse van de eerste stappen [The non-judicial enforcement of the EU Charter]', 37 *NJCM-Bulletin* (2012), pp. 295–310.

Mowbray (2005)

A. Mowbray, 'The Creativity of the European Court of Human Rights', 3 *Human Rights Law Review* (2005), pp. 57–79.

Mowbray (2004)

A.R. Mowbray, *The Development of Positive Obligations Under the European Convention on Human Rights by the European Court of Human Rights* (Oxford, Hart Publishing 2004).

Muir (2014a)

E. Muir, 'The Fundamental Rights Implications of EU Legislation: Some Constitutional Challenges' 51 *Common Market Law Review* (2014), pp. 219–246.

Muir (2014b)

E. Muir, 'Fundamental Rights: An Unsettling Competence', 15 *Human Rights Review* (2014), pp. 25–37.

Muir (2013)

E. Muir, 'The Court of Justice: A Fundamental Rights Institution Among Others', in: M. Dawson, B. de Witte and E. Muir (eds.), *Judicial Activism at the European Court of Justice* (Cheltenham, Edward Elgar Publishing 2013), pp. 76–101.

Nieuwenhuis (2011)

A. Nieuwenhuis, 'Het EHRM en de ontwikkeling van de positieve verplichtingen [The ECHR and the development of positive obligations]', in: A. Nieuwenhuis, J.H. Reestman and C. Zoethout (eds.), *Rechterlijk activisme: opstellen aangeboden aan prof. mr. J.A. Peters* (Nijmegen, Ars Aequi 2011), pp. 187–195

Nussbaum (2006)

M. Nussbaum, *Frontiers of Justice: Disability, Nationality, Species Membership* (Cambridge, The Belknap Press of Harvard University Press 2006).

Pech (2012)

L. Pech, 'Between Judicial Minimalism and Avoidance: The Court of Justice's Sidestepping of Fundamental Constitutional Issues in Römer and Dominguez', 49 *Common Market Law Review* (2012), pp. 1841–1880.

Peers (2014)

S. Peers, 'Article 52', in: S. Peers (ed.), *The EU Charter of Fundamental Rights - A Commentary* (Oxford, Hart Publishing 2014), pp. 1461–1468.

Polakiewicz (2010)

J. Polakiewicz, 'The Execution of Judgments of the European Court of Human Rights', in: R. Blackburn and J. Polakiewicz (eds.), *Fundamental Rights in Europe* (Oxford, Oxford University Press 2010), pp. 55–76.

Prechal, De Vries & Van Eijken (2011)

S. Prechal, S. de Vries and H. van Eijken, 'The Principle of Attributed Powers and the "Scope of EU Law"', in: L. Besselink and F.J.L. Pennings (eds.), *The Eclipse of the Legality Principle in the European Union* (Alphen aan den Rijn, Kluwer Law International 2011), pp. 213–247.

Prechal & Corthaut (2010)

S. Préchal and T. Corthaut, 'Competence Creep and General Principles of EU Law', 3 *Review of European Administrative Law* (2010), pp. 5–22.

Prechal & Widdershoven (2011)

S. Prechal and R. Widdershoven, 'Redefining the Relationship Between 'Rewe-Effectiveness' and Effective Judicial Protection', 4 *Review of European Administrative Law* (2011), pp. 31–50.

Ress (2005)

G. Ress, 'The Effect of Decisions and Judgments of the European Court of Human Rights in the Domestic Legal Order', 40 *Texas International Law Journal* (2005), pp. 359–382.

Rosas (2011)

A. Rosas, 'Is the EU a Human Rights Organization?', CLEER Working Paper 2011/1.

Russell (2010)

D. Russell, 'Supplementing the European Convention on Human Rights: legislating for positive obligations', 61 *Northern Ireland Quarterly* (2010), pp. 281–294.

Sanchez (2012)

S. Sanchez, 'The Court and the Charter: The Impact of the Entry into Force of the Lisbon Treaty and the ECJ's Approach to Fundamental Rights', 49 *Common Market Law Review* (2012), pp. 1565–1612.

Sarmiento (2013)

D. Sarmiento, 'Who's Afraid of the Charter? The Court of Justice, National Courts and the New Framework of Fundamental Rights Protection in Europe', 50 *Common Market Law Review* (2013), pp. 1267–1304

Sathanapally (2012)

A. Sathanapally, *Beyond Disagreement: Open Remedies in Human Rights Adjudication* (Oxford, Oxford University Press 2012)

Sen (2010)

A.K. Sen, *The Idea of Justice* (London, Penguin Books 2010).

Senden (2011)

H.C.K. Senden, *Interpretation of Fundamental Rights in a Multilevel Legal System: An Analysis of the European Court of Human Rights and the Court of Justice of the European Union* (Antwerpen, Intersentia 2011).

De Schutter (2014)

O. de Schutter, 'Bosphorus post-accession: redefining the relationships between the European Court of Human Rights and the Parties to the Convention', in V. Kosta, N. Skoutaris and V. Tzevelekos (eds.), *The EU Accession to the ECHR* (Oxford, Hart Publishing 2014), pp. 177–198.

De Schutter (2004)

O. de Schutter, 'The Implementation of the EU Charter of Fundamental Rights Through the Open Method of Coordination', Jean Monnet Working Paper 07/04.

De Schutter & Butler (2008)

O. de Schutter and I. Butler, 'Binding the EU to International Human Rights Law', 27 *Yearbook of European Law* (2008), pp. 277–320.

De Schutter (2008)

O. de Schutter, 'The Two Europeans of Human Rights: The Emerging Division of Tasks Between the Council of Europe and the European Union in Promoting Human Rights in Europe' 14 *Columbia Journal of European Law* (2008), pp. 509–561.

Shue (1980)

H. Shue, *Basic Rights* (Princeton, Princeton University Press 1980).

Spielmann (2012)

D. Spielmann, 'Allowing the Right Margin: The European Court of Human Rights and the National Margin of Appreciation Doctrine: Waiver of Subsidiarity of European Review?', 14 *The Cambridge Yearbook of European Legal Studies* (2012), pp. 381–418.

Spijkerboer (2009)

T. Spijkerboer, 'Structural Instability: Strasbourg Case-law on Children's Family Reunification', 11 *European Journal of Migration and Law* (2009), pp. 271–293.

Stachel (2006)

C. Stachel, *Schutzpflichten der Mitgliedstaaten für die Grundfreiheiten des EG-Vertrags unter besonderer Berücksichtigung des Grundrechtsschutzes in der Gemeinschaft* (Berlin, Duncker & Humblot 2006).

Stubberfield (2012)

C. Stubberfield, 'Lifting the Organisational Veil: Positive Obligations of the European Union Following Accession to the European Convention on Human Rights', 19 *Australian Journal of International Law* (2012), pp. 117–142.

Suerbaum (2013)

J. Suerbaum, 'Die Schutzpflichten der gemeinschaftsgrundrechte', 38 *Europarecht* (2013), pp. 390–416

Sutton (2010)

I.N. Sutton, 'The Power of the European Court of Human Rights to Order Specific Non-Monetary Relief: A Critical Appraisal from a Right to Health Perspective', 23 *Harvard Human Rights Journal* (2010), pp. 51–73.

Temple Lang (2008)

J. Temple Lang, 'The Development by the Court of Justice on the Duties of Cooperation of national Authorities and Community Institutions under Article 10 EC', 31 *Fordham International Law Journal* (2008), pp. 1483–1532.

Triantafyllou (2002)

D. Triantafyllou, 'The European Charter of Fundamental Rights and the "Rule of Law": Restricting Fundamental Rights by Reference', 39 *Common Market Law Review* (2002), pp. 53–64.

Trstenjak & Beysen (2013)

V. Trstenjak and E. Beysen, 'The growing overlap of fundamental freedoms and fundamental rights in the case-law of the CJEU', 38 *European Law Review* (2013), pp. 293–315

Tulkens & Van Drooghenbroeck (2012)

F. Tulkens and S. van Drooghenbroeck, 'L'Évolution des Droits Garantis et l'Interprétation Jurisprudentielle de la CEDH' (Lecture at the University of Grenoble on 27 September 2002), available at <http://cejm.upmf-grenoble.fr/userfiles/TULKENS.pdf> (last visited on 12 December 2012.

Urwin (1995)

D.W. Urwin, *The Community of Europe: A History of European Integration Since 1945* (London, Longman 1995).

Van der Velde (2009)

J. van der Velde, 'The Protection of Fundamental Rights within the European Union – a historical approach', in: J. Wouter, L. Verhey and P. Kiiver (eds.), *European Constitutionalism beyond Lisbon* (Antwerp, Intersentia 2009), pp. 61–79.

Vasak (1977)

K. Vasak, 'Human Rights: A Thirty-Year Struggle', 30 *UNESCO Courier* 1977, pp. 28–32.

Villiger (2007)

M.E. Villiger, 'The Principle of Subsidiarity in the European Convention on Human Rights', in: M.G. Kohen and L.C. Caflisch (eds.), *Promoting Justice, Human Rights and Conflict Resolution Through International Law: Liber Amicorum Lucius Caflisch* (Nijhoff, Leiden 2007), pp. 623–637.

De Vries (2013)

S. de Vries, 'Balancing fundamental rights with economic freedoms according to the European Court of Justice', 9 *Utrecht Law Review* (2013), pp. 169–192.

De Vries (2011)

K. de Vries, *Integration at the Border: The Dutch Act on Integration Abroad in Relation to International Immigration Law* (Amsterdam, Vrije Universiteit Amsterdam 2011).

De Vries & Van Mastrigt (2013)

S. de Vries and R. van Mastrigt, 'The Horizontal Direct Effect of the Four Freedoms: From a Hodgepodge of Cases to a Seamless Web of Judicial Protection in the EU Single Market?', in: U. Bernitz, X. Groussot and F Schuylyok (eds.), *General Principles of EU Law and European Private Law* (Alphen aan den Rijn, Wolters Kluwer, Law & Business 2013), pp. 249–280.

Waldron (2006)

J. Waldron, 'The Core of the Case Against Judicial Review', 115 *The Yale Law Journal* (2006), pp. 1346–1449.

Weiler (2013)

J. Weiler, 'Epilogue: Judging the Judges – Apology and Critique', in: M. Adams, H. De Waele, J. Meeusen and G. Straetmans (eds.), *The Legitimacy of the Case-law of the European Court of Justice* (Oxford, Hart Publishing 2013), pp. 235–253.

Weiler (2001)

J. Weiler, 'Epilogue: the Judicial Après Nice', in: G. de Búrca and J. Weiler (eds.), *The European Court of Justice* (Oxford, Oxford University Press 2001), pp. 215–226.

Weiler & Fries (1999)

J.H.H. Weiler and S.C. Fries, 'A Human Rights Policy for the European Community and Union: The Question of Competences', in: P. Alston (ed.), *The EU and Human Rights* (Oxford, Oxford University Press 1999) pp. 147–166.

Weiler & Lockhart (1995a)

J. Weiler and N. Lockhart, '"Taking Rights Seriously" Seriously: The European Court of Justice and its Fundamental Rights Jurisprudence - Part I ?', 32 *Common Market Law Review* (1995), pp. 51–94.

Weiler & Lockhart (1995b)

J. Weiler and N. Lockhart, 'Taking Rights Seriously Seriously: The European Court of Justice and its Fundamental Rights Jurisprudence - Part II', 32 *Common Market Law Review* (1995), pp. 579–627.

Van de Westelaken (2010)

R.A. van de Westelaken, 'Het EVRM als wapen tegen straffeloosheid: over het recht van slachtoffers van ernstige mensenrechtenschendingen op een effectieve strafechtelijke aanpak van de dader [The ECHR as a weapon against impunity: on the right of victims of serious human rights violations to an effective criminal response of the perpetrators]', 35 *NJCM-Bulletin* (2010), pp. 135–152.

Wildhaber (2002)

L. Wildhaber, 'A Constitutional Future for the European Court of Human Rights', 23 *Human Rights Law Journal* (2002), pp. 161–165.

Williams (2004)

A. Williams, *EU Human Rights Policies: A Study in Irony* (Oxford, Oxford University Press 2004).

De Witte (1999)

B. de Witte, 'The Past and the Future Role of the European Court of Justice in the Protection of Human Rights', in: P. Alston (ed.), *The EU and Human Rights* (Oxford, Oxford University Press 1999), pp. 859–899.

Xenos (2012)

D. Xenos, *The Positive Obligations of the State Under the European Convention of Human Rights* (London, Routledge 2012).

Xenos (2009)

D. Xenos, 'The Human Rights of the Vulnerable', 13 *The International Journal of Human Rights* (2009), pp. 591–614.

INDEX

School of Human Rights Research Series

The School of Human Rights Research is a joint effort by human rights researchers in the Netherlands. Its central research theme is the nature and meaning of international standards in the field of human rights, their application and promotion in the national legal order, their interplay with national standards and the international supervision of such application. The School of Human Rights Research Series only includes English titles that contribute to a better understanding of the different aspects of human rights.

For previous volumes in the series, please visit http://shr.intersentia.com.

Published titles within the Series:

70. Helen Beckmann-Hamzei, *The Child in ICC Proceedings.*
    ISBN 978-1-78068-339-3
71. Karel De Meester, *The Investigation Phase in International Criminal Procedure: In Search of Common Rules.*
    ISBN 978-1-78068-305-8
72. Nelleke Koffeman, *Morally sensitive issues and cross-border movement in the EU. The cases of reproductive matters and legal recognition of same-sex relationships.*
    ISBN 978-1-78068-349-2
73. Roland Moerland, *The Killing of Death. Denying the Genocide against the Tutsi.*
    ISBN 978-1-78068-351-5
74. Andrea Broderick, *The Long and Winding Road to Disability Equality and Inclusion. The United Nations Convention on the Rights of Persons with Disabilities.*
    ISBN 978-1-78068-358-4
75. Christina Peristeridou, *The principle of legality in European criminal law.*
    ISBN 978-1-78068-357-7
76. Emilie Ellen Kuijt, *Humanitarian Assistance and State Sovereignty in International Law. Towards a Comprehensive Framework.*
    ISBN 978-1-78068-366-9
77. Lize R. Glas, *The Theory, Potential and Practice of Procedural Dialogue in the European Convention on Human Rights System.*
    ISBN 978-1-78068-375-1
78. Paulien de Morree, *Rights and Wrongs under the ECHR: The Prohibition of Abuse of Tights in Article 17 of the European Convention on Human Rights.*
    ISBN 978-1-78068-418-5

www.ingramcontent.com/pod-product-compliance
Ingram Content Group UK Ltd.
Pitfield, Milton Keynes, MK11 3LW, UK
UKHW051920100926
8556IPUK00021B/1278

9 781780 684550